CROSSING THE LINE

CROSSING THE LINE

THE OUTRAGEOUS STORY OF A HOCKEY ORIGINAL

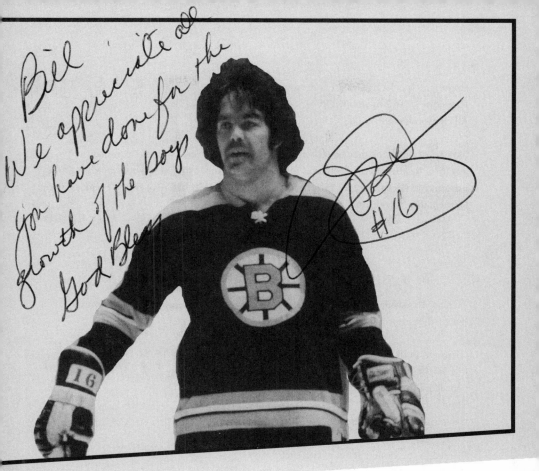

Bill
We appreciate all
you have done for the
growth of the boys
God Bless
[signature] #16

DEREK
SANDERSON

WITH KEVIN SHEA

FOREWORD BY **BOBBY ORR**

TRIUMPH
BOOKS

This book is available in quantity at special dicounts for your group or organization.
For further information, contact:

 Triumph Books LLC
814 North Franklin Street
Chicago, Illinois 60610
Phone: (312) 337-0747
www.triumphbooks.com

Printed in the United States of America
ISBN 978-1-60078-680-8

Published simultaneously in Canada by HarperCollins Publishers Ltd.

This book is dedicated to the great many people who helped me get on my feet again. Bobby Orr was always there for me. Being helped up when I fell was one thing, but to stay sober, you need something more than that. I believe it is love—unconditional love. Very few of us find that in our lifetimes. I was blessed with my wife, Nancy, who gave me a reason and the strength to become someone new. My boys, Michael and Ryan, are my pride and joy. To be blessed with the kind of love I discovered is a godsend. I could never stay away from the bottle without my family. They give me that purpose every day.

CONTENTS

FOREWORD

My first memory of Derek Sanderson dates back to when we played against each other in junior. Although we were both property of the Boston Bruins at that time, Derek ended up playing in Niagara Falls and I became a member of the Oshawa Generals. Even back in those days, Derek had great skills on the ice and was a tough competitor.

By the time Derek made the jump to the NHL with Boston in 1967–68, I had already completed my rookie year, and we won the league's Calder Trophy as rookie of the year in back-to-back seasons. Those were great times for both of us, but our greatest accomplishment as teammates was being able to hoist the Stanley Cup in both 1970 and 1972.

Unfortunately, Turk eventually decided to jump to the rival World Hockey Association, and things began to change in his life, often for the worse. He started down a slippery slope that no one could prevent, and all of us who considered him a friend could only wait and watch. At the appropriate time, many of us reached out to help Derek, and I am proud to say that he has beaten the demons that for so long controlled his life.

Derek and I have been friends for over 40 years, and I can tell you that he is a "salt of the earth" type of person. In addition, he has an opinion on most topics and is not afraid to share those thoughts. Undoubtedly, you will read many of those ideas plus a ton of stories as you turn the pages of his book.

During his lifetime, Derek Sanderson has been to the mountaintop and then to the valley floor as well, and now it is your turn to revisit both the good and bad times of his life. Derek's has been a unique life, and I have no doubt that everyone will benefit from his experiences along the way.

I'm very thankful to have been able to play in Boston with Derek, where we enjoyed so much success together. He will always be a legend of the game, but more importantly, he will always be my friend.

Bobby Orr
June 2012

PREFACE

Why would anybody want to read a book about a third-line centre who played in the National Hockey League more than 30 years ago? I mean, I read two books a week, and if that's all the book has going for it, I'm not interested.

I have a friend who told me, "Hanging out with you is like living in a movie." When I look back at it, I realize that every day, something crazy was going on, but when you're in it, you don't realize that. It's your normal.

I have no doubt that I should be dead or in jail. Thank God, I'm neither. Instead, in January 2011, *GQ* magazine named me one of the 25 coolest athletes of all time. My boys, Michael and Ryan, might argue that point when they see their old man hobbling down the stairs in the morning, hair all over the place and wearing an undershirt and boxer shorts! I try to tell them that, once upon a time, there was a day, but they only laugh.

People ask me all the time, "Where was the bottom for you, Derek?" That is the sensational sound bite searched for by TV producers, radio hosts and newspaper journalists. The truth is that the day you realize you can no longer stop drinking and that alcohol has you by the throat, when you realize you can't stop for more than a day before you begin to withdraw, every single hour is a bottom. You just can't see how anyone or anything can help you. There is no light at the end of the tunnel. Fear begins to take control of everything you do. You don't even know what you are afraid of.

There are times that this book will let you experience the joys of a kid who only ever wanted to play in the National Hockey League, and who got there and was able to play with the greatest player of all time and win two Stanley Cup championships. At other times, this book will take you to places you do not ever want to visit, experience things you don't ever want to do and feel things you don't ever want to feel. It will make you understand that alcohol is as dangerous to a person as heroin or cocaine. As they say in Alcoholics Anonymous, "a drug is a drug is a drug."

I do not take any pride in some of the things I have done through my life, and certainly am embarrassed about other things, especially when I told my wife and sons, who never knew *that* Derek Sanderson.

I have tried to entertain, to inform and hopefully help some people without lecturing. There were a lot of great times and a ton of laughs before hitting rock bottom forced me to rearrange my life.

Along the way, I was blessed with great parents, a terrific sister, great friends I knew would always be there for me, and one amazing alcohol counsellor in St. Catharines, Ontario. With an assortment of wonderful people to help me, and by the grace of God, I have survived, and am able to tell you my story.

Enjoy.

Derek Sanderson
June 2012

CHAPTER 1

CENTRAL PARK

How did I screw up my life so badly?

My only dream was to become a professional hockey player. Everything I did, I did to play in the National Hockey League. Now, I was 31 years old. I should have been in the prime of my life. I had found the girl I wanted to spend my life with. I should still have been playing hockey. Four years earlier, I was the highest-paid athlete in the world, and yet there I was, being quickly escorted into the bottomless pit of alcoholism and drug addiction.

I tried to blame everyone else for my situation, but I had only myself to blame for the situation I found myself in. When you realize that for the first time, it's quite a wake-up call. No one put a gun to my head and told me to drink. I was bad and I was mean. I'm telling you, I was ugly mean. By that point, I didn't give a shit, no matter what happened.

Fuelled by drugs and alcohol, I flew to New York and what proved to be the start of a three-year binge that was the worst nightmare you can imagine; out of control with fear that I might never get off the merry-go-round. You drink to control the fear and the loss of respect. Really, that is all you have.

I slid slowly into the depths of a hell I could never have imagined.

It started with a good-looking girl, as it so often does. We were both drunk. I had just come from Dallas, and while I was there, I broke the cap off my front tooth. It was ugly. The girl was staying with friends and invited me back to

1

the house. As we were heading there, she asked if I had any money. I gave her the last of the cash I had, which was about $1,500. She slid into the apartment before me and slammed the door. I could hear the click of the lock, with me standing on the outside.

It was late. I had no money and no place to sleep. The clothes I was wearing—the only clothes I had—weren't appropriate for a miserable New York night. I banged on the door for a long time. Through the locked door, she yelled, "Get away from here or I'll call the police!" There I was—no money, drunk and looking like hell. That was not the condition I wanted to be in when the cops arrived. I had one option—I hit the street.

I trudged over to Central Park and glanced around. There were a few people walking around, but the park was mostly quiet. The cold and rain made the night miserable, but I knew I just needed a place where I could close my eyes and drift away from my problems for a few hours. I saw an empty park bench and figured that was as good a place as any to spend the night. I grabbed a discarded *New York Times* and stretched out on the damp bench, pulling the newspaper over me like a blanket to keep dry and, hopefully, as warm as possible.

An old-timer came by, looked at me and shook his head. "You're obviously new at this," he sighed. "If you knew what you were doing, you would have wiped down the bench and then put the paper down before you laid down."

"Is there an art to this?" I asked facetiously.

"Yes sir," came the reply. "There actually is."

I appreciated the advice from a guy who clearly had spent a few years living in the park.

"Hey, one more thing."

I glanced up.

"You'd be wise to find a spot under the bridge in the western part of the park. You'll be out of the wind and out of any bad weather. Get there about 4:30 or five o'clock, before it gets dark, and claim a spot. I'll tell ya now, you're gonna have to fight for it, but it'll be worth it."

I asked him if that's where he stayed. "No, I'm too old to fight for a spot," he shrugged. "But you'll be fine."

I thanked him for the advice, but he offered more of his experience.

"In the alley behind the big appliance stores, get yourself one of those cardboard boxes that they ship refrigerators in. Lean it up against a building. It'll keep out the wind. Eventually, your body heat will warm you up. The temperature drops pretty good some nights."

The next day, I found one of those cartons, and it became my new home. A discarded paperback was my entertainment. I ate out of dumpsters, stole and panhandled. It was sheer survival at that point. When it came to panhandling, I discovered that there was a pecking order; the veterans had their corners, and you didn't mess with their seniority or you'd suffer the consequences.

My sign said: "Just Sober. Help Me Out. I Want to See My Family." People handed me tens and twenties. I made $150 to $200 cash a day. I realized that if you really wanted to get out of living on the street, it was possible. For some reason, I knew I would get out of this predicament. I had family and friends, but I was too embarrassed to ask anyone I knew for help. My ego simply wouldn't let me, but I realized that I needed help.

The expression "Pride goeth before a fall" was appropriate for me, but no one knew me, so what did I care? I was anonymous for the first time in my life. My hair was really long and unwashed, I hadn't shaved for a while and my clothes were filthy. People walked by and didn't recognize me. It wouldn't have mattered to me if they did.

After a couple of days, I started to shake. I needed a drink. I had no money, so I figured I was out of luck, but there was a liquor store nearby. Desperate for a drink, I lingered outside, and then, as soon as the guy at the cash was serving a customer, I grabbed a pint of vodka from near the front of the store. I ran, and before he knew where I was, I was out of sight. The guys in the park later told me that the employees at the liquor store wouldn't chase you for a pint, but they would for a fifth. It didn't matter to me—a fifth was too big to run with anyway.

I was going back to steal another pint the next day when I noticed a guy sitting on a bench wearing a nice camel-hair topcoat. It was clear that he was on a two- or three-day bender. He had a couple of bottles of booze stuck in the pocket of his coat. When I noticed that he was asleep, I snuck over and reached into his coat to take one of the bottles.

"What the hell do you think you're doing?" he barked, grabbing my wrist.

"Come on. Just give me a drink!" I begged. "We're both in the same spot."

"Get your own!" came the reply.

"Listen," I blurted. "Do you know who I am?"

That was the stupidest thing I have ever said. That was the first and only time I have ever said that in my life. I was desperate.

"Yeah, I do," he said. "You're a drunk just like me."

Those words stung.

CHAPTER 2

MOM, DAD AND THE WAR YEARS

There are many things I've done in my life that have left me embarrassed, but far fewer that I can admit I'm ashamed of. I have often veered off the path of good and right and have occasionally peeked into the darker sides of life.

Why are we the way we are? You and I can argue that until we are blue in the face. Are we products of our environment, or have our lives been predetermined through DNA? It's the nature-versus-nurture argument, and while we all have an opinion on it, who really knows the answer?

Because of some of the choices I have made in my life, some might question the way I was raised. I can tell you definitively that I had nothing but the most wonderful of childhoods. I had two parents who loved me unconditionally, who allowed me to be a kid but who taught me right from wrong and instilled strong moral values in me.

The times I strayed into life's darker corners were all conscious choices I made, and defied the values that I learned from my mother and father.

My cousin traced the Sanderson family back to Virginia. He discovered that the Sandersons were part of the Flagler family, a prominent family that settled in Florida. Flagler County is on the Atlantic coast of Florida and was named after a railway builder named Henry Morrison Flagler. My branch of the Sandersons must have been the poor side of the family.

The Sandersons remained loyal to the British crown, and when the American Revolution took place, they were told, "Grab what you can carry and get out," and sent north. My great-great-grandfather crossed the border into Canada and settled in Niagara Falls, Ontario.

My father, Harold, was one of seven kids born and raised in Niagara Falls. One of the moments that shaped his life came when he was 17 years old. He fell in love with a girl who dumped him for a guy with a '32 Ford because she didn't want to walk. My dad was devastated, so he quit school and joined the army. They gave him a uniform and, just to show her, he walked proudly past her house.

When he went home, he walked in the front door. His father saw him in uniform. "You stupid bastard! What have you done?"

"I enlisted," replied my dad.

My grandfather, who had fought in the First World War, punched my dad in the mouth and knocked him out cold. Seven weeks later, Dad was in England. The experience wasn't nearly as romantic as the posters had described. It was a whole different world.

My father never told me much about the war, but he was always proud to be a member of the Cameron Highlanders of Ottawa. They played a key role in the invasion of Normandy on June 6, 1944, and the regiment fought in almost every battle in the northwestern Europe campaign.

Dad was wounded in action. I asked him how, but he chose not to discuss it. "Derek, you won't understand. Someday, I may be able to tell you, but believe me, it's not what the movies portray."

Dad was recuperating in a hospital in Kirkcaldy, Scotland, a town on the northern shore of the Firth of Forth and the largest town between Dundee and Edinburgh. Kirkcaldy was just southwest of my mother's hometown of Dysart. Dysart had, at one time, been a coal harbour, but with no employment, the town was forced to merge into Kirkcaldy in 1930.

One weekend, my dad secured a pass, and he was told that when he returned, they were going to send him back out to the front line. He and his buddies, all wearing kilts, decided to go to the movies. They went to the first screening of the afternoon.

My mom, Caroline Hall Gillespie, was 17 and was an usherette at the theatre, using a flashlight to show people to their seats. When my father caught a glimpse of her, he leaned over to his buddies and said, "Oh my God, she's a beauty!"

He tried to talk to her, but she was having no part of him.

My dad was nothing if not determined. Hoping to introduce himself, he stayed at the movies all day and watched all five showings of the same film, but my mother avoided him. Unsuccessful by the end of the night, he returned to the base.

The next day, he went back and watched the same movie again! And again, he tried to talk to her, but she was afraid of the crazy Canadian soldier.

He stayed for all five screenings again, but this time, at the end of the night, when my mother climbed onto the bus to go home, my father also jumped on the bus and sat behind her. She refused to talk to him, but he was smitten and wasn't about to take her silence as an answer.

Dysart was at the end of the bus line. Mom got off the bus and the driver turned to my dad and said, "This is it. Out you go." My dad got off the bus and followed her home. She was scared. She ran up the stairs and her father came to the door.

When her father saw my dad in his uniform, there was immediate camaraderie. "How is the war going, son?" he asked.

"Fine, sir."

My mother's father invited my dad into the house for a drink. My mother had to stay up and wait on the two of them. They drank port and told stories through the evening. When my father got up to leave, he asked, "Is it okay with you if I write your daughter? And will she write me back?"

"Son, she'll write you every day."

My mother's father made the promise for her . . . and she had never even talked to this man!

My dad wrote her every day. After that weekend, he returned to the front and was wounded a second time. He asked to be transferred to Kirkcaldy to recuperate. When he was, he went over to Dysart. My mom was there, and she had fallen in love with him through his letters. To the end of her life, my mom laughed that she never met the man who wrote those letters. She never saw that side of my father again.

I asked my dad what was in those letters that made my mother fall in love with him. "Son, you don't know what you say when the shells are screaming in all around you. The sound is deafening and you can't shrink into a trench deep enough. You're scared, and you write some pretty amazing things."

My father and mother were married in Dysart by a local pastor. My mom's parents and her sister served as witnesses. Their honeymoon was getting the big bed in my grandparents' house for a couple of days before my dad had to leave to go back to the front. It wasn't long afterward that Mom learned she was pregnant.

A German bomb destroyed part of my grandparents' house and killed the family next door. With the war raging around them, my mom gave birth to my sister, Karen, in that house. Dad didn't get the chance to see Karen until she was nine months old.

After the war, our family, with my mother now expecting me, moved to Canada, back to my father's hometown of Niagara Falls. All her life, my mom retained a very thick Scottish brogue. Any time her sisters visited us, we could barely understand what they were saying to each other.

My father carried a lot of demons with him from serving in the war. He'd say, "War is never a good thing, but they were the proudest four years of my life because I went through it. Thank God I made it." Yet if I tried to pry information about the war out of him, he'd say, "War is an ugly thing, son. You don't understand it unless you go through it. Maybe when you're older I'll be able to tell you."

He never did.

Whenever we talked about his war service, he told me, "I fought that war so you would never have to. They told us it would be the last."

My father was awarded five medals for his service during World War II, but he kept them hidden away. I was around 18 when my mother first brought them out. I could never figure out why Dad didn't talk about the medals. My mom said, "You have no idea what your father's been through."

A few years ago, my father joined a group of veterans in returning to Europe. My mom convinced him it would be good for him to go, have a few beers and tell stories with fellow veterans. He said, "Son, I'm going over to Germany. The last time I was there, they were trying to kill me!"

He thought that was the funniest thing.

CHAPTER 3

CHILDHOOD

My dad enlisted in 1941, and after four years overseas, he returned to Canada with my mom, my sister, and me on the way, and the family needed a place to live. Towards the end of the war, Wartime Housing Ltd. built more than 30,000 houses to ensure that returning servicemen would have a place to live. These were cookie-cutter one-and-a-half-storey homes priced to make them accessible to veterans. The houses were assembled all in a row, and were intended to be temporary, but an awful lot of them are still standing today. Our little wartime house at 1267 Stamford Street in Niagara Falls cost my parents around $4,000. I lived there until I was 18 years old.

I was born Derek Michael Sanderson in Niagara Falls on June 16, 1946, very much loved by the greatest mother and father a kid could ever want.

After the war, my dad got a job in the Kimberly-Clark plant, where they manufactured feminine hygiene products. My father was mechanically inclined and could fix anything. He was great with machinery. By simply looking at things, he could tell you how they worked. He tinkered with anything mechanical. In fact, he made great toys for Karen and me. He was always down in the basement, working away on something.

My dad worked his butt off his entire life—weekends plus any overtime he could get. He had a tremendous work ethic, and took a lot of pride in putting in a good day's work. His philosophy was that anything worth having was worth working for, and if something was easy, everybody would do it.

One day, the management at Kimberly-Clark dropped a bombshell: they told the employees they were closing the plant and moving to Toronto. I can remember my dad telling my mom.

"Do you want to go?" she asked.

He hemmed and hawed. "Well, Derek's just going to start junior and I think we've got to talk." The two of them discussed the move and, unbeknownst to me, my father turned it down and took a job in quality control at the General Motors plant in St. Catharines. He gave up his seniority and four weeks of vacation a year so we could stay in the area while I was playing junior! He made a huge sacrifice for me.

Just like most men in that era, my dad would have a beer or two after his shift. He always came home. He was never unfaithful. It would never cross his mind to cheat on my mother. I never met a man who loved his wife more than my father loved my mother. When he met her, it was over.

My mom was the best mother on the planet.

Being a mother is a 24-hour-a-day job. There's no time off. My mom was always there, with a Band-Aid, some good food, a kind word or just a hug. Our house was always tidy, and my mom always washed my clothes and cleaned my room for me. She prepared every meal and was an incredible baker. She treated mealtime like she was running a private restaurant. My dad got what he wanted, my sister got what she wanted and I got what I wanted. When I was playing junior, every time I walked through the door for dinner, she had pork chops and french fries for me. That was my favourite meal, so that's what she made me. When I left home to play with the Bruins, I wondered how I was going to be able to fend for myself. I was living in an apartment by myself and I never picked up anything, so every time my apartment got dirty, I moved! My wife will tell you that I'm still sloppy.

One time when I was a toddler, my mother was cooking beans on the stove. I saw the bright red burner and was just tall enough to reach up to see what it was. My mom slapped my hands. "Derek, do not put your hands near the stove! It's very hot!" Of course, it didn't register, and when she wasn't looking, I reached up and put my hands on that bright red burner.

"*Owwwwwwwwwwwwwwwwww!*" I screamed bloody murder. Some of the skin from my hand remained on the burner.

My mother took me in her arms and whisked me over to the freezer. She took all the food out and put my hands on the ice. It took the sting away and kept them from blistering. It was a valuable lesson that I would use again later in my life.

I lived in my own little world when I was a kid. When I was about eight, my mother blasted me for leaving my clothes lying around. "Derek! How tough is it to pick up your clothes? Do you know that your pyjamas are inside out every other day? What is it with you, son?"

Without thinking, I said, "Mom, I'm harmlessly thoughtless. It's the waywardness of genius."

She gave me a look as if I was daft. "What?!"

I repeated it. "It's the waywardness of genius, Mom!"

I have no idea where I got that line. I never read it. I never heard it. It just came out of my mouth.

My mother looked at me as if I had three heads. "And what qualifies you for the genius category?"

"Because I think of the big picture, Mom." Using all the confidence that an eight-year-old can summon, I explained, "I'm not a detail kind of guy, Mom. I've got better things to do."

That's the way I've lived my life. I look at the bigger picture, but I never pay attention to details, and it has cost me dearly.

The four of us were always together. My mother and my sister, Karen, always did girl stuff together and my dad was always with me, taking me here and there.

As much as I loved my mother, I was closer to my dad. There was never an athlete or a recording artist that I idolized. My only idol was my father.

I was white-blond, a real towheaded little child, and skinny as a rake. I was always getting into something. In that regard, I don't know that I was any different from most boys my age. My best friend, Leigh Shelton, and I both got cowboy outfits for Christmas one year. The following summer, we pulled on our cowboy boots and hats, strapped our toy guns around our waists and decided to go down to the Queenston Quarry. We were about five. Of course, we were always warned that we were never to go there. The quarry had filled up through the years and there were now sandpits, but they had flooded over. Leigh and I built a raft and were floating in the sandpits.

My dad came home from work each day at 3:50. He'd kiss my mother and ask about us kids. "Karen's fine," my mom told him that day. "I'm not sure where Derek is."

My dad stopped dead. "You don't think . . . ?"

My mother shrugged. "Knowing him, absolutely."

My dad jumped into the car and drove over to the quarry. He parked at the top of the cliff, looked over and saw us there on our raft. We were there having fun, so he could relax. He lit up a smoke, sat down in the grass and watched his boy playing with his buddy.

Leigh and I were at opposite ends of the raft, but for some reason, I got it in my head that we'd go faster if both of us were on the same end.

My father shouted, "Don't!"

Too late! When I moved closer to Leigh, the raft tipped and threw the two of us into the water.

My dad was about 600 feet away, and as he was running towards us, our cowboy boots were filling with water. We were dropping like stones. Leigh stayed afloat by grabbing the raft. My dad dove in and grabbed me. I was thrashing away, going down for the second time when he pulled me to the surface.

When we got to dry land, my father just glared. "I knew you were going to do that! I just saw that in your little brain!" The next day, he signed me up for swimming lessons.

I used to terrorize my sister.

Karen was two grades ahead of me. She was very bright—a straight-A student. Although I was too young and self-involved at the time, I'm certain that a part of Karen must have resented me for all the attention given to me because of hockey.

My sister loved me and always looked out for me. She would wait for me every day and we'd walk to school together. There'd be times—many, in fact—when I tried Karen's patience. She would be ready for school, books in hand and about to walk out the door, and I'd still be dicking around. "You're going to be late for school! I'm not going to wait any longer!"

She'd storm out the door because she hated to be late, but it was all for show. She'd wait at the corner for me.

In the winter, the snowbanks would be piled up high on either side of our street. They never plowed the streets in our neighbourhood. Karen and I would be walking to school and I'd see a car going by, so I'd grab onto the bumper and let the car pull me through the snow-packed streets. We called it "jumping the bumper." I'd slide past my sister and, with a big smile, wave and yell, "See ya, Karen!" I'd get to school on time and then she'd be late. She'd be furious at me!

I was brutal to her, but that's what brothers do, isn't it?

Karen still lives in Niagara Falls and has three kids and a granddaughter who all live near her.

Ever since I was a kid, I hated the dentist. He terrified me. I went to my first dental appointment when I was five. One of my permanent front teeth came in on top of the baby one, and the baby tooth wouldn't leave. My teeth have really long roots.

My father took me to my appointment. The dentist said, "We've got to get this one out of the way," and with no anesthetic, he started yanking on it. The tooth wouldn't budge. I was screaming, and through the walls, my dad heard the wails. That was an alarm for him. He came flying around the corner. "What are you doing to my son?" Just as he turned the corner, he saw the dentist slap me.

My father didn't say a word, but he hit the dentist and lifted me out of the chair.

"Don't you ever touch my boy again or I'll break every bone in your body."

I was bleeding like a stuck pig. My dad took me home. He examined my tooth and tried to wiggle it around in my mouth. "This bugger doesn't want to come out, Caroline."

My mother had a solution that she probably saw in a Little Rascals movie. "Let's tie it to a door."

They attached one end of a string to my tooth and the other to a door and slammed it repeatedly, but the tooth still wouldn't budge. I guess the roots were damaged badly enough that, a few days later, I pulled it out myself. I was thrilled.

As a result, I've always been deathly afraid of dentists. It's the needles I really hate. Considering all the drugs I took through the years, I would never go near a needle. Even if I were having unbelievable withdrawal symptoms and you gave me a needle filled with heroin, I absolutely couldn't do it. I have this phobia of needles.

I even hate the smell of a dentist's office. If my mother told me that I had a dental appointment, I wouldn't be able to sleep the night before. Her solution was to show up at school, knock on the door of the room I was in and say, "I'm here to take Derek to the dentist." If I knew before that point, I would never go. While on our way to the dentist's, my mom would lecture me. "I just don't understand you, Derek. If you took better care of your teeth, you wouldn't get cavities, you wouldn't have pain and then you wouldn't have to see the dentist. Doesn't it make sense to you?"

I'd just shrug.

When I was a kid, my mother used to ask, "Did you brush your teeth before bed?" My dad would ask, "What for, Caroline? He's only going to lose them playing hockey anyway." He thought that was hilarious!

My dad hated doctors, too. I remember being about seven when my father was building a shed for our house. He had a sawhorse out and was cutting a two-by-four with a rusty saw. I'll never forget hearing him say, "Measure twice, cut once. Living your life like that wouldn't be a bad thing."

Dad was sawing away really fast. I was standing there holding the two-by-four when the saw hit a knot and jumped out of the groove. The blade went right between my father's thumb and forefinger into that meaty part in between. Blood poured out of the wound. That was the first time I ever heard my dad swear: "Son of a bitch!"

He never cried—that was beneath him—but he was furious at himself. He told me to run and get his tackle box. And he hollered for my mother. She was cooking, but she ran out to see why he was calling so frantically. "Get me the sulfa powder."

He ran his bleeding hand under the kitchen tap, poured on the sulfa powder and wrapped his hand in a tea towel. He told me to get the leader line out of the tackle box. Then, he hooked up a needle to it and stitched himself up. After 12 loops, he tied off the end, poured more sulfa powder on it and wrapped it in a bandage.

I just stood there in awe.

"Pain is a state of mind, Derek. If you let physical pain take over, it will control your life." When I was older, he also told me, "If you let emotional pain take over, it'll destroy you, too."

The idea that pain is a state of mind was carried with me through my life. Everybody fears pain, but as my dad taught me, "Your brain will not retain pain." I asked him what he meant, and he told me that the brain isn't capable of remembering pain. Pain is an instantaneous way to get the message to the brain that there is trouble. But pain is only the message. It's not debilitating. It's there to tell you that you've been hurt.

I started playing hockey when I was eight, and that was one of the first things my dad had me thinking about: conditioning myself to ignore pain and never allowing it to intimidate me. And it never did. Getting beat up? That didn't bother me. Cut, bleeding, broken bones? That didn't bother me. Fear of embarrassment and fear of rejection—that bothered me. Losing a fight in front of all those people, whether it was in junior or the NHL, was my greatest fear in hockey.

My mother and father are both gone now and I miss them terribly, but they gave me a wonderful childhood and supported me through my entire life, even when they had every reason not to.

CHAPTER 4

SCHOOL DAYS

From kindergarten through Grade 8, I went to Valley Way Public School in Niagara Falls. I was a bright kid but didn't apply myself, as the teachers would inform my parents. But while my mom and dad instilled great morals in me, it was at school that I developed my social skills.

In Grade 6, I threw a snowball with a stone in it and hit Mr. Brooks, one of my teachers, in the head. I got caught. My dad had taught me that if you do something wrong, you don't run away. You stand there and 'fess up. I stood there, but I knew I was in trouble.

Mr. Brooks gave me a detention. He kept me after school for a week. My father wondered why I wasn't home. I told him I had been at school, studying, but he knew better. "No you weren't. You got a detention, didn't you?"

I admitted that I did and told my dad about the snowball. He asked me how I was being punished. I told him that I had to take a pencil and fill in a blank sheet of foolscap, which is legal-sized writing paper.

"You've got to be kidding me!" he roared.

He grabbed me by the scruff of the neck, threw me in the car and marched me into the school. We walked into Mr. Brooks's office. "Are you the one who gave my son a detention?"

"Yes," said Mr. Brooks. "Your boy threw a rock and it hit me."

My dad said, "That was a mistake and he certainly deserves a detention. I have no problem with that, but put him to work! Make him do mathematics or something. Don't have him waste his time filling in a sheet of paper! And if you are going to give him the same punishment in his detention tomorrow, he will not be there. And that's with my permission! Put him to work constructively!"

My father never bailed me out, but he looked out for me and did the right thing.

I hated bullies and people making fun of others. My English teacher, Miss Escott, suffered from rheumatoid arthritis and had a hard time writing and walking. It was heartbreaking to see a teacher I respected so much experiencing so much pain.

Two kids mimicked the way Miss Escott walked down the hall, so I walked up and cuffed both of them right behind the ear. *Bang!* Dropped them both. Books flew everywhere.

"Principal's office, Derek!"

In the office, Mr. Fullerton demanded that I tell him why I hit those kids. I refused. It would have broken Miss Escott's heart if she knew that kids were mimicking her behind her back. I was suspended.

My dad came home from work, and it was always the same routine. He'd ask my mom, "How are the kids?" My mother would say, "Karen is fine." But this time, she stopped before she finished her answer. I heard my dad stomping up each one of the 13 stairs it took to get to my room. I knew I was in big trouble.

He kicked open the door and, through a clenched jaw, asked, "What the hell is this about?"

"Dad, if I tell you the truth, will you believe me?"

"Of course," he said. "But this better be good!"

I told him.

He said, "Fine," and left my room. Nothing more.

I never would have allowed anyone to hurt Miss Escott. When she put her head on the pillow at night, she didn't need to think about kids laughing at her. She was in tremendous pain every day. She cared.

I was in Miss Escott's 10th-grade English class, and we studied Shakespeare all that winter. She said, "Class, you won't believe it! For nigh on 35 or 40 years of my teaching career, this is the first perfect paper I have ever seen on Romeo's soliloquy from *Romeo and Juliet!*"

I was looking around to see who had the perfect paper.

She continued. "Colons and semicolons in all the right places. I have never seen such a perfect paper!"

Then, the penny dropped. "Derek, you did such an outstanding job on the paper. Will you please stand up and recite the soliloquy for the class?"

Caught!

I started. "But soft! What light through yonder window breaks?" Then I stopped. I gave her the first line, but that's all I knew. I looked down at the ground. "Miss Escott, I cheated."

"I thought so," she replied. "The next time, don't copy it straight from a book with all the colons and semicolons."

I was an athlete, even in elementary school. One of the kids in my class never got picked for team sports in the schoolyard. There were two boys who picked on this kid unmercifully. What were they proving by being bullies? The kid was shy, and he was never going to challenge them . . . but I did. "If you keep messing with this kid, I'm going to hurt you!" They hit him one day, so I took a bat to one of the kids. They never touched him again.

We played outside with our buddies all the time—road hockey, baseball, cops and robbers, hide and seek. You sure didn't want to be stuck inside, because if your room was anything like mine, there was a single bed and a dresser and that was it. When I got sent to my room, that was real punishment. It was a dungeon. All I could do was open the curtains and stare out the window.

I had a BB gun when I was 10 and a pellet rifle when I was 11. There'd be a gang of about 14 of us who would go down to Queenston Heights and Fort Drummond and pretend we were soldiers. We used to follow the Canadian army when they were on drill and then copy them. They'd run 20 yards, drop and then fire live rounds. Every once in a while, a live round would fall out of their gear or they'd drop it when they were trying to load up. These were .303-inch cartridges for Lee-Enfield rifles.

We built a fort out of old plywood. There was a big tree there and we built a campfire beside it. Our gang collected five live rounds from the army. We pretended we were in the movies, so we tossed the shells into the fire and then ran like hell, thinking they were going to explode immediately.

We waited and waited and waited. Leigh Shelton said, "It didn't work. This is a lie. In the movies, it happens right away."

I said, "Yeah!"

"Did they go in the fire?"

"Who's going to check?"

"I ain't going. How about you?"

"No way! I'm not going!"

I said, "I'll go."

Leigh begged me not to go. "What if they go off when you get there, Derek?"

I said, "They're not going to go off for about half an hour."

The fire died out, and just then, *poof!* The first one went off!

"Get down, get down!"

We started to argue. "How many went off?"

"I think it was four."

"No way! I think it was five!"

"No, I counted and it was four."

"No, it was five—two quick, one slow and then two more. I think it was five."

None of us had a clue as to how many shells had exploded.

We had to decide who was going to approach the fire to find out if all the rifle shells had gone off. Those damned shells would kill you from 700 yards! I lost, so had to go check out the shells.

I held a piece of plywood in front of me like a shield, peeking around it as I went. I saw a couple of casings that had bounced out of the fire after they had gone off. But then I saw another one, leaning against a rock. I bent over to pick it up and it went off. *Bang!* It hit me in the forehead and split my head open.

My buddies all ran home and left me there, bleeding. I was a mass of blood.

I went home, caked in blood. I didn't know how bad it looked, but my mother took one look at me and nearly had a heart attack.

"Mom, I ran into a tree."

I later told my dad the truth. He was livid. "You stupid bastard! If I had any idea you were doing that, I'd have put you under lock and key!"

"But Dad, we were just fooling around," I explained.

"Oh yeah? Do you know how many kids are dead because they were just fooling around?" He stayed angry for days.

It didn't knock me out, although it dazed me a bit. It scorched my hair and I had to get some stitches. By the grace of God. God protects drunks and fools.

It wasn't that I was a bad kid, but trouble always seemed to find me. My mother told me, "Don't ever lie, cheat or steal. It's not in you, and if you do, you will get caught." Sure enough, she was right. I always got caught.

I started to get interested in girls when I was in Grade 7. Before *Hockey Night in Canada* came on on Saturday nights, we watched "From Miami . . . *The Jackie Gleason Show.*" It featured the June Taylor Dancers, and that's when I fell in love with women in lingerie. I got some *Playboy* magazines and hid them under my mattress, thinking my mother would never find them, but after washing my bedding, she found them when she was tucking in the sheets. My dad just laughed. "You silly bugger. You know your mother knows every inch of your room."

When I was 12 or 13, my buddies and I made a deal. We would meet at the pool every day at four o'clock. We loved to splash around, but even more than that, we loved to ogle one of the girls from school who was our age but had already developed.

This girl was cute. Black hair and green eyes. I was in the eighth grade when I saw her and, at that moment, my life changed. I had to get near her. Some jerk, whom I hated for the rest of the school year, got to sit next to her.

I stared at Louise for four or five days. I was too afraid to talk to her.

I started an inane conversation with my dad, but after much hesitation, I blurted out the one question I didn't know the answer to: "Dad, how do you get girls to like you?"

"Oh, you're at that stage, are you?"

I asked, "Stage? You knew this was going to happen and you didn't tell me?"

I was one of the tougher guys in the neighbourhood. My buddies used to call me "Skull" or "Footballhead." One kid might say we were going to play baseball that day, but if I wanted to play road hockey, for instance, I'd give him a slap and we'd roll around on the ground in a spirited wrestling match.

"Son," my dad barked, "you can't control people. When you're with girls, you've got to grow up or they won't like you. You have to treat girls with respect, kindness and patience. You have to be caring, giving, warm and receptive. And you have to have a smile."

The only word I got out of my dad's diatribe was "smile."

The next day, I walked into school and said hello to this girl with the biggest, goofiest smile. She looked at me as if I had two heads. "Who's this kid with all the teeth?"

I knew that hadn't worked, so I tried it again the next day.

"Hi!" Big, goofy grin.

Nothing. I started to question whether my father knew what he was talking about.

This went on for a couple of weeks. Finally, one day, she smiled at me and said hi back to me, so I leapt at the opportunity. "Can I walk you home from school today?"

"Sure!"

I met her after school. She lived about a mile and a half away—the longest walk of my life at that age. She brought home every textbook and notebook she owned every single day! And every single day, I said, "Here, let me carry those." In my head, I said, "Don't you dare drop any of these books." My right arm was paralyzed by the time we got to her back porch. She gave me a kiss on the cheek and thanked me, then went into the house.

That was it. That was the beginning. By the ninth grade, I'd mustered up a bit more courage. We used to go to the YMCA dances every Friday night. The Y made the boys wear a sport coat. I was playing junior at the time, so was wearing my Niagara Falls Flyers blazer. You think you're cool, but it didn't do you any good.

I had a crush on a girl, and each Friday, I tried to summon the courage to ask her to dance. Finally, after seven weeks, I walked up to her and asked her. She said the greatest word a woman can say to a man: "yes."

Out on the floor we went, and six bars into the song, she started laughing. "That's the way you dance?" She turned to her girlfriend, still laughing, and said, "Look at this!"

I have never danced again in my life. Not even once. The fear of being humiliated remained with me through my entire life.

CHAPTER 5

THE START OF
MY HOCKEY CAREER

I have to guess that it was around 1950. My dad was sitting in the living room, leafing through *Maclean's* magazine.

"Listen to this, Caroline," he said to my mother. "*Maclean's* has a story here that ranks the most respected professions in Canada. What do you think is the most respected profession?"

"Doctor?"

"You'd think so, wouldn't you?" he answered. "They say playing hockey is Canada's most respected profession! I'll be damned."

Without missing a beat, he added, "My boy's gonna be a hockey player."

And so began my destiny.

My dad was an extremely intelligent guy, in spite of his lack of formal education, and with a boatload of common sense, he took a practical approach to everything he did. He wanted me to find my balance on a pair of skates. To prepare me, he took a couple of butter knives, cut them off and taped them to my shoes and then had me walk around on the hardwood floors. I was four years old.

Like most kids in our neighbourhood, and in communities across Canada, we played road hockey by the hour. During the winter, our roads used to get all packed with snow, and the surface resembled ice. Instead of using a beat-up old tennis ball, we could play road hockey with a puck. Inevitably, somebody's shot would miss the net and the puck would slide down the street, seemingly forever.

My dad was walking home from work one day and saw me chasing after the puck about 200 feet away from where the game was being played in front of the Quinlans' house on Detroit Avenue. There were two Quinlan brothers, both older, bigger and tougher than me.

"Hey son," my dad called out. "What're you doing?"

"Playing street hockey," I answered.

"What are you doing here?"

I told him I was getting the puck.

"Did you shoot it?" my dad asked.

"No," I replied. "Peter Quinlan did."

"Oh yeah? Then why are you getting it?" he asked.

"They told me to."

"Oh yeah? Doesn't that bother you?" he continued. "Do you always do what they tell you?"

I shrugged. "Never thought about it."

"Well, I'll tell you what," he explained. "I'm going to stand right here. Leave that puck right there. I want you to go back and tell Peter that he shot it so he gets it."

I looked up at my dad. "If I say that, he's going to punch me in the mouth!"

"Then punch him right back, son. And every time he punches you, you punch him."

I walked back and Peter Quinlan asked, "What the hell are you doing, Sanderson? You didn't get the puck."

I said, "I didn't shoot it."

Just then, Mike Quinlan, the older brother, grabbed me and demanded, "Do what you're told. Get the puck!"

"No!" I said. "Peter shot it, Peter gets it. When I shoot it, I'll get it."

Mike pushed me and we got into a fight. I took a bit of a beating, but they never, ever asked me to get another stray puck.

I was harmlessly naive. I didn't look at being sent after pucks as any kind of dominance thing. I was just happy to be accepted, playing with the older boys. It was part of the sacrifice you put up with.

Learning to skate on a backyard rink was a rite of passage for most young Canadian boys. We took it for granted, never thinking about the hours our fathers spent, with frostbitten fingers, creating a rink that we could use to fuel our NHL dreams.

Our backyard was a pretty good size, but my dad wanted a rink closer to the size of a real rink, so he asked the next-door neighbours if he could stretch it across their yard as well as ours. That would give us a good 160-foot ice surface in our backyard, almost regulation size.

The neighbours said no, so instead, my father made a deal with the guy who lived behind us. We would give him all of our broken hockey sticks to stake his tomato plants, and we'd let him grow his tomatoes in our backyard in the summer. In return, we could use his backyard in the winter to create a much larger rink.

My dad made real boards, and brought home some old discarded pipes from the Kimberly-Clark plant, along with old mesh from the Niagara Falls Memorial Arena, to make nets.

Every morning, my father would get up at 5:45 and flood our backyard rink before his seven o'clock shift at the plant. He'd be out there in a World War II–issue coat, with a scarf wrapped around his neck and over his head. I'd ask him to wake me up before he left for work. In the winter, if it didn't snow, there'd be this beautiful, fresh ice to skate on for an hour or so before school. Then, I'd scarf down some porridge and a hot cocoa and head off to school.

After school, the big kids would come over. "You're not playing hockey unless you help scrape the snow off the rink," my dad would bark. "You don't just show up and expect to play. You've gotta work here. And guess who runs this rink?" He'd point to me. "He does."

I would have been five or six years old, playing hockey in the backyard with my buddies, when my father noticed that I had a little bit of talent. He couldn't have been prouder. He insisted that I work at hockey, so I did.

The Canadian Legion sponsored hockey in our area, and there were the Little NHL and the Little AHL, with six teams in each age group. When I was seven years old, I didn't want to play in a league. I was way too shy to go into a room full of kids to sign up. I just liked playing hockey for fun in the backyard with my buddies. My best friend, Leigh Shelton, and I were inseparable. Leigh's family couldn't afford to register him for hockey. They couldn't even afford a pair of skates. To be truthful, neither could we.

Unbeknownst to me or anyone else, my father went over to Leigh's house and asked him if he'd like to play hockey. Leigh said, "Sure, I'd love to, Mr. Sanderson, but I don't have any skates." My dad went out and bought him new skates, but there was a catch. "Leigh, the only thing you have to do is take Derek with you and both of you sign up for the Legion's hockey league on Saturday."

Leigh was so excited. He ran over to my house and shouted, "Derek, I've got new skates! Let's go down and sign up for hockey!"

"Okay," I said, and that Saturday, the two of us went down to the hall and signed up for hockey. My father volunteered to be our coach. At our second practice, I got hit in the head with a puck. Parents in the stands were looking at me. My teammates were staring at me. I was working hard and could feel some sweat on my forehead. When I took off my glove to wipe away the sweat, I realized it wasn't sweat. "Holy cow! I'm bleeding!"

I went over to my dad, but he showed no expression. He believed that when parents overreact to a child's injury, it's the look of terror on the adult's face that scares the child.

"Dad! Dad! Look at this!"

He shrugged it off. "There are only 20 minutes left in the practice. You won't bleed to death!"

I figured if it didn't bother my dad, it shouldn't bother me.

He asked me, "Does it hurt?"

I said no.

"Then why are you flipping out?" he asked.

"Well, I've never bled like this before!"

He said, "It'll stop." He put me on the goal line and shouted to the team, "Line up! Stops and starts!"

The whole team lined up. On the whistle, it was blue line and back, and then red line and back. I was leaving a trail of blood behind me. It was all over my face and sweater. My teammates thought I was the toughest guy in the world! I loved the admiration. It didn't hurt, yet they were saying, "Wow! Are you ever tough!"

I shrugged. "Yeah." I wasn't, but I sure wasn't going to tell them that.

Later on, my head started to ache. After the practice, while I was taking off my equipment, my dad said, "Now we get to go for stitches."

I didn't know what it felt like to get stitches. I wasn't very happy when I found out!

About a week later, my dad removed the stitches himself, using a pair of needlenose pliers and a little knife. He wasn't going to pay any doctor to take them out. And he saved them, just like the rest of the 400 that followed. He used to put them in a grey velvet watch box.

My dad made getting stitches seem like the red badge of courage, so whenever I got cut, I just kept playing. And I noticed that when you do that in hockey, people can't believe it. You get attention. "That kid's tough!"

That was part of growing up.

I didn't get any goals that first year, but I did get eight assists and my first penalty. I tripped a kid, and when the referee sent me to the penalty box, I cried. I didn't think I'd done anything wrong, and I felt frustrated because there was nothing I could do about a bad call.

The next game, I got a penalty for charging. This time, I went to the penalty box laughing. It wasn't that I was happy about it; it was just that I figured you had to be able to laugh to get along in this game and take things as they come.

Leigh lost interest in hockey early, but he did finish out the year. I am pretty sure that he only registered so he could get the skates my dad bought him.

My father became a disciple of Lloyd Percival, who hosted a popular CBC radio program called *Sports College*. The show gave listeners tips on how to be a good athlete and a good sport. Many of Percival's ideas were revolutionary, and ran contrary to popular thinking at the time. He also wrote a book, published in 1951, called *The Hockey Handbook*.

Lloyd Percival was a pioneer in physical training, and many athletes from various sports followed his fitness regimen. Hockey didn't really embrace Percival's ideas in North America, but Soviet hockey coaches devoured his ideas. My dad thought Percival was brilliant, and had me following a lot of his fitness tips. He had me skate around our backyard rink while carrying the puck 200 times in one direction, and then 200 times the other way. It was my dad's theory, learned from Lloyd Percival, that a hockey player had to be able to turn left or right equally well. He'd tell me I had to work on my shot. I came home from school one day, and my father had placed linoleum on the driveway and made me a beautiful net. He also put up targets in all four corners.

After work, Dad would stop by the arena and walk through the seats, picking up any pucks he found. After a while, we had five full buckets—probably a couple of hundred pucks—and I was expected to stand on the linoleum, which served as an ice surface, and shoot all 200 pucks every day. My dad would come home from work and ask if I'd shot my pucks. I'd say, "Yeah," but my father was sharp. He would put a piece of paper under one of the buckets, and if it hadn't been moved, he knew I hadn't shot my pucks.

"That isn't fair," I'd protest. "That was the one bucket I didn't use."

"Do you want me to look under the other one?" he'd ask.

"No, don't do that." I'd been caught.

My dad didn't really push me all that hard. He simply knew I had some talent and wanted to help me with what I was good at. When I was 10, he told my mother that I had something special and was a surefire NHL-calibre player. He told her he could tell because I had so much desire, which I did. "Don't give up hockey," he'd say. "You're good at it."

Nobody knows if they are going to make it to the National Hockey League, but I never really doubted I would. Everybody pooh-poohs it, telling you the odds are stacked heavily against you, but as I got older, I realized that the dream might be within reach.

On Saturday nights, our family would sit in front of the TV and watch *Hockey Night in Canada*. In the late 1950s and early '60s, the opening faceoff was at eight o'clock, but the telecast didn't start until nine—usually, just in time for the second period—and we would have a friendly wager amongst us as to what the score would be when the game signed on.

I was always a fan of the Toronto Maple Leafs. I never had a favourite player, although there were guys I really enjoyed watching and learned from. My dad had me watch Teeder Kennedy because he was good on faceoffs. He said, "Study him, son. The man does more than one thing. He's gifted at forehand and backhand. It's the little nuances of the game you have to learn. Anybody can skate. Anybody can shoot. Anybody can score. But not everybody is good on defence, and not everybody is good at picking up their man. You've got to cover well. There are two ends to the building." He always told me that. He also said, "Hockey is a game very different from football, baseball and basketball. In those three sports, they give you the ball. In hockey, you have to take it away."

He also told me to watch Davey Keon. "He really knows how to play the game." Keon could dance on skates; he was always moving. He was a great checker and I watched how he forechecked. He came in on the side and flushed the puck out on the other side. He never wasted steps, and he read the play well. Keon was a lot better than people think he was. When I made it to the NHL, I played against him and ran him a few times, but I really admired the way he played.

It wasn't just forechecking. My dad taught me the sweep check by having me watch Norm Ullman and Davey Keon. I got really, really good at the sweep check, and it really became a big part of my game when I joined the Bruins. Nobody could do it. It used to look like I was going to run you, and then I'd step left, drop down on one knee and put my stick out. Everybody would look to protect themselves from the hit, and when they did that, they lifted their stick and stopped protecting the puck. I'd drop down, slide my stick and turn the blade over and pull the puck right into me. The momentum of the play was going the other way, so I'd be heading the opposite way with the puck. It really worked well. I learned the sweep check when I was about 13. I was amazed that players never protected against it.

I was about 11 years old and becoming a pretty good hockey player but had never been to a National Hockey League game. The cost of tickets was out of reach for my dad. Somehow, my uncle got three tickets through his job on the railroad, so he and my aunt invited me to go to Maple Leaf Gardens to see Montreal play Toronto on a Saturday night. My aunt was a big Canadiens fan.

I seem to remember the game ending 0–0, and I loved watching the players fly up and down the ice. I remember the grace and beauty of Frank Mahovlich. And there was Jean Beliveau and Maurice and Henri Richard for Montreal. It was really something to watch.

My aunt thought it would be fun for me to get some autographs. She had a pen and an autograph book, and after the game, she took me to the spot where the Canadiens filed out of the arena, boarded a bus and were taken to Union Station so that they could take the train to Chicago.

All the players were leaving the rink wearing dark blue blazers and red, white and blue ties, with their London Fog overcoats draped over their arms. There had to have been a hundred people standing there, but my aunt pushed through the crowd so I could get close enough to get them to sign the auto-graph book. I was standing there with my pen and my book and I held it up. There was a big guy walking by, but I didn't know what to say to him. I knew he spoke French and I didn't *parle le français.*

It was Jean Beliveau, the star of the Montreal Canadiens, wearing number 4. He was a gentleman and an exceptionally good centre. He could make a play on his backhand just as easily as talk. I held up the autograph book, but he pushed me back and said, "No, no. I've got to catch the train." I didn't realize until later that there was very little time to spare between leaving the rink, getting to Union Station and then catching the train. They had to hurry because the train left on time and waited for no one.

When he pushed me away, I was embarrassed. I was certain I looked like an idiot in front of all those people. I watched him climb onto the bus, and my aunt said, "Oh well. He must have been busy."

"I didn't want his autograph anyway," I huffed.

Years later, when I was breaking in with the Bruins, we played an exhibition game against the Canadiens at the Montreal Forum. I thought, "If I ever get the chance, I'm going to knock Beliveau into the middle of next week for not signing that autograph when I was a kid." I know I harboured resentment towards him.

There was a scrum along the boards, and the referee blew the whistle. And there was my chance. Beliveau was standing there with his head down. I threw my gloves off and punched him right in the face.

His teammate John Ferguson went ballistic. I was behind the net, and I swear Ferguson was trying to climb over it to get a piece of me!

Beliveau said, "Play hockey! Play hockey." That's all he said, but Ferguson glared at me with a look that told me he'd kill me if he got hold of me. All I could think was, "Jesus Christ. I hope the linesman can hold onto him, because this man is going insane."

Fergie was in an absolute rage. Nobody attacked his captain! I finally spat out the reason I had punched Beliveau.

"He never signed my autograph book when I was 11," I said. "I promised my dad that someday, I'd get him back!"

Ferguson stopped, and I thought he was going to start laughing. He thought I was nuts. It calmed him down, and then I said, "That's over. I won't hit him again. I'm going to leave it at that."

I had it in my head that I was going to be a hockey player, and around our house, I played it for all it was worth . . . much to the chagrin of my sister.

Everybody in our neighbourhood had a push mower to cut the grass. We were the first to have a gas-powered lawn mower. I was cutting the grass and hit a rock, throwing it so hard that it hit the slate on the side of our house and broke it.

I ran into the house. "Dad, I was cutting the grass and a big rock flew out and broke the siding on our house! What if that rock had hit me in the ankle? It would have broken it, and then there goes hockey!"

"Karen," my dad called out. "Go cut the grass."

This was too easy.

My father asked me to trim our hedges. "But Dad, what if I bruise my thumbs?"

"Karen. We have an investment in your brother. Go trim the hedges."

There was a blizzard one Saturday night. We were trying to watch the hockey game, but the reception was extremely poor. My dad scrambled like a mountain goat up a ladder to the roof and discovered that winds had blown the aerial off the roof.

"Son, come up here and help me. I just need to screw in a couple of base plates."

"But Dad, if I slip, I'll never play hockey again!"

"Karen, get your coat."

I sat inside and sipped a hot chocolate while Karen and my dad fixed the aerial.

My dad coached me from the time I started hockey. He actually made the first trade in peewee history. He traded the two best players on his team—the two best players in the league, by the way—for me. Billy and Ricky Foley were really great players. They were both a little older than me. Ricky went on to play in the NHL with Chicago, Philadelphia and Detroit, as well as for the Toronto Toros in the WHA. The team had a chance to win the championship until my father made the trade. Everybody on the team hated me as a result.

I've been known as "Turk" from the time I was a teenager. There are kids from that neighbourhood in Niagara Falls who still call me "Turk," and most of the Bruins alumni call me "Turk," too.

We were studying Turkey's Ottoman Empire in school when I was about 13. One of the kids drew a cartoon of me, the fanatical Whirling Dervish, wearing a turban, hockey pants and skates with long, curled toes like Aladdin would wear. There was a thought bubble above the cartoon that said, "Derek thinks he's Turkish." From that point on, my friends called me "Turk."

But it seems there might be another story.

My friend Tommy Cottringer swears Turk came from an incident on the rink from about that same time. We were in a close game and I stole the puck from an opponent, and the next thing I knew, we had a three-on-one. I heard someone shout, "Derek! Drop it," so I left the puck for the guy skating behind me. Unfortunately, it was a player from the other team who happened to know my name. He grabbed my pass, turned around and scored in overtime to win the game.

We decided as a team that instead of using our names, we'd make animal sounds. When you wanted a pass, instead of shouting your teammate's name, you might bark or moo. That way, you knew who you were passing to and didn't make the mistake I had made. The sound I was given was a turkey. When I wanted a pass, I'd yell, "Gobble, gobble," and they'd know it was me. Tommy swears that that is how I ended up getting called "Turk." He has never lied to me, and was always one of the guys I could count on through my life.

When I started high school, I picked up an attitude from some of the kids I was hanging out with. I was mouthy, and it was going to get me into trouble. My father drilled an important lesson into me. He knew that I loved hockey and wanted to advance. He told me that when the coach was addressing the team in practice, I was always to stand in front, look at the coach and say "Yes sir" and "No sir." He said, "The coach wants that kid in the front row looking up at him, listening to him and doing exactly what he's told. He doesn't want the jerk in the back fooling around with the puck while he's talking. He expects respect. Always be respectful of your elders."

To this day, I still say "Yes sir" and "No sir," and say it to people who are younger than me. They look at me as if they've never heard the word "sir" before.

When I was 12, I begged my dad to buy me a pair of CCM Tacks. They were actually called Tackaberrys, and all the NHL players wore them. They cost $100, which was a month's salary for my father. I pleaded my case, and finally, my dad agreed to buy me a pair, unbeknownst to my mother. My father had put a few bucks away each week for several months because he didn't want to disappoint his boy. But we made a deal the day we went to the sports shop. "Son, I'll buy you your Tacks, but when you win the Stanley Cup, I get the ring."

"Sure, Dad. Whatever you say." I wasn't thinking about anything but the beautiful kangaroo leather of my new skates.

I was a rink rat when I was 14. I'd skip church on Sundays and help out at the rink all day. There were a bunch of us. That's where I first met Eddie Westfall. At the time, he was a big shot with the Niagara Falls Flyers, the local Ontario Hockey Association junior team. This was prior to the arena getting a Zamboni. We used to flood the ice by pulling barrels of water around the ice surface. For working on the rink all day, they gave us free ice time. Of course, you know when they gave us our ice time? At midnight, when they shut the lights off! Luckily, the street lights threw off enough glow to play. It's amazing how your eyes adjust. You really learn how to play hockey when you're doing it in the dark. The other perk I got was getting to watch the Niagara Falls Flyers play for free.

Tommy Cottringer was my best friend and a great goaltender. He and I moved up through the ranks together, from peewee to bantam and then on to midget. I was playing midget even though I was bantam-aged.

Tommy and I were the one-two punch of the Niagara Falls Midgets, even though there wasn't much of a punch. We were getting beaten by scores of 14–4. I'd get four goals and Tommy would be named the first star. I've never seen a goaltender let in six, seven or eight goals and get the first star, but he was making 60 saves. Tommy was better than Bernie Parent, Doug Favell or any of the goalies in Boston's system at the time. He was the most competitive player I've ever met. He hated to lose, but we always got shelled. We had bad teams, but came out every night with renewed hope.

Stamford always beat the snot out of us. They were bigger than us. They had the best midget line in hockey at that time—Fred Bassi, Albert Boone and Brian Cornell. They beat every previous record for a midget line in Canada, and held the records until Wayne Gretzky came along. They could score from all over the building. The three of them would come out of their zone and tic-tac-toe, *boom!* You couldn't stop them. You'd trip them, hit them—it didn't matter. I tried everything. In 1961–62, their team went undefeated and averaged better than five goals a game on their way to the Niagara District championship and then the All-Ontario midget championship. They were unbelievable!

We had back-to-back games against Stamford on a Friday and Saturday night. We knew we were going to get killed. During the warmup before the first game, we were skating around and I saw one of their players, an older kid, wearing a leather helmet with a pink tassel on the top. I pointed him out to my teammates—"What is that?"

We were losing 5–2 in the first period—which, for us, was a moral victory. They were upset when I got a third goal late in the period because we were back in the hunt. The ref then dropped the puck and I won the faceoff. I kept the puck as though it had a string on it and stepped around the guy with the helmet and pink tassel. He dropped his gloves and punched me right in the mouth. *Bang!* My head snapped back and I just looked at him. I still had both my hands on my stick. He hit me again twice—*bang, bang!* I didn't do a thing. The referee pointed at him and at me. "You're both gone."

This guy banged me around all game. I got my fourth goal in the second period, but we got pounded again and ended up losing something like 14–4.

My dad always took me to games, watched and then took me home. I climbed into the car after the game and in a routine that played out following every game, I asked, "What did you think, Dad?"

My dad wasn't saying anything. I asked, "What's the matter? You're quiet. I got four goals."

He said, "You disappointed me."

"Why?" I asked. "We can't beat them."

"No, no. That isn't it," he replied. "Did you get a penalty?"

"Yeah," I said. "But I didn't do anything."

"That's the problem," he said. "Did you get five minutes for receiving? All you were was a punching bag."

I said, "Dad, I didn't think I'd go to the penalty box for that."

"Always," he said. "The ref will always send you both off, five and five. So defend yourself. You're playing the same team again tomorrow night, so I want you to straighten that guy out right away. Show him you're not there to be pushed around."

"Okay," I nodded.

The next night, we were skating around in the warmup. The guy with the helmet was skating around like a big shot, so I timed it so that I'd reach centre ice at the same time he did. As he circled along the red line, I stepped over and hit him with a right hook. *Bam!* I suckered him and then jumped on him.

I got kicked out of the game, but there was never a happier guy on the planet than my dad! He beamed. "Now, you see how much respect you get next time you play."

My teammates gave me more respect, and the word went out: "Don't hit Sanderson—he's crazy!" Once that message starting circulating, it was amazing the respect I got. I liked that!

At the time, we were only an A team playing against AA and AAA teams, and we were getting slaughtered regularly. It was during that season that I got hit harder than I'd ever been hit. We were playing Fort Erie, and I got hammered by some kid. That did it. I wanted to pack it in. I said, "If you can get hit that hard, then I'm going to quit."

I asked my mom if I could talk to her. I told her I no longer wanted to be a hockey player, and that I now really wanted to be a doctor.

She said, "Oh fine, Derek. That's a wonderful profession. I think you can do that and you can choose to do anything you like. Let me talk to your father."

My father came home at 11 o'clock that night, and I was supposed to be in bed. But there was a grate that fed the heat to the second floor, and if I took the grate off and stuck my head down, I could listen to my parents talk on the first floor.

I heard my dad come in and give my mom a kiss. Like always, he asked how we kids were doing. My mother said, "Karen's fine, but I had a conversation with Derek that I'd like to speak to you about."

"Oh yeah? What was it about?"

She said, "Derek wants to quit hockey and pay attention to education and be a doctor."

My dad was puzzled. "Oh, he does, eh?"

"Yes. He got hit really hard last night and now, all of a sudden, he wants to quit."

My dad wasn't having anything to do with that change in career path. "No, he's going to be a hockey player. I'll take care of this."

I quietly put the grate back in its place and went to bed. I heard my father say there was no question but that I was going to be a hockey player, so I forgot about it.

A couple of days later, my dad said, "Derek, your mother tells me you want to be a doctor. That's a wonderful profession if you've got the ability. After five years in high school, you've got four years of university, then four years of medical school, and then you get an internship. You'll start paying back your debt when you're 34. Of course, you have to buy malpractice insurance. You'll work 12-hour days. Are you sure you want to do that? Or would you rather work hard in hockey for an hour and a half each day?"

I said, "I think I'll stick to hockey."

He asked me why I considered giving up a game I loved and did well at.

"Dad, it was just a thought."

"No it wasn't," he replied. "That kid walloped you, and all of a sudden you wanted to give up hockey to be a doctor."

"Dad! He hit me really hard, you know!"

"Yeah, but he hit you clean, son. Keep your head up and it won't happen to you again. Hockey is a tough game. You've got some tough people out there. Don't ever think you're the biggest, baddest boy in the land. Always keep your eyes up. If you play dirty instead of tough, then remember that those who live by the sword also die by the sword. If you have talent, that's great, but if you've got talent and toughness, that's unbeatable."

I really loved playing hockey and I was pretty good at it, but you never know if you're going to make it. As I got to be about 17, I thought, "I can do this. I can make it in hockey." I never really doubted that I'd play in the National Hockey League. I firmly believed that if I wanted to play in the NHL, I would.

CHAPTER 6

HIGH SCHOOL HIJINX

I thought I was pretty cool by the time I started high school at Niagara Falls Collegiate Vocational Institute in 1960. There were about 1,400 students, maybe 50 of whom were bound for university. At the time, girls were directed to the commercial stream and guys to the technical part. There was an academic component, but it wasn't the primary focus of the high school. The school is gone now.

The community we lived in was a tough, working-class neighbourhood. Nobody had any money. Everybody was a working stiff. I hung out with some great guys. Leigh Shelton was my best friend when I was young, and Tommy Cottringer was my best friend later on. We had tough guys and we had guys who excelled in their field. My next-door neighbours were Denis and Jimmy Callaghan. Denis is a doctor in Hamilton and Jimmy is serving a life sentence in Kingston Penitentiary for murder.

I've known Rob Nicholson, who is now Canada's justice minister and attorney general, all my life. I'm six years older than he is. In fact, I used to walk him to school when he was in kindergarten. Later, I'd get him to shag the balls when we were playing road hockey if one of our shots missed the net and went rolling down the street. When I was in junior, I used to play a little game with some of the neighbour kids. I'd play goal on our driveway, and Robbie and some of the other kids had to try to score on me. For every shot I saved, they would owe me a penny. For every goal they scored, I'd pay them a nickel. I was pretty good in goal, and the kids had a tough time beating me. I'd usually win about 12 cents from a couple of them. We had fun.

Eddie and Brian Greenspan lived around the corner from us. Eddie was a little bit older than me and Brian was a year younger. They were really bright kids. I didn't know until recently that I ended Brian's hockey career. We were about 13 years old and playing hockey in my backyard. He was the goalie. It was just pickup, so nobody was wearing any equipment. I fired a pretty good shot and hit him right in the balls. He threw down his goalie stick. "That's it. I'm done." Maybe hockey wasn't his game, but he did all right for himself. Brian and Ed became two of the most highly regarded defence lawyers in Canada.

I was also hanging with some tough kids. By then, I had started to smoke and was pretty mouthy. I also started stealing. I always did it on my own; if I was going down, I wasn't going to get caught because of somebody else's stupidity.

I noticed how none of the stores kept watch on their customers. It didn't matter whether it was a five-and-dime or a grocery store, they were all pretty lax. I was taking orders from the guys and was getting away with stealing things. When you get away with it the first time, you think, "That was pretty easy. These store-keepers are pretty stupid."

I used to watch, wait and linger. If I thought somebody was watching me, I'd leave. Woolworth's was easy. They left their rings out on the counter, and even though they weren't really expensive, everybody at my school went steady with the rings I stole.

When I was about 13, I turned to stealing cigarettes. I took orders for cartons by brand. I wasn't driving yet and knew I could get a lot more cartons if I had access to a car. One of my customers ended up driving me everywhere. I think I got 16 or 17 cartons of cigarettes from different grocery stores. We had an old bathtub in the backyard. My dad threw it out when we got a new one, and it was upside down in the yard. I figured that was a perfect place to hide the cartons until I found buyers.

It was a Saturday afternoon, and my father and I were watching the Cleveland Indians on TV. They were our team. The phone rang and my mother answered and said, "It's for you, dear," and handed the phone to my dad.

I just had a gut feeling that my driver had ratted me out. "Great," I thought. "The first time I trusted somebody enough to bring them into my game, *bang!* It only took a week for the dirtbag to give me up."

My intuition was right. My driver's father found his cigarettes and asked him where he got them. "Where'd you get the money for all this stuff?" He told his dad that Derek Sanderson gave them to him, so his father made him call my dad.

I was sitting beside my father and could hear his half of the conversation: "Yeah, you certain? . . . You better be certain . . . All right, goodbye."

I glanced at my dad's face, and he was steaming mad. He was trying to figure out how to handle the situation. He had to make a point, but how does a father handle something like that?

I tried to deflect the inevitable by making stupid small talk—"Hey Dad, wasn't that a good hit? Do you think they'll win this game?"

He didn't answer. He just sat there, and then, all of a sudden, he demanded, "Where are they?"

Damn! "They're in the backyard under the bathtub."

"All right," he barked. "Go get them!"

The two of us walked into the yard and he saw them, all 16 cartons. I saw a little smirk on his lips. I could tell he was thinking, "How could this kid be smart enough to steal 16 cartons?"

"Put them all in the car," he demanded.

"What for?"

"We're taking them back," he said.

We went to every single store I had stolen from, and at each one, my dad insisted that I talk directly to the manager. When the manager arrived, Dad introduced himself and said, "My son wants to talk to you."

"Sir," I stammered each time, "I stole these cigarettes from your store yesterday."

The managers usually said, "You're kidding? Well, what are we going to do about this?" Every one of them, except for one, deferred to my father, who said, "I hope you trust me. I'll handle this." They agreed, and I'd give them back the two or three cartons I'd stolen from their store.

But one guy said, "I'm calling the police."

My dad was quick to reply, "You call the police and I'll break every bone in your body."

We went home, and my father punched me right in the chest. My mom and my sister cried. Karen was hysterical, screaming, "Don't hurt him! Don't hurt him!"

I thought, "What the hell was I thinking?" The punches didn't hurt me physically, but they certainly did emotionally. "What did I do to my family?"

My father gave me a left and a right, but then I balled my hand into a fist. He had always told me not to take shit from anybody. When he saw the fist, he growled, "You pull that and it'll be your last day on this earth!"

I took the punishment, and he snarled, "Am I raising a common thief? I'm done with you!"

He walked outside, sat on the porch and lit up a cigarette.

My mother insisted that I go and apologize. "Grow up, Derek, and tell your father you are sorry."

I was trying to be tough. Here I was, 14 years old, thinking I could take a few punches, but when I went out to my father on the porch, I noticed that he was crying.

I never stole again.

The tears really got to me. I later realized that if he had given me a beating or grounded me, it wouldn't have worked. But to make me go back to the managers and observe the respect they had for my father for forcing me to own up, really made me grow up.

I sat down beside my dad. "Son, do you think your friends think you're cool? They don't! You're the fool. They're laughing at you." He said, "Friends never laugh at you, they laugh *with* you. Learn the difference."

I learned a valuable lesson that day. Every once in a while, my dad would ask if there was any more stealing going on. I'd tell him there wasn't. "Your word is your bond, you know, son. Don't ever lie to me."

I never did lie to my father again.

I realized that I had hurt my family over some stupid cartons of cigarettes. I had let everybody down. When my buddies—former customers—asked if I wanted to go steal some cigarettes with them, I said, "Nope. Not me. I pay for them now. That shit's over."

Every teenager in Niagara Falls hung out on Centre Street in Clifton Hill. Twenty or 30 of us would gather at Borelli's Billiards. There was Carmen Barillaro, Albert Cavelli, John Clary, Tony DeGiorgio, Gino DiPietrangelo, Louie Gallardi, Denny Goldfinch, Billy Prestia, Domenic Vaccaro. I was a skinny punk; the youngest of this group of guys. I was the gopher—go fer the coffee, the paper, go get this, go get that—for the older, bigger kids. This was a gang in every sense of the word. Some of these boys were tough and got themselves in some trouble through the years. But every one of them looked out for everybody else. And we had a lot of fun, too. There were a couple of the guys who were really funny.

My dad always warned me, "Son, be careful who you associate with. Those guys will get you in trouble."

I said, "Dad, don't be so judgmental. Let me tell you about my friends. They make sure I don't get into any trouble. You know why? Because I can play hockey and they don't want me to ruin my career. They tell me, 'With your hockey, you can get out of here. We can't.'"

The guys knew that I had been signed by the Bruins. I was 15. Albert Cavelli and Louie Gallardi sat me down one night and said, "Look, Turk. If you don't leave us to find your own path, you're an asshole. See that parking meter over there? We'll still be hanging on that when we're 60. You don't need to. Get out of here. If you get pinched, you're going to end up like us. You're going to be a big shot some day."

They really looked out for me. We'd be hanging out on the street corner, telling stories and having some laughs, and the same cop, a British guy, would tell us to move along. "Hey, you guys. No loitering! Come on, move along!"

We'd tell him we were waiting for the bus, and he'd say, "Now come on, boys. You are not waiting for the bus. Move along."

All 30 of us would shuffle three or four feet to the left.

"All right. Don't be smart. Move along."

We'd all then shuffle three or feet to the right. The poor guy.

One day, we faked a fight in the alley. He came running in. "Hey, hey!

What's going on here?" We threw a sack over his head and took his clothes off. Then, we put his gun belt back on him and put him on the corner of the street.

"I'm going back to England. You people are crazy!"

He had a nervous breakdown and quit.

Every day, we'd entertain ourselves somehow. We didn't really do anything wrong, but it was a tough group. Tough, but very loyal. We were all good friends.

One night, one of the guys got into trouble in Fort Erie. Everybody got their car and was ready to go. I said, "I'm all set, guys," but Billy Prestia said, "You aren't coming. There are pipes and chains and it's going to be a big fight. You might get hurt." They wouldn't let me go.

A bunch of the guys later apprenticed with my dad at General Motors. He wanted to help them out, so he got them into the apprenticeship program as machinists.

When I was in the NHL, every time I went home to Niagara Falls, I'd play golf with Tommy Cottringer, Johnny Lombardi and Carmen Barillaro. Carmen was a funny bastard. He was a hairdresser. He was convicted of heroin trafficking in 1978. Two years later, he was out on parole, but got nabbed for selling heroin to an undercover cop and they put him away for three years. He was also involved in some other illegal stuff. Carmen was well known in the underworld. He reported directly to John Papalia, head of the Magaddino family and one of Canada's highest-level Mafia members. You didn't mess with Carmen.

A rival faction, the Musitanos, tried to take over the Magaddinos' drug turf. John Papalia, the head of the Magaddinos, was shot and killed in May 1997. Carmen took over as *capo,* but not for long. Two months later, Carmen's wife and kids had gone shopping, and he was home by himself in Niagara Falls. The doorbell rang, and when he opened the door, he was shot twice in the face and killed. The guy accused of killing Carmen was a hired killer for the Musitanos—and the same guy who killed John Papalia.

Carmen was a good guy. I said to Tommy, "I didn't know he was a killer." Tommy said, "Turk, how do you think he lived so well?" He did what he had to do. When Johnny and Tommy and I went golfing afterwards, we'd laugh about how Carmen would bitch and moan about shots.

When I was 16, one of my buddies was a guy named Tommy. Tommy was only 17, but he already had the reputation of being a guy who was getting a lot of action with the girls. It certainly helped that he had a purple '55 Chevy with four on the floor.

There was a girl in town whom all the boys practised on. She was a couple of years older than me, had a stunning figure and it was well known that she never said no to the boys.

Tommy and I were in the parking lot at a Red Barn fast-food restaurant having a cigarette when I spotted her. She had just finished work, and she looked fantastic. I asked Tommy if I could borrow his car. He asked, "What the hell for?" I told him I was going to get laid.

I was a virgin. Talk about working on a mystery without any clues! I had absolutely no idea what to do, but I had bravado and bluff. I wanted Tommy to think I was getting as much action as he was.

Tommy was very particular about his car. Nobody but Tommy was allowed to drive it. And the girls were all impressed with his '55 Chevy. He agreed to let me borrow his car. He tossed me the keys. I pulled across the street and wheeled up beside the girl.

"Do you want a ride?"

"Okay!"

I opened the door and she slid in. It was summer and still light out at 8:30. I had to kill some time before it was dark enough for me to make my move.

Now that I had her in the car, I didn't know what to do. I asked her if she had to go straight home. She rolled her eyes and yawned, "No." I didn't know where I was going to take her. I figured that going to a bar was the right first step. I didn't know any spots, so I decided to just drive around and we'd find a place.

We drove across the border to Niagara Falls, New York, and ended up at a place called the Ontario House—the "OH." We found a table and the waitress came over and asked us what we'd like. At the time, if your eyes could get to the top of the bar and you had cash, you got served in Niagara Falls, New York.

There was no carding, no checking a licence, ID or anything. I was sitting there getting served and I hadn't even started shaving.

I was trying to be so gallant. "Ladies first. What would you like?"

She ordered a beer.

Then it was my turn, but I had no idea what to order. I had never ordered a drink in my life, and there I was, ordering a drink with a girl in an American bar. I ordered a whiskey because I saw it in a cowboy movie. From the facial expression of the waitress, I knew she was laughing at me.

She said, "You want that on the rocks or neat?"

Shit!

I said, "Neat." "Neat" sounded cool to say.

My date gave me a look that said, "What the hell are you doing?"

The waitress came back with a beer and a glass, plus a shotglass with whiskey. I proposed a quick toast, we touched glasses and I fired back the whiskey just like they do in the movies.

Oh my God! It felt like someone stuck a torch down my throat. I wanted to puke, but I had to fight the feeling. I took a deep breath and said, "Oh crap, I drank that too fast!" I started making excuses, but she just laughed at me.

The waitress came back a little later with another beer for my date and another shot for me. By that time, I was already feeling light-headed. But then it was time for the bill. I had no concept of prices. I had $12 on me. The beers were two dollars each, but the shots were $3.25 each. I started to do the math in my head. "Four bucks and $6.50. Holy shit, I owe this waitress $10.50!"

I tossed the $12 on the table, told her to keep the change and stumbled out the door. Then I realized that I had to pay a toll to cross the bridge! "Oh shit. I don't have any more money."

My date sighed and handed me a dollar from her purse.

I was nervous as hell. We were driving along and I said, "Do you have to go straight home?"

Exasperated, she said, "I didn't have to go straight home when you asked me at 8:30. We had a couple of drinks and I didn't have to go straight home then. And now that we're over the bridge, I *still* don't have to go straight home."

"Do you want to go someplace?"

"Yeah."

It was dark by then, and I took the girl over by the Niagara Gorge Golf Course. I was really nervous in spite of having a couple of drinks in me. We found a parking spot. All the cars around us were parked and couples are making out. I turned off the ignition in Tommy's car and these purple lights came on and it made the interior look like it was in a porno movie.

I messed around with the lights and finally got them turned off. I looked over at the girl and said, "Come here." She looked at me, rolled her eyes, pulled off her blouse, unhooked her bra, pulled off her panties, and that was it.

I wrestled to get my pants off, and in the process, I leaned on the horn twice. When the moment of truth came, I didn't have a clue where to put things—not a clue.

With my date's guidance, things started to happen, but she started screaming. All I could think was that she was loving it, but then I realized that every time I thrust, her head was hitting the door handle. I felt terrible when I realized, so I stopped what we were doing, went over and opened the door. When I did, her head fell off the end of the seat and the interior light came on. I panicked. I slammed the door and nearly broke her neck. At the same time, I was at the point of no return and the inevitable happened. And not where it should have occurred.

She screamed, "Take me home, you stupid idiot!"

Embarrassed, I said, "Okay, okay. I'll take you home."

I went back to the Red Barn alone. Everybody had seen me leave with the girl, so they assumed I had got lucky. Tommy asked, "So, did you get laid?"

"No."

He was astonished. "She doesn't say no to anybody, and she said no to you?"

I just shrugged. "Had a couple of drinks and took her home. That was it."

Some of the girls from school were within earshot. I didn't know that by telling my pal nothing happened, it sent my stock through the roof. All the girls assumed that I had gotten lucky but was the only guy who didn't brag about his conquest. I didn't kiss and tell—it's true—and I ended up being a hero . . . but I was still a virgin!

CHAPTER 7

JUNIOR ACHIEVEMENT

I became the property of the Boston Bruins when I was 14.

Weston Adams Sr., the Bruins' president, was a wonderful man and he became a dear friend. His father, Charles Adams, owned a grocery store chain called Finast, and he was also the first owner of the Boston Bruins. Weston was wealthy because of the family money, but his heart was in hockey. He played goal when he attended Harvard.

Weston took over from his father as president of the Bruins in 1936. When he served in the Second World War, the team struggled and Adams was forced to sell the team in 1951 to Walter Brown, the owner of Boston Garden, but he became chairman of the board of Boston Garden five years later.

In the late 1950s, the Bruins' farm system wasn't nearly as developed as those of the other five National Hockey League teams. Boston struggled along, and while they were able to get into the playoffs most seasons, it was clear they would have to upgrade their talent in order to be competitive with the rest of the league and get back to winning the Stanley Cup. Weston took an active role in looking for talent. He'd jump in his car—no flying for him—and make the trek across Canada, looking for hockey players. That he would sit in cold rinks during the winter, looking for talent, was really quite amazing to me.

The Bruins sponsored junior teams in New Westminster, British Columbia; Estevan, Saskatchewan; and Oshawa and Niagara Falls in Ontario. Mr. Adams discovered so many guys who went on to play with the Bruins—Wayne Cashman, Gary Dornhoefer, Doug Favell, Bill Goldsworthy, Reggie Leach, Rick MacLeish, Bobby Orr, Bernie Parent, Jean-Paul Parise, Jean Pronovost,

Joe Watson, Tommy Webster and me. In fact, if the Bruins could have kept the players they lost to expansion in 1967, we would have been a dynasty. Weston Adams Sr. did a masterful job scouting, and he did it himself, with the help of a head scout named Harold Cotton, a former NHL star who went by the nickname "Baldy."

The Boston Bruins acquired my rights when I was playing in a bantam tournament in Paris, Ontario. I played well, got four goals, and Baldy Cotton came down to our dressing room to find my dad.

Mr. Cotton said, "I understand Derek Sanderson is your son."

My dad replied, "Yeah."

"Well, sir, the Boston Bruins would like to buy your son's negotiation rights." For signing, he gave my dad a cheque for $100. My father cashed it so fast it would make your head spin. For him, that was a month's pay. For me, it didn't really mean anything, but it gave me bragging rights in the neighbourhood.

You had to be 18 years old to sign a C form, which formally assigned your pro rights to an NHL team, but clubs also had negotiation lists that included players much younger. They called them "negotiation lists," but it's not like you had a chance to negotiate. It was modern-day slavery. You remained the team's property for two years. If they wanted to get rid of you or if you didn't want to sign with them, you had to stay out of hockey for two years to get your amateur status back. It was like being suspended.

The Bruins traded me twice at the age of 14. Then, when I was 15, Weston Adams came to see me play in Stamford. "Sanderson is a great competitor," he said. "There are players in this league who can do things better than he does, but nobody is the competitor he is. Derek looks at hockey the same way I do. Once they drop the puck, he hates the hell out of the opposition."

I had just turned 16 when the Niagara Falls Flyers sent me a letter inviting me to training camp. I didn't even know that they were watching me. I didn't even know that they knew me. The Flyers were a big deal in Niagara Falls. Their owner, Hap Emms, had moved the franchise from Barrie to the Falls for the 1960–61 season. I used to go to some of the games. Gil Gilbert was the star. He had a cup of coffee with the Bruins a couple of years later. Eddie Westfall was on that team, too. The next season, I watched the Flyers even

49

more. By then, they had Donny Awrey, Terry Crisp, Gary Dornhoefer, Wayne Maxner and Ronnie Schock.

I attended training camp in Niagara Falls in the fall of 1962, but when I showed up, there were 138 guys trying out for four spots! I had never seen anything like that in my life. For two days, we scrimmaged nonstop. Everybody was out to impress. If you carried the puck 15 feet, you were really doing something special, and then *boom!* Somebody would run you over. You bled, spit your teeth out and kept going, and the management in the stands would put a check mark beside your name. "That kid's got some balls." That was old-school hockey. Courage was supreme.

Hap Emms's philosophy was that if you could skate, he could teach you how to play hockey. My father was a big believer in that himself, as was Lloyd Percival.

I had been told that my nemeses—Fred Bassi, Albert Boone and Brian Cornell—had been asked to try out, too. They were so good that I wouldn't stand a chance of making the team with them around. Boone was a better centre than I was, Cornell was as smart a right winger as I had ever seen and Bassi was a bull on skates. All three could have played in the NHL.

The three of them told Emms they wouldn't attend camp unless they were paid. Emms was cheap, and told the three that he'd give them the opportunity to play, but they insisted: "Not unless we're paid."

So, Hap Emms called me. "Do you want to come out and practise with the Flyers?" I couldn't say yes fast enough!

Bassi, Boone and Cornell used to laugh at me because I wasn't getting paid. I didn't care. I was learning the game and they never got a shot. Freddy Bassi later played at Boston University and then in the Eastern Hockey League. Brian Cornell played a bit of junior with Niagara Falls and then, ironically, at Cornell University. He went on to be an executive at Price Waterhouse. I lost track of Al Boone through the years. He definitely was talented, but I guess he didn't want it badly enough.

I really was all that Hap Emms had left at that point. He took me aside and told me he liked my effort. Then he said, "You've got your family father, and I am now your hockey father. I don't want the two to meet."

I was stunned.

"I don't want any irate father coming down here telling me his son is better than we think he is. I wouldn't tell him how to do his job; I don't want him to tell me how to do mine. I want you as part of this team. When you sign this A form [tryout form], I want you to go from here directly to your father and tell him that he's no longer to interfere with your hockey life."

So I did. That was difficult. I'd always gone to my dad for advice about my hockey career.

Hap Emms had me practising regularly with the club. "You're only 16, Derek. I want you here, sitting on the bench, to watch and learn."

My dad suggested, "Pick somebody that's good at their position and watch what they do so that when you're out there, you can do what they do." The best player on the team in those days was the captain, Ronnie Schock. I watched Schock and how he cut back and curled and took player position. I learned a lot sitting on the bench. I shut my mouth and minded my business. I was very coachable, despite popular opinion.

I was up and down between playing midget and playing with the Flyers. I got into two games during the regular season. No points, but 10 penalty minutes. Niagara Falls finished first in the Ontario Hockey Association Junior A loop. I played a game in the playoffs, too, as the Flyers eliminated the Hamilton Red Wings, Montreal Jr. Canadiens, Neil McNeil Maroons and Espanola Eagles to earn a berth in the Memorial Cup final against the Edmonton Oil Kings.

The Oil Kings were a powerhouse. I didn't make the trip, but followed the results religiously. Edmonton absolutely ran the Flyers out of the building and won the series four games to two to claim the junior championship, but in the process, both Gary Dornhoefer and Gary Harmer suffered broken legs. Niagara Falls did not have a physical team. They were fast, but not very aggressive. The Oil Kings had a tough team with guys like Bert Marshall, Pat Quinn and my future teammate, Glen Sather.

Hap Emms, the owner of the Flyers, would get money from the Boston Bruins to help run the team, and in return, it was expected that the Flyers would prepare players to play in the National Hockey League for Boston. Part of that was incorporating the Bruins' system into the Niagara Falls coaching scheme, so that players who made the transition played the way the Bruins played. So, for two and a half hours each day, they drilled into us six ways to come out of our own end under pressure without panicking and losing the puck.

In exchange for giving the Flyers hand-me-down equipment, Weston Adams Sr. got one personal pick per training camp—somebody who had not been picked for the team by the Flyers' staff. There were a lot of very talented hockey players in camp in 1963. I was a 16-year-old runt compared to some of the 20-year-olds who were already married with kids.

Adams came to training camp and told Emms he was going to choose me. "No," Emms said. "Get somebody else. Sanderson's never going to make it."

"What's our deal?" Mr. Adams reminded him.

Hap said, "You get one player."

Adams came back with, "And you're telling me I shouldn't take Sanderson?"

Hap said, "I just don't want you to waste your pick. He isn't going to make it."

Boston's head scout, Baldy Cotton, and coach, Milt Schmidt, agreed with Emms that I'd never play in the National Hockey League. I wasn't very big, and I could tell by the line they had me on that they had no faith in me. I was playing with a couple of linemates who were not going to make the team either. Every player knows who is going to make the team, even before management does. And when management makes the wrong choice, it is demoralizing to a team and has profound repercussions for that season— and sometimes longer.

I hadn't been told of the behind-the-scenes management discussion, but I could tell I wasn't in the Flyers' plans for 1963–64. I was sitting in the dressing room, discouraged and taking my stuff off. Just then, the trainer, Ken Carson, told me that Hap Emms wanted to see me. I was crushed. I thought, "This is it. I'm going to get cut and sent back to the Stamford Junior Bs."

I met with Emms. He was cheap, but he never bullshitted you. He said,

"Well, against my better judgment, Weston Adams Sr. would like to see you. He has some news for you."

I met Mr. Adams and we walked around outside the Niagara Falls Memorial Arena. He was wearing a coat worth more than my father made in a year. He said, "Derek, you're not the most talented player out there, but you show me something every time you step out onto the ice. I'm impressed with you. I think you have the look of the eagle."

I didn't know what that meant, but it sure sounded good to me!

Mr. Adams continued. "You're my ugly duckling, because no one thinks you can make it. They all think I'm a fool. I think you, me and your father are the only ones that believe in you. I would really appreciate it if you'd help me prove them wrong."

I was smiling like the butcher's dog. "Yes, sir! You won't be sorry!"

"That's good," he said, and then winked at me. "If you've only got one guy believing in you, it's not a bad thing that it's the guy who owns the Boston Bruins. Let's make a pact—I'll back you, but I need you to be the best player you can be. Don't be disappointed if they don't play you a lot. You're going to do just fine."

I was going to be paid $40 a week. Christ, my hard-working Dad only made about $25 a week!

My father cried with joy when I told him the news.

That day, my mother read my horoscope from the *Niagara Falls Evening Review*. It said: "Today you will benefit from someone else's folly."

Hap Emms was like a second father to me while I was playing in Niagara Falls. He was the owner, general manager and the coach. Bill Long was the assistant coach, although he really was our head coach. Bill lived for hockey and was a brilliant coach. He was a patient man. Emms was a very religious man who refused to coach on Sundays, so he had Long take over for him then. As Mr. Emms got older, he eventually handed the team over to Long and stayed on as the GM.

As I mentioned, the Flyers got all the Bruins old hand-me-downs. I was given equipment, including long underwear, that had Cal Gardner's name on it, and the sad thing was, he hadn't played with Boston since 1957.

I got a fair bit of playing time. They had me on the fourth line, but they used to send me out for key faceoffs and penalty killing. My dad always told me, "If you excel in the little things, the big things take care of themselves."

A couple of times, my dad had to remind me to play the game they wanted. "Son, stop, get back into the play and get aggressive. You're floating. You're looking for goals. You've got to skate. You've got to bang and bruise. And remember, if someone takes the puck off you, stop! At that instant, you will never be closer to the puck than when you lose it. Don't go for the big skate—stop!"

I knew he was right.

Hap Emms asked my dad to put me on his insurance policy so that the team didn't have to insure me. Sure enough, I needed a knee operation later in the season.

We were playing the Peterborough Petes. There was a brawl in Peterborough one night and I beat the snot out of one of their guys. They were waiting for me the next time we came in. I knew there was going to be a donnybrook. It was always an animal house when we played there. They were up 5–3 and were looking for any excuse to run me.

I always played with my head down but my eyes up. After the whistle, I was watching for Bill Plager, but I left my right side vulnerable. Two or three seconds after the whistle, one of the Petes, Bob Jamieson, kneed me in the knee and popped my cartilage. I played with it the rest of the season, but it hurt like a bastard.

Kenny Carson was a fabulous trainer. He later went to work for the Toronto Blue Jays. This is a guy who took his training seriously. He helped me through the injury during the season. The team doctor was Dr. Williams, a former World War II army surgeon. He had witnessed a lot of death during the war. His bedside manner was tough. We usually practised each evening from six o'clock until eight, and he'd come by after he left the office to check us out.

You did not mess with Doc Williams. Towards the end of the season, he examined me and told me I had a meniscus tear. "I've got to go in and see how bad it is."

Dr. Williams operated on me the next morning at seven o'clock. I was on medication and had a nice little buzz, but the anesthetic wore off by midafter-noon. I was worried. I was just 17 and had never had surgery before. I wiggled my toes, not knowing what to expect, but could move both feet, so that was a good sign. Half-afraid, I slid the sheet to one side in order to look at my knee.

Expecting to see a cast, I was quite surprised—maybe even horrified—to find that it was only bandaged. Dr. Williams explained that muscles atrophy in a cast, and that bandaging a knee after surgery, while experimental, was his preferred method of treatment. I was fascinated. He explained that a cast smothers the muscles, and when they don't get any exercise, the body over-compensates for what has been injured.

The doctor asked me if I had started doing my exercises.

"Doc, it's four o'clock and you cut me this morning at seven o'clock! I'm still bleeding!"

Without any sympathy, he asked, "Before I go through the roof on you, were you not told to do exercises?"

I hemmed and hawed. "Yeah, I guess so. The physical therapist came by and showed me what to do—quadricep squeezes and lifting my leg. But Doc, I said I couldn't! I tried, but it really, really hurt!"

"It won't hurt compared to what's going to happen." He grabbed my big toe and lifted my leg up about four feet. The pain shot through my body.

"*Whoaaaaaaaaa!!!!*"

I reached for an ashtray—anything that I could throw at him—but it wasn't within arm's reach. I tried to kick him, but couldn't.

"Quit struggling," he commanded. "Tighten your quads. Hold them up. When I count to three, I'm dropping your leg. One, two—"

"Doc! Don't drop it!" I screamed.

Boom! He dropped it. The pain was off the charts.

He started again. "We can do this all day, Derek. Are you going to man up and start doing your exercises?"

"I will," I begged. "But why do I have to put myself through all this pain?"

He answered, "That's what we've got medication for." He kept working my leg, but I knew what to expect and could slow my leg when he released it.

"I want those quads built back up," he explained. "You've got to toughen up your quadriceps so they'll protect your knee. If you have big, strong quads, it'll help protect you."

While he was not a kind and gentle soul, Doc Williams was a wonderful surgeon and very proud of his work. He loved hockey, and I said to him, "Isn't it a shame that you have all this talent and yet the fuss is being made about my knee and the ramifications to my career?"

He just smiled. "Derek, no one would pay to watch me operate, but millions will someday pay to watch you play hockey. I've got my job, and you've got yours, and we are both very good at what we do and very proud of our chosen professions. But I can't play hockey and you could never become a surgeon."

The Flyers finished fourth in 1963–64. I scored 12 goals and had 27 points. Ron Schock and Bill Goldsworthy, both of whom also went on to play with the Bruins, were our big guns that year. Bernie Parent had the best goals-against average in the league. The Toronto Marlboros eliminated us in the first round of the playoffs and went on to win the Memorial Cup.

In my opinion, I would really come into my own the following season, 1964–65.

CHAPTER 8

MEMORIAL CUP MEMORIES

I was never really much into working out, especially during the summer. My dad, on advice he heard from Lloyd Percival, did not believe in bulk. Long, sinewy muscles were preferred so that, even if you were slightly built, as I was, you could still be very fast and very tough. My father would tell me, "The more meat you have on you, the more you have to carry. This isn't football. You have to be quick and agile."

But he did have me work on strengthening my wrists so I'd be better on faceoffs. He took a broomstick, drilled a hole through the middle of it and then knotted a hockey lace on one side and attached a weight to the end of the lace. I started using one-pound weights and worked my way up to four pounds. And I would turn my wrists to lift the weight and then roll it back down. I repeated that over and over again. I really feel it built up my wrists and fingers, giving me a strong grip on my stick and making me better able to win faceoffs.

Hap Emms, our general manager, and Bill Long, our coach, taught a little of the Lloyd Percival methodology—the team concept and puck control. We did the same thing for two and a half hours at every single practice in junior. We had the six ways to come out of our own end under pressure drilled into us. Bill Long said, "After you cross that red line, create. But I always want one of you—I don't care which one—to stay high. Let two work the corners and one guy stay high. That way, if we lose the puck, the guy turns to take a winger and the defencemen can stand up on the puck carrier and the open guy. And if it's two on two, nothing happens." And that was their simple way to play the game. It was the Bruins' way to play the game, too. They were preparing us for the National Hockey League.

I was wearing number 17 and centring a line with Brian Bradley and Teddy Snell. Bradley could really dangle. He was smart, and I'd say, "I'm gonna come down the boards and flush the puck out right. I want you to be there when the defenceman is looking for a winger. If it doesn't happen and he uses his centreman, I'll take the other side."

He'd say, "Okay, Turk," and it worked like a charm. We had it figured out and timed.

Our rivals were the Hamilton Red Wings, who played in the old barn on Barton Street. They didn't have glass behind the net—they had chicken wire. But we did like playing in Hamilton because they televised the games. When we were on TV, we made a point of looking good. "New laces, boys. CHCH-TV tonight." We'd comb our hair and everything.

The Flyers were playing well, and I was having a pretty good season. One night, I got three goals and a helper and we won 4–3. The next day, I was at practice, feeling pretty good about myself, dipsy-doodling and playing like some Fancy Dan. I was skating down the wall, cutting to the middle, splitting the D and *ping!* I'd fire one home. I was on a roll. Hap Emms always made us do line rushes and I was feeling pretty good carrying the puck.

Emms sat up in the corner of the rink. He walked down and called Bill Long over. Bill blew the whistle to stop the practice, and we all gathered in front of the bench. I was in the front row, as always.

"I have something important to say," began Emms. "You guys are truly blessed. Do you understand that? Do you know how lucky you are that, playing on this OHA Junior A team, you are playing with the best player that has ever played the game?"

I looked around to see who he was talking about. We had Doug Favell and Bernie Parent in goal. We had guys like Gilles Marotte and Rick Ley on defence. Bill Goldsworthy, Rosaire Paiement and Jean Pronovost were solid forwards. We had maybe 12 guys who went on to the NHL, but I wasn't sure who he was talking about.

And then Hap said, "You guys get to play with Derek!"

I wanted to crawl in a hole!

He continued. "After sitting up in the corner there for 20 minutes, I've watched him handle the puck. He takes it alone, he can go through people, split the defence and can score! Amazingly gifted player! You should all be humbled by Derek's excellence. In fact, I'm going to show you how good he is. We're going to scrimmage."

Then he said, "Wait a second. Hold everything. Derek, a player like you probably doesn't need wingers. You can handle the puck really well. You don't have to pass. The way you played yesterday in Hamilton only shows how good you are alone, so you probably don't need your wingers, right? Pronovost and Goldsworthy, go sit down."

Bill Long, the coach, knew exactly what Emms was doing.

"Tell you what, Derek," Emms continued. "You probably don't need defencemen, either. Guys, let Derek play alone. He's good enough."

And he looked at me. I didn't know what to say or do. Should I apologize? This was definitely going downhill.

"Derek, I think you probably need a goaltender. I'll give you a goalie."

Bernie Parent said no to that, but I knew Doug Favell wouldn't leave me stranded.

Hap then turned to the team. "And, if he's standing on his feet for any more than 10 seconds in a row, you'll all do a hundred laps each, both ways."

I got the puck off the faceoff and I was dancing with it. *Boom! Boom!* I got knocked down every time I stood up. I practically crawled to the bench. My tongue was dragging on the ice. "I got the point," I said, exhausted.

"No, you're good enough," Bill Long said. "Take the next shift!"

I got the shit beat out of me. Hap gave me a half-smile. "Don't you think it's a little easier playing with wingers rather than using them as decoys?"

"Yeah, I do."

"And don't you need a couple of defencemen behind you? Do you understand that this is a team game? You cannot play this game alone. Ever! No one can."

I learned humility the hard way. I apologized to Hap and Bill Long and told my teammates I was sorry. I explained, "I was just having fun."

Emms stopped me in my tracks. "No, you weren't. You were showing off. This game is not for show-offs."

We went back to a full team scrimmage, and after an hour, we headed for the dressing room. Hap came into the room and said, "Was that a little better, playing with linemates, Derek? You've got some pretty good players in this room, you know."

"Yes, sir," I said. "I know."

Bill Long was sporting a shit-eating smile. While I was out on the ice, he had Kenny Carson, our trainer, drill a hole through a puck and put a skate lace through it. After I changed into my clothes, the coach told us he wanted to make a presentation. "To the best player in the world, Derek Sanderson! He loves the puck so much that he's going to wear it around his neck at school for two weeks. And if you take it off, I'll know about it and you'll wear it for the rest of the school year." Then, Bill turned on his heel and walked into his office.

For two weeks, I was the jerk walking through Niagara Falls Collegiate Vocational Institute with a puck tied around my neck. Everybody laughed at me. Even people who didn't know me thought I was an asshole. Never again did I hog the puck. From then on, I decided to play with the guys and I always looked to pass first.

That wasn't the only time I was humiliated in front of the team, and again, I had to take full responsibility.

Maybe a month earlier, we'd played Peterborough. It was a big game and we were up 3–2 with a couple of minutes left. We were two men short and I was out killing the penalties. I was really working my ass off. I broke up four or five plays, sweep-checked two or three times and dumped it down the ice. They weren't moving the puck the way they wanted to because I worked hard and forced them. They never got the puck near our end.

Then, the Petes finally broke into our end. Bernie Parent was in net for us. He came out of his crease to cut the angle and committed to a good, hard shot off the wing. He always told me, "You take away the pass. Give me the shooter." The puck was shot, but it hit a skate and popped into the air. Bernie was moving right and the puck was going away from him. I tried to bat it out of the air, but I missed it. It bounced in the crease and dribbled in.

"You asshole, Bernie!" I shouted in frustration. I was standing in the crease with my arm on the crossbar. "You've got to work harder than that!"

I skated over to the bench, and Hap Emms was waiting for me. His face was beet red. "If you ever do that to your goalie again, you won't be wearing a Flyers uniform again. Don't you ever insult a teammate in front of our fans!"

The next day at practice, all of my equipment was gone from my stall. In its place was all of Bernie's equipment.

Hap was angry. "You want to shoot your mouth off and tell 4,000 people that your goaltender made a mistake? That two of your teammates happened to get penalties and this is all about you? Then *you* are going to play goal! Until you play, you won't understand what it's like to be a goalie."

I skated out wearing full goaltending equipment, including the skates. The guys started to warm me up. Bernie was laughing. Gilles Marotte was shooting from centre ice and I was able to knock them down with my blocker. Then they started to shoot from the point, and I could still stop most of the shots. But when the team started to scrimmage, I was a fish out of water. They put seven past me so fast it'd make your head swim. A little head shake, a shift—I was one way and they were the other. I was totally useless. Believe me, I had a new appreciation for my goaltenders.

I loved everything about playing junior. Well, almost everything. It was really tough to keep up my grades during the season. We used to go on long road trips—to Montreal, for example, and we'd play Peterborough on the way back. Six-hour trips. We'd take our books, but I told my teachers I couldn't write while we were driving. Almost all of my teachers were jerks except the ones who were hockey fans. They knew I had a hockey game and would say, "Derek, we'll give you an extra day to get your homework in."

I figured I would really show the teachers who didn't appreciate that I was playing hockey by failing their subjects. How stupid was I, but that was the way things were going. My history and English teachers understood. They told me to get as much done as I could, and I always got their work done. They told me if I got a detention, I should go to them and they'd go over some work. They were educators. My Latin teacher didn't understand, but Latin came easily to me. *Semper ubi sub ubi*—always wear underwear. Languages came fairly easily to me. Everything I read, I remember.

I hated public speaking. The teacher told me I had to speak to my class in French at an assembly. I said, "No, no, no. Me? Give a speech? Have the kids all laughing at me?" I was too cool to be doing that shit. I used to get help in French from some of my teammates. Gilles Marotte, Bernie Parent, Jean Pronovost—they all tried to teach me French. I got pretty good at it . . . after I quit school.

I had 12 days to prepare my public speech. I didn't panic because I had no intention of delivering it. I intended to quit school before I had to give the stupid speech.

I always rationalized everything. I figured that my life was too busy and I had to choose two of the three things going on at that time: career, social life and education. It was pretty easy to figure which one wasn't going to make the cut.

I approached my dad. "None of the French guys on the team go to school."

He looked up from his book and asked, "What are you trying to say?"

"Dad," I continued, "think about it. They're on the ice from nine until noon every day while we're in school. They've got two goalies, they choose sides and they scrimmage for three hours. That's an unbelievable advantage."

Back then, people weren't making big money. Hockey players in the NHL were making around $6,500 a year. My dad was likely making $3,700, so I worked that angle on him every day. After four or five days, he looked at me and asked, "Son, what are you trying to do? Are you trying to quit school?" He said, "You'll rue the day you quit school. Don't you ever even think about that. You need your education. Not many make it playing hockey."

I turned his words around on him. "What are you saying, Dad? Don't you have faith in me making the National Hockey League?"

"No," he replied. "I think you'll make it."

"Then why are you stopping me from playing hockey each morning with the French kids?"

He gave it some thought, and then, on the Sunday before I had to make the speech to the class, he told me I could quit. I went to school on the Monday and visited all of my teachers to tell them of my decision. I never liked my physics teacher or my Latin teacher. But I loved Mrs. Downey, my history teacher, and Miss Escott, my English teacher. Miss Escott begged me to reconsider, but I had made up my mind.

We ran away with the league that season, finishing first overall. I finished second on the team in scoring with 65 points (19 goals and 46 assists). Jean Pronovost finished with 70 points, including 30 goals. My future teammate Ken Hodge, playing with the St. Catharines Black Hawks, led the league with 61 goals and 123 points. We were a tough team and didn't take shit from anybody. Bill Goldsworthy, Gilles Marotte, John Arbour and I all had more than 100 minutes in penalties. Bernie Parent won the Dave Pinkney Trophy again for having the best goals-against average in the league.

We dumped Bobby Orr and the Oshawa Generals in the first round of the playoffs, then eliminated the defending Memorial Cup champion Toronto Marlies to win the J. Ross Robertson Cup as OHA champions. Our series with the Garson-Falconbridge Native Sons, the Northern Ontario Hockey Association champs, was a joke. We buried them four straight in the best-of-seven series, outscoring them 43–5. Then, we beat the Lachine Maroons of the Montreal Metro Junior League for the Eastern Canadian championship and the George Richardson Memorial Trophy. We had earned a shot at the Memorial Cup as the junior champions of Canada. Our opponents: the Edmonton Oil Kings.

The Oil Kings had reached the Memorial Cup final for an unprecedented sixth consecutive season by 1965. But that streak of success had been virtually matched by a string of futility that had seen them lose four out of five finals going into our series in 1965. Unfortunately, the one they won was against the Niagara Falls Flyers, two years earlier. Edmonton had some tough boys on that 1963 team, but we weren't short on physical players, either. It was a brutal series and the Oil Kings roughhoused their way to the championship. So, even before the '65 series started, there was no love lost between the teams.

The West was not as dominant as the Ontario Hockey Association. Nobody was. But the West got to pick up a couple of players to supplement their team when they went to the Memorial Cup final. They chose Fran Huck from the

Regina Pats and Jim Cardiff from the Weyburn Red Wings. Their goalie, Gary Simmons, got hurt, so they picked up Wayne Stephenson from Winnipeg.

We travelled to Edmonton, ready to exact revenge by coming back with a tougher team in 1965. We intended to dominate, and we did—we hit them at every opportunity. The Oil Kings also had a hard time dealing with our speed and passing, and we won game one 3–2. I scored the winning goal. All three players on Edmonton's first line were injured during the game. Both coaches began posturing early. "I think we played pretty well, considering this was the opener," shrugged Edmonton coach Harry Allen. "It was far from our best. We're bound to improve." Bill Long, our coach, responded, "If we'd played that badly all year, we'd have wound up at the bottom of our league!"

Two nights later, Fran Huck picked up the Oil Kings' only goal as we bombed Edmonton 5–1. Boris Debrody scored twice for us and Bill Goldsworthy, John Arbour and I picked up goals. Hap Emms complained about the officiating. "That guy [referee Jim McAuley] is worse than the one we had two years ago in Edmonton. We play just as hard in the OHA, but the penalty box isn't always full."

Some kind of evangelical meeting had been booked into the Edmonton Gardens, which forced a three-day break in the series. It gave time for injuries to heal a bit, but in the meantime, many of the Oil Kings came down with the flu.

Even the fans knew that game three was going to be intense. Midway through the first period, Brian Bennett of the Oil Kings tangled with Dougie Favell, so I jumped in to protect our goalie. Some of the fans got into it with me. Then, just as the first period ended, Goldsworthy ran Edmonton's Ross Perkins into the boards. They said it was after the whistle. Their big defenceman, Bob Falkenberg, came to Perkins's rescue and speared Goldie right in the gut. Goldie was doubled over. Falkenberg got a major, but as our team was leaving the ice, a group of Edmonton fans got into it with us. They were swearing at us, spitting and throwing shit. One of our guys tried to retaliate, and in the process, Ken Reid, the linesman, broke his hand. He finished the game with his hand in a cast. It took 11 police officers to help the linesmen settle everything down.

Goldsworthy was spitting blood. He returned for one shift in the second, but was checked by Al Hamilton and didn't come back after that. We found out later that he had internal bleeding. The spear from Falkenberg had ruptured his spleen, but he didn't know it. He nearly died sitting on the bench. While he was sitting on the bench, he could barely talk, but he said, "Turk, if you get the chance, get that prick." I had every intention of running him.

Favell was tossed out of the game for the altercation, so Bernie Parent replaced him in goal at the start of the second period. Through the rest of the game, the Edmonton fans threw eggs at him. A battle had now evolved into a war.

Tensions were already high when, midway through the third period, Ricky Ley and Edmonton's Ron Anderson got into a stick-swinging duel. They both received majors and game misconducts. Then, with three and a half minutes left in the game, Rosaire Paiement started a fight with the Oil Kings' Al Hamilton at our blue line. Hamilton had a bloody nose. While the linesman, Ken Reid, was trying to break up the fight with a big cast on one hand, one of our tough guys, John Arbour, got into a fight with Ace Bailey from Edmonton, and when they did, the benches cleared. Everybody was fighting!

I had already received two minors, a major and a misconduct. I asked Cardiff if he wanted to go, and he said, "No! I've got no loyalty to these guys."

I didn't know what to do. Everybody was paired off and there was nobody left. Then, I saw Falkenberg come over the boards. He was a big boy—six foot two. Everybody was brawling, but he hadn't gotten into anything. Goldsworthy nodded and pointed at him, so I thought, "All right, here we go." I snuck around in a semicircle, laid my stick and gloves down and said, "Hey!" He turned around and I belted him with a right hook that dropped him like a stone. I jumped on him and hit him two or three more times, but then I realized, "Holy shit! This kid ain't moving!"

I got up, but he was out before he hit the ice. He started twitching. I thought, "Oh my God! I hurt him."

Eleven Edmonton policemen scrambled onto the ice, slipping and sliding around like the Keystone Kops. They started clubbing people. The fans were out there, too, with their boots on. They were easy prey. When they came at us, all we had to do was duck and then pound them. *Bang!* Down they went. They couldn't stand up on the ice. It was stupid.

Johnny Arbour hated authority. He was a tough kid. He looked at the cops and yelled, "Hey! What's with the clubs?" He grabbed a goal stick off the bench and challenged a cop who was going to drill him. He said, "Now, you wanna be tough?" The cop had a billy club, but Johnny hit him and snapped his arm like it was a twig. The officials and the cops tried to stop the fights, but they continued for 10 more minutes. Fights broke out randomly as the teams milled around the ice. Meanwhile, Falkenberg was carried off the ice on a stretcher, unconscious.

I was the last one off the ice. The police surrounded me, but when I walked by Edmonton's dressing room, I got pulled into the first aid room. *Zip!* Right in! I threw a roundhouse right and the first guy ducked, but it caught the second guy flush and he went down. Then I started kicking with my skates. I was scraping my skates against legs and trying to take out insteps. Somebody nailed me and I was out cold. Next thing I knew, I was lying in the corridor, handcuffed. The cops had pulled me out of the first aid room and arrested me for assault and battery. I asked the cop, "Are you insane? Do you think I'm going to go into their dressing room? I'm not crazy! They pulled me in there! How can you arrest me and let them go?"

He said, "I don't know who they are, but I know you were in there."

I had cuts on my face, but I finally got to the dressing room. Art Potter, the Edmonton-based past president of the Canadian Amateur Hockey Association, ordered referee Jim McAuley to end the game with 3:30 left in the third period. We lost 5–1. I got our only goal, but they also gave me a major and a game misconduct for intent to injure.

Potter called the brawl the most brutal he had ever seen. Bill Long, our coach, said the fans that attacked me were like vultures. Hap Emms thought it was one of the worst things he had ever seen in his hockey career and recommended that the Memorial Cup series continue in another city.

When we went to the bus, the Edmonton crowd was yelling, "We want Sanderson! We want Sanderson!" I jumped into the crowd and said, "Here I am!" Johnny Arbour jumped in behind me and said, "I got your back, Turk.

Let's go!" No one did a thing. I couldn't believe it! We turned and walked out of the crowd arm in arm and climbed onto the bus.

After an overnight stay, Falkenberg was released from the hospital. I was greatly relieved. I hadn't meant to hurt him, just to stand up for Goldie.

The future of the series hung in the balance while Gordon Juckes, the secretary-manager of the CAHA, launched an investigation into the brawl. "The series could easily be over," Potter said. "I've been told the Garden is closed until this is settled." The next day, Juckes meted out sentences. Anderson and Ley were tagged with one-game suspensions, and I was suspended indefinitely for deliberate injury of a player, although Matt Leyden, the president of the Ontario Hockey Association, appealed and got it reduced to a two-game suspension.

The series continued, but for game four they added extra policemen to monitor the proceedings. They weren't needed. The game was cleanly played with no hint of what had happened in game three. I was dressed in my blazer and tie, watching, as we whipped Edmonton 8–2. Brian Bradley scored five times and Bill Goldsworthy, whom we didn't expect to play, scored twice, opening and closing the scoring on breakaways. Their goalie also stopped Goldie on one other breakaway, and again on a penalty shot in the second period. Jean Pronovost scored the other goal for us.

We wrapped up the championship in game five by bombing Edmonton 8–1. Dave Woodley and Donnie Marcotte both scored twice. My pal Goldie scored another goal, too. Debrody, Marotte and Paiement got the others. Cardiff scored the only goal for the Oil Kings. It was the game's first goal, and it gave Edmonton the lead for only the second time in the series. That lead lasted less than four minutes.

We received Memorial Cup rings and cowboy hats for winning the championship. We were all so happy for Hap Emms. It was the third time one of his teams had won the Memorial Cup. He won in 1951 and '53, when the team was based in Barrie. Even though I couldn't play in those last two games, I ended up scoring seven goals and six assists—and was credited with 70 minutes in penalties.

It was a double victory for us—we won the Memorial Cup *and* we avenged Niagara Falls' defeat in the 1963 final.

CHAPTER 9

NHL DEBUT

knew the Boston Bruins had been keeping an eye on me when I was invited to attend their training camp in London, Ontario, in 1965. I felt quite comfortable—there were a lot of guys I knew from playing in Niagara Falls. But there was something else that helped me: Hap Emms, my coach and mentor with the Flyers, had been named general manager of the Bruins, replacing Lynn Patrick.

Having learned the Bruins' system with the Flyers, I was comfortable on the ice, too, although every single guy in that camp was really good. I had to keep my head up at all times.

Hap told me to go back to the Flyers and continue to work hard. He promised me that if I showed the kind of effort he had seen the previous two seasons, he would give me a shot with the Bruins for a few games.

We were on a high coming off our Memorial Cup win, but the 1965–66 roster was quite a bit different than the one that had won the championship. We lost both of our goalies—Bernie Parent joined the Bruins and Dougie Favell was in Oklahoma City, Boston's Central Hockey League affiliate. Brian Bradley and Bill Goldsworthy were also in Oklahoma City, and Gilles Marotte was promoted to the Bruins. Along with veterans like Johnny Arbour, Donnie Marcotte, Rosaire Paiement and Jean Pronovost, I was expected to take a leadership role with the Flyers.

My neighbourhood friend, Robbie Nicholson, now a member of Parliament and cabinet minister, was the oldest of six great kids in a wonderful family. When I was playing junior, I had a Shelby Mustang, and Rob used to ogle my car. Even though I was about six years older, every once and again I'd invite Robbie to go for a ride. He was thrilled.

Robbie's uncle, Al MacNeil, was an NHL defenceman. He played parts of four seasons with the Toronto Maple Leafs in the late 1950s, and I remember watching him on *Hockey Night in Canada*. Then, he played a season with the Montreal Canadiens and, in 1962–63, he joined the Black Hawks and spent four seasons in Chicago. MacNeil used to give Rob sticks that had been rejected for one reason or another by the Black Hawks to share with the kids in the neighbourhood. There were sticks with wicked curved blades that had come from Bobby Hull and Stan Mikita. We were thrilled. Those guys were the biggest stars in the National Hockey League at the time, and here we were, using their sticks.

I was the first kid in junior to use a curved blade. I used to love to roof the puck. When you're in close to a goalkeeper and they put their legs out, you're not going to score, but what they can't stop are pucks that are fired up under the crossbar. Al MacNeil also taught me how to curve my stick. We'd heat up the stick and bend it under a door. All I wanted was the toe curved a little.

In 1965–66, only two points separated the top three teams in the OHA. The Peterborough Petes had 58 points and the Montreal Junior Canadiens had 57. Both were sponsored by the Montreal Canadiens. We finished third with 56 points. I was selected to the OHA Second All-Star Team at centre. I finished seventh in scoring with 76 points, including 33 goals. I also led the league in penalty minutes, with 238. I think that set a record at the time for penalties by a junior.

We were stunned when we got knocked out of playoff competition by the Kitchener Rangers in the first round. They'd finished seventh in a nine-team league!

In December 1965, I got my first chance to play in the National Hockey League. The Bruins were in a losing skid and hadn't won in six games, and during that stretch, they got bombed in back-to-back games—10–2 by Detroit and, two nights later, 10–1 by Chicago. Hap Emms told the team he was sick and tired of losing. "You don't care! I'll bring up guys from the American League. I'll bring up juniors." Next thing I knew, I got a call from Hap. "Can you get to Toronto tonight?"

"What for?"

"I want you to play with the Bruins tonight," he explained. "Ed Westfall is coming in a day early. He'll be taking the bus, so meet him and come in together."

I had known Eddie Westfall since I was a kid. He was one of the stars with the Flyers when I was watching them. It seemed that every Friday, he was named the first star and they'd award him a shirt from Ben's Men's Wear. He had more shirts than you can imagine. But Eddie was also the lifeguard at the local pool in the summer. I was 15, and he used to stop me from running on the deck and made me sit against the fence. There were four or five of us who went to the pool all the time. Our schoolboy libidos went crazy seeing the girls in their bikinis.

I met Eddie on the bus and we went to Toronto. I was nervous. There I was, with my skates, wearing my Flyers blazer. I asked him, "What the hell do I do?"

He said, "Derek, you know the system. The way you play in Niagara Falls with the Flyers is the same way we play in Boston with the Bruins. You know the six ways that we come out of our own end, and you've been practising it for four years."

I said, "Okay. Nothing different?"

"Always the same," he said. "We go behind the net, pause and wait. The defenceman leaves it for the centreman. The centre comes in the weak side and goes out the strong side. If the defenceman tucks it, you let him handle it. He can see the ice ahead of you, and you can't. You know our system. It's the same way we play. You're one of us."

I said, "Okay. Fine!" But I was a wreck. Eddie said, "Don't be scared. You can't panic. You've got four of us on the ice with you, and we all know what you're trying to do." He added, "I don't know whether I'm going to be playing wing or defence, but if I'm on the ice, I'll look after you."

It was December 11, 1965. We got to Maple Leaf Gardens and went into the visitors' dressing room. I knew who some of the guys were, but the only guy I actually knew was Eddie Westfall.

I introduced myself to Dan Canney, the trainer, and asked him where I'd find my stuff. He barely looked up. "Go over there and get dressed, kid." Of course, every rookie gets the seat close to the washroom. Frosty Forristall, the assistant trainer, handed me sweater number 27. At that time, you had no choice of what number you wore. I was so excited to be playing in "the show" that I'd have gone without a sweater if they had asked me to. I was sitting there, nervous but trying to pace myself. I started to pull on my equipment. I pulled on the pants, but they were too tight. "Okay, that doesn't work. How the hell am I going to do this?" I was figuring things out, not saying anything to anyone. Ron Stewart, one of the veterans, came over wearing a towel around his waist and nothing else. He stood in front of me, then got down on his knees. "Are we supposed to bow to you, great saviour?"

"What the fuck are you talking about?" I asked.

He said, "You're going to take us by the hand and lead us out of the woods so that we have a winning season."

All the guys were laughing. I shrugged, "Somebody's going to have to. You haven't made the playoffs in six years, so it might as well be me!"

You could have heard a pin drop. I wasn't putting up with that shit. I said, "Get up off your knees, asshole." It never got to blows, but there was no love lost between the two of us.

I didn't play at all in the first period. I sat on the bench, trying to watch the game, but I caught myself looking around at Maple Leaf Gardens, where I had watched the Leafs play so many times on *Hockey Night in Canada*.

At the end of the first period, I think we were down 4–0. One player came in and said, "Fuck 'em! We'll get them next year." It was December 11, for God's sake! They still had to play Toronto 10 more times that season! What do you mean, get them next year? What are you talking about? I could never understand that attitude, but that's what losing did. There was so much frustration. No player likes to lose.

I got my first NHL shift in the second period. I tried to plot what I was going to do before they dropped the puck. I noted that Allan Stanley was playing right defence for Toronto. When we were going over the Leafs' roster, my dad said, "Stanley is so slow. If you get a chance, son, go around him like a hoop around a barrel." They called him "Snowshoes" because he was so slow.

The faceoff was just outside our blue line. I won the draw, and the puck was taken back behind our net. As we had practised, I went in the weak side, came across the back of the net and went out the strong side, where there was a partner. I curled out while the winger came off the boards. I was on the left wing and cut across. I glanced up and saw Stanley about 40 feet from me. I looked back and was all alone when I got a soft pass. I was trying to gauge it before I hit centre ice so I wasn't offside. I got the pass and turned to go around Stanley as my dad had suggested. But he came and hit me so hard it knocked me back into the middle of next week. I said, "Holy shit! Can he ever hit!" I was by our bench and had to crawl off the ice on my knees. When I got to the bench, they had to give me smelling salts. People might have thought that Allan Stanley was slow, but he didn't waste any steps getting to where he needed to be. I tell you what, that guy could play! It was the first time in my life that my dad had been wrong.

My next shift didn't come until the third period. We were behind 7–1. Our coach, Milt Schmidt, asked me how I was doing, and I told him I was fine. He sent me out for a shift. The scenario was very much the same. I came up from the left side again and cut across the blue line. *Bam!* Bobby Baun jumped and hit me in the chest with his hip. Same bloody thing—it knocked me straight back and I struggled back to the bench.

Later, I got one more shift. I was in the corner, and Bob Pulford nearly put me through the end of the building. "Fuck this!" I dropped my gloves, but Pulford just looked at me and that was that. Nothing happened. At least I had to show him that I was game.

We got our asses handed to us, 8–3. I was knocked out twice during that game. When Schmidt approached me after the game, all I could muster was "Send me back to junior." I wasn't ready to play pro. I didn't have the mechanics in place. I knew I had to go back to junior because I had a lot to learn.

All the guys on the Niagara Falls Flyers watched the game. They wanted to know what it was like to play in the NHL. I said, "Let me tell you something: the National Hockey League is the toughest league in the world. They can all play; every one of them. Every time I had the puck, there was no time to think. You had to know what you were going to do with it before you got it."

Our family was preparing for Christmas when the Bruins called me up again. I was to report to the Garden in Boston for the game on Christmas Day against the New York Rangers. This time, I wore number 23. I didn't see the ice in that game. I travelled with the Bruins to New York for a game at Madison Square Garden the next night, December 26. I don't remember much about that game, other than we lost, 6–4.

Back in the 1960s, if your junior team was eliminated in the playoffs, you were allowed a 10-game tryout in the minors without having to turn pro. When the Flyers got beat out in 1966, the Bruins sent me to Oklahoma City. I knew a few of the guys there from junior, including Dougie Favell, Brian Bradley and Bill Goldsworthy. It's also where I first met Gerry Cheevers and Glen Sather.

Cheevers was our goaltender, and what a character he was. You had to be within 12 feet of Gerry to catch his wit, because he'd throw out lines under his breath. Glen Sather took care of me in Oklahoma City because I was away from home for the first time. I was only there for a couple of weeks, so it was like a little vacation.

Harry Sinden was the playing coach in Oklahoma City. I didn't know Sinden from Adam. He took me aside and said, "Derek, this is the same system you played in junior. Nothing's different. We play a Bruins system. All you have to do now is execute. Energy and execution."

I was the extra forward, so I didn't play much when I got to Oklahoma City. The idea was that I'd watch and learn, get a few shifts and get a feel for the transition from junior to pro. In one of my first games, I was sitting on the bench during a game against the St. Louis Braves when Sinden, skating behind the goal, got hit and his skate got caught up in the loose mesh in the back of the net. He couldn't get loose, and Wayne Maki began pounding him. I jumped off the bench and gave Maki a thumping. Beat the snot out of the little prick. They gave me five for fighting and a 10-minute misconduct. Harry skated over to me in the penalty box and said, "Thatta boy, kid!" We always got along famously after that.

Harry sent me out to shut down players. I was a penalty killer and a faceoff specialist. I did those same things in junior, so the transition was seamless. I was comfortable with the speed of the game and the system wasn't complicated. Harry got to know me as a coachable player.

In the Central League playoffs, the Oklahoma City Blazers swept the Tulsa Oilers, the Toronto Maple Leafs' farm team, and won the Adams Cup championship. It felt good.

CHAPTER 10

FINAL JUNIOR CAMPAIGN

I was 20 years old entering my last year of junior in 1966–67. I was honoured when Bill Long, our coach, made me captain of the team. A lot was expected of me. I'd had a strong season the year before and had been up to "the show." I was definitely part of Boston's future, but in my final year of junior, I wanted to show everyone what I could do.

By Christmas, I was leading the OHA in scoring with 43 points in 19 games, 12 more points than Garry Unger of the London Nationals. Bill Long was worried that he'd lose me to the Bruins should they call me up. They had done that with Gilles Marotte the year before and we'd been eliminated in the first round of the playoffs. Bill felt that with Marotte, we could have won the OHA championship for a second straight year.

Mickey Redmond of the Peterborough Petes and I chased each other for the scoring championship through the last half of the season. With two games left in the regular season, I had a five-point lead.

We were playing on a Friday and Sunday, while Peterborough played Thursday and Saturday. On Friday morning, a bunch of us were sitting at Billy's Lunch and looking at the newspaper. My jaw dropped when I read that Peterborough had won 8–1, and Redmond got eight points in the game.

"Eight points is unheard of!" I said. "How many goals did he get?"

One of my teammates counted them. "Five . . . six . . . he got seven, Turk."

Seven goals! I couldn't believe it! I could see him passing and getting some helpers, but *seven goals?* I thought to myself, "Jesus, this guy is the real deal." So my five-point lead in the scoring race had not only been erased, but Redmond now had a three-point lead. But I had two games left to play and he was down to one. On Friday night, we won 6–3 and I got five points—one goal and four helpers—and I was back in the lead by two. On Saturday night, Redmond got two points, so we were now tied for the scoring lead, but I still had a game on Sunday, against the Marlies at Maple Leaf Gardens.

End of the first period—no points. End of the second—one point. Then, I assisted on five goals in the third. I finished the regular season with 101 points—41 goals and 60 assists. Redmond had 95 points—51 goals and 44 assists. I won the Eddie Powers Memorial Trophy as the OHA scoring champion; Redmond was given the Red Tilson Trophy as the league's most valuable player. I also led the Flyers in penalty minutes with 193, just three behind the league leader, Jim Dorey of the London Nationals. Through my time with the Flyers, intimidation was part of our game. We were a tough team, and in many ways were a forerunner to the Big, Bad Bruins.

The Flyers finished second to the Kitchener Rangers that year. Oshawa missed the playoffs altogether; a year after winning the OHA championship and playing in the Memorial Cup final, they ended up finishing last. Of course, they had lost their greatest player ever to Boston. Bobby Orr still had two years of junior eligibility when he joined the Bruins in 1966–67 and won the Calder Trophy as the NHL rookie of the year. The Generals also lost a great goaltender. Ian Young caught a Mickey Redmond shot in the eye and it ended his career.

We faced the London Nationals in the first round of the playoffs and eliminated them four games to two. Then, in the semifinal, we met our archenemies, the Hamilton Red Wings. It was a strange series. At that time in the OHA, you could have tie games in the playoffs, and after seven games in the series, both teams had three wins and a tie. That meant an eighth game would take place, played in Niagara Falls. It was expected to be a bloodbath. Almost like a scene out of *Slap Shot*, there were ambulances circling the building.

It turned out to be a night of fights. There was a rule that said three fights in a game and you were out. I already had been involved in two fights. The Red Wings had an extra defenceman named Jim Young. He didn't play a lot, but he knew about the "three and out" rule. He suckered me into a fight—

took one swing at me and then held on for dear life. I kicked the crap out of him, but ended up getting kicked out of the game.

I thought their coach, Eddie Bush, had sent the kid out after me, so I went over to the Hamilton bench and challenged him. The Wings backed away. I was tossed out, and the Red Wings went on to win the game and the series. The Marlboros ended up beating Hamilton for the OHA championship, and they went on to win the Memorial Cup.

That was the way my junior career ended.

I ended up with 25 points in 13 playoff games, and I also had 70 penalty minutes.

That year, the OHA coaches made me and Mickey Redmond unanimous choices for the All-Star Team. I was selected at centre and Redmond at right wing. We both got the maximum 40 points. The others selected were Gerry Meehan of the Toronto Marlboros at left wing, Tom Reid of St. Catharines and Brian Glennie of Toronto on defence and Peter McDuffe from St. Catharines in goal.

Just before my last junior year, Hap Emms signed me—illegally. Hap, who had always treated me well, said, "I want to take care of you, Derek. I want to ensure that you are the highest-paid junior ever."

I liked the sound of that!

He offered a three-year contract with the Bruins. I'd get $8,000 in my first year, $10,000 in my second and $13,000 in my third. As excited as I was, I was cautious. "If I sign, doesn't that mean I automatically am professional and can't play my last year of junior?"

"It will probably be my last move as GM of the Bruins," he admitted. "I want you to get a good deal."

One of the things he promised was that if I signed the contract, he would bring me up for more games with the Bruins that season. That really is why I signed. At the end of the day, at least in his mind, I think he really did believe that he treated me fairly. He just didn't think very progressively. He believed 10 bucks was a lot of money. I don't think it was his fault, per se. But the contract was terrible, and after my rookie season with the Bruins, I fought to get out of it. And I also found out that I was nowhere near the highest-paid junior.

In December 1966, the Springfield Indians of the American Hockey League went on strike. The team was owned by the legendary Eddie Shore. On the ice, he was one of the greatest defenceman of all time. As an owner, he was one of the biggest pricks of all time.

During their training camp, a couple of players—Dale Rolfe and Bill White, two All-Star defencemen—decided to hold out for a $500-a-year raise. Shore, who was tighter than bark on a tree, begrudgingly gave them the raise, but when the team lost an early-season game, he fined them for "indifferent play." The amount of the fine? Not so surprisingly, it was $500 each.

The team went on strike to support the players.

Shore's methods were infamous. If players were injured, Shore still got his money out of them by having them shovel the parking lot or sell programs. If Shore felt that a player's stride was too wide, he'd make him practise with his legs tied together. Marcel Paille told me how Shore solved his habit of going down as a butterfly goaltender by attaching a noose to his neck during practices so that if he started to go down, he'd choke himself.

When the Indians went on strike, they contacted a lawyer to see if he could help them against Shore, and it was this lawyer who was brought in to negotiate with Shore on the players' behalf. Shore was prepared to let the players strike and bring in other players—scabs, really. The Bruins contacted a bunch of us and told us to report to Springfield to play in place of the striking players. This didn't sit well with my dad. He was a staunch union man and he called the Springfield newspaper to get the whole story. When he was informed that it was a wildcat strike to support the players' rights, he told me, "No way are you going to play for Springfield to replace hard-working guys who have walked off the job in protest of poor treatment." He had me call around and tell other guys that I wasn't going and why they shouldn't go. Some were disappointed, but I convinced all the guys not to report. I think Toronto sent a couple of players from Tulsa, but after a day, they also decided they didn't want to be involved in the strike.

Eventually, Eddie Shore was forced to give up day-to-day operation of the team, although his son Ted took over, and I suspect Eddie manipulated him from outside. He continued to own the team until the end of the season.

Conditions for the players, I am told, were not ideal but significantly better. At the end of that season, Shore sold his players and leased the franchise to the expansion Los Angeles Kings. The National Hockey League Players' Association really grew out of that incident.

I had played two games with the Bruins as a junior in 1965–66, and was supposed to play 10 in 1966–67, but I ended up playing just two that season. I could really have used more games to help me make the transition from junior to pro—the familiarization, and learning how difficult it is to play in the National Hockey League. The Bruins decided I was a shit disturber because I'd phoned the players and told the press how my dad didn't want me interfering with a strike. So they buried me.

CHAPTER 11

ROOKIE SEASON: 1967-68

From 1959–60 until 1966–67, the playoffs had eluded a dismal Boston team. There were few bright spots, other than forward Johnny Bucyk. And yet, the Boston faithful never abandoned their Bruins, filling the Garden's 13,909 seats virtually every night.

Life changed for the Boston Bruins in 1966–67. Harry Sinden, who had been the playing coach in Oklahoma City and had just led the Blazers to a second consecutive Adams Cup championship, was promoted to coach in Boston. Bucyk was named captain prior to that season, and the long-awaited Bobby Orr joined the Bruins, sporting a brush cut and a face that barely looked his 18 years of age.

There was no doubt that management, players and fans regarded Bobby Orr as the player who would lead the franchise out of the darkness. When the Bruins played Toronto at Maple Leaf Gardens earlier that decade, a few of the players went over to Oshawa to watch Bobby and the Generals. He didn't disappoint. He seemed to own the puck, skating with skill and monopolizing possession of the puck.

While the Bruins finished last once again in 1966–67, it was the last time they would dwell in hockey's cellar. Milt Schmidt, the Bruins' GM, was fed up with missing the playoffs. He and Sinden realized that the team, as it was, couldn't win, and they planned wholesale changes. They decided that they liked their goaltenders, Eddie Johnston and Gerry Cheevers. There was no doubt they would keep Bobby Orr and Ted Green. At forward, it was Johnny Bucyk and Eddie Westfall. That was the nucleus that they would build around.

In May 1967, Milt pulled off a couple of trades that changed the course of the Bruins' history. He sent Murray Oliver to Toronto for Eddie Shack, but that trade was dwarfed by one that is regarded as the greatest heist in NHL history. Defenceman Gilles Marotte, forward Pit Martin and goalie Jack Norris were sent to the Chicago Black Hawks for three forwards: Phil Esposito, Ken Hodge and Fred Stanfield.

Martin was the key man for Chicago, and for us, of course, it was Esposito. I was a little surprised that they let Marotte go, because I know management figured that he and Bobby gave us a great one-two punch on the blue line. He was young and aggressive and really promising. But the sleeper in the trade was Freddie Stanfield. He was a great number-two centre for us.

We couldn't believe that Chicago would make that trade. "I really don't think Tommy Ivan will ever make another trade with Milt Schmidt," laughed Johnny Bucyk.

Esposito brought a larger-than-life personality to the Bruins. He was a real joker, which was a rare commodity in the Bruins' dressing room, but above all, he wanted to win, and that attitude rubbed off on the guys. When the Chicago trade was made, Esposito, Hodge and Stanfield came in and talked positively in the dressing room. That hadn't happened for a long time. It gave guys like Teddy Green a new lease on life.

During training camp that fall, Esposito told the team, "We're going to make the playoffs this year." He added, "And you know something else? The Bruins are going to win the Stanley Cup within three years. I mean it. You wait and see!"

No one knew that Phil Esposito could predict the future.

I was very pleased to have played a few games during the "Original Six" era, but it was a whole new ballgame starting with 1967–68. The National Hockey League was expanding, doubling the size of the league from 6 to 12 teams. Each of the new franchises had to stock their team, and did so in part through an expansion draft that was held in June 1967. The Bruins protected goalie Gerry Cheevers, defencemen Don Awrey, Gary Doak and Ted Green and forwards Johnny Bucyk, Phil Esposito, Ken Hodge, Johnny McKenzie, Eddie Shack, Fred Stanfield, Eddie Westfall and Tommy Williams. Bobby Orr and I weren't eligible to be drafted because we were still of junior age. Then, every time Boston lost a player to one of the new teams, they got to move a player they hadn't protected to their protected list, so they ended up keeping John Arbour, Brian Bradley, Ron Buchanan, Wayne Cashman, Bob Heaney, Ted Hodgson, Skip Krake, Bob Leiter, Wayne Maxner, Ron Murphy, Jean Pronovost, Glen Sather, Dallas Smith, Ted Snell and Dave Woodley.

The Bruins lost some good young talent. The California Seals claimed Ron Harris and Jean-Paul Parise. The L.A. Kings picked Ted Irvine and Poul Popiel. The Minnesota North Stars selected Wayne Connelly, Bill Goldsworthy and Bob Woytowich. The Philadelphia Flyers got Dick Cherry, Gary Dornhoefer, Doug Favell, Forbes Kennedy and Keith Wright. The Pittsburgh Penguins chose Bob Dillabough and Gil Gilbert, and the St. Louis Blues selected Terry Crisp, Wayne Rivers, Ron Schock and Ron Stewart.

Training camp opened on September 8, 1967, in London, Ontario. Baldy Cotton, the Bruins' longtime head scout and the guy who discovered me, had just retired that summer, although the Minnesota North Stars quickly convinced him to join their new franchise.

I was a little concerned when I discovered that Hap Emms had been fired as general manager and replaced by longtime Bruin Milt Schmidt. Hap had been like a father to me, and I thought that if I could present myself well, I might get the benefit of the doubt from Hap, whereas I was just another prospect to Schmidt. He had never believed I had what it took to play in the National Hockey League. Still, there were only nine holdovers from the team that finished last the previous spring, so we all felt like we had a legitimate shot at making the team. Along with the new guys acquired by trade, there were 11 guys from Oklahoma City and eight amateurs, including me. Bobby Orr was out with a bad knee that he injured in a charity game during the summer.

Because I had signed a pro contract, I knew I would be going either to Oklahoma City or sticking with the Bruins. Harry Sinden told reporters when I arrived at camp that he thought I had ability, but that he didn't know whether I was ready to make the jump from junior to the NHL. I figured if I worked hard, I might be lucky enough to stick.

A bunch of us were sitting at the Holiday Inn in London. Eddie Shack and Ted Green offered me a beer. I told them I didn't drink, but they insisted. Cheesy said, "If you don't drink, you're fucked. You need to drink to handle the pressure." But Esposito told me, "Kid, if you don't drink, don't start."

I wanted to belong. For virtually every decision in life, there are two choices: left or right, right or wrong. Nobody held a gun to my head to drink, but I wanted to be part of this group of teammates. I had one beer, and then another, and then I had a third. I started to act like an asshole. Phil shrugged and commented, "It doesn't take much for you, does it, kid?"

I started to drink during training camp that year. Not a lot, and I certainly didn't drink until nighttime, and it was almost always around a girl, as I tried to summon the courage to talk to her. I seldom went out and had a beer with the guys. Occasionally, I'd order a beer at lunch, but I hated the taste.

After my first year, I was drinking two or three beers to feel good. After my second season, it was three or four. By my third season, I was drinking five or six beers to get the same buzz.

During training camp, all the management guys sat up in the corner and watched us. The Bruins used to pick sides for scrimmaging, and it was always Bucyk's Biggies against Green's Hornets. The management wanted me playing against Ted Green because he and I were yapping at each other. I'd have my head down but my eyes up, and I'd watch him. He'd come at me and I'd give him a little deke, then cut back and say, "Goodbye!" as I was skating by him. He wanted to kill me. He'd swing at me and just miss me with his stick. "You asshole."

If you've got your head down, people will take a run at you. If your eyes are up and you're watching the puck with your peripheral vision, they don't know that. They think your head is down, you can't see them and they're going to kill you. But you just move your head, drop your shoulder, and when they go one way, you take the puck the other way and you beat them all night long. So the greatest myth in hockey is that you should keep your head up.

Teddy Green was a tough, surly bastard in practice. He tried to catch the brash rookie with his head down, and because he wanted a piece of me, gave me a couple of slashes. I'd bait him. "Learn how to play the fucking game!"

He'd be incensed. "Don't you talk to me like that, you punk!" I'd just laugh at him.

He was a miserable prick. He came over to me and said, "So, you think you're a tough guy, eh? Fucking junior punk. We'll see how tough you are!"

"I didn't say I was tough," I replied. "But I'm meaner than any other bastard out here."

"You've got a big mouth," Green barked.

I said, "Fuck you!" I wasn't going to back down from him, even though I really wanted to. I couldn't show him that he had me rattled. He was not someone I wanted to be looking to get me.

Milt Schmidt and Weston Adams were up in the stands laughing. They agreed, "The kid will stand up and he won't take any shit from him."

There were a couple of times that I was down and thought I'd be shipped out. When you are at training camp, you can tell how you are doing by looking at the line you are skating on. I had been practising with Eddie Shack and Tommy Williams, but Harry took them away from me and had me centring two guys from college, so I figured I was toast.

There was a drill where you take the puck at centre ice and skate in to warm up the goalers. When my turn came, I just shot the puck from centre ice. I was pouting. After the practice, I approached Harry Sinden and said, "Either play me or trade me." Six days into training camp, I was demanding a trade. I was making $10,000. What was I, stupid? Truthfully, my contract was for $8,000, but the Players' Association got the minimum up to $10,000. I hadn't even played yet and I'd got a $2,000 raise.

Eddie Shack really helped me. He told me not to worry and to keep on working. There were a few other veterans who also helped. Phil Esposito took me out to dinner one night and had a talk with me. "What do you think you're doing? They're just seeing if you're man enough to take a little adversity. Work your way out of it! This is the humility test. It's how they work." He told me to stay cocky, to keep my cool but to cut out the silly rough stuff and the pouting. "I've been around a while and you are going to be on this team," he said. "I know it, they know it and now you have to believe it."

I stopped pouting. It wasn't doing me any good. About a week later, we had another exhibition game against the Canadiens, and I made the trip to Montreal with the team. A big brawl broke out to the right of the Canadiens'

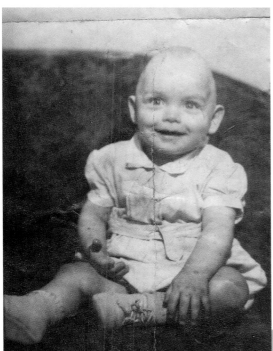

I was born Derek Michael Sanderson, the second of Harold and Caroline Sanderson's two children, in Niagara Falls on June 16, 1946.

My dad was determined that I would become a hockey player. He had me walking with table knives attached to my shoes by the time I was three.

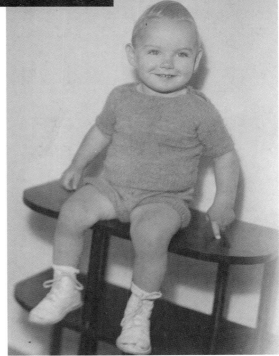

Being forced to stay indoors was punishment for us. We created all kinds of games to play outside, but we especially loved being cowboys. Here, some neighbourhood kids and I have strapped on our six-guns. I'm the cattle rustler on the left.

Leigh Shelton, my best buddy (*right*), and I were inseparable as kids. In this picture, we pretend to throw our balls at the camera during a game of catch.

My mom was a beautiful woman who taught me morals and manners. We lost Mom, Caroline (Gillespie) Sanderson, in March 2012.

It upsets me when people attribute my battles with addiction to problems within my family. I had an idyllic childhood, with parents and a sister who loved me dearly. Here, Dad is taking me and my sister, Karen, fishing.

I was likely playing peewee on this team in Niagara Falls. I'm in the back row, fourth from the left. My dad, on the extreme right of the back row, was my coach that year.

I was 16 years old and already part of the Bruins organization in 1962–63 when I joined the Stamford Bruins of the Niagara District Junior B Hockey League.

My final school picture was taken at the start of the 1963–64 year. I left school over public speaking and focused instead on playing hockey.

I joined the Niagara Falls Flyers of the Ontario Hockey Association full time in 1963–64 and played four seasons of junior before becoming a full-time member of the Boston Bruins in 1967–68.

It was a big deal when we played the Hamilton Red Wings at the Barton Street Barn because CHCH-TV televised the games. We'd put new laces in our skates for the occasion. This was my first TV interview.

The 1964–65 Niagara Falls Flyers were a powerhouse team. We won the Hamilton Spectator Trophy for finishing first through the regular season, the J. Ross Robertson Cup as OHA champions and the George Richardson Memorial Trophy as Eastern Canadian champs. Then we dumped the Edmonton Oil Kings in a fight-filled Memorial Cup final.

The Edmonton Oil Kings had beaten us for the Memorial Cup—the national junior championship—in 1963, so we exacted revenge on them when we got our chance. I was suspended for the championship game in 1965, which we won. When we returned home, Niagara Falls hosted a reception in our honour, where I faced my fear of public speaking.

I was named captain of the Flyers after Ronnie Schock went to the Bruins. Steve Atkinson, who spent most of his career with the Buffalo Sabres, is circling behind me.

GRAPHIC ARTISTS/HOCKEY HALL OF FAME

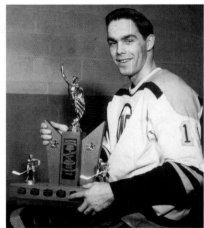

In 1965–66, I was awarded the Drummond Cycle & Sports Trophy as the most valuable player on the Niagara Falls Flyers. In 1966–67, I was the OHA's leading scorer, receiving the Eddie Powers Memorial Trophy, and was named to the OHA's First All-Star Team.

At the end of the 1965–66 and 1966–67 junior seasons, the Bruins brought me up for a few pro games with the Oklahoma City Blazers of the Central Hockey League. Although I was only a bit player, I was proud when the Blazers won the Adams Cup both years. I'm second from the left in the back row.

The Bruins had missed the playoffs eight years in a row by the time the 1967–68 season began. I was surprised that I made the team. With Phil Esposito, Fred Stanfield, Ken Hodge and, of course, Bobby Orr, we finished third in the East Division of the NHL. Here at a Bruins practice, Dallas Smith chases me as Teddy Green looks on.

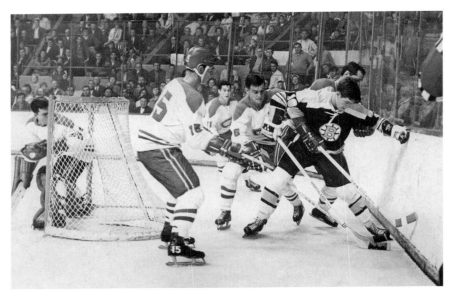

I was very proud to follow Bobby Orr in winning the Calder Trophy for rookie of the year in 1967–68. Although I scored 24 goals, Harry Sinden asked me to become a defensive specialist. Here, I'm fending off (*from left*) Montreal's Bobby Rousseau, Claude Larose, Ralph Backstrom and Jacques Laperriere while we are two men short.

AL RUELLE/KEVIN SHEA COLLECTION

When I made my NHL debut, most players were sporting crewcuts and wearing team-issued blazers and grey slacks. Nobody else our age dressed like that. I was just the guy to shake things up. AL RUELLE/AUTHOR'S COLLECTION

net. Teddy Green and John Ferguson went at it. I first fought Claude Larose and then Terry Harper. Harper never won a fight in his life, although he was a tough kid. He'd laugh at you and stand there taking punch after punch. He couldn't fight, but I'll tell you, he wasn't afraid of you.

The crowd was going nuts. They wanted my head. After two fights, I was so dead tired that I could barely lift my arms. Ted Harris pointed to me and wanted to go. Harris was one big, tough mother. He'd have beaten the snot out of me, but I couldn't back down—there were 19,000 people watching—so I said, "Fuck you. You're crazy." You get a little shot of adrenalin. I figured if I could just hold on, I'd get through it.

Harris said, "I'm gonna take care of you!" And then, out of nowhere from behind me, came Teddy Green. He looked at Harris and said, "What're you gonna do?"

"I've got no problem with you, Teddy," said Harris, but Green said, "If you want him, you do. If you want him, you got me or you've got both of us. What do you want to do?"

Just then, the linesman came in and calmed it down.

From that point, Teddy Green and I were fast friends. That night, we flew back to Boston, and when we landed, he said, "Hey kid, you got a ride?" I told him I was going to take a cab because I lived downtown. He insisted. "Come on. I'll give you a ride. I want to talk to you."

While he was driving me back to the Madison Hotel, right by the Garden, he said, "Look, I fought here alone for a long time. It's great to have somebody else who's got some balls." Even though we hadn't really got along to that point, he told me he liked the way I played.

"But Ted, I haven't made the team yet."

He said, "Oh yes you have."

That meant a lot to me.

People always ask me for my proudest moment in the game. They expect me to say, "Winning the Stanley Cup," but as great as both of those victories were, my proudest moment in hockey was when Teddy Green said to me, "Oh yes you have."

And he added, "The guys know. We all know. You're here."

I said, "Geez, there's a lot of talent out there," but he assured me: "You're here. Don't worry. But don't ever quit working."

With that, we buried the hatchet. I really felt confident after that. I went to practice with some zip and I wasn't afraid of trying new things or making mistakes.

I made the Boston Bruins. I was one of the boys. Teddy Green was a great mentor.

Harry Sinden congratulated me, telling me I had impressed him and that I had made the team. He liked the fact that I worked hard, wasn't afraid to drop the mitts and could add some scoring to a team that desperately needed it.

A bunch of us came into the league around the same time—me, Ace Bailey and Wayne Cashman. It was a young team, but we took care of each other. Bobby Orr made a rule that no one was ever to be in a fight alone. You were only alone until the second guy got there. If you hit one of us, the closest teammate was going to clock you—just drill you in the back of the head, cross-check you or sucker-punch you. *Pow!* Whatever it took. Eventually, the NHL instituted the third-man-in rule to eliminate this.

All of a sudden, the team that got pushed around the year before looked like it was going to be entirely different. The Bruins had an all-new look, with three centres who hadn't been part of the team in 1966–67—Esposito, Stanfield and me. The team had size, skill and sandpaper. This is the moment the Big, Bad Bruins were born.

I got a $7,500 signing bonus when I joined the Bruins. I bought some clothes and a banana-yellow, four-on-the-floor GTO with mag wheels and all the fixings. It cost $7,900, and I paid $72 a month on it. My signing bonus was gone in a heartbeat. I drove it to London for training camp with the Bruins in the fall of 1967 and then drove it down to Boston. On the third day I was there, the damned thing was stolen. They stripped it right down. They even took the engine. They threw a chain over a street light and lifted the engine right out. And the car had been parked two doors down from a police station! The police called me. "Derek, we've got your car, but you're not going to be happy." It was an absolute shell of what it had been.

Welcome to Boston, kid.

Leo Labine wore number 16 all through the 1950s for Boston. He wasn't very big, but he was tough. They called him "Leo the Lion." He visited our training camp, and said to Frosty, "Let Sanderson wear my number, because he'll toughen it up." Murray Oliver had worn the number, but after his trade to Toronto, it was available. I liked the idea of wearing 16, although it didn't really matter to me. I didn't want a number that had a reputation with it. In those days, defencemen, for the most part, wore single digits. Stars wore numbers like 7 and 9. Guys like Frank Mahovlich had made 27 a special number, so why couldn't I make a number like 16 special?

I started the season playing with Eddie Shack on my right and Glen Sather on my left wing. Sather was a pretty feisty guy. He was one of the guys who jumped me in Edmonton when we won the Memorial Cup, but when we played together in Boston, there was no problem. Slats is a class guy and a real bright hockey guy. We became good friends.

I was staying at the Madison Hotel, and Slats wanted to look out for me because I was totally naive. He said, "Don't worry, kid. I'll take care of you. I've got us a great place in Saugus." We went out to Saugus, a suburb on the north shore of Boston, and I looked at the place. "Slats, this is a boarding house."

He said, "Yeah, it's only $60 a month and we get our meals."

I looked at him and said, "Slats, I didn't make the National Hockey League to be living in a boarding house."

Saugus is in the suburbs, and I wanted to know where to find the action. There's lots of action anywhere if you look for it. Glen knew of one girl and said, "Listen, take her home and she'll give you a jump."

That was great! The problem was that when I came home late, I couldn't get in. The landlady locked the door at midnight, and if you weren't home, too bad. I'd bang on the door, but everybody would be asleep. There were a few nights that I slept in my car and just about froze my butt off! I decided that I wasn't doing that anymore.

I lived with Glen until December. There's a road in Boston called Storrow Drive that runs along the Charles River, and it leads to the Mystic River Bridge that goes into Revere and then north into New Hampshire. It's bumper-to-bumper traffic every day. I was stuck on Storrow Drive after practice one day and saw a big sign positioned beside a new apartment complex: "If you lived here, you'd be home now." I turned right, went to the office and got myself a studio apartment.

I was living alone. That proved to be a big mistake. I had always lived at home and thought I was ready to be on my own, although I don't think Glen would have agreed. I was late for practice 13 times. I learned how to get dressed in seven minutes—strip down, into my equipment and *boom!* Out the door. Frosty used to help me—left skate, right skate. Then I'd dash out. Practice was at 10:30 every morning that we were home. After being late so many times, I promised Harry I would never be late again, and sure enough, there I was, late once again. I came out and all the guys were tapping their sticks on the ice in mock celebration. "Nice of you to join us!"

Harry presented me with an alarm clock! I was pretty prompt after that. I had never even thought about buying an alarm clock.

Bobby Orr was only in his second year, but he was definitely the leader of the Bruins. They wanted to make Bobby captain right away, but he wouldn't take it. So, Chief (Johnny Bucyk) was captain in 1966–67, and then we went without one until 1973–74.

Bobby was a big believer in seniority and respect for the guys that had come before—Leo Boivin, Leo Labine, Fleming Mackell. We sailed in their wake. Bobby used to say, "They gave us the game and we have to respect it."

Bobby instituted a rule that really pulled the team together. It was simple: the Two-Drink Rule. After every game, all of us had to go out with the rest of the team for two drinks, and then you could go wherever you wanted. It didn't matter whether it was two beers, two Cokes or two coffees. Even if you had your girlfriend, your parents or your friends with you, you had to go with the guys, but you could meet them afterwards.

I scored my first NHL goal on October 19, 1967, against the Red Wings at the Olympia in Detroit. Teddy Green and I broke away on a two-on-one rush. He carried the puck into the Detroit zone, drew the defenceman to him and slipped the puck across the crease to me, and I tapped it in. The goal came against Roger Crozier, in the second period of a 6–3 win. Greenie grabbed the puck for me. It is one of the few things I kept throughout my career. My dad was there to see me score. He was so excited.

I had my first heavyweight fight in the National Hockey League on November 18. We were facing the Rangers, and in the first period, I got into a scuffle with Orland Kurtenbach, who was one of the best fighters in the game. We used to go at each other in the faceoff circle. This time, the puck dropped and I missed it, but took a second swipe, and the next thing you know, I saw a pair of Ranger gloves on the ice at my feet. I looked up and this big prick wanted to go.

He was six foot two (but looked six foot seven) and could fight with both hands. I always got inside bigger guys. You can't stand on the outside and throw a punch at a guy his size. You're balanced on one-sixteenth of an inch of steel. Fighting on the ice isn't like fighting in a bar. You don't have the ability to grip and rip and throw haymakers. Any bar brawl is over in 30 or 40 seconds, unless you're in shape. Aerobically, hockey players are in great shape, so we can go a longer time.

I went to get inside on him in order to get my elbow underneath his right armpit and to make sure I grabbed his sweater to pull over his head. Then, I'd get my right going. Back then, most players were not left-handed, so my right hand against his left was going to work.

Teddy Green was on the bench and yelled, "Don't go in." I stepped in anyway, and then thought about it and backed up. When I did, Kurtenbach threw a right hook that just missed my eye. If that punch had landed, it would have knocked me into the middle of next week and I'd have starved coming back. And when he missed, he lost his balance. I got inside and I was all right after that. It wasn't something I ever wanted to do again.

I won a clean decision, which really gave me a boost. Later, I scored the winning goal in the third period in a 3–1 win.

My first interview on *Hockey Night in Canada* was on January 6, 1968. Ward Cornell asked what my biggest thrill so far was, and I said, "Getting in a fight with Kurtenbach. That was one of them. I picked up a couple of goals. I guess that was the biggest thrill so far."

Then, he asked me about my reputation from junior. "A lot of it [publicity] is good; a lot of it is bad," I said. "Whether it's good or bad, it doesn't matter, as long as they keep saying something about you."

My rookie season was going along quite well. I was contributing to the effort by playing a good, tough game, but I was also racking up points. In a pregame speech one night in Boston, Harry said, "I just want those guys in the other dressing room to know that they're playing the toughest team in the league."

I think I got six minor penalties in the first period. They were all tough penalties—two for charging, two for roughing and two for interference. I was in the box for 12 of the 20 minutes! At the end of the period, we were down 2–0. I was walking by Harry's office and he reached out, grabbed me by the sweater, yanked me into his office and slammed the door. "What the Christ do you think you're doing? You took six goddamned minor penalties and they got two power-play goals! How the hell do you expect us to beat this team when you're in the box all night? You keep that up and I'll bury you so far that *The Hockey News* won't be able to find you."

He stopped for a moment, and then threatened, "I've got a good mind to send you to Oklahoma City tomorrow."

I said, "Harry, hold it a second. If there was somebody in Oklahoma City that you thought was better than me, he'd be here. If there was someone in Oklahoma City making less than me, they'd be here. Cut that shit out."

Harry wanted to say something further, but I had him, and he knew it. He slapped me on the back. "All right, I'll give you that point. But I don't want any more selfish play, okay? A tough guy doesn't have to show off how tough he is. All he has to do is play hard every night. I want you to tighten up. You've got to learn how to play this game."

I'd do anything he wanted after that.

That's how a good coach does it—stand up, man to man. He was so smart, and the two of us really got along. I didn't take any more penalties that night. We hit them all night, but they just passed the puck around and beat us 5–2.

In January, Pat Hannigan of the Philadelphia Flyers high-sticked me right in the middle of my forehead. I was sure the bastard did it on purpose, and I wanted to pound the living shit out of him, but Harry's strict warning stuck with me, so I just bled and the bastard got five minutes.

Harry said, "You're growing up! That's a good sign." It was a major turning point for me. From then on, I realized I had to be a hockey player first and a fighter second.

The humour on that Bruins' team was outrageous. Johnny Bucyk, Phil Esposito, Johnny McKenzie and Freddie Stanfield used to like to play euchre. They never stopped, even while walking through the airport—they had the rookies carry a suitcase on its side so that they could continue dealing the cards and playing.

The guys used to check into the hotel and they'd all throw their keys at me. "There you go, kid." They'd expect me to carry their suitcases and suitbags up to their rooms. For the first little while, I did it, but I finally got smart and handed $20 to the porter and had him do it.

Every team has some initiation rite for its rookies. Today, a lot of the teams go out for a huge meal and stick the rookies with the bill. We did that, too. But that wasn't all. We played the Red Wings in Detroit on New Year's Eve in 1967. I got a call in my hotel room from Dallas Smith. He said, "Hey Turk, come on up to the room. I've got a couple girls." Now, that was about as improbable as anything could've been. Dallas Smith was no more likely to have a couple girls in his room than he could fly through the air. He would never cheat or do anything like that. In fact, unless he had a few drinks, Dal barely spoke. He was the most straitlaced guy in the world, but he set the trap with a lure he knew I'd fall for.

I went up to his room and he opened the door. "Come on in." I looked, and sure enough, there were three girls, and they were beautiful. They were stewardesses. Somebody on the team had lassoed them. I was thinking, "This is great." But something wasn't right. This was completely out of character for Dallas.

I walked in and turned the corner. Damned if there weren't eight of my teammates. One of the guys asked if the girls had ever seen anyone initiated in the National Hockey League. That's when I knew. "Oh no. Don't. This ain't right. Don't be doing this, boys!" The guys tackled me, pinned me down and stripped me down. Eddie Johnston walked out of the bathroom with a towel around his neck and holding his hands up like he was a surgeon preparing to operate. The other guys dried his hands off and everybody was killing themselves laughing. Well, everybody but me!

The guys each took a hand and had me spread-eagled on the floor. Eddie took out one of those old Gillette safety razors, loosened it to the point that the blade was just about falling out, and they started to shave me . . . everywhere. They weren't being particularly careful—they cut me. I was bleeding, but that just made the guys laugh harder. One girl left, and another one was going to leave too, but the boys convinced her to stay. "No, no. Stay. This might be interesting." Meanwhile, I was begging them. "No, get out of here! Get out of here!"

So they shaved all the hair on my body below my neck, and carved me up pretty good. Then they sprayed Freezone on the areas and took Aqua Velva, poured it onto towels and dabbed it on the shaved areas. Holy Christ, did that sting! A couple of the cuts got infected and I had to go to the team doctor, who told Harry Sinden.

"How the hell did this happen?"

"I don't know, Harry. I guess I cut myself shaving."

Harry hit the roof and addressed the team. "What the hell are you idiots doing? What did you use, a straight razor? Are you guys stupid? This hazing bullshit has got to stop!"

Another time, Johnny McKenzie set me up at Gene and Georgetti's, a steak house in Chicago. Pie had played for Chicago and knew all the great spots. All the boys went for a steak dinner one night. That evening, the owner came over with a high chair. The guys put me in the high chair, taped my arms to the armrests and taped my mouth. They had great steaks, a few beers and a lot of laughs while I was forced to watch. The meal went on for three hours, and then they left me there. As they all walked out, they said, "Don't worry about the bill. Derek's got it."

As weird as it sounds, that's when I knew I was part of the Boston Bruins.

The Bruins were very close knit, and when we were on the road, we all went out together. We had strong leadership from guys like Esposito and Bobby. Each of the 18 players would fight for any of the other 17, and if someone got taken out and couldn't get the bastard that did him in, then someone else stepped in and picked up the banner. Sooner or later, one of us got him.

Harry had me taking regular shifts. I was on the top penalty-killing unit with Eddie Westfall and he had me on the left point on power plays. He was showing confidence in my abilities, and I was feeling good about my game. The media always surrounded Bobby and Phil, and because Cheevers and McKenzie were so funny, they often had a microphone in their face, too. The reporters found out fairly quickly that I was always quotable. I understood that hockey was entertainment as well as a sport. I believed that thoroughly. Rookies were supposed to be seen and not heard, but I didn't believe in that. If the media asked me a question, I'd give them an answer. Sometimes I'd embellish an answer because it made for a better story. My father had always taught me to be good to the media because they had a job to do. And if I was good to them while I was on my way up, they'd be good to me through my career.

I used to sit next to Phil in the dressing room. He asked me, "Derek, why do you say outrageous things? You're going to get yourself in trouble!"

I told him, "Phil, you score the goals and get publicity. Bobby is the greatest player in the game and he gets publicity. I'm a third-line centre. How am I going to get publicity?"

I knew that the reporters were going to be all over Orr and Esposito, so I decided on a different tack. Anybody with a little charisma could have done the same thing. I guess I was a little flaky and wasn't afraid to express my opinion about anything. But I exaggerated, and so did the writers. Ultimately, it put my reputation all out of proportion, but I must admit, I enjoyed myself immensely.

At the halfway point of the season, I had 13 goals and 13 assists and was leading all rookies in voting for the Calder Trophy. The voting that season was unique—they had the 12 NHL coaches vote instead of the beat writers in each city because they didn't think the writers in the six expansion cities knew enough about hockey to vote fairly. I didn't even know the other coaches knew who I was!

Phil Esposito said, "You deserve it. It's a landslide. Nobody can catch you." But I started to pressure myself to play better. I knew I could play better. I used to call my dad every night after a game. He'd ask how I had done, and I'd tell him I had played all right. He was unbelievably supportive. He might have offered a tip every once and again, but he was just so proud of me. And then, I fell into a slump early in the new year. I had received that early praise and recognition and started to look for goals. I wanted the easy ones that would add to my stats. Harry Sinden grabbed me and gave me shit. He said, "All of a sudden, you're getting strong consideration for rookie of the year and you want to play out at the logo at centre ice? It's a two-way game! Smarten up and play your game. If you get away from that, you are going to have nothing but problems."

Esposito really helped me, too. Frustrated, I said to him, "Phil, how can you play this game and go six games without a shot? Not a goal, not a point— a shot! I'm at a standstill here. I'm going backwards."

He said, "Slow down, Turk. You're not going backwards. All you need is one and you'll start again." He calmed me down. "You've got the rookie of the year locked up. Stop thinking about points. Points come from working hard. Goals and points will come."

I went back to fundamentals—win the draw and go from there. I worked my ass off. Harry came to me many nights when I didn't get a point and told me it had been one of the best games I'd played. He knew how well his players performed with or without points. Points didn't mean anything to him. I thought that was impressive.

We were in Detroit, and I was standing in front of the net when I got cross-checked from behind. Teddy Green took a slapper and scored. He went over to the referee, John Ashley, and told him I had tipped it. I couldn't believe it! I was on my ass. Ashley knew there was no way I had tipped it, but Greenie persisted. "I'm telling you, Derek tipped it." Ashley shrugged and went over to the scorer and reported that it was Sanderson from Green. The next night, I got two goals and two assists. My fortunes changed.

I scored my 20th and 21st goals of the season on February 29 against Toronto. By that time, I had 44 points. The press called it "an exceptional output" for a rookie, but I now had confidence in my play. That was my fourth two-goal game of the season, and before the season started, I'd told management I would score 22 goals. We played the Philadelphia Flyers at Maple Leaf Gardens in Toronto on March 7, 1968. The Flyers were forced to play home games at neutral sites because the wind had torn holes in the roof of the Spectrum and the rink was closed for repairs. Because it was close to home for my father, he came in to watch me play.

It was a brutal game. Eddie Shack and Larry Zeidel of the Flyers got into a stick-swinging duel in the first period that resulted in both players bleeding from gashes to the head. Shack was suspended for three games. In that same game, Dallas Smith fired a bullet from the point. It got tipped and caught me right in my left eye. *Boom!* I went down like a stone, holding my face. There was blood everywhere. I was scared to death.

Eddie Johnston always wanted our tickets for games in Montreal, and we were going to be playing the Canadiens a week later. He was from Montreal and had family and friends he wanted to take care of. So Eddie saw me lying in the crease bleeding and skated like hell from the other end of the ice. He leaned over me and said, "Turk, that's maybe the worst cut I've ever seen. Listen, can I still have your tickets for Montreal?"

Through the pain, I said, "Oh yeah, Pops. Sure."

Teddy Green leaned over and said, "Oh kid, that's ugly." I asked him if it was really that bad and he admitted he couldn't even see my eye. The swelling was so bad that it looked like somebody put half a basketball on the left side of my face. They took me by ambulance to Wellesley Hospital, which wasn't far from the Gardens. Besides the overwhelming pain, I had blurred double vision. My dad, Milt Schmidt and Harry Sinden arrived just as an eye specialist was inserting some tool that separated the eyelids in order to examine the retina, the cornea and the blood in my eye. He told them, "My best guess right now is a blowout fracture of the retina."

My dad asked, "What does that mean?"

The doctor explained. "Between the blow from the puck hitting him in the eye and the pressure building up, it would blow out the back socket of his eye. We have to go in, temporarily remove his eyeball, fill up the back and place the eyeball back. Time is of the essence. If it is what I think it is, we must act quickly, because the mucus of the membrane will leak into the sinuses and the eye will dry out. If that happens, he'll lose his eye. But if we can keep that fluid from leaving the eye socket, we have a 50–50 chance of recovery. If we don't, there is a good chance he will be blind in that eye." The doctor arranged for the operation to take place the next morning at seven o'clock.

I was lying in the hospital bed and the night nurse came in. She was a first-year nurse. They told her to keep her eye on me because of a possible concussion. She leaned over and spoke to me. "I know the doctors are brilliant and I'm just a first-year nurse, but common first aid sense tells me we need to bring down the swelling. I'm not supposed to do anything without a doctor's written permission, so please don't tell anybody because they'll fire me, but I'm going to apply some ice to your eye and see if I can't bring down the swelling." She got some gauze, crushed some ice and applied it to my eye. She stayed with me off and on all night, and between her other responsibilities would come back each time with new ice and fresh gauze.

Early the next morning, she told me, "I've got to take the ice off or else it'll be red and they'll know I did something." Not long afterwards, the doctor arrived, and as they were readying me for surgery, she gave me a little wave and left. They wheeled me into the operating room. The doctor took another look at my eye and expressed surprise at how much the swelling had gone down overnight. I was barely able to function, but as the doctor separated my eyelids before surgery, I shook my head aggressively and indicated that I could see. The doctor couldn't believe it. He cancelled surgery and, upon further examination, discovered that my vision problems were tied to bleeding into the retina.

That nurse likely saved me from having to endure that operation, and I never did get the opportunity to thank her.

Ultimately, there was no damage to the eyeball, in spite of my blurred vision, which cleared up in a week or so. They sewed me up with 47 stitches under the eye and another 10 in my eyebrow. I also had a depressed fracture of the cheekbone. My cheek and teeth still hurt today.

We finished third in the newly created East Division and made the playoffs for the first time since 1958–59. Montreal swept us in the opening round. Gump Worsley played great and we had trouble coping with their speed. They went on to win the Stanley Cup. Even though the press said we had come a long way from last place in 1966–67 to making the playoffs, it was still a big disappointment to the team. We really believed we had what it took to go all the way.

I finished the season with 24 goals, falling just short of Roy Conacher's Bruins' rookie scoring record of 26 goals in 1938–39. I finished with 49 points. I also had 98 penalty minutes. Then the league announced I had won the Calder Trophy as rookie of the year. As Esposito had predicted, I won by a large margin. I received 92 points to 41 for runner-up Jacques Lemaire of the Canadiens and 36 for third-place Doug Favell of the Flyers. When I arrived at training camp, I was just hoping to make the team. Milt Schmidt had told me at the time that it would be good to see me score 12 to 15 goals. It was a real honour to follow my teammate Bobby Orr as winner of the Calder. But, almost as important as the award was the $1,500 bonus the league gave me, which the Bruins matched. I was only making $10,000, so the extra $3,000 was important. I wasn't as thrilled when the league office called me and told me to be in Montreal on May 10 to receive the award. It meant I had to cut short a vacation in Daytona Beach.

I went to the award ceremony but felt out of place. I was just a kid. I didn't really feel like I'd done anything. All the big guns were there. Mikita won the Art Ross as the scoring leader, the Hart for most valuable player and the Lady Byng as most gentlemanly player. Gump Worsley and Rogie Vachon of Montreal shared the Vezina and Bobby won the Norris as top defenceman—his first of eight.

"That's what you call one hell of a rookie season," Johnny Bucyk said. "His forechecking was very effective, he had a solid shot and was a fine skater. The only thing that bothered me about him was that he was always in trouble, being a scrappy, knock-'em-down type of player. But then again, he fitted in well with the club because that is the type of player the fans like in Boston."

CHAPTER 12

SIDEBURNS AND A NEW ASSIGNMENT: 1968–69

When I first arrived in Boston, I was standing outside a bar having a smoke. Another guy came along and lit up a smoke, too. He looked over and said, "Aren't you Derek Sanderson?" I nodded and said, "Yeah." He introduced himself and said, "I understand you golf. Wanna go to the International and play a round?" The International is one of the premier courses in New England, so I told him I'd love to. Jimmy McDonough became one of the first friends I made in Boston who wasn't an athlete. His father, Sonny, was able to get me a membership at the International. Both Jimmy and Sonny have been important people in my life.

Jimmy and I were sitting around with a beer or two one day and I mentioned that I was leaving for Banff, Alberta, the next day. Glen Sather, who'd been with me in Oklahoma City in the spring of 1967 and then with the Bruins in 1967–68, asked me if I'd go out and help him with his hockey school. He could only afford to give me gas money, but we were friends, so I agreed.

Jimmy said he'd never been to Canada, so I suggested that he join me. He packed a shaving kit and threw a couple of pairs of underwear and a shirt into a gym bag. We drove along, and six hours later, we arrived in Syracuse, New York.

Jimmy asked, "Derek, where the hell is Banff?"

I said, "It's a little farther."

We stopped at my parents' house in Niagara Falls. My dad pulled out a map, pointed out Boston, showed us Niagara Falls, and then, on the far left side of the map, showed us where Banff was located.

"Holy shit!" said Jimmy. "That's a damned big country!" He had no concept of how big Canada was. We had a great time driving to Banff, but we continually struck out with the ladies. Back in Oklahoma City, I'd gotten laid for the first time. She was a really cute little thing. So I phoned her from Banff, and then drove off to Oklahoma City to get lucky. It took 46 hours to drive from Boston to Banff, and then 28 hours to get to Oklahoma City and get laid. And then, another 28 hours back to Alberta. Damn, she was good, but nobody's *that* good!

In 1968, all the guys my age were wearing "mod" clothes—bell-bottoms, boots and things like that—and were wearing their hair long, with beards and moustaches.

All except hockey players. Players from that era all looked like old men—clean-shaven with crew cuts and wearing blazers, ties and grey flannel slacks. Hockey needed colour, and I was just the guy to add it.

When I arrived at the Bruins' 1968 training camp sporting sideburns, Milt Schmidt, the general manager, said he felt sick. "Sanderson, cut those things off!"

"Don't worry about how I wear my hair," I told him. "How I play hockey is all you've got to worry about."

Bobby had a brush cut and I told him, "Kid, the brush cut—forget it. It makes you look like a kid of 16." I got him to go to a hairstylist, and as his hair got longer, it looked a lot better.

And then there were the clothes. Ken "Hawk" Harrelson of the Boston Red Sox and Joe Namath of football's New York Jets were great dressers, and I learned from them. I'd never really paid much attention to fashion until I started to hang out with Hawk and Joe Willie. Both of them loved entertaining people and understood that sports were entertainment.

Hawk Harrelson had 60 pairs of golf shoes. I had two. But if a reporter asked me, I would tell them, "I don't really know how many pairs of golf shoes I have—40? Maybe 50? I've lost count." And the reporters would write it. They used to ask about my clothes. I told them I had 47 suits and 60 pairs of shoes and boots when, in fact, I had four suits and four pairs of shoes. I was pretty good at mixing and matching, which gave the appearance of having a bigger wardrobe than I did. I was good at embellishing, and the reporters ate it up. It was a joke to me, but they went with it. The problem was, I lied so often, I began to believe my own stories. I didn't realize that, in fact, I was creating a Frankenstein.

Later on, Bobby introduced me to Marty Alsemgeest, who owned Marty's Custom Tailor and Shirtmaker in Toronto. Until I met Marty, I had no real style. I was completely haphazard fashion-wise. I wore whatever was the current fad. Marty is the best tailor on the planet and he got me dressed to the nines. Marty explained that fads come and go, but style stays.

I used to buy seven or eight suits at a time. My logic, shared by Marty, was that there are 20 business days each month, so if you buy eight good suits and rotate them, you're only wearing them twice a month. And that's just over 20 times a year. Not bad. Classic clothes last for years that way. I would also buy 12 white shirts and maybe four or five blues in various shades. I would never buy stripes and patterns because they go in and out of style. Finally, Marty taught me to spend my money on ties. That's all that people look at. And always use the double Windsor knot. Classy way to go.

Later, when I showed up dressed in a turtleneck, Nehru jacket and bell-bottoms, Milt ordered me to change. "Straight shirt and tie, kid. What do you think you're doing?" I went along with his demands most of the time, but at one point during the season, I showed up for a road trip dressed in mod clothes. We were boarding the bus and Harry wanted to fine me $100 because I wasn't wearing a tie. He looked me up and down and asked, "What the hell is that thing you've got on?"

I said, "Harry, it's a Nehru jacket!" He said, "Nehru? No way! Jacket and tie." He pulled a clip-on tie out of his pocket and handed it to me. "Here."

I said, "Thanks anyway. I'll take the $100 fine."

None of us ever questioned Harry. We might bitch and moan, but no one ever thought of disrespecting him. All decisions were his and all lineups were his alone. While we were on the road, he was alone with one trainer. Today, coaches couldn't imagine not having three assistants, a video guy, a road secretary, trainers, equipment managers and a marketing team.

My teammates thought I was flaky, but hockey was too old-fashioned. Eventually, I was able to persuade a bunch of the other guys to adopt a hipper look. Bobby, Phil, Eddie Johnston and Gerry Cheevers began dressing more like me. I'd like to think I influenced them, but truthfully, it was simply the times. Milt and Harry eventually relaxed the dress code rules. Soon, most of the players in the league, especially in Montreal, started getting with the trends.

Once, half-jokingly, I asked the Bruins if I could wear white skates. Namath was wearing white cleats with the Jets and the Oakland A's were wearing white baseball spikes, so I thought it'd be a nice touch for me. The Bruins didn't see it the way I did. Harry Sinden said, "Sure, you can wear white ice skates, Derek, on the condition that you wear a pink helmet to go with them." Milt Schmidt asked me not to wear them, so I dropped the idea. Our trainer, Frosty Forristall, thought it would be a fun idea to use my backup pair of Tacks as a joke, and the next day at practice, I went to my spot in the dressing room and there were white skates. Frosty had whitewashed them! Harry just looked over and warned, "Don't even try it."

Heywood Hale Broun was on CBS television, and he was the first guy to do a major story on me. He put me on the national stage. He told viewers that certain athletes had *duende*—something that gives people chills. He rhymed off a list of athletes who had *duende*, including Muhammad Ali, Joe Namath and me. That really escalated my reputation.

Once, I was in Las Vegas and Muhammad Ali came over to my table and knew who I was. He said, "I'm a big fan of yours. I like that game." I couldn't believe it! It was a humbling moment because Ali was the best boxer in the world. Maybe the greatest athlete ever.

Our league stymied any individuals who hoped to stand out from the rest, but it was slowly coming around. League president Clarence Campbell, a Rhodes scholar and a lawyer who had helped prosecute war-crime cases in the aftermath of World War II, stood for class and leadership, but even he knew that we were in the entertainment business.

A few key players were missing from training camp that September. Bobby Orr was recuperating after having surgery and Johnny Bucyk, Teddy Green and Eddie Shack were all holdouts. I didn't hold out, but I also found myself at odds with management.

After I won the rookie of the year award, I wanted my contract renegotiated. I thought I was better than what I was getting paid. I asked my lawyer to look into it. He met with the Bruins but came back and told me, "Forget it. You have to honour the contract." When I told the press what I made, they became allies. So did the fans. It was David versus Goliath—the young player against big, bad management. Up until that time, no one had ever tried to renegotiate a contract. Milt Schmidt told me to quit bitching, and Harry told me to grow up. "One good season does not a star make. Do it again." The players were on my side because if it worked for me, it might work for them.

At training camp in London, I was told that Mr. Adams wanted to speak to me. I thought I was going to be told that I would get the money I'd asked for. I met Mr. Adams in his room. He opened with, "You have proven to me that you are as good as I said you would be. Congratulations on being named rookie of the year." After a pause, he continued. "You are very close to your father, am I correct?"

I proudly said, "Yes, sir!"

"He raised you to be loyal and a man of your word."

"Yes, sir." My father had always said that you have nothing in this world but your word. "Don't give it lightly," he said, "but when you do, always honour it."

Mr. Adams handed me a piece of paper. It was my contract.

"Is that your signature?" he asked.

I could see what was coming. "Yes, sir," I replied.

"And doesn't that signature represent your word?"

"Yes."

"Well?"

"But that's not fair!" I stammered. "I'm better than that."

"Yes, you are," he said. "But when you signed this contract, weren't you happy?"

"Yes, I was."

He continued. "Well, if you broke your neck and couldn't play, doesn't my signature on this contract mean that I promise to pay you anyway?"

I agreed.

"Well," he said, "just because I made a good deal this time and you did not is unfortunate. Come see me when your contract ends."

I shook my head in astonishment. I couldn't say anything but, "Yes, sir, you're right."

I had been spoiled in my rookie season. Harry had me playing in every situation—five on five, left point on the power play and killing penalties. This year, he sat me down at training camp and we had a great talk. He said, "You're the best defensive player I've got. I'm sorry, but you're not going to be on the power play anymore. My power play is going to come from my first two lines. I need you to do something for me. I've got to have you shut down the opposing teams' best forwards—Beliveau, Mikita. I want to know that I can depend on you to take care of them so I don't have to worry about them." He continued, "You'll get your scoring chances by playing good, solid defence. You've got that sweep check. You'll steal pucks and away you'll go. You'll get your due."

I can't say I wasn't disappointed, and I guess Harry could see it in me. "Harry, I won't make any money because I'm going to give up power-play points," I protested. He just looked at me. "Derek," he said, "I want you and Eddie Westfall to bring penalty killing to an art form. I'll know it and your teammates will know it. That's all that matters. Be ready when you see a delayed-penalty call because you're going out right away."

Harry gave me a challenge and told me I was the best faceoff man he had and that I was key in the Bruins' penalty-killing plans. I always played the last minute and a half in games that were tied or within one goal. I was determined to be the greatest penalty killer the National Hockey League had ever seen.

I also set my sights on scoring 26 goals in 1968–69. I was in a somewhat different role, but with more confidence and with the Bruins cooking along, I was confident I could hit that target.

I got off to a slow start. Now, I don't go in for that "sophomore slump" business. I knew what I was doing wrong and I worked on it. For one thing, I was shooting off my wrong foot. Fortunately, my linemates, Eddie Shack and Eddie Westfall, were getting their goals.

Both goalies, Cheevers and Johnston, were playing well for us, and then, Johnston got hurt during the pregame warmup on Halloween in Detroit. Unlike today, where they've got a ton of pucks on the ice during the warmup, at that time, they usually only had one puck on the ice to warm up the goalie. Somehow, Shack got hold of a second puck. Bobby Orr fired a shot from the blue line, but Johnston was distracted by Shack and took his eyes off the puck. Bobby's shot clocked him on the side of the head and put him out. He didn't come out of the hospital until just before Christmas. The incident really bothered Bobby, because he and Eddie had been best friends since 1966. Popsy was a great competitor and a great friend. He had been with the Bruins since 1962–63, and had seen more rubber than roadkill on a highway. Although he was 11 years older than me, he was a guy I enjoyed spending time with, especially on the golf course.

We played back-to-back games against the Montreal Canadiens just before Christmas. We skated to a scoreless tie in Boston on December 21, and the next night, we played the Canadiens in Montreal, which was where the NHL's head office was. Before the game, Orr and I were scheduled to receive our awards from Clarence Campbell, the league president. I made myself a salmon sandwich after the game in Boston and ended up with ptomaine poisoning! I woke up at three o'clock in the morning, running from both ends. I had a fever of 103 and I thought I was dying. It was all I could do to call the dressing room and let them know I was sick. Frosty Forristall answered, and I was so weak that he didn't even recognize my voice. He grabbed Harry Sinden and said, "It's Derek, and he's sick."

Harry got on the line. "You got a broken leg?"

"No. My legs are good, Harry, but I'm sicker than a dog."

"Get over to the rink," Harry demanded. "Hockey players don't get sick. They only don't play when they break their legs."

I played that game and got two goals in a win over Tony Esposito and the Canadiens.

The pregame award presentation was a photo opportunity, nothing more. But after the game, Teddy Green came up to me in the shower. I was dripping wet, just wearing a towel, and he said, "Congratulations, kid. You deserved it."

"Thanks."

He replied, "Oh, you think I'm talking about winning rookie of the year."

"Yeah, isn't that what you meant?"

He said, "No. I meant getting that body through this league. You're skinny enough to bury yourself in a gun barrel."

I laughed and said, "Fuck you." He slapped me on the back of the head. It was really a close team.

I got my first National Hockey League hat trick in a road win over Los Angeles on January 30, 1969. I had just come back after spending a month recuperating from a pulled hip muscle that forced me out of the lineup for nine games. My three goals were part of a six-goal burst for the Bruins over a five-minute stretch that started late in the second and carried over into the third. We ended up winning the game 7–5. The game was also notable because I got into a slashing duel with Kings goalie Gerry Desjardins.

I had two goals and was parked with the puck behind Desjardins and the Kings net. I had no play. They had me shut off. The defenceman was staring at me, and I was cuffing the puck, waiting for a play. Everybody was covered and the Kings weren't challenging me. If they had come at me, I could make a move because it would leave someone unprotected. I noticed the goalie's left pad was bent and maybe four inches off the post. I had to try. My shot hit him on the pad and bounced in.

"Sorry," I taunted, "but you didn't cover the post!"

The only guy who knew I had banked it in like that was Esposito. He'd been on the bench and came on the ice when we changed lines. He laughed, "You planned that, didn't you, you little prick?"

A couple of weeks later, I sprained my left knee hitting J.P. LeBlanc of the Black Hawks. I nailed him with his head down but injured my knee in the process. It hurt at the time, but not that badly. I aggravated it later when I used my skate to jam the puck against the boards while I battled Bobby Hull. Later, I hit Doug Mohns and really felt a twinge. I finished the period and felt okay, but it stiffened up between periods. We ended up winning 7–3, but I damaged the medial lateral ligament and was out for a couple of weeks. Dr. Adams put me in a cast to rest the knee.

Our lineup was seriously depleted. We were without Orr, Esposito, Johnny McKenzie, Gary Doak, Tom Webster, Tommy Williams and me. We got crucified in back-to-back games, shut out by Pittsburgh 3–0 and 9–0 by the Rangers, but then won four in a row.

I was back in the lineup in mid-March, and we had back-to-back games against the Leafs. On the 15th, in Toronto, the Leafs beat us 7–4, but that was the least of our worries. Bobby was trying to dig the puck out from Bruce Gamble's pads when Pat Quinn cross-checked him into the crossbar and, when he fell to the ice, kicked him. "I gave him a kind of half-hearted kick, but it was in the seat of the pants," Quinn told *The Globe and Mail.* The next night, we played them in Boston. We wanted Quinn's head. Nobody touched our guys without repercussion, but Quinn didn't dress because of an injury. Believe me, Quinn was a big, tough guy afraid of no one, and if he could have played, he would have.

The game ended with us on top, 11–3. We set an NHL record with eight goals in the second period. We drove Bruce Gamble out of their net in that period, and they put in Al Smith. I tied a club record with six points, including my second NHL hat trick. Harry had me centring Wayne Cashman and Ace Bailey, who was brought up to fill in for Shack. Ace got five points that night. That set the stage for a first-round playoff matchup between the two of us.

Boston finished second in the East Division—and the league—with 100 points, trailing only Montreal, who had 103. We scored an NHL-record 303 goals, 23 more than the Black Hawks. Esposito set a record by collecting 126 points to take the Art Ross Trophy. He later was awarded the Hart Trophy as the regular season MVP. Bobby Orr won the Norris Trophy as the league's best defenceman, combining his great defensive play with an unbelievable 120 points from the blue line.

I hit my target, scoring exactly the 26 goals I predicted, to go with 46 total points and 146 penalty minutes.

On April 2, the Bruins met the Leafs in the first game of the quarter-finals. We wanted to hurt them in every way a team could be hurt. We kicked their asses 10–0, but the game included the infamous Quinn–Orr incident. In the second period, Bobby was coming up the boards, trying to fend off a forward, when Pat Quinn stepped into him and sent him into the middle of next week. They took Bobby out on a stretcher while the crowd chanted, "Get Quinn! Get Quinn!" From there, it was a continuous brawl. You don't hit Bobby like that.

I fought Tim Horton. Forbes Kennedy of the Leafs went crazy, fighting Cheevers and getting a minor, two majors and a game misconduct. He was later suspended for four games. There were 132 minutes in penalties called in that game. Harry told the papers, "I wouldn't say our team is the best to play that style against. The Leafs have two or three people who want to play that way. We have 18. The toughest job I've had all year was trying to hold our team back."

Bobby told *The New York Times*, "We're just like a bunch of animals. When we see blood or one of our guys getting hurt digging out the puck, we're in that corner like a bunch of animals."

We walked all over the Leafs the rest of the way. They were a broken team and we had something to prove. The next night, we blanked them 7–0. Bobby was really sick, but played and set up the first goal. There was only one fight, a tilt between Don Awrey and Larry Mickey. We beat the Leafs 4–3 in game three, and I was lucky enough to get the winning goal. Quinn took a poke at me, but I just skated away. That was too big a game and I wasn't going to take a penalty and cost us anything. We then finished off Toronto with a 3–2 win in the fourth game. I got two goals, including the winner. The story in the *Boston Globe* ran under the headline, "Sanderson's Play Draws Raves."

Immediately after the game, Leaf owner Stafford Smythe fired Punch

Imlach. I went on record as saying it was a huge mistake and that Toronto would suffer because of it. Imlach might have been a tyrant, but he delivered them from obscurity to four Stanley Cup championships. They haven't won since.

During that series against Toronto, I hurt my leg and it was really bothering me, but there was no way I was coming out of the lineup. We faced the Canadiens in the East Division final. We knew that if we could get past Montreal, the Stanley Cup was ours. The Stanley Cup final would be against the winner of the West Division—made up of the six expansion teams—and in a best-of-seven series, we could take them. But we also had an incentive to beat the Canadiens because they had embarrassed us the year before by sweeping us in four straight games.

Before the series, a headline in *The Hockey News* read, "B's Sanderson Rocks in Playoffs. Could Be Club's Next Super Star," but the one I really appreciated was from the *Toronto Star:* "Habs Fear Sanderson More Than Espo." One of the greatest compliments I ever got was from John Ferguson. He and I were at each other all the time. I always respected Fergie as one of the fiercest competitors I ever played against, and was surprised but flattered when, before our series, he said, "If we're going to beat the Bruins, we've got to stop Sanderson."

In the first game, played in Montreal, I potted a couple, but the Canadiens edged us 3–2. I fought Yvan Cournoyer and Dickie Duff. They beat us again, 4–3, in game two but, riding amazing fan support back in Boston, we shut them out 5–0 in game three, even though Kenny Hodge and Pie McKenzie were out with the flu and Cashman with a broken hand. We felt really good going into game four. In the first period, I scored a shorthanded goal and raised my stick to celebrate. Ferguson came barrelling at me from 20 feet away and hit me right in the thigh where there was no protection. It practically crippled me. I had hurt my leg in the series against Toronto, but this one hurt like a mother. It bothered me so much that I only played one shift in the second and then pulled myself out of the game. That was it for me for the night.

Ferguson competed hard and he was out to win. I couldn't really fault him for the hit. I would have done the same thing to him if I had the chance.

We went on to win 3–2 to tie the series at two. I was diagnosed with a charley horse, and Dan Canney, our trainer, announced that I'd be out for 10 days.

We believed we had Montreal on the ropes. We won both games in Boston, and then, in Montreal for game five, we were ahead 2–1 with a couple minutes left to play. Eddie Shack picked up a stupid penalty when he jumped up in the air and wrestled John Ferguson, laughing. Under my breath, I said, "You asshole! What a stupid penalty!"

Montreal was on the power play. There was about 1:45 left in the game when Ferguson came down the wall and took a slapper from just inside the blue line. It fluttered on Cheevers and the puck caught the far post and went in. Now it was 2–2. Then, Shack got another penalty. Montreal had momentum on their side.

We needed somebody to carry the puck out of our own end. When Phil had the puck on his stick, he was magic. He held the puck really well. He never gave it away. He was a big, strong man and a very good defensive player, which is something no one gives him credit for. He backchecked better than most players, and he always worked his ass off.

I was put on the ice for the draw in our end. I had won six in a row but couldn't get the puck out, so we kept freezing it and eating up the clock. Harry made a change, putting Esposito out for the faceoff against Jacques Lemaire. Lemaire won the draw and unloaded a bullet just under the crossbar. We ended up losing the game, 4–2. Right after the game, we flew back to Boston. Fog forced our plane to circle Logan for a few hours, but we finally landed around three in the morning.

I tried my best to play in game six, but was pretty limited in what I could do. Gump Worsley was out with a swollen hand, so the Canadiens had Rogie Vachon in net. We fought hard and held them to a 1–1 tie through regulation, but in the second overtime, Claude Provost scored to give them the win and the series.

Before the series, I had predicted we'd blow Montreal out of the rink. "We have a better team and more guts." After losing in game six, I was deflated. How do you explain it? They didn't have the team, the guts, the defence or the talent, but they got goals. We should have won that series, because if we had, we would have been able to defeat the St. Louis Blues. Instead, Montreal beat the Blues in four straight to win the Stanley Cup.

That spring should have been the first of four straight Stanley Cups for Boston. Even though Montreal beat us, we knew we had the team that could win.

CHAPTER 13

BACHELORS III

I got a call one day in June 1969. "Hi, is this Derek Sanderson? This is Joe Namath."

My reaction: "Yeah, sure. Okay, who's screwing around with me?"

"No, it really is Joe Namath," he said. "I've got a proposition for you. Any chance you can come to New York?"

"Right!" I said. "Sure," and I hung up on him.

He called right back. "Look, Derek. Call me at this number," and he gave me a New York City number. I called it and, sure enough, Namath answered. He laughed and admitted anybody could have said they were him, but he asked if I could meet him the next day.

"Sure," I agreed.

Joe Namath *was* the American Football League. He was the rookie of the year in 1965, a four-time All-Star and set all sorts of records for passing. On January 12, 1969, Joe led the AFL's New York Jets to one of the greatest upsets in football history when they beat the NFL's Baltimore Colts in the third Super Bowl. A couple of days earlier, he had guaranteed a victory, and after the game, he was voted the MVP of the championship game. Joe was the future of football, especially after being a winner in New York.

Joe had opened a bar in Manhattan called Bachelors III, but the National Football League's commissioner, Pete Rozelle, ordered him to divest himself of his interest in the bar in order to protect the sport's reputation. There were too many bookmakers in the joint, and the NFL didn't want the association with gambling. Joe didn't, either, but he had a very viable, growing business.

"No one's going to tell me I have to get out of the bar business," Joe said, and he held a media conference to announce he was quitting football. The owners panicked. Joe had brought a ton of cash to the sport through increased TV revenue. Joe and Pete Rozelle had a long meeting, and in the end, they decided that Joe would sell his shares in the New York location of Bachelors III, but if he followed through with his plans to open locations in Boston and Fort Lauderdale, he could keep those shares. After missing most of training camp, Namath came out of retirement and reported to the Jets.

Bachelors III was the first real dating bar for singles in America. The timing was unbelievable. The world was changing rapidly in the 1960s, and my generation was at the forefront of the changes.

Namath asked me to meet him at the Green Kitchen on First Avenue in New York. I told the guy at the door that I was there to see Joe Namath. He led me to a booth, and there was Joe Willie, feet up on the table, wearing New York Jets shorts, a T-shirt and sneakers. He was talking on the phone and eating a salad.

He stuck his hand out. "Hey Derek. Joe." Then he introduced me to the guys he was sitting with. Joe didn't go anywhere without them. I slid into the booth and asked, "What's this all about?"

"You may have read the news that I quit football, but now they want me to come back. But in order to go back, I have to leave Bachelors III in New York."

The Bachelors III were Ray Abruzzese, Bobby Vannuchi and Namath. Abruzzese was Joe's roommate at the University of Alabama and had gone on to a pro career with the Buffalo Bills and New York Jets of the AFL. Vannuchi was another pal of Joe's. He called himself Bobby Van. He was the host who'd greet people at the door.

"In Boston," Joe said, "it's going to be me, Bobby Van and you. You'll be the third bachelor."

"Why me?" I asked.

"I gave it a lot of thought," Joe explained. "The first guy we thought of was Kenny Harrelson. He's an action guy. He was in the running for MVP, but the Red Sox just traded him to Cleveland. I have to have my guys in Boston. I thought about Tony Conigliaro. He's a good-looking guy, but he's got an ego bigger than mine, so that wouldn't work. I thought about Bobby Orr, but he has a 'milk and cookies' reputation. I don't think the kid drinks, so that wouldn't work."

He looked up from his salad. "So, I hear you have some charisma. You're in. I figure you'll stick around for a while and we'll build a business. Everything will be good."

It sounded too good to be true. I said, "Okay, what's the deal?"

He said, "You get a salary of $30,000 a year." I liked this deal already! That was more than twice what I was making with the Bruins. "And you get a new Lincoln." It was a brand new, gold Lincoln Continental Mark III. I got the licence plate BRUINS 16 and had to have it welded on or else it would've been stolen every day.

"How much money do I need to put up?" I asked.

"None," Namath replied. "And you also get power of the pen."

"What's 'power of the pen'?" I inquired.

He said, "When your friends and people you've invited come into the bar, you pick up their tabs. Just sign the cheque. We write it off as marketing."

That's how I learned how to pick up the tab. Unfortunately, I ended up buying the world a drink. Every night was sensational fun. There were lineups around the block. When the Bruins were in town, we were there until two in the morning every night. All the waitresses were great-looking. It was a beauty contest. They all wore V-neck sweaters to show some cleavage and hot pants with high boots. I was thinking, "This is unbelievable! And I'm the boss!"

Two doors down from Bachelors III was the Playboy Club, which had opened in Boston in 1965. I had earlier met Mary, the Den Mother. She oversaw 64 of the best-looking women on the eastern seaboard. Playboy Enterprises had strict rules for the girls. They didn't want the Playboy brand to get tarnished. The girls could only pose nude if it was for *Playboy,* they couldn't have their boyfriends or husbands on the premises and there was to be no interaction with customers in the parking lot. It was really prestigious to be a Playboy bunny in those days. I'd gotten to know all the girls.

I went to Mary and said, "How about inviting them two doors down to my new bar, Bachelors III, after work? The girls can drink for free."

She was astonished. "They don't have to pay?"

"Nope," I said. "All they have to do is show their Bunny Card and the drinks are on the house."

"Wow, I'll tell the girls," she exclaimed. She posted a note to that effect on the Playboy Club's bulletin board. That was it. It was insane! Thirty-two of the best-looking women in the country were in my club every shift—morning, afternoon, lunch and dinner. They would come in after work and party until two, three, four o'clock in the morning. And where beautiful girls go, guys are sure to follow.

I also went to the Red Sox and Patriots and told the players they could drink for free at our club. Same with my teammates on the Bruins. Any time you have athletes and beautiful girls, the bar will be jammed. It was party time! Guys trying to pay for a drink were five deep at the bar all day. We had the best bar in town.

When the Jets were playing the Patriots, Namath was in the bar and everybody knew it. He'd come in Friday, Saturday and Sunday, joking and announcing that it was time to party. The best-looking women in the city showed up. It was just a zoo. Joe drank Johnnie Walker Black and talked football. That's all he ever talked about. He never did understand hockey.

The lineups went around the block. Jerry McCullough, the only male employee at Bachelors III, would go out, inspect the line and decide who got in. You have to know that the most beautiful single girls got preferential treatment. There were so many beautiful women in our club every night that I was like a kid in a candy store. This was all brand new to me, so I was quite taken with the whole scene. The girls were flirty and often quite forward. I was always a one-on-one guy, but I slipped a few times. If you want insanity, go to bed with three or four women at once. It was unbelievable. You'd have four queens in bed with you and they want to go all night. What are you going to do? Fuck two and then breathe through your ears until you were ready for the other two? I later learned a great lesson, and that was that one girl was sufficient.

I used to look around the room and think about which one I was going to take home, but it often seemed that at the end of the night, I'd end up pounding my own pud because all the girls had left. I got a lesson in picking up girls from Namath: "Derek, don't worry about getting the pick of the litter. If you don't isolate early, you're going to end up alone. Find the one you like and stick with the girl you've chosen. Treat her well. Get a couple of drinks into her and get her out of there. And if things work out well, come back for last call and find another one to take home for breakfast. I watch you. You've got four or five girls on the go and you're table-hopping. At the end of the night, you're going home with Rosie Palm and her five sisters."

One night, we returned late after a road trip to New York. I was walking to my car when a stunning blonde walked into the bar with four or five suitcases. It was about 1:30 in the morning and all the cabs had left for the night. I walked up to her and said, "Excuse me, are you looking for me?" She said yes! I asked her if she needed help and she said that she did.

Oh boy!

She was a Norwegian beauty named Liv. She ended up living with me. She was stunning, and not possessive at all. One day, she came to me and said, "There's a guy who says he's from Playboy Enterprises and he wants to take my picture." I was a little protective because I wasn't sure how legitimate this guy was, but he assured me he would only take pictures in my apartment, needed no more than four hours and I could be there if I wanted to be.

I shrugged and said, "Sounds okay to me." I told them I'd leave and come back later so they could do their shoot in private.

They sent the photos to *Playboy*'s head office and they contacted her to say they needed her in Los Angeles as soon as she could get there. She was Playmate of the Month in January 1971 and was selected Playmate of the Year in 1972. I never saw her again after she left for L.A.

I'd started to run with a new crowd. One of my new friends was Ken Harrelson. He was a really colourful guy who had helped the Red Sox win the pennant in 1967. He had an MVP season in 1968 and the city loved him. They called him "the Hawk" because of his nose. He was traded to the Cleveland Indians in April 1969 and, in protest, retired briefly.

I really hit it off with the Hawk. He had style, and I admired that. Kenny was a really "mod" dresser—lace shirt, Edwardian jacket, bell-bottoms and square-toed suede shoes with buckles—and wore his hair fairly long. Kenny and I became really good friends. I lived with him for a while when I was first with the Bruins.

The Hawk lived pretty fast, and he knew all the angles to get the hottest girls. In those days, to be a stewardess—now called a flight attendant—was a beauty contest. Every single one of them was drop-dead gorgeous. Harrelson had a friend who was involved in crew scheduling for the stewardesses. Because their schedules were flexible, you had to find out which days they had off and where they were flying. The Hawk used to trade baseball tickets and I traded hockey tickets with the guy so that he'd schedule certain stewardesses so that their schedules matched ours. We got whatever we wanted at the time.

One time, Gino Cappelletti, Kenny Harrelson, John Havlicek and I decided to have a contest to see who was the best athlete. The four of us each represented a major sport—Cappelletti with football, Harrelson with baseball, Havlicek with basketball, and I was hockey. These guys were no slouches! Cappelletti played for the Boston Patriots and was the AFL's most valuable player in 1964. Harrelson was an All-Star first baseman and outfielder. Havlicek played 16 seasons with the Boston Celtics and was a major reason why they won eight NBA titles during that time. He's in the Basketball Hall of Fame.

We made up some rules. Each guy had to play the three other sports, and would earn a score out of 10 for each one. You got an automatic 10 for your own sport. In the basketball drill, you had to shoot free throws. In baseball, with the Hawk pitching, you had to hit the ball to the Green Monster at Fenway Park. With football, we had to kick a field goal and throw a football through a moving tire. All the guys did pretty well. In basketball, I rated 6 out of 10, in baseball, I was a 7, and in football, I was a 7—a total of 20 points out of a possible 30. All the other guys got a zero in hockey because they couldn't skate. Cappelletti and Havlicek didn't even try—Havlicek joked that they didn't have size 15 skates for him to wear. But Harrelson said, "I'm not taking a zero in hockey. What do you have to do?"

I said, "I will lay a two-by-four across the goal mouth, and from 20 feet out, you have 10 shots to see how many goals you can get." So, first of all, he had to skate, and secondly, he had to raise the puck over the plank.

The Hawk asked, "Can I do it wearing my boots?" I told him no, insisting that he wear skates.

"That's not fair! Normal athletes play on the ground."

I said, "Yeah, I know, but that's how difficult it is to play on frozen water, my friend."

He came out wearing skates and his bell-bottoms, and the first thing I heard was, "Holy shit! This game is insane. You guys go 30 miles an hour on these things?" He held on to the boards while he tried to stand upright on his skates, and when he got to the hash marks, Ken Hodge and Phil Esposito helped him out to the front of the net.

I dropped the puck in front of him and placed the two-by-four across the net. He took a swipe at the puck and missed. He asked Kenny Hodge to show him how to shoot a puck and raise it, but he couldn't get the pucks in the net.

Harrelson was frustrated. "This thing is stupid."

I said, "Wanna see me hit the left post, the crossbar and then the right post?"

"Holy shit, can you really do that?" he asked.

I said, "Yeah, watch." I went back to the blue line and took some slappers. I said, "Left post, crossbar, right post." *Bing, bing, bing!* Hit all three in order. We used to do it all the time after practice. Bobby Orr used to do it from centre ice!

He just shook his head. "Screw you." He finally conceded defeat, saying, "As far as athletics go, I guess you're the best, Turk."

I won simply because none of the other guys could skate.

The Hawk introduced me to the man who became my lawyer. I was starting to get a little attention, and Kenny suggested that I consider getting an agent.

"Why do I need an agent?" I asked.

"Agreements, deals. He can get you signings and things like that."

"Okay," I shrugged. "I didn't know that." I had no idea about the business side of the game.

I have chosen not to include the name of my lawyer. We had major differences through the years, and while he has since passed away, I refuse to even dignify him by mentioning him by name.

My lawyer had just started out when Earl Wilson, a pitcher with the Boston Red Sox, asked him to handle his career. That was in 1965. Because of his work with Wilson, he picked up Carl Yastrzemski, the Red Sox superstar, as a client, and by 1971 he had abandoned his law practice and concentrated solely on athletes. He also represented John Havlicek of the Boston Celtics. I was walking into his office for the first time as Havlicek was walking out. Havlicek turned to me and said, "Do yourself a favour and turn around. He is not a good guy."

Kenny Harrelson took me into the office to meet this guy. I sat down, put my feet on his desk and said, "I need a lawyer."

He asked me why. I said, "Actually, I don't really need a lawyer. I need an agent."

He replied, "Well, I'm not an agent. I'm a lawyer."

"Look," I said, "I need someone who can handle my legal work. I'm going to be a millionaire, and en route, I'm going to have things that I'll need a lawyer to check out for me."

"Oh," he smirked. "So you're going to be a millionaire?"

"Uh-huh."

"How much do you make now?"

"Eleven thousand a year."

"Okay," he laughed. "And how do you plan to get your million?"

I told him I could create a nice stable of clients for him. "Everywhere I go, I'll mention you. I can create a mystique about myself by mentioning that I have a team working for me—not an entourage, but a team. If I have someone who is intelligent and can speak clearly about legal matters, that will start to carry some clout. And if I'm going to talk to the Bruins and negotiate anything, I can say, 'Talk to my lawyer.' That's all I want to be able to say. That will not make me seem self-important, but it will create an aura."

He said, "Okay, I can see your point, but you still haven't told me how you're going to get to be a millionaire."

I said, "I will. It just takes a little time. It's not going to happen overnight."

My lawyer never recruited players as clients. As part of my deal, I would recruit players for him, and in return, he wouldn't charge me for the work he did on my behalf. I would talk to guys and say, "You should talk to my lawyer." I'd give them his card and that would be it.

We had a great relationship . . . for a few years.

CHAPTER 14

A TEAM OF BROTHERS: 1969–70

Entering my third season, I hoped to get $70,000 a year in a newly negoti-
ated contract, but still had a year left on the deal I had signed with Hap
Emms. I missed the first day of training camp while my lawyer talked with
Milt Schmidt about my contract, but I wasn't going to get anywhere, so I
showed up the next day.

I had been letting my hair and sideburns grow since the previous season,
but showed up at camp this year with a moustache. My hair wasn't really
that long, but by the NHL standards of the day, it was likely longer than just
about anybody else's in the league. The comments from some of the old guard
were pretty ridiculous. These were guys who couldn't accept that hockey was
changing with the times. A sportswriter from *The Globe and Mail* commented,
"You get the impression that if he combed his hair, Joe Namath would fall
out." The coach of the Baltimore Clippers of the AHL, former NHLer Rudy
Migay, cheekily asked, "Is that Derek Sanderson or a buffalo?" Even my own
GM, Milt Schmidt, stated, "He doesn't look like an athlete." Billy Speer, whom
the Bruins got from the Penguins, had trained as a barber, and he threatened
to cut my hair, but that never happened.

The moustache actually caused more problems than the long hair. I simply hadn't shaved for a week before training camp, but Milt got bent out of
shape over it. "What the hell is this moustache?" he asked. "The rules I set say
no facial hair. This isn't the Rolling Stones." I laughed at his reference, but he
insisted I shave or I wouldn't get any per diem.

I said, "Milt, my dad has a moustache. You're insulting my father. If it's good enough for my dad, it's good enough for me." He couldn't argue with that.

If I thought my hair or moustache interfered with my game, I'd have shaved both right off. I would have done anything for the good of hockey, because I owe everything to the game, but my hair wasn't about to hurt my performance.

In 2011, Barry Melrose, an ESPN analyst, listed his all-time top NHL teams, and ranked the Boston Bruins of 1969–70 as fifth greatest. "This team scored a ton of goals, they were in a ton of fights, they had a bunch of free-spirited guys and they loved to play. It was an awesome team to watch."

The team was remarkable. Bobby Orr once referred to the Boston Bruins of the 1969–70 season as a "team of brothers." We truly were exactly that. Harry Sinden moulded that team out of a diverse group of characters. Harry is, without question, the smartest hockey man I ever met, and he never, ever got his due. You always knew where you stood with Harry Sinden. He didn't play games. Coincidentally, Harry was also a disciple of Lloyd Percival.

Bobby Orr, without question, is the greatest player who ever played. He used to curl around that net two or three times and everybody would be drawn to him like a magnet. The point man would drift in, so I would quietly position myself at the logo at centre ice, and while opponents were watching him, mesmerized, Bobby would go around the net on his forehand, fire the puck to centre ice waist high, I'd knock it down and I'd be gone. Westfall would be right there beside me. We had more breakaways than you could shake a stick at.

Bobby did things that were absolutely off the charts, things that guys had never done before and never since. People don't realize that they only saw him for nine years and he was never healthy during that time. He always had bad knees. The greatest thing about being on the ice with him was that you could take extra risks because he never lost the puck and he always had your back. Bobby was just a brilliant playmaker, but he could do it all. He was just the best, without question. He was our leader.

Eddie Westfall and I were the Bruins' penalty killers, and we had it down to a science. We used to call Eddie "the Shadow" or "Lamont Cranston" because it was his role to cover—or shadow—the best wingers in the league. Guys like Bobby Hull, Rod Gilbert and Gordie Howe. Harry would move Eddie from wing to wing just to cover certain players.

Eddie and I were very innovative. We never gave the opponents the same look twice. We started with Eddie Shack as the other winger, then it was Glen Sather, then Wayne Carleton and finally, Donnie Marcotte.

What made that team so special was that we had grown together since 1967. The Bruins had nicknames for everybody. Garnet Bailey was Ace. Johnny Bucyk was Chief. Wayne Carleton was Swoop. Wayne Cashman was Cash. Johnny McKenzie was Pie. Dallas Smith was Half-Ton because he was a farmboy who drove a half-ton truck. Rick Smith was Five To. It didn't matter where we were going, he would always arrive five minutes before we were leaving. At airports, they had to hold flights for him. Gerry Cheevers was Cheesy and I called Eddie Johnston "Pops" because he was older than all of us. Eddie always called me "Twilight" because I was in a different zone than everybody else.

We had so much fun on that team. We made up games on the bench during games. We'd pick players who belonged on an All-Ugly Team, an All-Wussy Team, a Should Not Be in the NHL Team or a Bad Look with a Helmet Team. And as hard as we played on the ice, we played just as hard off it.

We also had the greatest trainers in Danny Canney and John "Frosty" Forristall. Today, they've got five or six guys in the room doing things. In those days, we had Frosty and Danny. I think people misunderstand how important the trainers are to a Stanley Cup run. I think they're the most intricate part of keeping a team together. Dan and Frosty watched us. They knew if we were injured, even in some minor way. And hockey players are notoriously superstitious, and the trainers had to address all of our quirks. For example, Phil couldn't stand to see sticks crossed in the dressing room. That would make him crazy and really throw him off, so Danny and Frosty ensured that no sticks were crossed in the room. The trainer really owns the room. A hockey teams has 25 egos. Winning teams have great trainers because it's an important part of the makeup and personality of the team. When you have a bad apple in the bunch, the trainers are the first to know, and if they're good, they have ways to deal with it. Our guys were really good.

I often wondered how the trainers ever lived on what they got paid. They slept at the rink a lot. They didn't really have a life. Players come and go, but good teams keep their trainers. The guys gave the trainers tips at Christmas and at the end of the season as well. This was very important to their income. You had to take good care of the trainers.

We had an exhibition game in Ottawa, against the St. Louis Blues, on September 21, 1969. A bunch of us, including Teddy Green, were holding out for new contracts. Ted had come off a great season where he was voted to the Second All-Star Team. Just before the game, he verbally agreed to a new deal. He considered sitting out until he had actually signed the contract, but hedged his bets and decided to play that night.

I told him, "Don't play! What if you get hurt?" He shook his head. "Nah, we agreed to terms and I'll play. I've got to hit a few players and get my timing before the season starts. And this is a good organization, so even if something happens, they'll still pay."

Wayne Maki was a young guy trying to crack the Blues' lineup. He wasn't a tough guy. Midway through the first period, Green and Maki collided, and Greenie came back and gave Maki a jab to fend him off. Maki went down to his knees. Teddy hovered over him and Maki speared him, which gave him some room so he could get up on his feet. If they had dropped the gloves and fought, Maki wouldn't have stood a chance against Teddy. But this confrontation turned even uglier.

There was an American Hockey League referee, Ken Bodendistel, and he was hesitant to get in between the two of them. An NHL official would have waded right in, because players know that if you ever hit a referee, you're finished. Bodendistel and the linesmen stood back. They didn't know how violent these guys were. Greenie looked tough at the best of times. His scowl would scare you.

Teddy turned and took a step towards the penalty box, but Maki went up on his toes and brought his stick down on the right side of Greenie's head. Teddy dropped, but the blow didn't knock him out. He had a compound skull fracture, but he never lost consciousness. He mumbled, "Help me up, but nobody's going to carry me off the ice!" But then, the left side of his face started to slip. You could really see his mouth contort. He skated a few strides and then collapsed.

Medical staff knew that Greenie was in big trouble and insisted he be taken immediately to the hospital. Dr. Michael Richard, a leading neurosurgeon, was at dinner with friends when he got the call to report immediately to the hospital for an emergency.

Teddy underwent extensive work to save his life. A few days later, he had a second operation to remove a blood clot and, shortly afterwards, was released from the hospital in Ottawa to return to Boston. A few of us went to visit him as soon as he was allowed visitors. He squeezed my hand. "I let my guard down," he mumbled. "First time, and I got clocked." It took me a while to understand what he was trying to say.

The league assessed the stiffest suspensions ever handed out at that time. Maki was suspended for 30 days, meaning he couldn't play in 14 games with the Buffalo Bisons of the AHL, where he had been assigned. It seemed doubtful that Teddy would ever play again, but he was suspended for the first 13 games after he was declared physically and mentally fit to play again. Both players were fined $300.

When he was able, Teddy came out to a few games to see us. He made a courageous comeback, but missed the entire 1969–70 season. When we won the Stanley Cup that year, we voted to have his name engraved on the Cup and to give him a full share of the money we got from the league for winning the championship. He was as big a part of the team as anybody that skated with us. He returned to the Bruins in 1970–71 and played on our Cup-winning team in 1971–72. When the WHA started, he left Boston to join the New England Whalers. He was named their first captain and led the Whalers to the first-ever Avco Cup championship.

After my contract issue was resolved (I was told that the contract I had signed had to be honoured), I reported to camp. But in the first of several injuries I'd suffer that season, I got run by John Ferguson in my first exhibition game and injured my knee, forcing me to miss most of training camp. I had to wear a brace on my knee. It took me a while to get up to speed that season.

On November 21, 1969, we played the Black Hawks in Chicago. I got into a scrap with Ray McKay, a rookie defenceman with the Hawks. It evolved into a wrestling match, and when the linesmen finally pried us apart, I came out of the tussle with McKay's sweater in my hands. I skated towards the stands and tossed it over the boards into the crowd. The fans in Chicago went crazy and the media ate it up, but it made me a hero with the Boston fans, and that's all I cared about.

I was really getting a lot of media attention. Between the fights, the controversy over my hair and clothes, Bachelors III and the girls, reporters knew that they'd get good copy if they talked to me, so my stall in the dressing room was always surrounded by reporters. It was just a part of what was happening with the Bruins at the time.

My dad had always told me that if I went out of my way to speak with a reporter, they would treat me fairly, and he was right. Every once in a while, some jerk would rip me and I'd get pissed. Most of them, though, were really good to me. I also learned to be colourful. If you say the same old thing, nobody wants to read that. Give them some meat; throw them a bone.

The press was always asking me about my love life, so I gave them good copy. "The girl has to be feminine but she has to have a head on her shoulders and know what she's doing," I told them. "My whole theory is that a woman can interest you with her body but she can hold you with her mind. I like a girl who is really good-looking, feminine, sensitive and soft. The type of girl who can fit into a dinner at the Waldorf or drink a draft beer down at the beach. Very few girls can do that. And she has to be the kind of girl who can make a man feel like a man."

A writer asked which NHL cities were best for meeting the type of women

I preferred. "There are no better women in North America than in Montreal," I stated. "Pittsburgh is terrible. The good cities are Los Angeles, San Francisco, Boston, New York, Montreal and Toronto." I was sounding like a connoisseur. They asked if there was anyone special in my life, so I told them, "I'm not fighting love. If it comes my way, I'll take it, but right now, I'm not looking for it."

Every day was a new adventure. I was at Bachelors III every day that I was home, and there was always something going on. The writers asked me about my game-day preparation. "I plan everything I do with the game in mind. That's the most important thing. It's my whole life," I told them. "If I'm going to be with a broad the night before a game, I'll take her to dinner at eight o'clock, get home at nine, be with her until midnight then go to sleep. I know I've got to have my rest."

And then there's the quote that still circulates today. When I was asked what I had for a pregame meal, I cockily replied, "A steak and a blonde."

If people ever found out what I was really like, I'd have been finished.

Joe Namath did set me up on a few dates in New York. Through him, I met Judy, a stunning brunette from Texas. She really turned my head. She generally wanted nothing to do with athletes, but told me I was different. I used to make her laugh by doing bad impressions of celebrities like Howard Cosell and Kirk Douglas. We got along well and she made me want to give up adding to my conquests. I moved her into my place in Brookline, a town bordering Boston, in June 1970. *Life* magazine did a story on Judy and me in April 1971, and it caused a mild controversy by including photos of us lying on my eight-foot circular bed.

The new year didn't start well for me. During the warmup before our game against Los Angeles on January 3, I had a terrible pain and thought it was a groin injury. I decided I'd play, but had to call it quits after taking one turn on the ice. I played the next game, which was against the Seals in Oakland. I was on a breakaway when Bert Marshall tripped me from behind. I slid into the post and my calf hit the back of the post full on. In my day, the net didn't move from its moorings. My mother always loved Johnny Bower of the Leafs because, in one game during my rookie season, I got tripped by Tim Horton. I lost the puck, slid full speed and was about to crash into the post when Bower threw out both legs to block me from hurting myself. He knew I was in trouble, and he saved me from an injury.

I was in unbelievable pain after being hit by Marshall, and I knew that a hospital visit was in order. While I was waiting for the ambulance, a fan came up to me, stuck out his hand and introduced himself. "Hi Derek. Darryl Tishman. I'm from the Tishman family—666 Fifth Avenue. I'm a big fan of yours."

"Oh, yeah," I nodded. "I think I know of the Tishman family."

When I came out of the dressing room, an ambulance was waiting. And so was Darryl Tishman. I had never seen this guy in my life. The ambulance guy asked him, "Who are you?" He said, "I'm Darryl Tishman. I'm his agent. I'm making sure you guys do the best thing. Is he getting the medication? Are you doing what you're supposed to do?" The guy had balls. He jumped into the ambulance. Just by being assertive, he actually controlled the drive to the hospital. The poor ambulance attendant didn't know what to do. He was taking me over to Massachusetts General and finally just said, "To hell with it. Sit here and shut up."

I was lying there in great pain. The attendant said, "Derek, we're going to try to bring down the swelling." Tishman jumped in. "I don't want swelling, so pack him in ice. Jesus, do you guys know what you're supposed to be doing?" He was scaring the shit out of the medical people.

Mass General was five or six minutes away. We pulled into emergency, and because I was a Bruin—*zoom*, in the back. Darryl Tishman was right there beside me, holding on to the stretcher. He waved me in.

"Who are you?" they asked.

"I'm his rep and I'm taking care of him."

I was in too much pain to question anything. Darryl hollered out, "This man needs medication!"

He asked me, "Derek, what do you like?"

Through the pain, I winced and told him I was used to Demerol.

"Demerol!" Tishman barked. "Let's get the Demerol, now!"

The nurse ran and got me a shot! She shot me in the ass and I was stoned out of my skull.

All of my clothes were there. Tishman said, "I'll take his stuff."

The hospital staff asked, "What's your name, sir?"

"Darryl Tishman. I'm from the Tishman family—666 Fifth Avenue, New York. I'm his agent." They all believed him.

Through the pain, I wondered why this guy was doing this. I sensed he was a fraud, but he seemed to take control of things for me. Nobody from the Bruins was there—they didn't send anybody—but the folks at Mass General knew that the Boston Bruins had a protocol. You were taken to Phillips House, so when I came out, Darryl was sitting there. "I got all your stuff," he assured me. "I've got everything taken care of. Don't worry about anything, Derek." I was kind of groggy, so I nodded.

He took my keys, jumped into a cab and went back to Boston Garden. He stole my car, and because he had my licence, he had my address. He went to my apartment and took my address book with the names and contact information of everybody I had dated and was going around to bars, selling the names in my address book. He was making up stories and selling the numbers for 20 bucks each! I got more phone calls from irate women than you could shake a stick at. "What the hell are you doing, selling my number, you bastard!"

I said, "No, no, no! You've got to believe me! This guy Tishman stole my address book!"

I was in the hospital for three or four days. It was time for me to leave, so I asked where they had put my clothes. "Darryl Tishman's got them."

I said, "I don't know any Darryl Tishman!"

About a month later, Tishman tried to con my lawyer. He arrived at the office and announced, "I want to work with you. You're one of the best and I'd like to learn from you." He almost got a job with him!

Another time, he went into a Ferrari dealership. He said, "I'm here representing Bill Russell [of the Boston Celtics]. Bill's looking for a Maserati. I'd like to take it for a spin to see if there's enough legroom for him to get in and out easily. The salesperson asked, "Are you sure you rep him?" "Yes I do," Tishman replied. "And I don't need anybody coming with me. I know what I'm doing."

They picked him up just outside of Nebraska! Everybody was so embarrassed that he hustled them that nobody pressed charges.

"Darryl Tishman. I'm from the Tishman family—666 Fifth Avenue, New York City."

Whoever that guy was, he wasn't any Mr. Tishman from Park Avenue. Goddamned con artist!

As it turned out, the injury was a deep contusion, but there was calcification of the calf muscle from hitting the post—it's called *myositis ossificans*. The doctors were concerned that they might have to cut that part of the calf muscle out if it didn't respond, but fortunately, it did.

The era of train travel in the National Hockey League ended, for all intents and purposes, with expansion in 1967–68. In the six-team era, Chicago was the most westerly team, and the only city not in the Eastern time zone. Train travel was efficient. But with 12 teams, including two in California, trains were no longer a feasible solution.

I hated flying. I thought, "I'm going to play hockey for about 15 years, and during that time, fly 100,000 miles a year. That's a million and a half miles. And probability and chance tell me that over the course of more than a million miles, one of these planes is going down." You've got to look at probability and odds. I wasn't taking into account that there were 75,000 flights a day around the world that weren't crashing. I was just thinking about the ones that I was on, and I didn't like it. I hated not having any control over my destiny. The Bruins sent me to a shrink, and that was the first time I ever had drugs. The guy gave me 10 milligrams of Valium. He said, "Take one of these before a flight and you'll be fine." That was nice. I just smoked and relaxed. But I found that I was tired, depressed and really irritable. I was short-tempered, and when I got on the ice, all of a sudden I was getting in all kinds of fights. Harry Sinden was flipping out on me. He said, "You cannot be in the box all the time! You're the guy I depend on to kill penalties!" He used to get mad at me all the time, but never belittled, insulted or demeaned me or any player.

I said, "Harry, I don't know why I've got such a short temper." I was taking Valium for the anxiety, but was finding it all too much. I went back to the doctor and he said, "Okay, if you don't like the Valium, and find that it makes you groggy and irritable, stop taking the Valium." I stopped taking the Valium, but still needed something to calm me before flying. The doctor asked me if I drank. I said, "No, not really. A couple of drinks with the boys occasionally, but that's the extent of it."

So the doctor said, "The best drink to help your nerves, that has the least effect on the body, is Scotch, and the best Scotch to drink that has the least effect on the body is Dewar's White Label."

That's when I really started drinking. I would take four, five or six fingers of Scotch. I'd fill an eight-ounce glass almost to the top for a West Coast flight, halfway for a trip to Chicago and maybe four fingers for a flight to New York. Then, laid out in front of me would be a lit cigarette, a glass of 7-Up, a glass of Coca-Cola and a piece of Dentyne gum. When the announcement came— "Preboarding the Boston Bruins"—I'd take the Scotch, hold my breath and drink it all down, take a mouthful of 7-Up, a mouthful of Coke, chew the Dentyne, take a drag off my cigarette and hold my breath. It went down like a bomb! It hit my stomach and by the time I got to my feet, I was goofy. I'd stagger to my seat, close my eyes, and by the time Phil Esposito shouted, "Turk, it's time to wake up," I was at our destination.

It calmed the anxiety, but after a while, they started pouring me onto the plane. I had headaches. I was sweaty, tired and sick. And that's when I started eating poorly. My diet suffered because I was too sick to eat. Even though the mix of drinks helped my fear of flying, it wasn't healthy at all. No one really knew I was doing it. And then the alcohol got a hold of me.

I feared things I couldn't control. I drank to cope. When relationships fell apart, I drank to cope. When I was in the air, I drank to cope. I didn't feel as though I was in control of things, and I didn't realize that I was using alcohol as a coping mechanism for fear.

The Bruins' doctors finally told me I might need professional help. They suggested that I be sent to an aviators' school. They had such a thing in those days for people who were afraid to fly. There were seminars at the control towers of the airport. They taught you the fundamentals of avionics and aero-dynamics so that you would comprehend how planes flew, and that would help you eliminate your anxiety about flying.

The final road game of the 1969–70 regular season was in Toronto on April 4. In fact, it was the first game of a home-and-home series with the Leafs. We had already made the playoffs, so it was a bit of a meaningless game, but it was sold out, like all games were wherever we went, because Bobby Orr was there.

Our flight took us from Boston to Providence, and then Providence to Toronto. The plane had bench seats, where the seats faced each other in the middle. There were nuns sitting in those seats with me. It's 37 miles from Boston to Providence. The plane never went above 4,000 feet. We had a clear path, and the pilot took the plane up over the buildings. But this time, it felt like a hurricane. The plane was bouncing and jigging around and I was terrified. I looked at the poor nuns, and they had their rosaries out and were praying.

I said, "God, please! If you get me out of this, I promise I will never, ever fly again. I just want to play hockey."

The plane jigged and jagged so much that it threw the door of the cockpit open. All the stuff in the overhead compartments came tumbling out. I looked out the window and saw the ground and the runway. We weren't 300 feet off the ground and we were going down like a dart. I said, "Oh God, this is it!" The pilot brought the plane back, and then *bang!* We hit the runway and the plane bounced. He brought it back down, but that's when I got up. As soon as he shut the engines off, I got up and ran. Cashman tried to grab me, but when they opened the door, I was out like a bolt of lightning. I was on the tarmac before Cashman and Ace Bailey grabbed me and held me so I couldn't move.

I calmed down a little while they changed crews on the plane. The crew coming out was the Boston crew, and when they saw the commotion on the tarmac, one of the guys asked, "What's going on?" Harry Sinden came out and said, "Sanderson's afraid to fly. Don't worry. We have to corral him once in a while." Harry was really embarrassed. The new pilot said, "If you're afraid to fly, come in to the cockpit with us." I sat up there and was shocked. When I sat up front, I was not afraid at all.

The guys were having a cigarette and a coffee while they took the plane up to 26,000 feet, then put it on auto-pilot. The pilot turned to me and said, "That's it."

I said, "This is what you guys do?"

He said, "Yeah." Then he explained to me more about flight. Once he explained it to me and I saw his calmness in the cockpit, much of my anxiety was gone. So then the pilot gave me a demonstration. "Derek, they don't want us to turn any more than 13 degrees, so watch." The plane angled right. "Now, I'll put it back." The plane veered back to where it had been. "If I want to go up a foot, this is what I do." The plane's nose moved up and then he levelled it.

Just then, there was a knock at the cockpit door. A flight attendant stuck her head in and said, "I don't know what you're doing up here, but I've got 65 people back here terrified for their lives!"

The pilot gave an embarrassed chuckle. He had forgotten that there were dozens of passengers who had no idea why the plane was veering side to side and going up and down. Today, they would never dream of doing such a thing.

Sitting in the cockpit completely erased my fear of flying. I talked to my shrink about it. He said, "Just take a look at your personality, Derek. Have you ever driven long distances in a car with a friend?"

I said, "Yeah, of course."

He asked, "Do you drive?"

"Yeah, always. All the way."

"Have you ever sat in the passenger's seat?"

"Sure! With my dad, but I could never sleep. But I would never trust my friends to drive."

He just looked at me. "Derek, you have control issues. You must always be in control. You had no fear of flying when you were in the cockpit because you were within reach of the controls that could change your fate and destiny."

The doctor was right. But . . . my drinking days had begun.

Bobby Orr used to give me shit all the time. He would never let me get drunk. He'd say, "What are you doing? You're acting like an ass."

While I was going through the anxiety, I played an unusually aggressive game. I was always feisty, and I admit I had a mean streak and would play dirty when the occasion called for it. That's the way the game should be played. I didn't mind fighting. Sometimes I got the worst of it, but everyone knew I'd get the guy eventually. The theory I went on was that I didn't care who I fought. His face would bleed just as easily as mine. And with that stick in my hands, I wasn't afraid of anybody.

Fighting is part of the game. It polices itself. Guys would butt-end me, spear me, kick me. If I asked the ref what he was going to do about it, he'd say, "You handle it. I didn't see it." So they'd let you go, but you had better want to fight, because one mistake and you got the shit beat out of you.

No coach ever sends you out to get anybody. Nobody's that stupid. Nobody ever said that to me. It didn't mean I didn't fight. It meant I knew what the situation called for. We all did.

The last couple of months of the 1969–70 season saw me fight the league's toughest guys—Bryan Watson, Bob Plager, Reggie Fleming, John Ferguson and Orland Kurtenbach. I took a cross-checking penalty against Plager when we played St. Louis in early March. I dropped the gloves, but Plager didn't. As I was skating towards the penalty box, I raised my arms in what the *Boston Globe* called a "gesture of triumphant derision." The crowd went nuts. When I sat down in the penalty box, these two clowns started taunting me, and one waved a rubber chicken at me. He had a professionally made sign that said: "Sanderson—biggest chicken of them all." I told him to fuck off and he spat at me. I don't put up with that shit! I climbed the glass into the stands, and Ace Bailey and Wayne Carleton raced over to help me. The cops and the ushers got to them first, and the two jerks were removed from their seats. I probably shouldn't have done it, but they were asking for it. My dad always taught me that you don't take shit from anybody.

Boston played the Black Hawks in mid-March, and the fans gave it to me good. There was no love lost between the Bruins and Chicago anyway, as we were both clawing to see who'd finish first, but after I threw McKay's sweater into the crowd earlier in the season, well, I guess I had to expect it. The fans got on my case and were booing me even before the game. During the game, I got a misconduct for some stupid thing. After the referee told me I was gone, I turned around and gave him the "up yours" move. Harry Sinden went ballistic on me. "What the hell do you think you're doing? You can't behave like that! Jesus Christ!"

I said, "Harry, What do you want me to do?"

He said, "Clarence Campbell is going to call you and you're going to have to apologize."

"Apologize for what?"

"For the gesture. For behaving like that."

I said, "C'mon, Harry. What are you talking about?"

He said, "I'm telling you right now that he'll be calling you, and you had better treat him with respect."

I was sitting in Harry's office with my practice jersey on, ready to go out on the ice, when Clarence Campbell, the league president, called. He wanted me to fly to Toronto.

I said, "Clarence . . ."

Harry Sinden just about choked. No one called the league president by his given name. It was always Mr. Campbell.

I said, "Clarence, don't make me fly all the way to Toronto. The ink is already dry on the fine, I know that. The punishment is set, so why do you need me to go to Toronto? To grovel in front of the press? Fine me, do what you want to do. You're going to do it anyway. What good does it do me to fly to Toronto? I'm not going to talk myself out of it."

Campbell said, "Well, Derek, who do you think you are, giving the fans of Chicago an obscene gesture, and with the game televised, too!"

I played dumb. "What obscene gesture?"

"That arm gesture," he replied.

I said, "Oh no, Clarence, you're the one who is making it obscene. Where I grew up in Niagara Falls, that's the way we say hello to everybody!"

I don't think he bought it. Harry started laughing, but tried to stifle the giggles so that Campbell wouldn't hear him. I was fined $2,500.

Campbell also spoke to Weston Adams, the Bruins' owner. Adams also fined me and I was forced to apologize. I told Weston, "I've never said I'm sorry for a thing in all my life." He told me it was a condition of his agreement with Campbell.

"I sincerely regret my actions in Chicago last Wednesday night," I told the media. "All I can say is that at the time, I was very angry with both the Chicago team and their fans and reacted without thinking. I know my action was wrong and I hope all the fans will accept my apology." When the writers pressed me, I told them Clarence Campbell was a "stuffed shirt." That hit the papers faster than the apology. I felt it to be true, but grew to regret the statement.

Shortly afterwards, my lawyer was asked to comment on me as a client. "I hope to see Derek independently wealthy, financially secure for the rest of his life when he leaves hockey. I'd like him to be prepared to go into business at the executive level. He has a sharp mind and he can be articulate. His problem, perhaps, is that he comes off a little rough."

One of the greatest compliments I ever received came from Campbell, of all people. He said, "Of all the athletes that have ever come through the National Hockey League, Derek Sanderson is the only one that understands that this game is all about entertainment."

In the first shift of a game against the Rangers in late March, Vic Hadfield stumbled and I fell on top of him. He tore his Achilles tendon and was out for the rest of the season. Early in the second, I scrapped with Orland Kurtenbach. We had history. He was the first guy I ever fought in the NHL. As I was being escorted to the penalty box, the fans booed me, so I flashed a peace sign to the crowd. They went apeshit.

At least I used the proper fingers that time.

CHAPTER 15

THE FIRST STANLEY CUP

The Bruins and Chicago Black Hawks both finished the regular season with 99 points, but Chicago was awarded first place in the East Division because they won more games than we did. Once again, Boston led the NHL in goals scored with 277, twenty-seven more than Chicago. I had a decent season in spite of being plagued by injuries, collecting 41 points in 50 games.

We dominated the NHL awards, too. Bobby Orr astounded even us by winning the scoring race with 120 points—Phil Esposito was second with 99. Both were named to the NHL's First All-Star Team. Pie McKenzie was selected to the Second Team. Bobby also took the Hart Trophy as the league MVP and the Norris Trophy, again.

The Bruins and New York Rangers hated each other. It had been like that for decades. For years, the two teams had finished at the bottom of the NHL standings. Between 1959–60 and 1966–67, the Rangers made the playoffs just twice and the Bruins didn't make the playoffs at all. The sportswriters used to laugh and claim that Boston and New York were playing for the mythical Patrick Cup—Lynn Patrick was running the Bruins, while his brother Muzz was in charge of the Rangers. Both teams' fortunes improved in the late '60s, and the rivalry showed no sign of cooling.

The two teams met in the first round of the 1970 playoffs. We blew them out in game one, winning 8–2. Ranger coach Emile Francis yanked Eddie Giacomin when the score was 7–1 and Terry Sawchuk finished the game. Pie McKenzie laid a beating on Walt Tkaczuk, and the game turned into a slug-fest. I guess it was retribution, but I got mugged by Brad Park and Tkaczuk.

The game was out of hand, and in the last minute of play, I jumped Billy Fairbairn and punched him in the head. I said, "That's for nothing. Wait'll you do something!" My dad used to use that line as a joke.

Game two was also in Boston, and we beat them 5–3. Sawchuk was in goal. It was a pretty subdued game. The welcome to Madison Square Garden for game three was nothing short of hostile. The fans booed us and gave us the finger as we skated out. They pelted Cheevers with eggs. All the while, the organist played "Talk to the Animals." I didn't know it, but the Rangers had professed, "We're going to get that prick tonight," so when I skated out, the fans went berserk.

Esposito's line started for us, and Eddie Giacomin was back in goal for the Rangers. Phil got off a shot that Giacomin saved, forcing a faceoff. A minute and thirty-one seconds into the game, Harry Sinden sent me out to take the draw along with Westfall and Marcotte. The fans screamed and taunted. I stopped and glanced around to determine who was playing defence and where they were positioned. I then decided how I was going to win the draw. I skated past the Rangers' bench and pointed. Their coach, Emile Francis, shouted, "Use your head!" I skated back to the faceoff circle, surveying the Rangers' zone. Giacomin skated out and told Walt Tkaczuk, "He can shoot right off the draw. Don't let him shoot."

I said, "Get back in your net!"

He said, "Fuck you!"

"Fuck *me?* Fuck *you,* asshole! I'll put one around your ears!"

He snarled, "Fuck you," and returned to his crease.

As soon as the puck was dropped, it went into the corner to Giacomin's right. I took off for the opposite corner, looking for a pass. Donnie Marcotte picked up the puck and fired it behind the net, past Eddie Westfall, to the area where I was heading. When I went to get it, I got sandwiched into the boards by Arnie Brown and Walt Tkaczuk, who had their gloves off and could hardly wait to nail me, and then the Rangers ganged up on me. Dave Balon and Brad Park jumped in along with Brown and Tkaczuk.

When I got jumped, I elbowed somebody in the side of the face and then went at it with Arnie Brown. Somebody else jumped on me, and both Brown and I went down. He was lying on my left leg. Then, Balon and I went at it, which brought Fairbairn onto the scene. Donnie Marcotte was quick to get into the donnybrook. There were so many Rangers trying to hit me, but I ducked underneath the pile and managed to emerge on top, punching anything in blue that moved. When I did get up, the linesman got in between me and Billy Fairbairn. I wanted him to move so I could sucker Fairbairn, but he didn't, so we just wrestled.

Through it all, I never got hit once.

I got bounced with a game misconduct. I screamed at John Ashley, the referee, "Francis sent 15 players after me. They didn't even do that for Maurice Richard! Hell of a compliment!" Ashley kicked me and Balon out of the game. That pissed me off. If I had to get kicked out of a game, at least I'd like to have taken a better calibre of player with me.

Harry Sinden flipped out on the bench. He had to be restrained from running out onto the ice. He stood on the boards, grabbing onto players' sweaters in order to keep from falling.

"What are you doing? What the hell are you doing? Sanderson for Balon?! What kind of trade-off is that? Jesus Christ! Throw somebody out of equal skill, for Christ's sake!" They should have sent off Tkaczuk or Fairbairn. Or even Brad Park.

The fans were going wild and started tossing eggs, apple cores, coins—you name it—onto the ice. Rangers fans tried to attack our bench. It took 19 minutes to play the first 91 seconds of the game.

I really felt badly about getting tossed out of a very important game. We ended up losing 4–3. After being ejected, I was sitting in the dressing room, and Paul Anka, the recording artist, walked in. I had met him that summer and we had become friends. Great guy. Big hockey fan from Ottawa. It was through Paul that I met Joey Heatherton, who later became a friend. I don't know how Anka got past security, but there he was. So I was sitting there talking to him when all the reporters streamed in.

"What happened between you and Giacomin? What did he say?"

I looked around at the eager expressions on the faces of Paul Anka and the press guys and I knew I had to give them something to write, so I announced,

"Giacomin told me that William Jennings, the Rangers' president, put a $5,000 bounty on my head to any Ranger that could maim me."

I had had a run-in with Jennings earlier in the season. He had called the Bruins names. We hated him. Even after the game, he commented that if he was going to put a bounty on any Boston player, it would be Orr—certainly not Sanderson. I knew my comment would create a controversy. You can't go out and intentionally maim somebody! It was a complete fabrication, a total and farcical lie, but the press ate it up and ran with it like crazy.

Giacomin and I later became good friends when we played together on the Rangers. Great goalkeeper, great team guy. He tells this story at banquets. He says, "The kid made me famous." He told me that he gets more attention because of that incident than anything else he did during his National Hockey League career.

There were 24 penalties called for 132 penalty minutes in the first period alone, both of which were NHL records. We got nailed for 93 penalty minutes through the game. The two teams combined for 174 penalty minutes in the game.

In game four, the New York fans were no less vocal, but the game was far less violent. During the warmup, I skated around and looked at signs that read, "Derek is Dead" and "We Will Bury You." Giacomin stoned me on a shorthanded breakaway. The Rangers evened the series, winning 4–2.

We took the next game, 3–2, at home, and returned to New York for game six. The fans were disgraceful. I scored the final goal in our 4–1 victory, which eliminated the Rangers, but when the outcome was no longer in doubt, they threw eggs and ball bearings onto the ice, and some jerks set fires in the mezzanine of Madison Square Garden.

We had all sorts of fights through the series, but at the end of the game, we shook hands. Eddie Giacomin and I laughed as we shook hands. It was over. The Rangers stated that the difference in the series was Bobby Orr. Well, of course. Face it—he was the best player that ever played. The Rangers were a very, very good team and that was a tight series. The result was by no stretch a foregone conclusion. Whoever won that series was going to win the Stanley Cup because the West Division still wasn't as strong as the East.

By the way, the *real* circus opened at Madison Square Garden the next day.

No one knew I was in the hospital during that series with the Rangers. We kept it out of the press, but I was being treated with steroids for a bowel condition I had developed, though I continued to play. The abdominal cramps were so bad that I was doubled over on the bench. During one game, I was in such pain that I had to leave the bench and head to the dressing room. The team doctor came in and asked me some questions. I told him I had had terrible cramps for a couple of months. He then looked at me and asked, "How long have you had colitis?"

He told me to get undressed. "You're not playing." They took me to the hospital in an ambulance. There, they took blood samples and gave me pain medication to knock me out. The next day, they put me through a battery of tests. At the end of the tests, a doctor sat down beside me. "Derek, you've got chronic ulcerative colitis. It's an inflammatory bowel disease that affects the lining of the large intestine and rectum. It's debilitating."

I was scared because the pain had been so bad, but I had to play. The Bruins were in the playoffs, and that's where my heart and responsibilities were. Harry Sinden came to the hospital the next day and asked the doctors for the diagnosis. They told him about the ulcerative colitis and explained that my immune system had been compromised and I couldn't take the risk of being exposed to germs that might affect me, so they had me isolated in a private room.

Harry looked at me and then at the doctors. "Hockey players can't get sick. I've got to have him play." The doctors recommended prednisone. It's a steroid that had only been on the market about 10 years, so they really didn't have a full and complete handle on the long-term effects. The doctors warned that prednisone had side effects, including leaving patients susceptible to infections because it suppressed the immune system. What they didn't know then was that prednisone also burned your joints, and the first joints to go are usually the hips.

Harry asked me how I felt about taking the prednisone. "Give it to me," I said. They injected me with massive doses. It stopped the bleeding in the capillaries—the small blood vessels in your intestines. That's all I cared about at that moment. That, and getting back on the ice.

Our semifinal series against the Black Hawks should have been epic, but it was a complete non-event. We swept Chicago in four straight, and outscored them 20–10 to earn our chance to play the St. Louis Blues for the Stanley Cup.

The city of Boston was in a Stanley Cup frenzy. That's all you heard about, no matter where you went. WBZ Radio staged a "Win a Date with Derek" contest to coincide with the final. The station was at 1030 on the AM dial, so 103 girls won a date—all at the same time—with me at Bachelors III. It was silly but fun. At that time, I also appeared on *The Merv Griffin Show,* a talk show that ran on CBS opposite Johnny Carson's *Tonight Show.*

We were heavily favoured to beat the Blues. St. Louis had finished first in the West Division, but they had trailed the Bruins by 13 points in the regular season. St. Louis reached the finals for a third straight spring.

The best-of-seven final opened in St. Louis. We breezed to a 6–1 victory in game one. Chief Bucyk collected a hat trick and I scored once. Both Eddie Westfall and I scored twice in game two, a 6–2 win. The series shifted to Boston for game three, and again we dominated, with Wayne Cashman netting two in a 4–1 win.

Facing a third straight loss in the Stanley Cup final and down three games to none, the Blues refused to roll over and play dead. Game four was played in Boston on Mother's Day—May 10. We traded goals in the first period. I assisted on a Rick Smith goal that was followed by Red Berenson's goal for St. Louis later in the period. Gary Sabourin put the Blues up 2–1, but Esposito tied it for us before the end of the second. The Blues put a scare into us when Larry Keenan gave the Blues a 3–2 lead just 19 seconds after the puck dropped to start the third. We pressed, and Chief tied the game midway through the third.

Regulation time concluded with the score tied at three. Just before the overtime period began, Harry shocked us. "I'm going to start Sanderson, Westfall and Carleton," he said. "Orr and Awrey on the blue line."

We all fully expected that Phil's line would be called. It was Harry who contended that overtimes were usually won and lost in the first minute. He used to insist that we not get scored on in the first or the last shift. Get us into the period and get us out of the period and we'll score in the 14 to 16 minutes in between. He said, "I don't want them scoring on us right away, so Derek, you start." That was his logic. But in fairness, we were the hot line, too. Eddie and I both were having good playoffs.

Red Berenson beat me on the opening draw, and the Blues moved the puck into our zone. Donny Awrey carried the puck out of our end. I shot it into the St. Louis zone, and Swoop Carleton raced in after it. The puck was loose in front, but Jean-Guy Talbot cleared it. Awrey's shot was blocked by Talbot. I fired a shot that went wide and Larry Keenan cleared it but didn't get it out of the Blues' zone. Bobby Orr kept it in at the point, dumped it behind the net to me and went straight to the front of the net. I put the puck right back on Bobby's stick and he beat Glenn Hall. All Bobby was trying to do was redirect it. He knew he had a chance. He was looking for a rebound. Glenn Hall was expecting to shut the post off, but he gave Bobby the five-hole and Bobby scored 40 seconds into overtime!

As he scored, Bobby was tripped by Noel Picard, the Blues defenceman standing in front of Hall. The iconic photo of Bobby soaring through the air—his arms stretched out in front of himself in triumph—has become one of the defining images in hockey.

I skated around to make sure it was a goal. I looked at the referee, thinking, "Does that count? His arm is in the air. I think this is official!" And then I went around the net to Bobby. "Kid, we did it!"

"I got a little lucky," Bobby admitted. "The puck was coming up the boards and if it had got by me, it might have been a two-on-one against me, but it hit me. I did see Derek. I threw the puck back to him and I went to the net. That's the way I played and Derek gave me a great pass right on the stick. As I started to move across, Glenn Hall had to move with me and it's pretty difficult to move across and keep your legs closed. I was just trying to put the puck on net. When it hit my stick and I started across, I was just trying to get it on net."

Winning the Stanley Cup was a great feeling. I was happiest for Bobby. It was a Cinderella year for him, and it seemed only fitting that he should score the winning goal. No one has the heart, the guts or the toughness that he did.

While we gathered around at centre ice, Clarence Campbell handed the Stanley Cup to Chief, and he skated it around the ice. I thought, "To hell with that. I'm not following the Cup around the ice," so I started towards the dressing room.

I was so happy for Bobby, but equally happy for someone else—my father. When I was 14, I had made that deal with my dad. I had wanted that pair of Tacks so badly that I agreed that if he bought me a pair, I would one day give him my Stanley Cup ring. My dad sacrificed so much for me, but saved up a few dollars each week and bought me the skates I wanted so badly. I loved those skates, and wore Tacks through my whole career. And truthfully, I forgot all about our agreement.

When we won the Cup, the fans went crazy. In those days, the glass was lower and you could get onto the ice. The players were milling about on the ice, but the fans began to converge on us. People were grabbing at me. Out of the corner of my eye, I saw a guy sliding along the ice and reaching for me. I couldn't tell who it was, so I turned fast and hit the guy with my shoulder pad. *Poof!* Hit him right in the face and knocked him to the ice. I turned around and it was my dad! Oh God! It gave him a little mouse under his eye. My own father! He lay on the ice and laughed, "That's the only time you hit anybody all series!"

"Dad, I'm sorry," I blurted. As I was helping him up, he looked at me and said, "Do you remember the promise we made when I bought you the Tacks? That ring is mine!"

So I gave him the ring, and I also gave him the second ring after we won in '72. When I started seeing Nancy, whom I later married, I brought her home to meet my mom and dad. She had never seen the rings, so I said, "Dad, have you got the rings? I'd like to show them to Nancy."

"Oh yeah, son." He got up, walked over to the curtains in the living room and grabbed the hem.

"Dad, what're you doing?"

He said, "They're sewn into the hem of the curtains. I didn't want anybody to steal them!"

I was shaking my head and laughing. "Dad, why don't you wear them?"

"I would never do that, son," he replied. "That would be pretentious."

I said, "Dad, why the hell do you think I gave them to you?"

He simply smiled. "Only those who win the Cup have the right to wear the rings."

Dad gave the rings back to me. When the boys were born, I gave one to each of them.

After the celebration in the dressing room, family and friends joined us at the Colonial in Lynnfield. I don't even think the Cup was there. To tell you the truth, the first time I actually saw my name on the Stanley Cup was when I did an appearance for Sullivan Tire in the winter of 2011. They're a big tire chain in New England. They had the Stanley Cup for a day for their district managers. I took pictures with the managers and employees with the Cup. Back when we won, players didn't get the Cup for a day like they do now.

A parade through downtown Boston was held the next morning at 10 o'clock, and concluded in Government Center Plaza in front of City Hall. It was insane. There were more people in one place than I had ever seen before. Girls were throwing their bras at our cars during the parade. There were so many fans crowding the platform that they couldn't do the presentations, so they moved us inside City Hall. Mayor Kevin White presented each of us with Paul Revere water pitchers. Johnny McKenzie filled one with beer and dumped it on the mayor's head. Thank goodness Mayor White was a good sport!

After the parade, the only celebration we had was a Bobby Orr Day in Parry Sound, Ontario, Bobby's hometown. There was a parade and a banquet held at Parry Sound High School. Eddie Johnston, Milt Schmidt, assistant coach Tom Johnson and I were there from the Bruins. Bobby's girlfriend, Peggy, and Mike Walton, his business partner in a hockey school, were also there. So were Terry Crisp and Gary Sabourin, both with the losing St. Louis Blues team and both also from Parry Sound.

How many times, playing on that backyard rink so beautifully made by my father, had I dreamed of one day winning the Stanley Cup, and now that dream had become reality.

CHAPTER 16

DAISY'S AND THE DYNASTY DENIED: 1970–71

All of that ridiculous publicity about my moustache coupled with a Stanley Cup win and further fuelled by stories of my wild life had elevated me in the public's eye, and who was I to turn down publicity? I played it for all it was worth. In June 1970, my lawyer contacted me and told me that WBZ-TV was running a "Win a Date with Derek" contest. He thought it would be a great promotion for me, but I was always fearful of those things.

"Can you run shit like this by me first, please? What if it bombs?"

He chuckled. "It isn't bombing, Turk. They've received 13,000 entries in a week!"

It was an essay contest, and entrants ranged in age from 15 to 73, and entries came from 30 states and three provinces. The five finalists all came to my door, and I could handpick the winner. I was nervous. I wasn't worried about my image, but it would have been easy for something to go wrong. The girls were very pretty and they were wild, but I was thinking, "No, no. Too dangerous." So I picked the 73-year-old—Mabel Hocking of South Boston. She was a grandmother of eight and great-grandmother of 13. I figured I was safe.

Wouldn't you know, her husband was upset. He was 80 and jealous as can be. "You think this is funny, huh? I don't think this is funny."

I told him, "Don't worry, sir. There'll be nothing untoward."

He said, "Yeah, that's right that there'll be no monkey business, because I'm coming along for the date!"

We went to a steak house and he sat out front. Partway through our dinner, he came in and said, "I'll take it from here." I drove around the corner and went to a bar. It was fine by me. She told the TV station that I was "a perfectly charming young man."

I loved playing hockey with the Boston Bruins and loved having a very active social life. The atmosphere around Bachelors III was electric, but after a while, it got to be pretty methodical. I would go to Bachelors III after practice, have lunch and then hang around in the afternoon, sipping a couple of beers. Then, I'd find somebody, take them to dinner and then go home to bed, sometimes alone.

My partner, Joey Cimino, and I were sitting in Bachelors III, counting the money one night, when he turned to me and asked, "Why are we doing this for Namath, Turk? Why don't we do it for ourselves?"

"I don't know," I said. "Joe Willie's a good guy."

"I know," Joey agreed. "But we could be doing this for ourselves. It's our town."

I hadn't really thought about it before. "Interesting," I mused. "What are we looking at?"

He said, "I'm looking at building our own place." I liked the sound of that. "I've got a spot picked out," he said. It was at the corner of Newbury and Fairfield. Great spot, but it was too close to a church, too close to a school and, to complicate matters, the residents of Back Bay didn't want a bar there. Joey said, "I need you to go see Sonny McDonough and convince him that we can zone the area for our bar. He'll do it for you."

Sonny McDonough was an influential member of Boston's city council and chairman of the Massachusetts Governor's Council. His chauffeur was the head of the Alcohol Beverage Control Board, which granted licences. McDonough was my friend Jimmy's father and a terrific guy who had helped us out in the past.

I drove up to Second Cliff and called on Sonny. He welcomed me with a smile. "It's favour time, is it, Derek?" He knew.

I told him about our vision and explained our predicament. He made me go through the process, but told me, "I'll get you your licence, don't worry about it, but I don't want Jimmy and Joey to know right away. I don't want them to think it's that easy. I worked a lifetime to get the power to have the ability to help my kids." All four of Sonny's boys did very well. Jay is a clerk for courts in Massachusetts, Jimmy got his law degree, Dicky became a lobbyist and Paul became a well-known fashion designer.

In September 1970, we opened Daisy Buchanan's, named after the Great Gatsby's lover in F. Scott Fitzgerald's classic novel. Daisy's held 85 people, but we used to put 200 in there every night. It was a zoo! A plaque on the wall displayed our motto: "Living well is the best revenge"—a quote from the poet George Herbert.

We were doing very well at Daisy's, and then Joey told me we were going to open up another bar. I was concerned. The bar and restaurant business is really tough. Sixty-five percent of bars fail in the first six months.

"Are you kidding me? Where?" He didn't know at that moment. All he knew was that he was going to get another bar opened. Joey was a terrific partner, owner and manager. Eventually, we had four: Daisy Buchanan's, The Great Gatsby's, Scott's and Zelda's, all reflecting Joey's appreciation of F. Scott Fitzgerald.

When we opened Daisy's, I simply walked away from Bachelors III. I just didn't give it a second thought. I never told Namath I was leaving, and that's not like me. He was miffed, and he had every reason to be. We haven't spoken since. He was a great friend to lose. It certainly wasn't the way to handle the situation, and I admit I went about it all wrong.

As it turned out, Joey, Jimmy and I were the triumvirate—a great team. We did everything together, so it ended up going well. Joey ran a tight ship. He taught me things about the bar business that I still consider amazing. For example, he told me to put the television at the far end of the bar because people need a focal point when they come into an empty bar. He wanted the bottles dusted down every night. He handled the staff. He told me, "If you listen to them, they'll have you working for them!"

I was really into Daisy's and spent most of my spare time there. It was aimed at a younger college crowd who just wanted to go out and see beautiful women and the athletes that came in every night. It was a fun place . . . and still is.

After helping mould the Boston Bruins from an afterthought to a Stanley Cup champion, Harry Sinden walked away from the team and his coaching career following the victory on Mother's Day in 1970.

Before Christmas 1969, with a two-year contract about to expire, Sinden went to Milt Schmidt, our general manager, and asked for a raise of $8,000. Schmidt thought the amount too rich and, after consulting with team president Weston Adams Jr., returned with an offer of a $3,000 raise. That was short-sighted. They just did not know what they had in Harry, who was the best coach in hockey at the time and has proven to be one of the best of all time.

Harry contacted a good friend, David Stirling, owner of the Stirling-Homex Corporation in Rochester, New York. The two had grown up together in Toronto, and Stirling had previously offered Harry a summer job with his company. Stirling-Homex built prefabricated components for low-cost housing. *Forbes* magazine called David Stirling "the Henry Ford of the housing industry" and predicted that Stirling-Homex would be "the salvation of the housing crisis."

"A couple of days after my meeting with Schmidt, I called Dave and told him I wanted to get out of the hockey business," Harry told *Sports Illustrated*. The two friends worked out an arrangement that would see Sinden earn more than he had asked from the Bruins, but also looked to guarantee a bright and stable future.

Three days after the Bruins won the Stanley Cup, Harry told management he was leaving. All they said to him was, "Okay, we don't want to stand in your way." Harry was pissed. He said, "The Bruins weren't very interested in my future. There was no doubt in my mind that the decision I had made at Christmas, the decision to hold out for more money at the end of the season, was the right one." The Bruins placed Harry on the voluntary retired list, which prohibited him from taking a position with another team for a year. Harry joined Stirling-Homex right afterward.

All fans question management, especially if they love their team, but to let Sinden go for such a small amount of money was a sin. Now, I was worried.

Maybe the Bruins' management didn't know what they were doing. In the meantime, Tom Johnson was hired to take over the team's coaching responsibilities. Tom had his own style. He was a fabulous guy and Harry's best friend, but when a team is used to one guy's style and all of a sudden they change, it changes the room and the atmosphere.

We knew Tom well because he had been the assistant general manager and was around the rink all the time, helping with coaching and other duties. Tom had been an All-Star defenceman with the Canadiens, and after an injury, he finished his career with the Bruins. His theory as head coach was to let opponents try to beat us. By the time Tommy took over, we were a dynamite hockey team. We were breaking all sorts of records.

The Bruins didn't realize the genius of Harry Sinden at the time. I did, although I was being labelled "unruly." I wasn't. I did what I was told. I was very coachable. Harry used to come up to me privately and say, "Listen, Derek. I need you tonight. I have a lot of things to think about, and I want you to take those things off my mind." He gave players individual assignments. When I found out the Bruins let Harry walk away because of a piddly amount of money, I told them, "You just cost us the Stanley Cup." It made headlines, of course, and I got shit for it, but the comment was quickly forgotten because our team was so good.

In 1969–70, the last year of my original contract, I made a basic salary of $13,000. It was now time for my compensation to increase to represent my contributions to the Boston Bruins. I wasn't looking for an exorbitant salary, just what I thought I deserved. I decided to hold out until my contract got settled and didn't show up for training camp in London. In the meantime, I flew to Montreal for two days to shoot my part in a movie. I think they paid me $1,000, and my role was to walk into a party and tell people I was a scout for a girls' hockey team. I was onscreen for about 90 seconds. The movie was called *Loving and Laughing*. It got pretty good reviews when it was released in Canada, but it got an X rating. When it was going to be released in the

U.S. in 1972, I demanded that they edit out my part, even though I was fully clothed. The last thing I needed was to have people say I was in a porno film. Thankfully, my part was edited out in the American release. After my part was shot, I went to the airport, but found out that flights were cancelled. I should have checked to see if there was a train back to London, but I didn't. I missed a team practice, and Milt Schmidt announced to the press, "Derek Sanderson is suspended for not reporting for practice."

I had arrived at camp in good faith in order to get myself in shape, even though I didn't think I needed to be there because I was unsigned. Then, Clarence Campbell, the NHL president, ruled that contracts run from October 1 to October 1, so I was in breach of my original contract. When I returned, I was called into a closed-door meeting with Johnson and Schmidt. They laid down the law, but lifted my suspension.

The worst thing a player can do is think he is bigger than the game. I didn't want to alienate my teammates or disrupt the team. The Bruins said they were tired of me grousing about the bad contract I had signed and made the unprecedented move of revealing to the press that, although I repeatedly stated that I had earned just $13,000, I had also received a $1,000 bonus from the league because Boston had finished second in 1969–70; that the Bruins had matched that amount; that I had earned an $11,000 team bonus; that my share of the Stanley Cup win was $8,750, plus the Bruins had picked up pension and insurance fees of $3,000. But that didn't change the fact that my base salary was a pittance, and I felt I was underpaid.

I held out for as long as I possibly could, but it reached a point where it would have harmed me to miss games over money matters. My lawyer negotiated a new contract. I originally asked for $60,000, but finally signed a one-year deal for $37,500 plus bonuses. I received $17,500 and the rest was deferred. I signed, but I still didn't think it was fair. The base was lower than I wanted, but the bonus provisions were much better than what I was asking. That was probably the most they would have paid at that time. I signed the deal on October 12, two or three hours before the season opened. I wasn't allowed to play in the home opener against the Red Wings because Tom Johnson thought I had made some prima donna moves. For my part, I promised myself I wouldn't go popping off to the press and would just play hockey.

The Bruins were hot, and I was still a prominent member of the team, so WSBK-TV, channel 38 in Boston, offered me my own TV show. *Everybody's Talkin' at Me: The Derek Sanderson Show* debuted on October 17. It was a weekly half-hour show taped in front of a live audience, and it aired on Saturdays at six o'clock. The theme song was "Everybody's Talkin'," the Harry Nilsson song from the film *Midnight Cowboy*.

I had a lot of high-profile guests on the show. Ricky Nelson was on the show, and I gave Linda Ronstadt her first television appearance. She and the Stone Poneys performed their hit song "Different Drum." Linda was very pretty and exceptionally talented. We flirted back and forth and had a few good laughs, but the 24-minute show took three hours to tape. She had a mouth like a sailor! There was an audience in the studio. Parents were laughing uncomfortably and covering their kids' ears. She just lambasted us with the F-word. It was quite an experience. I shrugged and said, "Okay, I'll learn from that."

One night, Phil Esposito came on as a guest with Gerry Cheevers and Johnny McKenzie. We sat them down in the studio and the cameras were rolling. "Oh. So this is your little show, huh?"

I said, "Yeah. We've got a little show here and today, I'm with some of my boys. So Gerry, where did it all start for you?"

He kind of sucked his teeth and looked at Phil, and then Phil looked at him. They had made a pact that they weren't going to talk. I was dying, and I didn't know how to get out of it. I said, "Come on, guys. Don't do this to me. Do not do this to me! You can't do this." And they glanced around the studio and said, "Do you hear someone talking?"

I was exasperated. "Ah, guys, are you going to do this all night?" I was trying my best to get through it, and they were just having a ball making me squirm. The studio audience thought it was funny, but I don't think people at home stayed tuned in. I said, "This isn't right. These guys are more intelligent than this. I want everyone to understand that. Don't believe that hockey players are stupid. These guys are pretty smart. They just don't know any better at this point." I continued to ask them questions, but the three of them totally ignored me.

Everybody was smoking right there in the studio. That's what everybody did back then. So Cheesy lit up a cigar and said, "How come you've got an ashtray and I don't have one?" The guys broke up laughing, but they kept ragging on me. It was uncomfortable for me, but people liked it. Anything the Bruins did in those days was loved by the fans.

The show ended after 26 weeks. According to the *Boston Globe,* "Derek failed despite the fact that he seemed to have some pluses that other athletic stars usually lack. He possessed a distinctive lifestyle, was an easy conversationalist and was confident enough not to cave in front of the mike."

I liked doing TV. Who knew—maybe there'd be a career in it one day.

I did *The Tonight Show* with Johnny Carson twice. Carson's show in those days was the summit of television programs. Everybody watched it. The first time I was invited was right after the Bruins won the Stanley Cup in May 1970. Comedienne Joan Rivers and David Hartman, an actor who later hosted *Good Morning America,* were the other guests that night. The second time I was on was in December 1970, along with talk-show host David Frost, jazz singer Buddy Greco and comedian Alan King.

Carson could not have been more professional. He had the ability to make you feel important. I felt very comfortable and was just myself, but I got Johnny laughing. On the first appearance, he asked me why I had left my hometown. I said, "Well, Johnny, I had to leave Niagara Falls because the only good-looking chick in town didn't like me." Another time, he said, "Derek, you've got a pretty good career going for yourself, but what are you going to do when the game is over?" I smiled and said, "Your seat doesn't look too bad." He laughed! He thought it was the funniest thing he ever heard. His sidekick, Ed McMahon, let loose that big, deep, "Ha, ha ha! Hey-ohhh!"

I never saw a television show that legitimized anybody more than *The Tonight Show.* It made you into a bona fide celebrity. As I travelled, I would often meet people who recognized me from playing hockey, but more often than not, they'd say, "Hey! I saw you on Johnny Carson." The show was that powerful.

Television appearances never scared me. I found that by simply looking at the host, you come off as natural. I never tried to act, because acting was not something I did particularly well. By doing all these major TV shows and proving to be an entertaining guest, it put my image out of proportion, but I must admit, I enjoyed myself immensely. And the more I did, the more I got asked to do others. I also guested on *The Merv Griffin Show* and *The Mike Douglas Show,* and because I had done these shows, I was on a roll and *The Dick Cavett Show,* which in those days aired on ABC in competition with Carson, invited me to appear.

I'd been on the street all my life and knew an attitude when I saw one. So I could sense that Cavett had every intention of doing a cerebral interview with a *dumb* hockey player. He said, "Hockey player, huh? How many teeth do you have?"

I said, "You know, Dick, I have my own TV show, and if the producer leaves me short of questions, I struggle too. I know what it's like. That has got to be the dumbest question I've ever been asked." I said, "This is the best you've got? I really expected more from you."

That was it for *The Dick Cavett Show.* It was basically, "Get this punk out of here." It may have been the shortest interview I ever had.

"Garden Party Was a Brawl," the *Boston Globe* reported about our win over the Montreal Canadiens in Boston on November 8, 1970. I set the tempo for what was going to be a rough game when I picked up a double minor early in the first. Then, just before the end of that period, a donnybrook broke out. Wayne Cashman was duking it out with Guy Lapointe and Teddy Green was laying a beating on somebody else. Both benches cleared. Everybody paired up and there was equipment scattered all over the ice. A bunch of guys were naked from the waist up slugging it out. It was astounding!

Their coach, Claude Ruel, was yipping away at me. He had been a pretty good junior hockey player, but his career ended when he was blinded in one eye. Ruel sent Phil Roberto after me. Roberto and I had been friends in Niagara

Falls. He didn't want to hit me, so he just grabbed me from behind and put me in a chokehold. I tried to shake him, but couldn't. "Let me go, you bastard!" And then, all of a sudden, I couldn't talk. I started backing him up and he was still holding me. He leaned me back against the boards at their bench, and Ruel was still going at me. I managed to kick myself upright. I don't know why I thought of that, but Roberto had to let go of me or it would've broken his arm.

I was 10 feet away from Ruel. I yelled, "You asshole!" I went after him, and he turned and ran. I followed him down the corridor, across the linoleum, and he went up the stairs. I thought to myself, "I don't want to ruin my skates for this prick," so I yelled the only thing I could think of: "Come back and I'll blind you in the other eye!"

He yelled back, "You're crazy!"

I went to go back on the ice, but the Boston police wouldn't let me back. The brawl lasted 45 minutes.

It wasn't the only brawl we had with the Canadiens. We hated them. They stole the Cup from us in 1971. In Montreal, the bench was strange. The crowd could actually walk behind the bench to get to or from their seats. One time, somebody suckered one of our guys on the bench and I reached for the bastard and just missed him. He was with his friend and they started running, so I bolted after them. They turned down the corridor and ran down the ramp. *Boom!* Through one doorway. *Boom!* Through a second set of doors and out of the building, over top of a snowbank beside the TV trucks and then they cut right towards Sainte-Catherine Street. I chased after them in my skates. They ran through traffic and I lost them. There I was, standing on the corner of Lambert-Closse and Sainte-Catherine with my Bruins uniform on. I was still wearing my skates. I could see the TV production truck, and everybody was watching the fight on television.

A fan grabbed the guys and pointed at me, but I was done. Ace Bailey had followed me out of the Forum and was standing beside me. We looked at each other quizzically and he asked, "Turk, what are we doing out here?"

"I don't know, to tell you the truth," I answered. "I thought I had to catch the guys, but I couldn't. Whaddya say we go back?"

The two of us climbed back up over the snowbank past the TV truck. The Montreal Canadiens' security guard was standing there and said, "*Non, non!* You don't come in. You've got no ticket."

We were standing there in our full gear, including skates, begging the guy to let us back into the arena, but he refused. The RCMP came down and told him, "Don't be an ass." They opened the door to let us back in. Meanwhile, Tom Johnson was looking all around and asking, "Where's Sanderson? Where's Bailey?" One of the guys said, "I don't know, Coach, but I think they're chasing after somebody."

We got back to the bench and Tom asked, "Where the hell have you two been?"

"It's a long story," was all I said.

In mid-December, we were playing the Flyers in Philly. I was in the penalty box and a fan spit on me. I decked him, and a couple of other guys moved in. I knocked one down and was taking on the others when Swoop Carleton and Ace Bailey arrived and were in the box fighting these jerks.

I found a kindred spirit in Mike Walton when he arrived in February. Mike was a hell of a hockey player. He broke in with Toronto in the late 1960s, but he was pretty headstrong, and so was Punch Imlach, the coach of the Maple Leafs. The two of them were constantly in conflict. Imlach hated his hair and his agent and criticized his play on the ice. And it didn't help that Shakey married Candace, the granddaughter of former Leafs owner Conn Smythe. The tension and criticism eventually sent Shakey into a depression, and midway through the 1970–71 season, it was evident that he had to get out of Toronto to save his sanity and his career.

That February, he was traded twice in one day. The Leafs sent Walton, goalie Bruce Gamble and a draft pick to the Philadelphia Flyers for Bernie Parent and a draft pick. Then, Philly traded Walton to us for forwards Rick MacLeish and Danny Schock. Shakey fit in nicely. He was already a business partner with Bobby in the Orr-Walton Sports Camp in Orillia, Ontario, but his offence really fit in with the type of team we had at the time.

The two of us hit it off. Just after he joined the Bruins, we went to Daisy's for a few beers after practice. We were telling stories and laughing and the beers were starting to add up. I was under the impression that our flight was at 4:30. I had my bag packed for our road trip and it was in the car, but Mike hadn't packed yet. He lived right around the corner.

I said, "Hey, Shake, we've got to go home and shower."

He said, "No, we've got to go now! It's a 3:30 flight."

"What?! You're kidding me!" I sputtered. "It's 2:45! We'll never make it in 45 minutes!"

I always parked my Lincoln right in front of Daisy's, and Joey, my partner, always had the keys ready to go. We ran out of the bar, jumped in the car and set out to make the 3:30 flight. The traffic was a nightmare. We sat through two light changes and I had only inched up about eight cars.

Shakey said, "We're dead! And I'm with you. I'm *really* screwed!"

"What do you mean by that?" I demanded.

"You're already in the shithouse," he answered. "I just got here."

I said, "Come on, it isn't that bad. We'll just say we had car trouble."

Shakey was really worried. "It's a commercial flight. You have to be on time and they preboard. We're in big trouble."

I laughed. "Never fear, the Turk is here."

"Huh?"

I said, "Watch this move!"

It was bumper to bumper and some of the worst gridlock I'd ever seen. So, I honked, went over the curb, around a parking meter and beeped at a guy to get him out of the way. "Excuse me! Excuse me!" I was getting all these looks. "Excuse me! Late for a flight!" The car dropped off the curb—*boom-boom, boom-boom*—and I cut across traffic. I ran the red light and turned left. *Boom-boom, boom-boom.* I had two tires up the curb. On Commonwealth Avenue, a wide, tree-lined median separates the two roadways, and down the middle there's an eight-foot-wide cobblestone walkway, flanked by benches and full of people walking along. I had to catch that flight, so I drove along the median, honking my horn—*beep beep*. People turned around and saw a car driving down the median. Everybody was thinking, "What is this idiot doing?"

Shakey let out a big sigh. "All we need now is to have a cruiser stop us." Of course, not only were we driving through pedestrian traffic, but we were both hammered while doing it. He said, "What are you going to do? You can't go left and go around the Boston Common."

"Hmm. Yeah, you're right. I never thought of that." So, I kept running it. *Beep beep. Bump-bump.* I went over the top, through the big stone gates, over the duck pond, around the grass, through Boston Common and down the walkway, honking all the way to get people to move. *Beep beep!* We were driving down Charles Street when I realized it was a one-way street and I was going the wrong way. "Holy shit, Shakey! Oh well, I'm only going one way anyway." I cut right and got on Storrow Drive and was going over the top. I made a U-turn to enter the airport and all I can remember was opening the door of the car and throwing up. The left front wheel was bent backwards. As I was puking, I looked up and there was this guy standing there with knee-high boots and his hands on his hips.

"Shit! It's a state trooper."

"Sorry, trooper. Bad pizza!"

He shook his head. "What are you two assholes doing?"

I told him, "We're late for a flight and we're in serious shit."

"Get in the cruiser," he said.

I asked, "But what about the car?"

"It isn't going anywhere," he stated. "We're going to have to tow it and you're going to have to pay for the tow. We'll take it out of here and they'll put it in the garage."

The police were great, although things were very different then. The cop dropped us off at the departure level and Shakey and I made the flight.

Daisy's was turning out to be a great spot just to hang out with some great people. It was comfortable—sometimes just a little bit too comfortable because I was there all the time.

Jimmy Buffett and I were hanging out a little back in 1971. He was just a guy strumming a guitar. Who knew he would end up being one of the all-time great performers? Someone I knew got him a job working in a gin mill over in Cambridge. He had one album out, but it hadn't really done anything. His real success didn't come until a few years later.

We were both drinking pretty good back then. We'd get a little squirrelly sitting in Daisy's, telling stories. Jimmy had been drinking at Daisy's one night in February 1971. With a belly full of rum and tonic serving as antifreeze, he stepped outside to head back to his hotel, but couldn't find a cab. Then, he noticed one idling nearby, with the driver nowhere to be seen. Cold and buzzed enough that he didn't care about the consequences, Jimmy jumped in and drove himself back to the hotel. He swears he left the fare on the front seat. He wrote a song about the incident and released it in 1979. It's called "Boat Drinks." Whenever he plays the New England area, Jimmy usually plays "Boat Drinks" and mentions me.

I saw Jimmy at Great Woods, which is now the Comcast Center, an amphitheatre in Mansfield, Massachusetts. We got a chance to chat with a little more clarity on that occasion.

It was obscene how strong the Bruins were in 1970–71. We finished first with 121 points, winning 57 games—both NHL records. We set another all-time high with 399 goals that season—108 more than the next-best team. Phil Esposito led the NHL in scoring with a record-setting 152 points, including 76 goals, which shattered Bobby Hull's two-year-old standard of 58. Bobby Orr was right behind him with 139 points, including a league-record 102 assists, and he won the Hart Trophy as the most valuable player as well as his fourth consecutive Norris Trophy. John Bucyk and Ken Hodge also finished with more than 100 points. We had 10 guys with 20 or more goals—Esposito, Bucyk, Hodge, Bobby, Pie McKenzie, me, Eddie Westfall, Fred Stanfield, Swoop Carleton and Wayne Cashman. Bobby, Phil, Hodgey and Chief were all selected to the First All-Star Team.

My 29 goals were a career-best. I also added 34 assists. Not bad for a defensive centre. I was really proud that our penalty-killing success was better than 84 percent. We also scored 25 shorthanded goals: Eddie Westfall had seven, I had six and Donnie Marcotte, who was the other winger on our line, also had six. The Bruins were on fire and ready to repeat our Stanley Cup win.

In a game against Montreal in early April, Johnny McKenzie suffered a shoulder separation and I stretched the ligaments in my right wrist, which I had hurt a year earlier against Pittsburgh. I sat out the last couple of games of the season. I probably could have played, but the wrist was sore and Mike Walton was great filling in for me. The club didn't need me in those games, and as long as we kept on winning, the important thing was to get that wrist fully healed in time for the playoffs.

We faced the Canadiens in the opening round of the playoffs. They were no pushovers, but few had any doubt that we could handle them. During the season, we'd beaten them five of six times, outscoring them 29–14. They had a rookie coach, Al MacNeil—the same guy who had been so good to me by giving me sticks when I was a kid in Niagara Falls.

We weren't worried about the Canadiens. Our strategy was to let them come up with a plan to beat us, and that kind of rattled me. In my mind, it was the worst thing you can do to a team, no matter how good they are. Confidence is one thing, but cockiness is different, and after all, they were the Montreal Canadiens, a team you could never underestimate.

I was going to go up against Jean Beliveau. I watched him while I was growing up, and he was a great player. If we were going to win, I had to outplay him. And it wasn't just shutting down Beliveau; the Canadiens were fast. Another thing that amazed me was Montreal's ability to take a pass in their feet.

Late in the season, the Canadiens called up Ken Dryden from the American Hockey League to replace Rogie Vachon and Phil Myre. He was a big, tall, standup goalie, and he won all six games he played during the regular season. We played Montreal in two of our final three games of the season, but never faced Dryden. It came as a big surprise to everyone when the Canadiens named him as their starter. We expected Vachon, who was an experienced playoff goalie and had won the Vezina Trophy in 1968. About Dryden, we thought, "He's some big college kid in goal. It's not like we'll be facing Jacques Plante or Gump Worsley."

Dryden was highly overrated, in my opinion, but he was the first big goaltender. He covered the top of the net so well, and when he dropped and spread, he covered a lot of ground in the bottom part. You'd turn to shoot, and he would have that area covered because of his size. It took us a while to get used to that. It created problems we had never seen before.

Everybody told us to run the Canadiens out of the building. That was easier said than done. They had courage and they were dedicated, so you couldn't push them around.

We started the series with two games at home, and took the first one, 3–1. Cheevers played really well, so we were surprised when Tom Johnson named Eddie Johnston as the starting goalie in game two. We went into the third period of that game with a 5–2 lead, and then we blew it. It may very well be the greatest comeback in Montreal's history. They scored five unanswered goals. We just couldn't do anything right, and Dryden couldn't do anything wrong. They beat us 7–5 and completely knocked the wind out of us. Two nights later, the series moved to Montreal and they beat us 3–1. We evened the series with a 5–2 win the next night at the Forum. It was now down to a best-of-three. We pounded the Canadiens 7–3 back home in Boston, but they came back and hammered us 8–3 in Montreal.

Dryden didn't provide the stellar goaltending everybody continues to talk about. You could score on Dryden. He wasn't that good; he was just different. In the seventh and deciding game, he stopped us in our tracks. We took an early lead, but by the time the buzzer sounded to end the first, it was 2–1 Montreal. They added another goal in the second and a fourth goal in the third. The Canadiens eliminated us with a 4–2 win.

It was a huge upset. We were the Stanley Cup champions, for God's sake!

We sat quietly in that dressing room, still dressed with our heads hung down, almost as though someone had died. It had been a serious mistake to underestimate Montreal.

That should have been our third Stanley Cup in a row.

CHAPTER 17

SECOND CUP: 1971–72

I started playing golf when I turned pro. My dad taught me. The first time we went out, he showed me how to grip the club. The first swing I took, I missed the ball completely. He said, "You've got to keep your head still. Keep your head behind the ball." That was the first lesson I ever learned, and *bang!* Today, I hit the ball 300 yards straight down the middle.

The NHL had a lot of boys who were scratch golfers—Gary Dornhoefer, Stan Mikita, Bobby Rousseau, Dale Tallon. Hockey players can golf. The reason, in my opinion, is that it's not foreign to hit something at your feet, and a slapshot and a golf swing are similar acts. A golf swing is not unnatural for hockey players.

I love the game. I've played with Jack Nicklaus. I've played with Donald Trump. The Donald can play. He's a good guy, too.

The players today can flat-out play. I played with Dennis Wideman when he was with the Bruins. My God, can he hit the ball! These kids can hit it 340, 350, 360 yards. That's a long way to hit a golf ball. I play with Bobby Orr all the time. When Eddie Johnston comes to town, we play. When hockey players get together, they golf.

During the summer of '71, Eddie and I teamed up for the third annual American Airlines National Hockey League Golf Tournament in Woodbridge, Ontario. Bob Baun and Gump Worsley took the very first championship in 1969, and Gary Bergman and Frank Mahovlich won it in 1970. Popsy and I thought we had a good shot at winning in 1971. It was a best-ball tournament. I'm a pretty good golfer, but Eddie is really good, and he laid down the rules before we picked up a club. "Do not take a club out of your bag until I tell you which club to use and where to hit the ball."

I used to shoot an 85 and was a 14 handicap and hit the ball a lot farther than Popsy, but I did exactly what I was told. E.J. was off the charts and we won the tournament that year. The prize was $5,000, and I was already thinking about how I was going to spend my half. Eddie said, "I'd like to donate it back to charity," which was the Rotary Club of Toronto for physically challenged children and to the Canadian Olympic Association's youth development program. "What about you?"

I said, "I'm taking my half. I only made $13,000 last year. I need it. I'm not giving it back."

Popsy said, "Derek, don't take it. You'll lose your amateur status. You'll never play in a pro-am or any of those club tournaments."

"Come on, for taking the prize money?" I asked.

"Derek, trust me," he replied.

I wanted the cash. I didn't care about playing in any pro-am. That was nice spending money. I accepted my cash prize at first, but then E.J. talked me out of it, so I donated it to the charity. Even so, I was ruled out of the U.S. Golf Association and the Royal Canadian Golf Association for three years until they finally found proof that the cheque had been handed back to the charity. And I never even took the money!

Golf Digest invited me to the Doral Open later that summer. The Doral Open was a PGA Tour golf tournament played at the Blue Monster course at the Doral Golf Resort just outside Miami. They had a competition where if you put up $25, you could try to outdrive Jack Nicklaus, and if you beat him, you won $500 in the pro shop and got your picture taken with him. I just wanted to meet him, so I thought I'd try my luck.

Everybody else was sitting and watching, and he hit his ball 308 yards with a wooden club—the old persimmon head. Then it was my turn. I got up and hit it as far as I'd ever hit a golf ball. I know I couldn't put a better swing on it if God came down in the shape of a flaming bush and helped me. I tossed the club in my bag and said, "Is the ball still in the air? That's all I need!" I had heard that Nicklaus was surly, but I thought he was a great guy. He took my club out of the bag and looked at it. "If you get your pro to shave that club down, maybe you could hit that thing!"

I got to play two holes with him. That was a thrill. We both drove a par-4 and I think I was 12 feet from the pin and he was 20. He made his eagle putt and it took me three. Unless you learn to separate your head from those shoulders, you'll never be able to putt. That was my problem. On the second hole we played, we both drove it pretty well. He outdrove me, so I was hitting first and I decided to use a wedge. He said, "That's a figure-eight green looking at you. Not in this wind."

I said, "No, I'm driving it into the wind."

He shook his head. "You're going to hit the water on the left. That's a gale up there."

I insisted. "You'll see." I hit a beautiful shot, just outside the right-hand side of the green, up in the air. But then the wind got it and *splash!* All the way across the green, just like the master said.

He laughed. "I told you!"

Then he took a little 5-iron, choked it right down to the shaft and punched it. *Zoom.* One-jump stop. It rolled to within a foot of the hole.

"Holy shit." I hit a wedge and he hit a 5-iron.

"It's not what you hit," he told me. "It's how you hit it."

He was great to play with. He was witty and fun. Jack Nicklaus was a class act.

By now, I realized how fortunate I was to be playing hockey in Boston. I loved the city, loved the fans, loved the guys. But I wasn't getting much privacy. During the summer, I had attended the funerals of relatives of a couple of close friends, and fans approached me in the funeral parlour for autographs. I couldn't believe it! When I refused, they became indignant. Then, they go home and tell their friends that Sanderson is an asshole. You can't win. You can sit and sign a hundred autographs and people think, "Nice guy," but miss one autograph, especially for a kid, and people say, "I knew it! That Sanderson thinks he's a big shot."

I was always thankful for our fans, but I believe they should respect our rights to privacy. I was hounded while eating dinner, at the movies and even in washrooms. Autographs should be restricted to before and after games, and I'm more than happy to sign them at those times. Like my dad said, "Be nice to everyone on the way up, because you sure as hell are going to see them on the way down." Unfortunately, I did, but fortunately, people were very forgiving.

I met Judy through Joe Namath. She was what we called, in those days, a "stewardess." I moved her into my place fairly quickly, and we got along famously. Because she had seniority, she could often arrange her travel schedule to coincide with the Bruins' schedule. It didn't hurt that I knew the guy who made up the girls' schedules and would piece him off with tickets in order to make certain Judy was around when I was.

Judy had designs on being an actress and picked up a couple of minor roles. The two of us were offered leading roles in a western to be filmed in Spain, but I declined because it would have conflicted with my hockey schedule. We talked about marriage, but we were both too serious about our careers at that time.

In November 1971, there was a movie premiere for a film titled *Face-Off* that I had appeared in earlier that year. The film was based on a novel by Scott Young, a major Canadian sportswriter and the father of Neil Young, and was about a top Toronto Maple Leafs draft pick, played by Art Hindle, who fell for a folk singer, played by Trudy Young. The player gets a swelled head and runs into problems with referees and his coach, and the singer gets turned off by her boyfriend's violent profession.

Johnny F. Bassett produced the movie. His dad had co-owned the Maple Leafs with Harold Ballard and Stafford Smythe, and Johnny F. later bought the Ottawa Nationals of the World Hockey Association and moved them to Toronto, as the Toros, and later to Alabama as the Birmingham Bulls.

There were a lot of recognizable faces in the film, including John Vernon (the star of *Wojeck*, who later gained Hollywood fame as Dean Wormer in *Animal House*) as the coach, Austin Willis, three-year-old Carling Bassett-Seguso (as Kathrin Carling), George Armstrong, Harold Ballard, Ron Ellis,

Paul Henderson and Jacques Plante. My pal Jim McKenny was the stand-in for Art Hindle.

Karen Hazzard, the casting director, recalled that "Johnny F. used his considerable strings into the hockey world to get Derek. Derek was colourful, very good-looking and we thought he'd get along well with everyone, which he did."

"Derek was a natural actor—a little cocky but he listened to direction and he had a fabulous sense of humour. He laughed at all of my jokes," said Hindle. Trudy Young added, "I definitely remember Derek because he was so handsome and, being so insecure, I was shy and nervous around him."

We had a lot of fun. Much of it was shot in Toronto, and Howie (Jim McKenny) and I had a lot of laughs. The movie wasn't an earth-shaker, but it was a fun time. They released it in the States in 1972 as *Winter Comes Early*.

While I was in Toronto, I stayed with the Bassetts. At one point, I told Johnny F.'s son to round up the kids in the neighbourhood. "Let's get a road hockey game going!" John and his three sisters, Carling, Heidi and Vicky, all played, as did the neighbourhood kids. Some of those kids, who are now approaching 50, still talk about that afternoon.

The premiere was at the Odeon on Carlton Street, just down the block from Maple Leaf Gardens. Bassett really liked what I did, even though I was just being me, and in a cameo role at best. "He's so good that I've offered him parts in two future movies, both leading roles," he told reporters. "One is the title role in a western called *The Last of the Big Guns*. The other is the part of a disc jockey in a prairie town. Derek has all the instincts." *The Last of the Big Guns* eventually came out as *Paperback Hero*, starring Keir Dullea. I don't know what happened to that one, and the other film, I don't believe, ever materialized. I was also supposed to be in a movie called *The Love Machine* with Ann-Margret. I got busy at that time and she fell off a stage and was injured, so the movie never went ahead with the two of us.

Face-Off wasn't the last of my acting roles, but it is the one I'm reminded of most often. Everyone was so gracious. They made it memorable despite my inability to act.

In late October, Milt Schmidt called me in for a closed-door meeting. He had a number of concerns. One was that my off-ice lifestyle might affect my on-ice performance. I was drinking pretty good and smoked a fair bit. Milt also told me in no uncertain terms that he wanted me to cut back on the fighting—not my toughness, but just the scraps. He told me, "You're more valuable to us on the ice than in the box, Derek."

Why did I fight? I was always fiercely competitive, from the time I started taking hockey seriously. My father taught me to not back down from anyone. But I guess I was just a skinny kid looking for attention. I wasn't as big as some, or as good as others, but people noticed me when I fought.

I reduced my penalty minutes somewhat, but other than Stan Mikita, I can't think of many players who changed their games substantially during their career. After all, a leopard doesn't change its spots. The Mikita feat was quite impressive, as he led the league in scoring four times. In the first two seasons, he also finished third and seventh in penalty minutes, but after changing his game, he only had 12 penalty minutes in 1966–67 and 14 in 1967–68.

In April, we opened Zelda's. It was modelled after a great place in Toronto called Nepenthe, with lights and smoke coming off the dance floor. It was a hit.

Rumours swirled that I was on the trading block. One story had me going to Toronto and another had me being dealt to the Rangers for Walt Tkaczuk, who was one of the best left wingers in the game. My contract was up, and I wanted a good raise, but I didn't want to go anywhere—I might as well have had the Bruins logo tattooed on my ass.

There were some changes to the lineup that season, though. We lost a valuable team member when Wayne Carleton was picked by California in the intra-league draft before the season started. And Milt pulled off a trade in late February that sent Rick Smith and two of the four first-round picks we had in the 1970 draft—Reggie Leach and Bob Stewart—to the California Golden Seals for Carol Vadnais and Don O'Donoghue. The Bruins had been impatient with Reggie's development and dealt him before he exploded as an NHL sniper. One of the other picks we had in 1970, Rick MacLeish, would later join Leach in Philadelphia and help the Flyers win a couple of Cups.

In 1969, there was a popular movie called *Bob & Carol & Ted & Alice.* When we picked up Vadnais, we called our defence "Bob & Carol & Ted & Dallas" for Bobby Orr, Carol Vadnais, Ted Green and Dallas Smith.

We played the Golden Seals the same night as the trade for Vadnais. The Seals came out with their white skates, and midway through the second period, they were up 6–1. We were able to get two past goaltender Gilles Meloche before the period ended, but they were still up 6–3. I could tell by the feeling in the room that it was one of those "okay, this one's over" nights, and no matter what any coach might have said to inspire us to rally, it was done. Nobody was all that concerned about the Seals, but they'd dusted us off and were giving us a pretty embarrassing shellacking.

Then, Bobby Orr stood up. "Hey guys, what do you say we put on a show? Let's see if we can pull this one out." Having Bobby say that was the only thing on this planet that would've worked. He scored in the first three minutes, and then Freddy Stanfield scored his third goal of the night three minutes after that. He also missed on a penalty shot. Esposito was on fire and got two in the third, and then, with about 10 seconds left, I got one. We ended up beating them 8–6. I've never seen a team come back like that. We were dead. It was over. Nobody else could have made that happen. Bobby Orr had the respect of the room. All the guys trusted him and believed in him. He ended up with five points that night.

We were in Chicago in late February, sitting around and talking over beers. There were still a bunch of us on the team who had played on the Cup winner in '70. One of the guys said, "That was so much fun, let's do it again! It's up to us players!" Everybody bought in, and we kept reminding each other through the remainder of the schedule. We went on a nine-game winning streak. No one was going to deny us the Stanley Cup championship in 1972.

We finished first for the second straight season. Our 119 points were 10 better than the second-place New York Rangers. Phil Esposito won the Art Ross Trophy for the second consecutive spring, finishing with 133 points, including 66 goals. Bobby Orr won the Hart Trophy as the league's most valuable player for a third year in a row, and also won his fifth consecutive Norris as the league's best defenceman. The Boston fans have an award called the 7th Player, which goes to the player who goes beyond their expectations. I won it for 1971–72.

My drinking was getting a bit out of hand. It was entertaining to some of the boys, but a few of them, including Bobby, tried to get me to quit, or at least cut back substantially. People might argue with me, but I don't think it affected my game. I had 25 goals, including seven shorthanded, as well as 33 assists. I was moderately effective in curtailing the fights, but still spent 108 minutes in the penalty box.

My colitis had flared up again and I was hospitalized, although I was given clearance to play in the final. I hadn't played the last couple of weeks of the regular schedule or the first couple of rounds of the playoffs. Ace Bailey was dressed and took my spot between Westfall and Walton.

We met the Toronto Maple Leafs in the opening round of the playoffs and eliminated them in five games. The St. Louis Blues were next, and we rolled over them in four. The Stanley Cup final saw us facing our longtime enemies, the New York Rangers. It was the first Boston–Rangers Stanley Cup final since 1929.

I don't think anyone had forgotten our 1970 series. I told the New York press that I would run Giacomin at every opportunity. I didn't think the Rangers would let me, but I crashed the crease whenever I could to intimidate them. Ace did, too. The Rangers were plagued by injuries, but it didn't matter. We intimidated them.

I saw spot duty in game one, with Tommy Johnson using me to kill penalties. In the first period, I was killing off a minor, stole the puck and scored a shorthanded goal. Just 45 seconds later, Kenny Hodge also scored a shorthanded goal. We finished the first period with a 4–1 lead. We traded goals in the second, but the Rangers scored three unanswered goals in the third, including a Hadfield goal while I was in the box.

Ace Bailey was a key member of the team and a great friend. He was always there to help anyone. (We lost Ace in the second plane that hit the World Trade Center on 9/11.) He skated past Rod Gilbert on the left boards, then beat Brad Park. Giacomin dropped and Ace threw the puck over his shoulder to give us a 6–5 lead with a couple of minutes to go. We killed off the clock and took game one. Game two was much tighter than the opening contest. Chief scored for us in the first, and Gilbert tied it up in the second. With Walt Tkaczuk serving a penalty, Hodge scored on the power play, a goal that stood as the game-winner.

Up two games to none, we moved to Madison Square Garden for game three. The Rangers roared ahead and outscored us 3–1 in the first period. At the end of two, it was 5–2. We were pissed off because late in the period, Giacomin lost sight of the puck and Cashman located it behind him and tapped the puck into the net. The problem was that the referee lost the puck, too, and blew the play dead. No goal. Johnson sat me for most of the rest of the game.

Neither team scored in the third. With one second left in the game, I told linesman Matt Pavelich to fuck off and was given a misconduct and game misconduct and was fined by the league. The final score remained 5–2, Rangers. Game four was a tough game. Bobby scored two in the first period and we battled hard to get Eddie Johnston his shutout, but Rod Seiling scored late in the third to burst that bubble. The game ended in a 3–2 win for the Bruins. There were a lot of scraps. Bobby Rousseau and I fought early in the first period, and Donnie Marcotte and Gary Doak of the Rangers fought shortly after that. Don Awrey and Gene Carr paired off later. Near the end of the first, Bobby and Brad Park wrestled and McKenzie and Sather went at it. The third featured a bout between Vic Hadfield and Carol Vadnais. Ace Bailey jumped in and got involved. The referee handed out 72 minutes in penalties in the first period alone, and 104 in total for the game. Bobby Orr scored twice and added an assist on a goal by Don Marcotte. He controlled the puck for 40 minutes and let the other 35 players use it for the other 20. Bobby set a record for playoff points by a defenceman in this game. His three points gave him 22, two more than his record of 20 set in 1970.

We were up three games to one going into game five. My line faced the GAG (Goal-a-Game) Line: Jean Ratelle, Rod Gilbert and Vic Hadfield. Ratelle had been playing sparingly due to an ankle injury up to that point, but returned to the lineup in this game. Both teams were frustrated. Awrey was serving a double minor in the first, but we kept the Rangers from getting a shot. We had a two-man advantage for a minute and a half in the second, and couldn't put the puck in the net. Esposito was particularly snakebit. After scoring 66 goals during the regular season, and nine between the series with Toronto and St. Louis, New York held Phil scoreless in this series.

After the game, Phil was surrounded by writers. He said, "If the Rangers think they're going to beat us three in a row, they're full of crap. And you can spell that K-R-A-P. That's Park spelled backwards." I wish I were that witty. Some guys, like Jim McKenny, would say the funniest things, appropriate to the situation, off the cuff. It seemed like I always thought of great lines to retaliate with when I was ready for sleep.

We wanted to end the series right then, whether we were on enemy soil or not. Tommy Johnson put Cheevers in net to replace Eddie Johnston. Bobby was unbelievable in game six. He was the difference. He scored a power-play goal in the first period, but then a couple of minutes later, he picked up a misconduct for swearing at referee Art Skov. In the third, he fired a shot that Cash tipped past Giacomin for the second goal. Cash scored a late insurance marker, but the game and the Cup were ours. A 3–0 shutout for Cheesy, and Bobby scored his second Stanley Cup–winning goal. My philosophy was to give the puck to Bobby and let him do all he could with it. I said he was the difference in the game; he was the difference in the whole series.

May 11, 1972. Stanley Cup champions! Almost exactly two years to the date of our previous win. After the game, we lined up for the traditional handshakes. Cash and Greenie refused to shake hands with the Rangers, but there was Bobby, first in line to congratulate New York on a great series. After shaking hands with each of the players, he went over to the bench to shake hands with Emile Francis, the Rangers' head coach. I never would have thought of that. Clarence Campbell presented the Conn Smythe Trophy to Bobby, making him the first to win the playoff MVP trophy twice. Bobby had 24 points, which was a record for defencemen in the playoffs. His 19 assists set another playoff record for defencemen.

Phil Esposito shared the playoff point-scoring race with Bobby, even though he didn't get a goal in the final against New York. I toughed it out but finished with a goal, an assist and 44 minutes in penalties.

Although we didn't have a captain, Johnny Bucyk was the guy we designated to accept the Cup. Clarence Campbell said a few words and then handed the Stanley Cup to Chief. As we skated around Madison Square Garden with the Cup, the Rangers fans threw garbage at us, and I remember thinking how anxious I was to get out of there. It was sad. After the game, we got dressed and left to take our bus back to the hotel. The fans were rabid. Cops had to circle the bus in order to allow us to board and leave. The New York fans were screaming and swearing at us as we walked through the crowd to get onto the bus. I was carrying a leather bag. A kid broke through the ring of police, ran up to me and yelled, "Sanderson, you're an asshole." He then tried to stab me with a knife. I held my bag up to block the blow and he stabbed the bag. A cop stepped up and clocked him with a billy club. *Bang!* Dropped him like a stone.

Relieved, I turned to the cop and said, "Hey, thanks."

The cop said, "Look, I think you're an asshole too, but I'm just doing my job."

I laughed a little nervously and replied, "Okay, then. Thanks for doing your job!"

He nodded, and I climbed onto the bus. As we started to pull away, the fans rocked the bus, trying to push it over.

The bus took us to the airport and we flew back to Boston. We arrived just after midnight, and as we were descending, we could see state troopers' cars with their blinking lights and what looked like hundreds and hundreds of people. We were alerted to the fact that there was some kind of hoopla at the airport, but had no idea it was going to be as crazy as it was. Ten thousand fans were waiting there to greet the Stanley Cup champions. People parked up to four miles away in the middle of the Callahan Tunnel. Had there been an emergency, there was no way an ambulance could have made its way through.

We would have taken our lives in our hands had we walked through the airport. You just couldn't get through. Our plan was the same as it always was: send Bobby out first. Every city we'd go to, there'd be a bunch of kids waiting for the players. Bobby always drew big crowds. He always sat at the back of the bus. When I saw a crowd, I'd yell, "Hey, Four! Front of the bus!" He'd go out and be immediately swallowed up by the crowd. He'd stand there and sign every autograph. We'd step to the other side and be gone. Everybody wanted Bobby, so he'd sign 500 autographs and we'd get away with scribbling two or three on the way into the hotel.

When we landed in Boston, there were even more people than we thought—thousands of them.

"Bobby!"

He just laughed and shook his head. "Well, somebody at least take my garment bag, for Christ's sake!"

Cheesy said, "I'll take it."

So, Bobby went out first, and before he got 30 feet, he was half-naked. Fans ripped at his clothes for souvenirs, and even with all the cops around, they didn't stop.

You fear for your life when people lose it like that. I said, "No way am I going out there." I saw a ramp attendant, the guy who directs the landed planes into place with the orange batons in each hand. After he parked us, he boarded the plane to congratulate us. He was wearing overalls, a baseball cap and headphones. I had an idea.

"Hey, buddy. Come here."

He was all smiles. "Hey Turk, congratulations! What can I do for you?"

I told him I wanted to make a deal with him. "Do you like this top coat?"

"Yeah!"

"It's yours. Just give me your overalls."

He was puzzled. "What?"

I said, "Give me your overalls, your hat, your headphones and those two batons."

"Derek," he said, "I'll get fired."

"No, you won't."

I traded him clothes and grabbed a case of beer from the plane. I rode into the employees' entrance on the back of a baggage truck. Nobody noticed me, and I sat in the hangar wearing the Eastern Airlines overalls and baseball cap until the crowds cleared. Once the crowds thinned out, I jumped into my car and drove home.

We were invited by Boston mayor Kevin White to be honoured with a civic ceremony at City Hall. The mayor announced that he had a special award for spirit and enthusiasm, and asked Johnny McKenzie to come forward to accept it. Pie was happy as a pig in shit until Mayor White dumped a pitcher of beer on his head. We laughed so hard. Revenge is a bitch. The mayor had worn a pitcher of beer from Pie after the celebration in 1970 and, even though it took two years to get even, he finally did, much to the amusement of all of us.

CHAPTER 18

NEGOTIATING WITH THE WHA

After the final game of the 1971–72 season, I joked with Weston Adams Jr. that I would have to make a lot more money to continue playing for the Boston Bruins. I was shit-faced. One doesn't stay too sober after winning the Stanley Cup. He just laughed. In mid-June, I met more officially with him, and I brought my friend Jimmy McDonough with me. He worked with us over at Daisy's but had also attended law school. My attorney wasn't in town at the time, so I thought Jimmy could advise me should the need arise.

I threw a couple of figures out to Westy to see if the amounts were plausible. I wanted $80,000, and Adams said, "We're in the same ballpark. We are not too far apart." I also wanted a no-trade agreement for five years, but Weston told me that while he could likely agree to that point, it was not something he would be comfortable putting in writing. I was trying to find out whether I could relax for the summer or had to worry about being traded, but Adams assured me by saying, "Go ahead and have a good summer."

Later, Westy called me back and I was taken to the office of Charles Mulcahy, the Bruins' lawyer. Charlie told me, "You are about $20,000 too high."

I got up and left.

While driving down the expressway in Boston not long after winning the Stanley Cup, I glanced up and saw a billboard that read: "Paul Anka—Las

Vegas, Nevada—Caesar's Palace," and underneath, it said, "Opening Act—Joey Heatherton."

I'd met Paul Anka during the playoffs in 1970. It turned out he was a Bruins fan, and I was a fan of his. Since Paul Anka had visited my dressing room, I figured, why not visit his? On the spur of the moment, I turned right, went to the airport and jumped on a plane to Vegas. I only had the clothes on my back and figured I'd buy more when I got there. I had a little bit of cash in my pocket, but I used my American Express gold card for the whole trip.

When I arrived at Caesar's Palace, I approached the front desk. "I'm looking for Paul Anka. My name's Derek Sanderson." I didn't know that you didn't approach celebrities like that. The girl at the desk looked at me like I had six heads. She said, "I'm sorry, sir, but we don't give Mr. Anka's number out."

"I've got to see him," I told her. "Give me the manager."

The manager came out and I tried to explain the situation to him. "I'm a friend of Paul's. He'll be very upset with you if you don't tell him that I'm here."

The manager called up to his room, explained that there was a guy named Derek Sanderson claiming to know him. Paul said, "Send him up."

When I greeted Paul, I asked, "Do you really need that kind of security?"

"Oh yeah," he said. He asked me if I wanted to attend the show that night. "Absolutely."

We hung out and talked for a while. I asked him, "Is there any way I can meet Joey Heatherton?" Joey was a great dancer and really beautiful. She was really sexy.

He said, "Yeah! You're going to love her. She's great."

After the show, I went to Paul's dressing room and he brought Joey in. He introduced me as his friend who played hockey with the Boston Bruins. She smiled and said, "I'm going to an after-party with Sammy Davis Jr. Would you be my escort?"

"Yeah, sure." That's all it was. I took her there and kept her company. We walked in and I quietly said, "Listen. I know you're going to have to do your hellos and handshakes and work the room. I'll be here at the bar. Pick me up on the way out."

She said, "Wow, you're sweet," and she left. She did her thing—her Hollywood air kisses. "Hi, how are you? You were great." A little while later, she returned. "Are you ready?"

We drove out to the desert and talked. Nothing more. She was really nice and we became good friends. Like every other guy, I had been enamoured with her from her TV image, but I discovered that there was much more than a pretty face and a great body. She was a really good person and one of the sweetest people I had ever met. "Another myth destroyed," I thought.

She was in the midst of getting a divorce from Lance Retzel, the football player, and we talked about that. She was scared and hurt and didn't know what to do. That's when I started to realize that celebrities are really just ordinary people. The media escalates their profiles and makes them out to be something they're not. The thought fascinated me. "Why do they do that?" I never did understand that.

We hung out off and on through the summer. People saw us together and assumed there was more going on than there was. When I was in the audience at her opening at the Waldorf-Astoria in September 1972, the press descended on her like locusts. "Derek is more a friend than a boyfriend," she explained.

Joey Heatherton was a very classy lady, but I preferred girls who were a little more down to earth. Joey thought a simple meal began with caviar.

The World Hockey Association, while regarded as a joke by many, left its indelible imprint on professional hockey that resonates to this day.

In 1971, two entrepreneurs decided that professional hockey could sustain a league that would rival the NHL. Gary Davidson and Dennis Murphy were no strangers to the sports world, having previously founded the American Basketball Association (ABA). After recruiting "Wild Bill" Hunter, the president of the Western Canada Hockey League, a major junior circuit, the trio embarked on convincing nine other owners to pay $25,000 each for franchises in the new league.

My WHA adventure actually began in December 1971. Herb Martin, the owner of the Miami Screaming Eagles, approached me, through my lawyer, about whether I might have any interest in hearing what he had to offer. Martin was a land developer who planned to bring professional hockey to Florida. The Screaming Eagles were to be one of the WHA's 12 charter franchises. He planned to build an arena within the walls of four office buildings that would create what he planned to call the Executive Square Arena. The WHA was so excited about his plan that they had tentatively scheduled the league's first game, between Miami and Winnipeg, for October 6, 1972.

Martin had a pretty good plan. He intended to offer six-figure salaries to key players in order to lure them from the NHL to the WHA. I was one of his targets. He told my lawyer, "We think that by our second season, if you don't have a season ticket, you won't be able to see a hockey game in Miami."

I never paid much attention to the WHA. Who could possibly compete with the National Hockey League, the greatest league in the world? I was a Bruin, very happy in the NHL, but I wanted a good raise.

I heard about the cities they had picked for WHA franchises. They were going to go head-to-head with the NHL in four large U.S. markets: New York, Boston, Los Angeles and Chicago. My sense was you weren't just going to go into those markets and steal their fans. I read all the stories—WHA, rebel league, NHL trying to pooh-pooh it. No one was really giving the WHA a chance.

The WHA held what it called a General Player Draft in Anaheim over two days—February 12 and 13, 1972. The purpose of the draft was so the new franchises could claim WHA rights to players they hoped to sign for their inaugural season, 1972–73. The draft was held in two parts: a preliminary round in which teams made so-called "priority" selections, and then regular rounds to follow. The priority selections were the most sought-after players, consisting mostly of NHL veterans and highly touted prospects. The rest of the draft comprised players from the minor leagues and colleges. The draftees were under no legal obligation to sign with the WHA team that drafted them, but it prevented other WHA clubs from negotiating with these players who were drafted.

Twelve teams participated in the draft: the Calgary Broncos, Chicago Cougars, Dayton Aeros, Edmonton Oilers, Los Angeles Sharks (who had already changed their name from the Aces), Miami Screaming Eagles, Minnesota Fighting Saints, New England Whalers and Winnipeg Jets, as well as three unnamed franchises: one based in New York (later to be named the Raiders), one in Ontario (soon to be the Ottawa Nationals) and a third that had been conceived as the San Francisco Sharks but would be reborn as the Quebec Nordiques.

I chuckled when I heard that I had been one of the Screaming Eagles' priority picks. They also selected my junior teammate Bernie Parent from the Toronto Maple Leafs as well as Jude Drouin from the Minnesota North Stars and Bill White of the Chicago Black Hawks. Bernie signed a contract right away.

A few NHL players with some marquee value made the early jump to the WHA. Gerry Cheevers was chosen by the New England Whalers, and when the Bruins wouldn't budge on his contract demands, he signed with the new league for $1.4 million over seven years, a $10,000 interest-free loan and a free car rental each year as well as performance bonuses. His contract was sold to the Cleveland Crusaders in June 1972. J.C. Tremblay was selected by and signed with Los Angeles, but his contract was bought by Quebec. He earned $600,000 over five years, plus a $125,000 signing bonus.

But the WHA wasn't considered much of a threat to the NHL until Bobby Hull jumped. When he signed a 10-year, $1.75 million contract with the Winnipeg Jets, plus a million-dollar signing bonus, in June 1972, it opened every player's eyes to the possibilities of this rival league.

The WHA wasn't without its troubles. The Calgary Broncos folded within months, and their picks were transferred to a new franchise called the Cleveland Crusaders. The Dayton Aeros moved to Houston before the season began and the Edmonton Oilers changed their strategy, becoming the Alberta Oilers, with the intention of splitting home games between Edmonton and Calgary. Herb Martin's plan for the Miami Screaming Eagles began to fall apart when construction of the arena was halted. The league refused to accept Miami's $100,000 performance bond because of the lack of a rink, and while Martin proposed another site in upstate Florida until the Miami arena was completed, WHA president Gary Davidson notified Martin in April 1972 that his franchise agreement had been terminated and that the Screaming Eagles were no longer members of the WHA.

At a lawyers' convention in May 1972, a guy named Jim Cooper ran into a colleague who had just purchased the WHA's New York franchise. Cooper had an idea. He called a friend, Bernie Brown, who owned a trucking firm in New Jersey, to ask whether he'd be interested in investing in a professional hockey team. Brown was very interested, and the two decided to team up and buy the available Miami franchise, which was expected to sell for $4 million. Cooper arrived in Quebec City uninvited, and convinced the league executives and owners that he was prepared to buy the Miami franchise and move it, and the Screaming Eagles' draft picks, to Philadelphia.

I still didn't care in the slightest.

In an attempt to keep the WHA out of Atlanta and Long Island, the NHL quickly expanded to welcome the Atlanta Flames and New York Islanders for the 1972–73 season. An expansion draft was arranged, in which each of the 14 existing NHL teams could protect only 14 skaters and one goalkeeper. By that time, Teddy Green and Gerry Cheevers had jumped to the WHA. The Bruins decided to protect Eddie Johnston in goal, so we lost netminding prospect Dan Bouchard to Atlanta. Johnny McKenzie and Eddie Westfall weren't protected because Pie was 35 and Eddie was 32, and the Bruins didn't think that anybody would take these old guys. But both were in great shape and still had a few good years in them. The Bruins miscalculated.

I was playing golf when I heard that Boston had left McKenzie and Westfall unprotected. I picked up the phone and called Weston Adams Jr. in Montreal, where the draft was being held. "Westy, you can't lose Westfall." But Eddie was already gone, chosen by the Islanders. Pie wasn't chosen, but he jumped to the WHA, so we ended up losing them both. We had now lost a good chunk of our championship team. The Philadelphia Blazers grabbed Pie and made him the player-coach, which I thought was interesting because he had never coached a day in his life.

I never had any intention of going to the WHA. None. But McKenzie and I had been roommates, and he asked me to meet him at Daisy's. I had five or six beers in me by the time he showed up.

"Turk, I want you to talk to these guys in Philadelphia," he said. "They're good people. Just listen to the numbers."

I asked, "Is the league okay?"

"Not sure," he admitted. "There are court injunctions that the NHL is using to try to stop the WHA from starting, but don't worry about it. Everything is being worked out."

I asked Pie to have the Philadelphia owners meet me in my lawyer's office.

When they arrived, I was goofing around and had kicked my lawyer out from behind his desk because I wanted to sit in a comfortable chair. I'd also brought my partners in the bars, Joey Cimino and Jimmy McDonough, to the meeting. The Blazers' owners said, "Who are these guys?" I told them they were my partners and that we made all our decisions together.

The owners introduced themselves. "My name is Jim Cooper. I'm a lawyer and I own 50 percent of the franchise. This is Bernie Brown. He owns a very successful trucking company and he owns the other 50 percent of the team." Cooper guaranteed the franchise price, which was something like $125,000, and Brown guaranteed salaries, which was five or six million dollars. Two nicer guys you'd never want to meet. They admitted, "Derek, we don't know a lot about hockey, but this was a chance for us to own a sports franchise and have some fun, so let's do it." I could sense legitimate enthusiasm.

Cooper then stunned me. "I'm here to offer you $2,300,000."

I just sat there, speechless. That was more money than I knew what to do with. I paused and scratched my head. "That sounds great, and it's not the money that is making me balk at jumping at the opportunity, but when I first heard about you guys, weren't you the Miami Screaming Eagles?"

They explained that they had purchased the Miami franchise and moved it to Philadelphia.

"So, you're good? You've got a building? Because the National Hockey League is cast in stone. They're not going anywhere. They've solved their problems and they're not making up the rules as they go along."

Cooper said, "We're good. We're buckled in and ready to do business."

I didn't really want to go. "That's a lot of money, but let me explain my hesitancy. All of my friends are in Boston. Everybody on the Bruins is a friend.

I own four bars here, I do a lot of charity work in the community, and everywhere I go, people are great to me. I would really hate to lose that."

Without blinking an eye, Jim Cooper said, "Well, I'm authorized to go as high as $2,600,000." Within 15 seconds, he was offering me a $300,000 raise!

Quite the contrast with my dealings with Boston. After winning two Cups with the Bruins, I was holding out for $80,000. The Bruins wanted me at $75,000. When I met with Charlie Mulcahy, the team lawyer who handled negotiations, I told him, "Charlie, I'm not going to sign for $75,000. I want $80,000."

"Come on," he said. "You've got to sign it."

I said, "I don't have to do anything, Charlie. I don't have to do a bloody thing. Do you understand? Not a thing."

He said, "I get it, but let's get this over with so you can get in shape and go to camp." He added, "You'll never get $80,000."

I said, "That's fine. Then I'll go to the WHA." It was a total bluff, an out-and-out lie, and he didn't take it seriously, either. But now Jim Cooper had offered me $2.6 million, a million of which was in escrow. Philadelphia figured I was *the* guy to get. I was coming off a Stanley Cup championship, I was a pretty big name and I was available. According to sportswriters, I was one of the best two-way players in the game, provided strong defensive work, was good on faceoffs, could shut down the other team and could score a few goals. And I was colourful. I was a different sort of guy than the NHL was used to. And it's no surprise that I liked not being taken for granted. I thought it was pretty cool.

I realized just how eager Jim Cooper was to have me on his team, so I started to push the envelope. "Will you promise me that you'll never move the franchise again?"

Cooper said, "I promise that we will never move the franchise without your permission."

Wow. They wouldn't move the franchise without my permission? That was a pretty powerful statement. I said, "Put that in writing and initial it." He did.

"I know what you're going to do," I said. "You'll sell the team and the new owners will move it." He shook his head. "I promise we won't sell the team without your permission either."

I was stunned. That just did not happen in hockey. I insisted, "Write it into the contract and initial it." He did.

"I've got to be captain."

"That's not a problem," he smiled.

"I have to be on the power play."

"With the money you'll be making, you'll barely be off the ice!"

I thought everything was done. We agreed on every point and I was talking very positively about the future of the team, using lots of "we's" and "us's." He was happy and I was happy. Everything was good. Cooper added all the details to the contract and initialled each point. But I realized I could still ask for more.

"I want a driver and I want my girlfriend to have a driver to take her back and forth when I'm not around. And I want a two-bedroom suite on the road." I don't know why I asked for that, but when you had a roommate on the road, it really messed up your sex life.

"Jim, do you mind if I take the contract with me for a couple of days? I'll get back to you within five banking days." That gave me some time to figure out a couple of things. My partner, Joey Cimino, looked at me as if he wanted to strangle me. I imagined him saying, "Just sign it, Derek. Sign the fucking thing." But this was one of the smartest moves I ever made in my life. And it wasn't motivated by my being savvy; it was motivated by loyalty.

I got in my car and explained to Joey why I wanted five days. "I owe it to Mr. Adams." Weston Adams Sr., the owner of the Bruins, had known me since I was 14 years old. When no one else believed I had potential, he did. I loved the man and owed it to him, out of loyalty and respect, to talk to him about my future if my career with the Boston Bruins was in jeopardy.

My father always taught me to be loyal, and to be a man of my word, and I was, whether it was in hockey, in business or in my relationships. He had never been wrong before, so I followed his advice.

I heard that Mr. Adams was dying at the time. I drove to Marblehead, where he owned an incredible home. No player ever went to his house. That was considered irrational behaviour and a real taboo. Someone answered the door. "I'm here to see Mr. Adams." They called up to him and invited me in. Mr. Adams came to the door wearing a smoking jacket and asked me to join him in the library of his home.

I said, "Mr. Adams, I owe you this. You are responsible for me playing in the National Hockey League, but this is where the rubber meets the road. I would like you to read this contract." I handed him the deal the Blazers had prepared.

He put on his reading glasses and sat down. "It's true. It's really true."

He proceeded to go through the contract, page by page. Mr. Adams never, ever swore, but as he was turning the pages, he muttered, "Vandals, rogues, charlatans and thieves!" He said, "Sandy, look around you. Do you see all of the beautiful furniture in my home? Reading this contract makes me feel like they're hand-selecting the finest pieces and carting them away. There's something wrong in America when this can happen."

The WHA was a new league, and it was breaking all the existing rules in order to establish itself. Times were changing.

"Mr. Adams, I will do whatever you advise me to do."

"Well, then," he began. "If you're asking me as your friend, I have to tell you to sign this contract and take the money. It will ensure your family's security for life. But listen to me now, Sandy. One, demand the money up front and put it in escrow. And two, find a money manager, because you'll never understand this wealth. You are not bred to wealth, and you will rue the day that you took this money, Derek. The pressure will crush you. Money corrupts, you know. You're only 26 years old. This is so much money, and you can't comprehend its power. Do yourself a favour and don't ever consider yourself a millionaire—keep living at the $25,000-a-year level until you can grasp the magnitude of this contract."

I was surprised by his response. "Oh yeah? But what if I don't want to go?"

He said, "Am I understanding that you would consider turning down this offer in order to stay with the Boston Bruins?"

"Certainly," I replied. "The Bruins are the only friends I've got."

He said, "I truly admire your loyalty." After a pause, he added, "Under the circumstances, I think we can give you the $80,000 you are looking for."

I thought to myself, "Don't open your shirt or your heart will fall out!" But what I said out loud was, "That's decent of you." However, now that I had gone so far as to say that, I was having qualms about what I had done.

Mr. Adams asked me, "Will you sign with my son?" Weston Adams Jr. had taken over the team. I told him I would do that, but it gave me an opening.

"I do not want Charlie Mulcahy to get any credit for this," I said. "In fact, I don't want him in the room when I sign."

He said, "Sandy, I promise Charlie Mulcahy will not be in the building."

I thanked Mr. Adams for his time and he walked me to the door. After all of this, I had my $80,000. I was going to stay with the Boston Bruins, and the WHA be damned.

I went to Weston Jr.'s office. I had never been there before. His father had called him and summarized our conversation, so when I arrived, Westy was sitting behind his desk and he handed me a standard player's contract. I took the pen in my hand, but just before I signed, I looked up at him and said, "You know something? If people ever find out I turned down $2.6 million to play for $80,000, they're going to send me to Bridgewater!" Bridgewater was a state facility housing the criminally insane in Massachusetts.

While he was saying, "I really respect you for your loyalty," I was having serious second thoughts. All I could think was, "What the hell am I doing? All that money . . . vapour." I glanced up at Westy as I was about to put pen to paper and form the *D* in "Derek" when Charlie Mulcahy stuck his head in the door.

"I still think you're only worth 75," he said.

That was it. I took the pen and threw it at him. "Aw, Charlie! Why?"

Weston Jr. sputtered, "No, no! Derek! Wait a minute! Charlie, get out of here!"

I said, "Nope, it's too late, Weston. Your father promised me that Charlie Mulcahy would not be in the building." They breached the promise, lied, and I left. I walked out, and at that moment, I was no longer a Boston Bruin, so I had to go see Jim Cooper and give him my answer about joining the Philadelphia Blazers.

On the fifth day, as promised, I returned to see Cooper. I was terrified that he might have been angry and changed his mind, but I found him still eager.

"So, what happened?" he asked.

I told him that the Bruins had countered with a great offer.

"What do you mean? What did they do?"

I said, "Well, my dad is a good judge of hockey talent . . ."

Before I could even finish the sentence, Cooper blurted, "He can be a scout. Five years at $50,000."

Stunned, I said, "That's great!" But I didn't stop there. "The Blazers will be playing games in Los Angeles, Edmonton, Winnipeg, Houston. Plus, you have a team in the Eastern Hockey League, too. Where is it—Roanoke?"

Cooper nodded.

"My father hates flying, but if he could be allowed to station himself in St. Catharines and just watch the games from there—anybody from the Ontario junior league has to go through and he'd see all the guys."

Cooper agreed that that would be fine. And I couldn't resist pushing for one more concession.

"You know, I'm just as afraid to fly as my dad is."

He said, "Well, Derek, we would appreciate you getting to as many road games as you can by train."

"What?" I couldn't believe what I was hearing. "Does that mean I don't have to play road games if I don't want to?"

He responded, "Look, Derek, there are a lot of games you can get to."

I told him, "Okay, write those things into the contract and initial them," which he did. He was a great guy and a good lawyer, but I could tell he wasn't a hockey guy. He didn't understand the discipline that hockey players have to live under.

I was thinking, "Holy shit! I can do whatever I want." While he was writing those amendments into the contract, I said, "You know, Jim, the New York Cosmos just signed Pele for $2.6 million. Put another $50,000 in there and I'll be the highest-paid athlete in the world."

He lit up. "Yes! That'll be a good marketing angle! That'll get us headlines in magazines and newspapers!"

He gave me another $50,000.

My contract with the Philadelphia Blazers came down to $2.65 million spread over 10 years. I would get $300,000 for 1972–73 and 1973–74, $200,000 each year for the next five years after that and $250,000 a year for the final three seasons. In addition, I'd get $25,000 annually for doing public relations. And that final $50,000—a cash bonus.

The contract didn't require me to play for all 10 years, either. I certainly didn't plan to play that long. A clause stated that if I decided after five years that I no longer wanted to play, I'd become a scout at $100,000 a year for the remaining five years.

When I left, my lawyer also had them pay his fee, which he told me was 10 percent. He told me that they put $1 million in escrow and the rest was to be paid out according to discussions that would take place later.

Jim Cooper had been doing the negotiating, but he was giving me Bernie Brown's money.

Through this, I learned the golden rule about all negotiations. You win the negotiation if you're prepared to walk away. "Here's the number I want, boys. Before I reach the door, say yes or forget about it."

I was stunned. By agreeing to the Blazers' offer, I was now the highest-paid athlete in the world. But I was all alone. People say, "But you had all that money," but that was all I had.

CHAPTER 19

THE SUMMIT SERIES

While the fledgling World Hockey Association was preparing to launch, another monumental hockey event was about to unfold.

In 1972, for the first time ever, Canada's best hockey players were going to have the opportunity to face the best from the Soviet Union in a tournament. Never before had Canada's best players been allowed to compete against the best Soviet players. The Olympics, up to that time, only allowed amateurs to compete, so while Canada was sending senior teams or teams made up of university players, they were playing against Soviet players who were being paid to be in the military but, in fact, were playing hockey year-round. We called them "shamateurs." Canada had dropped out of international competition in 1970 because the country was denied the use of the nation's best players.

Alan Eagleson, the executive director of the National Hockey League Players' Association, was responsible for putting the tournament together in cooperation with Hockey Canada, a government agency. In April 1972, he announced that an eight-game tournament—four in Canada and four in the Soviet Union—would take place in September of that year, and would pit the best against the best.

After we won the Cup in 1970, Harry Sinden announced his retirement and wasn't afraid to tell anyone who asked that he'd left the Bruins because they had refused to give him a raise for the following season. The housing company he'd gone to work for, Stirling-Homex, had gone bankrupt in 1972, and Harry made it known he would like to return to hockey. In June, Eagleson hired him to be the coach and general manager of Team Canada in the tournament that would come to be known as the Summit Series. Harry suggested John Ferguson as a playing coach, but Fergie had been out of hockey for a year and said that there was no way he'd play. He took on the role of assistant coach.

Harry and I had remained friends, and when we discussed this series, he told me, prophetically, "Everybody thinks that these Russians can't play, Derek. I've been away from the game for a couple of years, but I know that they're mistaken. These guys can play, and if they think this is going to be a walk in the park, then they've got another think coming. We can only beat them with guys who really know how to play both ends of the rink. Their one weakness is that they are robots, and puck control is their game. We need checkers, hitters, guys who can kill penalties and who know how to work."

Harry was worried that Eagleson and the Canadian media were going to predict that Canada would blow out the Soviets. Harry told Eagleson that the Soviets could all play because they had learned the game from studying Lloyd Percival's *Hockey Handbook*. Anatoli Tarasov, the Soviet coach, had told Percival in a letter, "Your wonderful book introduced us to the mysteries of Canadian hockey. I have read it like a schoolboy."

He asked me to come to Rochester so we could discuss the roster. Harry admitted that he'd been out of the game long enough not to have a handle anymore on who the best checking wingers in the game were. I said, "Well, Jean-Paul Parise, for one. You've got to have him. And Bill Goldsworthy, too." Goldie had played with us in Boston, and Harry knew his game. I also suggested Ronnie Ellis, Claude Larose and Rosaire Paiement. They were guys who knew how to play.

Eagleson, Harry and Fergie compiled a list of 35 players they would invite to camp in Toronto for Team Canada. On July 12, they announced their roster. In goal, they had Gerry Cheevers, Ken Dryden and Tony Esposito. On defence, they selected Don Awrey, Gary Bergman, Jocelyn Guevremont, Jacques Laperriere, Guy Lapointe, Bobby Orr, Brad Park, Serge Savard, Rod Seiling, Pat Stapleton, J.C. Tremblay and Bill White. The players chosen at forward were Red Berenson, Wayne Cashman, Bobby Clarke, Yvan Cournoyer, Marcel Dionne, Ron Ellis, Phil Esposito, Rod Gilbert, Bill Goldsworthy, Vic

Hadfield, Paul Henderson, Bobby Hull, Dennis Hull, Frank Mahovlich, Pete Mahovlich, Richard Martin, Jean-Paul Parise, Jean Ratelle, Mickey Redmond and me. Even though Weston Adams Jr. was dubious about the series because he was afraid one of the Bruins might get injured, I was excited to be included. Being selected by Harry Sinden for Team Canada was probably the greatest honour of my life to that point.

From the outset, Clarence Campbell ruled that no NHL players would be permitted to play in the tournament. That summer, Eagleson, with help from Bill Wirtz, the owner of the Chicago Black Hawks, finally convinced Campbell that NHL players could compete in the series, but only if they had a signed contract with their NHL team. And at the same time, the NHL was getting into a long, protracted battle with the World Hockey Association, which was just then starting to take runs at signing NHL players. To protect the NHL and to strike back at the WHA, Campbell insisted that only NHL players would be permitted to play in the series. This ruling eliminated Bobby Hull, who had already signed with the Winnipeg Jets. That stunning declaration aroused public ire. Harold Ballard, the owner of the Toronto Maple Leafs, responded, "I don't give a damn if Hull signed with a team in China. He's a Canadian and should be on the Canadian team!" No less a figure than Pierre Trudeau, the prime minister of Canada, made an impassioned personal appeal to have Hull play for Team Canada. "You are aware of the intense concern, which I share with millions of Canadians in all parts of our country, that Canada should be represented by its best hockey players, including Bobby Hull, in the forthcoming series with the Soviet Union."

It was to no avail. Campbell ruled that the WHA had not entered into a relationship with Hockey Canada, which arranged all international games for Canada. Because the NHL had an existing agreement with the CAHA, only players who had signed a standard NHL contract would be able to participate in the series.

What bullshit.

Campbell and the NHL strong-armed the WHA, and everyone knew it. After I signed with the Philadelphia Blazers, I was advised that I would no longer be part of Team Canada. Nobody who had defected to the WHA was allowed to play. But instead of coming right out and stating that, they said that players participating on Team Canada had to have signed a standard NHL contract by the time of the series. Of course, because I had signed with the WHA, I hadn't signed an NHL contract, so I was not allowed to join the team.

This ruling eventually eliminated me, Gerry Cheevers, J.C. Tremblay and Hull. Imagine adding those players to that Summit Series lineup. Eagleson later said that the four of us, and a healthy Bobby Orr, who had undergone knee surgery in June, would have made a big difference, but Canada won the series, so I guess they did okay.

Replacing us were Ed Johnston of the Bruins in goal, Brian Glennie from the Leafs on defence, and forwards Stan Mikita of the Hawks and Dale Tallon of the Canucks. Jacques Laperriere had to decline the original invitation due to the health of his pregnant wife.

The Summit Series took place in September 1972, and as Harry predicted, the Soviets were much better than most hockey fans in North America anticipated. Team Canada did pull out the victory, with a goal by Paul Henderson late in the eighth and final game of the series. Immediately after the series, Harry Sinden returned to the Bruins. On October 5, he signed a five-year deal to become the team's general manager, just the fifth in franchise history, succeeding Milt Schmidt, who was promoted to executive director of the team.

I happened to be in Toronto, waiting on a connecting flight to Ottawa for my first exhibition contest with the Philadelphia Blazers, when Team Canada arrived after winning the greatest hockey series ever played. Thousands of well-wishers greeted them at the airport. I was anonymous as the team was welcomed home as champions. I said to myself, "I should have been there." Here I was, heading off to a meaningless game against the Ottawa Nationals when my countrymen were returning from the Soviet Union.

I boarded the flight, but with each passing minute of my trip to Ottawa, I regretted my decision more. I could sense my past getting further and further away. I knew I belonged on that team being celebrated at home. I knew I had made a mistake.

CHAPTER 20

THE RESERVE CLAUSE BATTLE

On August 3, 1972, the Philadelphia Blazers announced my signing at a media conference in the Bellevue-Stratford Hotel, a heritage hotel built in 1904 at the corner of Broad and Walnut. I wore a charcoal-grey pinstriped suit to the signing. After the obligatory photo opportunity of me signing the contract, I was whisked away in a police cruiser to John F. Kennedy Plaza, where thousands of fans were waiting. Four detectives stood behind me as I was welcomed by Philadelphia's commerce director, Harry Belinger, acting on behalf of Mayor Frank Rizzo. I was presented with a symbolic Liberty Bell as a welcoming gift to Philadelphia.

With my new million-dollar smile, I approached the podium to say a few words. "This really is a great opportunity being bestowed on me and my family." Afterwards, I signed autographs for a couple of hours, stopping regularly for television interviews.

Jim Cooper, the co-owner of the team, told anybody who would listen that there were only three players who could fill a hockey rink—Bobby Hull, Bobby Orr and me—and expressed how excited he was to have me join the team. The Blazers' marketing campaign was "Derek is Here!" A little premature, but marketing is marketing. My lawyer told the press, "Philadelphia is starving for a hero, and Derek is just the kind of person who can shake up a city like Philadelphia." I went back to Boston for a few days and we held another press conference at Zelda's.

The birth of the Blazers was a big deal for the city, but they still had the Flyers. They were building an impressive roster, one fashioned after the Bruins of the early 1970s that would become the Broad Street Bullies. The Flyers owned that town. It wasn't going to be easy. And I was going to be a big fish in a small pond rather than a small fish in a big pond that I had been sharing with guys like Bobby Orr and Phil Esposito.

It was peculiar to have money all of a sudden. One day, I was in a cab on my way to a movie. As we passed Keenan Motors, a Rolls-Royce dealership, I ordered the cabbie to stop and threw him a twenty. The fare wasn't very much, but at that point, I didn't care.

I was wearing jeans and a sweatshirt, jean jacket and cowboy boots and had long hair past my shoulders when I walked into the Rolls-Royce dealership. The salesman, who was sporting a three-piece suit with a watch fob and brogues that had been spit-polished to a glistening sheen, assumed that I was looking for a job as a mechanic. "Maintenance is around the back," he said.

"No, no," I said. "I'm not here for a job. What's the best car you've got?"

In his clipped British accent, the salesman said, "It is that one right over there, sir," and pointed to a Rolls-Royce Phantom. The exterior was burgundy, my favourite colour, and it had a beige interior. It cost $78,000—the equivalent of more than $400,000 today—and the thing would have cost me $4,000 a year to insure. And I still had my Lincoln Continental.

I walked over to the Rolls, looked at it, and tried to open the driver's door, but it was locked. The salesman never budged from his seat. He was a pompous ass. I played the game. "Hey, it's locked!"

I could feel him roll his eyes. He got up and sauntered over towards me.

"Well, sir. They are always locked."

I said, "Why would that be?"

He replied, "Well, sir, one traditionally orders a Rolls-Royce by phone."

"Wow," I said, shaking my head. "Attitude goes that far, huh?"

"Excuse me?"

I let it slide. He begrudgingly opened the car door and I thought to myself,

"You insulted me, so I'll give it right back to you." I said, "You know, for $78,000, it's not very comfortable."

"You don't say," he yawned. "Perhaps if you were standing where I am, you would notice the long wheelbase of this Phantom limousine. And I do believe if you purchased it, sir, you would be sitting in the back."

I said, "Yeah. I guess so." I sat in the back. It had a rollout tray, phone and everything. "Holy shit! This is pretty nice."

He said, "Yes, that is the accepted view, sir."

Now I wanted to kill him. I got out and walked around the car.

"What does she get to the gallon?"

"Pardon me, sir?"

"What's she get to the gallon? What's the mileage?"

"Oh dear," he muttered. "I'm without reply. I don't believe anyone has ever checked the mileage of a Rolls-Royce." After a brief pause, he tagged his reply with, "Does the expression 'penny wise, pound foolish' come to mind?"

That was it. I had had it with this jerk. "Who's the owner here? Is there a Mr. Keenan here?"

A man walked over to me and introduced himself as the owner.

"See that car right there?" I pointed at the Phantom I had been looking at. "Mine! Five o'clock today. Cash on the barrelhead. I'm not going to dicker on price, but I don't want this ass to get the commission."

"Done," Keenan said.

At that point, I didn't know if the money the Blazers were paying me was real. I nervously called the Bank of Boston, but was relieved (and excited) that all the funds were there. I went back to the dealership at five o'clock. The salesman was standing there, and I brushed right past him. I signed the deal and was handed the keys. Before I left, I went over to the salesman and gave him some sage advice. "Next time a young person comes in here and tells you they want to look at a car, you should really pay them a little bit more regard, because they just may have the money."

I flipped him the bird. He looked at me and went away.

I climbed behind the wheel of my beautiful new car, started it up and headed for home, but six blocks from the dealership, I ran out of gas. The bastard never filled the tank.

One of my pals, George Survillo, was the doorman at Daisy's. "Turk, you need a chauffeur for your Rolls."

"You interested?" I asked.

"Sure thing!"

The problem was that I didn't like other people driving when I was in the car. Most days, I ended up driving while George sat in the back.

People think that the money made my head spin. It didn't. I was really alone for the first time in my life. I had no friends in Philadelphia and no serious relationship. I looked at buying a seven-bedroom Tudor mansion, all done in stone, in Merion, northwest of the city. Each bedroom had its own fireplace. There were tennis courts and a pool, all on an acre of property. I had intended to live there on my own, but certainly could have envisioned having a chef and a maid.

Another place I investigated was the Edgar Allan Poe estate. Poe lived in Philadelphia from 1838 to 1844 because Philly was the centre of the literary world at the time. The place was glorious, and monstrous. The real estate agent took me around. I walked around the house, but never found all the rooms. The place even had its own gas pump on the property. That really intrigued me.

I looked at a place in Chestnut Hill, just outside Boston. It had 28 rooms, including 14 bedrooms, 17 fireplaces, a swimming pool, tennis courts, a greenhouse and a stable. But instead of buying, I ended up renting at the Latham Hotel. It was great to have room service.

We had our deal, but there were still complications between the World Hockey Association and the National Hockey League that jeopardized the start of the new league. The NHL tried to do everything in its considerable power to stifle and kill the WHA. The NHL hadn't intended to expand in 1972, but when word circulated that the WHA planned to put a franchise on Long Island, playing out of the newly built Nassau Veterans Memorial Coliseum, they quickly granted a franchise, the New York Islanders—and, to balance the schedule, another in Atlanta, to be called the Flames.

The WHA threw money at established NHL stars in order to establish credibility for the league and attract interest at the gate. The NHL tried to block the WHA from purging its ranks, but between July and October 1972, sixty-seven players had signed with the new league from either the NHL or teams affiliated with the NHL. Money talked, and it talked quite loudly.

The average salary in the NHL in 1972 was $25,000. That was lower than the average in Major League Baseball, the National Football League and the National Basketball Association. The arrival of the National Hockey League Players' Association in 1967 had helped remove the shackles of indentured servitude from hockey players, but salaries still were not where they should have been. The WHA knew that the only way it could compete on a par with the NHL was by promising much higher salaries.

In its bid to fend off the threat of the WHA, the NHL turned to the courts to block players from defecting. Although the Bruins let Teddy Green go to the New England Whalers without a fight, and left Johnny McKenzie unprotected in the intra-league draft because they knew he had signed with the Blazers as playing coach, they tried to stop Gerry Cheevers and me from jumping leagues. Candidly, they were most worried about stopping Bobby Orr from joining the Minnesota Fighting Saints. The Philadelphia Flyers claimed Pie in the draft, then went to Common Pleas Court in Philadelphia to try to bar him from playing with the Blazers. McKenzie claimed he would retire if the courts ruled against him. In Chicago, the Black Hawks got an injunction to keep Bobby Hull from joining the Jets.

In retaliation for players jumping to the WHA, the NHL tried to enforce its reserve clause, which had existed in player contracts since the league's creation in 1917. The clause meant that, when a player's contract expired, the team he played for retained his playing rights—even though the player had fulfilled his obligation to play for the team, he was not free to enter into a pact with any other team. He either negotiated a new contract to play with the same team, or requested to be traded or released.

Indentured servitude is what it was.

The reserve clause was the basis for the injunctions that NHL teams were seeking in order to prevent players from going to the WHA. The WHA wanted to mount a legal challenge against the reserve clause—to test its validity and, hopefully, have it stricken down as illegal. Jim Cooper came to me and asked for my help. My initial reaction was, "They'll bury me!" But I agreed to help in whatever way I could, and knew I could turn to Sonny McDonough, my partner Jimmy's father. I went to Sonny's office in Second Cliff, southeast of Boston. He greeted me by saying, "Jimmy tells me you're going to be making a ton of money leaving us."

I said, "It was an opportunity to set up my parents for their golden years, sir."

"You're a good boy, Derek." Then he asked, "So, what's the problem?"

I said, "It looks like the courts are holding up the World Hockey Association, which is where I'm contracted." I described in as much detail as I could what the reserve clause was and how it prohibited players from entering into another contract with any other team for a year. "If we can't get that changed, then the WHA contracts are null and void and guys like Bobby Hull, Gerry Cheevers and me will have to put our tails between our legs and go back to play for our NHL teams."

Sonny McDonough told me, "Have those brilliant lawyers change the venue from Philadelphia to Suffolk County, here in Boston."

On August 11, 1972, attorneys sought, and received, permission to transfer the suits to the United States District Court in Boston. We were aware that just about anything could happen. The NHL and its teams made it well known that they would sue players who jumped to the WHA, seeking injunctions and claiming breach of contract. I knew that I might be ordered back to the Bruins for a year, or might even have to sit out for a season. But that was a team problem, and I was protected financially against such eventualities.

I gave my deposition on September 6 in the law offices of Goodwin, Procter and Hoar in Boston. Also present were Milt Schmidt and lawyers for

I loved to wind up the sportswriters and tell them that I had a closet full of suits, jackets, shirts and shoes. I actually had only a couple of suits, a couple of jackets and two pairs of shoes, but I was creating a persona that later almost ate me up. Here, I'm doctoring my sticks for the game, dressed in my typical attire of the time.

AL RUELLE/AUTHOR'S COLLECTION

In my first few seasons in Boston, I spent summers in Niagara Falls with my mom and dad and was often asked to participate in civic events. Here, I'm assisting Miss Niagara Hospitality, Beryl Bird, at the start of the 1968 Greater Niagara Softball Association's season.

NIAGARA FALLS (ONTARIO) PUBLIC LIBRARY

Through my lawyer, I met Ken Harrelson (*right*), who had been a star ballplayer with the Boston Red Sox. The Hawk knew how to dress, and I learned a lot from his style.

JOHN FORRISTALL

After I partnered with Joe Namath in Bachelors III, Joey Cimino, Jimmy McDonough and I decided to open our own place. In September 1970, we opened Daisy Buchanan's. When the Bruins were at home, I spent most of my time between games at Daisy's.

NANCY NIKLAS

Our team was very close, and any time we competed, we expected to win. But as hard as we played on the ice, we played equally hard off the ice. Here I am with pals Bobby Orr (*left*) and Wayne Cashman (*right*), during the 1968–69 season.　　BETTMANN/CORBIS

The Bruins all bought in to the principle that no player was ever alone on the ice. If one of our guys got jumped, the closest Bruin was to immediately step in to help. Here, I'm tangling with Dickie Duff of the Canadiens with all three officials intervening.
BETTMANN/CORBIS

From the time I started learning the game, my dad emphasized the importance of winning a faceoff. Today, a centre who wins 60 percent of his faceoffs is considered amazing. I came close to 90 percent during my career.

Bobby Orr (*second from the right*) and Eddie Westfall (*far right*) celebrate one of Orr's
goals, along with Wayne Carleton (*second from the left*) and me.

On May 10, 1970, my overtime pass to Bobby Orr from behind the St. Louis Blues' net gave the Boston Bruins their first Stanley Cup championship since 1941.

FRED KEENAN/HOCKEY HALL OF FAME

Forty years after that momentous occasion, the City of Boston unveiled a commemorative statue called *The Goal* at the TD Garden.

NANCY NIKLAS

It's every kid's dream to win the Stanley Cup, and on Mother's Day in 1970, a team of men became boys all over again as the Boston Bruins realized that dream. Bobby Orr (*left*) and I are doused with champagne as we try to complete an interview.

BETTMANN/CORBIS

My name engraved on the Stanley Cup from 1970. My dad called it "a passport to immortality."

DAVE SANDFORD/
HOCKEY HALL OF FAME

BOSTON BRUINS 1969-70

WESTON W ADAMS SR CHAIRMAN
WESTON W ADAMS JR PRESIDENT
CHARLES W MULCAHY VP   E J POWERS VP
SHELBY MC DAVIS VP   DON AWREY   JOHN BUCYK
G BAILEY   W CARLETON   W CASHMAN   G DOAK
P ESPOSITO   TED GREEN   K HODGE   BOBBY ORR
D MARCOTTE   J MC KENZIE   D SANDERSON
D SMITH   R SMITH   B SPEER   F STANFIELD
E WESTFALL   G CHEEVERS   E JOHNSTON   J ADAMS
J LORENTZ   R MURPHY   B LESUK   I BOLDIREV
D SCHOCK   H SINDEN COACH   M SCHMIDT   GEM
T JOHNSON TR   D CANNEY TR   J FORRISTALL ASS TR

In 1971, I was asked to appear in a film called *Face-Off* (known as *Winter Comes Early* in the U.S.). The film starred Art Hindle (*right*) as Billy Duke. I made a cameo appearance along with George Armstrong, Paul Henderson and Jacques Plante.

COURTESY VIDEO SERVICES CORP.

Hockey was always a serious business for me—at least, on the ice. Off the ice, I liked to have fun with those around the rink. Here, I'm trying on an usher's hat at Maple Leaf Gardens in Toronto.

ART RICKERBY/TIME & LIFE PICTURES/ GETTY IMAGES

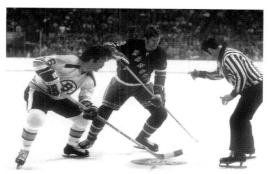

Harry Sinden regarded me as his shutdown centre, facing the opposing team's top centremen, like classy Jean Ratelle of the Rangers. My line also served as the Bruins' key penalty-killing trio.

AL RUELLE/COURTESY OF JAY MORAN

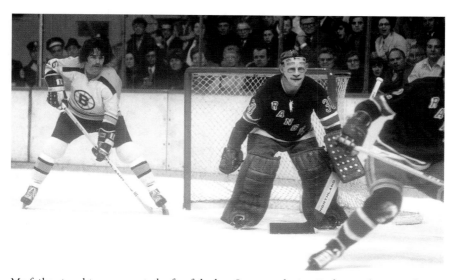

My father taught me never to be fearful when I was on the ice. I often took a pounding in front of an opponent's net, but I never shied away from going there. Here, I stand on the lip of the Rangers' crease beside Gilles Villemure.　　AL RUELLE/COURTESY OF JAY MORAN

There was no love lost between me and Ron Stewart. We were teammates in Boston, and then he was my coach with the Rangers. I bet he wondered if I would land on him skates first during this action.

The Bruins should have won three Stanley Cup championships in a row but lost to the Habs in 1971. We were hard to beat, though. We could skate, we could score and we were tough. Left to right, Phil Esposito, Ed Westfall, Don Marcotte and I cram into the penalty box.

the Boston Bruins, as well as lawyers for Gerry Cheevers and the Philadelphia Blazers, and the lawyer hired to represent me, Roger Stokey. I was questioned by representatives of Ely, Bartlett, Brown and Proctor, the law firm representing the Bruins.

On September 29, Andrew Caffrey, the chief judge of the U.S. District Court in Boston, denied the Bruins' motion for a preliminary injunction against Cheevers and me. "In the course of the balancing process, the defendants would suffer a much more serious hardship if the injunction was granted than the Bruins would suffer by the denial of the injunctive relief." He added that professional hockey was a leading candidate for an antitrust ruling.

Gary Davidson, the president of the WHA, planned an antitrust suit against the NHL, which would include seeking damages of $1 million for each of the 12 WHA teams. He stated, "We [the WHA] had hoped to avoid litigation. Since the NHL has filed suits seeking to enforce the invalid reserve clause, the WHA has elected not only to take its case to the public, but also the federal courts." The WHA's stance was that NHL expansion, specifically to Long Island, prevented the WHA from gaining access to that market, that the NHL used the reserve clause to monopolize hockey, and that it was unfair to prevent players who had jumped to the WHA from competing for Team Canada at the Summit Series against the Soviet Union that September. Sixteen lawyers from the Washington law firm of Covington & Burling presented 2,500 pages of testimony and briefs.

On November 8, Judge A. Leon Higginbotham of the U.S. District Court in Philadelphia handed down a landmark ruling. His judgment, which ran 124 pages, issued a temporary order that barred the NHL from using the reserve clause to block players from joining their WHA teams.

Judge Higginbotham ruled that the reserve clause was "the result of a common agreement, mutual understanding and conspiracy by the NHL and its affiliate minor league to maintain a monopolistic position so strong that the NHL precludes effective competition by the entry of another major professional hockey league."

He stated that prohibiting players from playing for their WHA teams would signal the death of the World Hockey Association, and added, "The record is devoid of any evidence implying, much less demonstrating, that the reserve clause has been retained as the result of serious, good faith, collective bargaining."

Judge Higginbotham didn't mince his words. He chastised the NHL for being "primarily a multi-state bi-national business where the fundamental motive was money. Despite the thousands of words uttered on this record by all parties about the glory of the sport of hockey and the grandeur of its superstars, the basic factors here are not the sheer exhilaration from observing the speeding puck but rather the desire to maximize the available buck."

In short, Judge Higginbotham's ruling announced that the days of slavery in hockey had come to an end. It was a clear and decisive victory for the WHA and for all players. It wasn't until February 19, 1974, that the two leagues finally reached an out-of-court settlement in the $50 million court case. The settlement eliminated the reserve clause and also stipulated that the NHL had to reimburse the WHA for its legal expenses, which came to $1.7 million.

Every player in the National Hockey League today should give me 1 percent of his salary for my role in getting the reserve clause eliminated from hockey, but no one knows.

CHAPTER 21

PHILADELPHIA BLAZERS

The Blazers initially tried to secure the Spectrum for home games, but it was owned by the Flyers, who were not about to share their arena with a competing league and team. Instead, we were forced to play our home games in the 9,000-seat Civic Center, which opened in 1930. When the Spectrum was built for the Flyers in 1967, the Civic Center had become virtually obsolete.

Even though we had the most hideous sweaters known to man—orange, white, red and yellow—we had a very good team in Philadelphia. It was probably the pick of the litter in the WHA that year. Bernie Parent was the best goaltender in the league and was already a fan favourite in Philadelphia from his four seasons with the Flyers. Our backup goalie was Marcel Paille, who was a really capable veteran with lots of NHL experience, although his last games in the NHL had been with the Rangers in the mid-sixties. He was one of the guys who fought with Eddie Shore on the Springfield Indians of the American Hockey League.

Johnny McKenzie was one of the toughest guys I knew, and we were good friends from playing together with the Bruins. Andre Lacroix had also played with the Flyers, and was a good scorer. Bryan Campbell was a veteran NHL player who came to us from the Black Hawks. Danny Lawson was a great skating winger with NHL experience. I knew Ron Plumb from the Bruins organization and thought he was really good. We had a handful of solid players and a bunch of kids with determination and promise.

My dad was the Ontario scout for the Blazers, and he brought my longtime friend Tommy Cottringer to the team. Tommy was a tremendous goalie when we played together as kids—better than guys I later played with in junior, like Bernie Parent and Doug Favell. Tommy could have turned pro with anybody. When he was about 14, his father died and he quit school, which derailed him a bit.

Tommy had been playing Senior B hockey in Niagara Falls when the Blazers signed him. I was happy that Tommy was finally getting his shot. It was tough, because Bernie and Marcel were no slouches in net, and they had this kid Yves Archambault in the wings, too, but Tommy got into two games for the Blazers that November. He looked good, winning one and losing one, both by a goal.

Incidentally, my dad also scouted Ian Turnbull and put him on the Blazers' radar. In 1973, both the Toronto Maple Leafs and the Blazers, who had moved to Vancouver, drafted him, but he chose to go to Toronto.

In addition to playing, McKenzie was our coach; the GM was a former NHL player named Dave Creighton, who had coached Providence in the AHL before the Blazers hired him. The director of player personnel was another former NHL player and coach. Phil Watson had played in the 1930s and '40s, and had coached for many years.

Philadelphia's amateur camp took place in early September in Roanoke, Virginia, home of the Roanoke Valley Rebels, their Eastern Hockey League affiliate. Then, the best of the amateurs joined us on October 1 in Sherbrooke, Quebec, for the Blazers' training camp. The Blazers were careful to make certain that those of us who had been under NHL contracts didn't report to training camp until October 1, which was when our NHL contracts concluded. Bernie Parent was being pursued by the Leafs, who offered to increase his salary if he returned to Toronto, but he decided to stay with us after all.

During our first exhibition game, a contest against the Nordiques in Quebec City, Pie crashed into a goalpost and broke his arm. Johnny wasn't there for practice the next day, so I was left in charge, along with a fly-by-night scout from Junior B. I was inclined to give everybody the day off, but figured I had better do the right thing. I got everybody out onto the ice and we set up drills. Then, this guy jumped over the boards in his white dress shoes and introduced himself to me as the acting coach. It was Phil Watson.

We played one exhibition game where I swear there were only 58 people in the stands, and 45 of them got in free because one of our players came from there. Bernie Parent looked at me and said, "Where are the fans, Turk?"

I replied, "Maybe they're just fashionably late."

Bernie disappeared into the dressing room. I went in after him and he was taking off his equipment! He said, "I don't risk my life in goal when there are no people in the stands." He talked me out of playing, too.

The World Hockey Association debuted on Wednesday, October 11, 1972, with the Alberta Oilers dumping the Ottawa Nationals 7–4 at the Ottawa Civic Centre. The next night, I returned to Boston Garden, as the Philadelphia Blazers played our first regular-season game on the road against the New England Whalers. The press made a big deal about the opening faceoff, as it was two former Bruins—Teddy Green, captain of the Whalers, and me, captain of the Blazers—facing off against each other in our former home. I scored the first goal in Philadelphia Blazers history at 6:52 of the first period against Al Smith. We ended up losing our first game 4–3.

Because there had been so much turmoil through the summer, and I hadn't been able to join training camp until October 1, I was out of shape—probably 20 pounds over my playing weight. The reporters were there to talk to me after that first game, and I had to admit that I couldn't remember having played a tougher game. I was soaking wet. Between the second and third periods, I had taken a shower.

Our home opener was set to take place on Friday, October 13, against the Whalers. There was an unbelievable traffic jam. People were late arriving, so officials delayed the game so that we could fill the stands.

You have to remember that the Civic Center was a joke. The elevator could only take four or five players at a time down from the dressing room. You either had to wait for this hydraulic elevator to return so more players could ride down, or you had to walk down three flights of stairs with your skates on.

The refrigeration piping ended about four inches away from the boards, and so there was this black slush all around the edge of the rink. We were losing pucks in the warmup. Not only that, but they had built the ice over sawdust. It created a crust, because when the wet sawdust slipped below the pipes, the top was a frozen shell with a hollow gap underneath. You could hear the echo when you skated over it. The ice had only been put in three days before our first game. It was extremely hard and chipped off in large chunks.

The referee, Bill Friday, was skating around during the warmup. I skated over to him. "Bill, are you going to pull the plug on this game? Look at the gap all along the boards."

He said, "Derek, we've got 6,000 fans looking forward to this game. We can't cancel."

I said, "Bill, then you've got to tell them to shovel snow into the corner and pat it down. Some guy is going to break a leg!"

Officials used watering cans and fire extinguishers to try to repair the ice while we finished warmup. I was heading back to the dressing room when the Zamboni, which had arrived from Wisconsin just that afternoon due to a manufacturer's delay, drove out onto the ice. I heard a crash and went back out. The Zamboni had broken through the ice and was spinning its wheels. The ice was all carved up, and there was smoke coming from the Zamboni.

I went over to Friday and said, "Maybe that's now sufficient to call the game?"

Nobody really knew what to do.

Now, there was also another lesson learned: never hand out souvenirs that can become projectiles before the game. The thousands of fans who were there to witness history had each been handed an orange Philadelphia Blazers souvenir puck.

Frank Rizzo, the mayor of Philadelphia, was there. He was a tough guy who had risen through the ranks from police officer to police commissioner and been elected mayor of Philadelphia in January 1972. He warned me, "Let me teach you something about politics in this town. This is not the time or the place to be magnanimous. Get out of here. This is a no-win situation." He ducked out underneath the stands and disappeared.

The crowd was getting restless. Bryan Campbell turned to me and said,

"This is one of those times where I sure as shit am glad I'm not the captain. You better get out there and say something, Turk."

I was stunned. "Soupy, I quit school because of public speaking. I can't talk to six people, let alone 6,000!"

He said, "You've got to, Turk. Just say sorry." He gave me a couple of things to say.

I figured that I had to do it, so I walked out onto the red carpet and took the microphone in my hands. "Ladies and gentleman, I'm Derek Sanderson, captain of the Philadelphia Blazers." *Ping!* The first puck banged off the glass. It missed me by about a yard. The second one was closer—missed me by about four inches. Then they started coming from behind me, so I backed up to the glass. The pucks were being tossed, bouncing off the glass. Some weren't even making the ice surface and were hitting people in the first few rows. I was blocking the pucks as they started to rain down, but I couldn't block them all.

While I dodged the orange pucks, I said, "I'd like to apologize on behalf of the team." I got hit with a puck and figured, to hell with that. "Don't give up on us because of this! We need your support after they get this ice fixed. I hope you can get out of the building—the parking situation isn't great. Remember that there was only one entrance to the parking lot when you came in? Well, there's only one exit going out. Goodbye!"

I was getting out of there, but the guy would not come to the end of the rink to let me out. The pucks were bouncing off the glass and I was getting dinged on the back and the leg. I was hunched over, protecting myself, yelling, "Open the goddamned door!"

The guy said, "No! The pucks will hit me!"

There were fights everywhere. We hid in our dressing room until one in the morning. Complete debacle. And it was Friday the 13th, too.

Jim Cooper, the owner, thanked me for going out there. He said, "It took a lot of courage to do something like that."

I laughed. "It's the first noble thing I've ever done."

We got a lot more publicity out of that than if we had played the game. You couldn't blame the fans for being upset.

Johnny McKenzie said, "I'm sure the fans realize that this wasn't a planned situation. It's a tough blow for the owners, but at least I didn't lose my home debut!"

"This is a major, major disappointment," stated the team's co-owner, Jim Cooper. "We're going to do everything in our power to rectify the situation. If we were able to put together this club in three and a half months, we'll be able to put down ice in five days."

Our next home game was scheduled for the 17th against Quebec. Joe Scott, one of the founding partners of the Philadelphia Flyers, offered the use of the Spectrum for the Blazers' next few home games, but Jim Cooper declined the offer. That Nordiques game was postponed.

We lost 5–0 to the New York Raiders at Madison Square Garden on October 15. Bernie Parent played the first two periods but was lit up for four goals, so they put in Marcel Paille for the third. In our third game, the Los Angeles Sharks doubled us 4–2. I got into a scrap in the second, and then late in the third, I was tagged with a misconduct and game misconduct. I picked up two minors and a misconduct in our fourth game, a loss to the Alberta Oilers.

Our next two games were against the Jets in Winnipeg. Before the first of the contests, Bobby Hull took me aside and gave me a pep talk. He stressed how important it was for me to play well and help sell the league. "Derek, we've really got to work hard on this. You've got to put a show on. Don't take your money and run."

I said, "I'll put on a show, but I'm not showing off. I'm out to win. If it's entertaining in between, fine."

Bobby Hull was everything the Blazers hoped I would be. The real problem was that the Blazers had identified me as both a goal scorer and a fighter, and while I could do both, I wasn't going to score 50 goals like Hull and I wasn't like some of the animals who made a living fighting and racking up 250 penalty minutes in a season. I was just one of the guys.

We had a lot of fun together. We all liked to party—I don't know many 26-year-old guys who don't, especially during those years. We laughed a lot, told stories and made the best of the situation. For fun, I'd load a bunch of the guys into my Rolls and we'd go to McDonald's. My car was filled with empty fast food wrappers.

I wasn't shy about spending my money. Because I was captain and we played the first six games on the road, we went out for dinner as a team and I picked up the cheque. A few of the guys thought I was showing off. I wasn't. I was simply trying to be a good teammate.

Some of the guys resented the money I was getting. Between periods, they'd make me get them Cokes and oranges and stuff. Soupy Campbell demanded, "Turk, unlace my skates." I did, but only to loosen up the guys in the room.

My supposed image—the freewheeling playboy—had been carefully cultivated, and it was one of the reasons Philadelphia signed me. I didn't do anything to dispel the image. I played the game and the media ate it up. I told them my idol was Bo Belinsky, a baseball pitcher who had been linked romantically to beautiful actresses including Ann-Margret, Mamie Van Doren and Tina Louise from *Gilligan's Island*. He later married a *Playboy* centrefold named Jo Collins. Ironically, he too later became an alcoholic. Belinsky used a line that I'd steal, telling the reporters he'd play for nothing if they lined up the 10 best-looking broads in town for him.

The playboy image really bothered my mother. She knew that the private Derek wasn't anything at all like the public facade I had helped create. She used to tell me to meet a nice girl, get married and have some kids. She warned me that my image was going to catch up with me. Moms know everything, don't they? Mine sure did.

This supposed image became like a Frankenstein monster that I later tried to kill for the sake of my career, but it never really went away.

I was playing badly, but was starting to get into better shape. Playing the Jets, I got an unassisted shorthanded goal to open the scoring, but we got beat 6–3. I was barking at the ref, and when he gave me a delay of game penalty, I called bullshit. That got me a misconduct. With less than a minute to play, Pie was arguing a call and tossed some towels on the ice. They gave him a bench minor and a misconduct. When I disputed, they gave me another misconduct, which earned me an automatic game misconduct. Two nights later, we played the Jets again. My frustrations were boiling over onto the ice. I picked up three minors, a misconduct and, with 19 seconds left, a game misconduct. We suffered our sixth straight loss.

I had never really wanted to be in Philadelphia. All the nonsense with attorneys and courts really took its toll on me. Most of the guys lived in New Jersey, while I was living in a hotel in Philly. I was basically by myself in Philadelphia. I wasn't there long enough to make many friends, but one highlight of my time with the Blazers involved some friends I did make—some unlikely friends. After a practice, I went out to my car and found a bunch of punk kids hanging out beside my Rolls. I figured that they were about to break into it or something, but they asked me if I wanted to buy some goalie equipment.

"Goalie equipment? Where the hell did you get goalie equipment?" I asked.

"We found it."

"Sure you did," I laughed.

It turned out they had stolen the equipment from the University of Pennsylvania men's hockey team, the Quakers, who played at the Class of 1923 Arena. I promised them I'd buy them some new equipment if they'd return the stuff they stole. Before I gave them the new equipment, one of the kids insisted I write a letter to his dad. "He'll never believe that some guy bought this stuff for me," he said. "He'll think I stole it."

I saw them regularly and used to take them for lunch. We'd go for spaghetti and meatballs. The kids thought they were in heaven. "If this is how a pro athlete lives, I want to be an athlete," one of them told me. I nicknamed them the "Under the Hill Gang." They were tough little bastards—good kids at heart but rough around the edges. They were all smart, but they put their energy into the wrong places. I saw a lot of myself as a teenager in them. They had their own moral code. One kid got thrown out of the gang after he snuck into the dressing room and stole Andre Lacroix's tickets.

One of the kids in the gang was Jim Evers. He liked to carry my sticks for me. The other kids starting calling him "Turk"—my nickname—because he spent so much time asking me questions. Turk eventually got into hockey, working his way up through the ranks until he became the equipment manager of the Philadelphia Flyers, which he did for 23 years. Funny how a little attention can make a big difference. Evers said, "Turk was the reason why I got into hockey. I'd be in jail if it wasn't for him."

We finally played our first home game of the season on October 25, this one against Gerry Cheevers and the Cleveland Crusaders. I bought tickets for all the kids in the Under the Hill Gang and they were just so excited. They loved going to the games. But we were spanked badly—an 8–2 loss in front of 5,075 hometown fans. I misunderstood my ego. I thought I could play great even if nobody was watching, but I was wrong. The Flyers were averaging almost 16,000 fans per game. We were averaging less than 5,000.

In the game's first minute, Bernie Parent broke a bone in his foot on an icing call. The doctors estimated that he'd be out for a month, recuperating. As we left the ice after the final buzzer, we were booed. I gave the crowd the finger.

While in a tussle with John Hanna, I hurt my shoulder. I finished the game but knew it was more than a strain. And Pie was still out with a broken arm. The three biggest stars on the team—the three biggest contracts for the Blazers—and we were all out with injuries. We had lost seven games in a row and were in last place, even though everybody predicted we'd be on top of the league. I resigned as captain of the Blazers; I found the responsibilities quite onerous. McKenzie surrendered the coaching role, and all of a sudden, Phil Watson stepped in. They also fired our GM, Dave Creighton, and gave Watson the dual role of coach and general manager.

Watson was absolutely certifiable. He had been hired by the Blazers as the chief scout and director of player personnel. A lot had changed since he had last coached in the NHL. He had coached both the Rangers and the Bruins, neither successfully. Everybody who had played for him hated him. Eddie Shack talked about him a lot when we played together on the Bruins. Shackie hated the bastard. In February 1960, Shack and Bill Gadsby were traded to Detroit for Red Kelly and Billy McNeill. Shackie was so happy, he decided to tell Watson what he thought of him as a coach. But then, Kelly and McNeill refused to report to New York and the trade was voided. Poor Eddie had to stay with the Rangers after he told Watson he was a shit coach. Shack became Watson's whipping boy. In the summer of 1960, Eddie actually went home to Sudbury and tried to get a job at the supermarket rather than return to the Rangers. But luckily for Shack, the Rangers replaced Watson with Alf Pike. And then in November, Eddie was ecstatic when he was traded to Toronto. It's really saying something when a guy preferred playing for Punch Imlach over Phil Watson!

Watson ranted and raved, and was always screaming at the players. I knew right away that Watson and I were not going to work.

While Parent was out, they called up a kid named Yves Archambault from our farm team in Roanoke to back up Paille. Wouldn't you know, with the team's three stars out of the lineup, Archambault was solid and we earned our first win of the season, beating Los Angeles 5–4. It figured, didn't it? They paid me millions and the team didn't win a game until I was out of the lineup. The fans had started telling me I was a bum, but I would turn around and say, "At least I'm a rich bum!" I told Cooper that no one was worth the money they were paying me. It was causing the team concern and was causing me anxiety. I even offered to give them back some of the salary they were paying me. I suggested that I'd return $200,000, but they declined. I told Cooper to rework the contract so that they paid me $100,000 a year, but he told me the team had made a deal and they would stick with it. He then told me that, in terms of building the World Hockey Association, my name alone was worth the money.

I sat out a 5–3 loss at home to Ottawa, and then, on November 1, I had my best night as a Blazer. I picked up a goal and two assists in a 7–5 road win over the Cleveland Crusaders. The attendance was just over 3,000. I felt like I was back playing junior.

In the second, I was in alone on Cheevers from just inside Cleveland's blue line. I knew he was going to come out of his net as soon as I ducked my head. That's when Gerry always made his move. He came racing out, but I pulled the puck back and as he sprawled, I flipped it over his head. He tried to back-pedal, but it was too late. I put the puck into the net easily.

Early in the third period, I picked up a minor penalty. The fans were throwing stuff at me while I sat in the penalty box. I said, "I don't need this shit." I jumped out of the box and went to stop the puck, but my left foot landed on a piece of garbage that somebody had thrown at me. I slipped and I could feel the pain go up my spine and right down my leg. *Boom!* I dropped like a stone. The left leg went out from under me and I kind of did the splits. My back took it all because I didn't have my weight balanced. I couldn't get up. I couldn't move.

My teammates helped me to my feet but I was in unbelievable pain. I thought my back was broken.

As it turned out, that was my last game in the World Hockey Association.

In spite of the excruciating pain, the doctors wouldn't give me any medication until they knew the nature of my injury. I tried to freeze the pain out of my back by lying on four bags of ice on the hospital floor. It didn't work. The next day, they got me back to Hahnemann University Hospital in Philadelphia. I have no recollection of how they got me from Cleveland to Philadelphia. They must have put me on a stretcher, because I certainly was not able to walk.

I was still in bed after a couple of days and the pain was severe. Unbelievably bad. It just pounded. After a couple of days, Dr. Arnold Berman, a back specialist, came in to see me, looked at the X-rays and told me I'd have to go into surgery.

"Okay," I said. "If that's what you feel is best, I'm fine with that. But I've drawn up this little agreement here and I just need your signature."

"What is that?" he asked.

I said, "It just says that if I cannot play hockey again, you are responsible for my salary for life."

His jaw dropped. "I won't be signing that!"

"I didn't think you would," I said. "No one's cutting me."

That was it. He said, "Then surgery is not going to be part of the process."

"Good," I agreed. "Look, Doc, I don't doubt your talent, but it's *my* back and I'm not going to be rolling over for anybody anytime soon."

You have to remember, this was 1972. The advances in surgery since then have put today's doctors light years ahead.

I held a press conference while I was convalescing in my suite at the Latham Hotel. In retrospect, I should have held my tongue, but my style was to say what was on my mind. I told the reporters that Philadelphia was the most negative sports town in the world. "This is a town where, as far as the fans are concerned, everyone is a bum or a loser. And the biggest reason the fans in this town are sour is the press. You guys never say anything complimentary."

The reporters scribbled wildly. I had more for them. "No athlete enjoys playing in Philadelphia. I know a couple of Eagles who'd be overjoyed if they could play a 14-game schedule entirely on the road."

While I was out of the lineup, the Blazers' owners had a falling-out. On November 18, 1972, my salary caused the disintegration of the partnership between Jim Cooper and Bernie Brown. They argued over my contract. Cooper left and Brown took over as sole owner of the team. Cooper had basically been using Brown's money to finance the team. He announced, "It's Bernie's team now. He can do with it what he wants." Brown was a trucking guy. What did he know about hockey? All he knew was he didn't like signing the big cheques.

The team was losing money hand over fist. People claimed that on paper we were the best team in the league, but at the time of the partnership dissolving, we had a record of 3–13. I talked to Brown and said, "Take a look around, Bernie. You've only got 10,000 seats in here. I'm no businessman, but if you add up the top six players' contracts, I don't think the economics make sense."

He asked me, "What do you mean?"

I explained, "The numbers don't add up, Bernie. If you sold out this building every night of the schedule, you still wouldn't make enough to pay the player's salaries." He hadn't realized that.

And we weren't coming close to selling out. There were only a thousand season ticket holders. The average attendance over the course of the season was only about 4,000. For the December 8 game against the New York Raiders, fewer than 800 fans bothered to show up. And we won!

Brown finally figured it out. "The goofball's right."

The drama was just beginning to unfold. The games had just begun.

The Blazers wanted to get out from under my contract. They were prepared to trade me or even give me away to any other WHA team. Rumours swirled that I was most likely destined to join the New York Raiders, although I was doubtful that they were prepared to carry my contract. Three WHA clubs said they were interested in me if I could secure my release. I know there were two NHL clubs that would like to have signed me. I also knew that I could get work with either Kansas City or Washington when the NHL admitted them into the league in the 1974–75 season. Milt Schmidt had been hired as GM of the Washington Capitals, and while we differed on clothing and hairstyles, we agreed about hard work producing results.

The Blazers found a physical therapist for me, a little Austrian guy. He was about five foot three, maybe 124 pounds. He was probably 65 years old, but was in better physical condition than any 20-year-old man I'd ever met. If he had been six foot two, he'd have been making movies. He was an example of what you could do to the human body if you work at it.

He told me point blank, "The team doesn't believe you're hurt, but I believe you are. We won't know until we find out. What I'm going to do is put you through a rather rigorous program to get you in shape so we can make a decision."

I wanted to feel better, so I was all for whatever he suggested. He bent me over at the waist and held my head. I went down as far as I could, but it was only three or four inches. The pain in my back seared like a knife.

"Dedicate, Derek. Dedicate." He worked me all day, from 8 a.m. to 5 p.m.

The team did ridiculous things to try to break me. They forced me to stand naked in front of a mirror in the dressing room and look at myself. I was thinking, "What do you think this is going to do? Make me give up $2.65 million? No, thanks." I'd been on the street too long to get broken down by that nonsense. Whatever they wanted, I did it. If they wanted me at the rink at 7 a.m., I was there. I could get up at seven o'clock for two and a half million!

This physical therapist got me into the best shape of my life. After hating him at the beginning, I really got to like the guy. He was exceptionally talented. He used interesting games to get me in shape. For example, he took two-inch-wide duct tape, rolled it into a ball and put me in a corridor six feet wide. He would throw the tape towards me and I had to catch it 50 times in a row. The tape ball took odd bounces, like a football would, so it was a real challenge. I had to get down and be quick in both directions in order to catch it, using one hand, two hands—whatever it took, but I couldn't let it get by me. We did that by the hour.

After a month on the sidelines, I was fully recovered from my back injury. I was ready to suit up for a home game against Cleveland on December 5. I skated in the warmup, but Watson ordered me out of uniform. I tried again on December 8 against the Raiders, the 9th against Ottawa and the 13th and 15th against Winnipeg. I was being paid and I wanted to help the team but they refused to let me play.

Bernie Brown told reporters that the decision was in the hands of the coach, but Watson denied that and said the order had come from above. When reporters probed and told him that Brown had denied ordering my benching, Watson said it came from executive vice-president Hal Freeman or from Dr. Arnold Berman. Freeman denied giving the order and Dr. Berman stated that he had cleared me to play several weeks earlier.

I was getting screwed over. I had no idea what was going on. Once I had been given the okay to play, I showed up for every practice and every game, but was not allowed out on the ice with the guys. Instead, the Blazers had me run around the rink while the guys were practising. It was humiliating. The guys were all good with me. They wanted me back on the team, but the management games dragged on.

I was physically ready but they were messing with me, looking for a way to get me to quit. Finally, Watson told me that Bernie Brown had told him I wasn't to play. Brown held the purse strings, so I could only conclude that he felt I was too expensive and wasn't bringing value to the franchise. I had tried to bring fans to the rink through my play and by being a little controversial, but that didn't work out.

They tried everything they could think of to break me. They counted on me being all huffy and quitting. They did whatever they could to get out of the contract. I said, "I'll stay here all day, boys. I'm good with this." They wanted to bury me. They wanted me gone. Long gone. I just wanted to play hockey, but they weren't going to let me do it—at least, not with the Philadelphia Blazers.

The fans didn't care about the Blazers. Attendance was pitiful and Bernie Brown was bleeding money. Clearly, he saw me as the main scapegoat for his woes.

The media pressed me for a response. "[The press] has created [an image of me as] a kid who wants to suck up the money and quit. But I didn't quit. I got hurt. You think I liked lying in the hospital? All I wanted to do was play hockey. That's what I'm getting paid to do. It's not my fault I'm getting paid an exorbitant amount."

It became evident that the Blazers' management was locking me out while they searched every sentence of our 28-page contract for a loophole that would free them from the pact. The team felt it had a chance to break even if it could get out of my contract, but no chance whatsoever if it didn't.

Just after Christmas, I went back to Boston. While I was there, I called Harry Sinden.

He asked, "What are you doing?"

I asked him if he needed a centre. He said, "You're still our property in the NHL." He had no qualms about legalities. "You're a Bruin."

On New Year's Day, I escaped to play golf in Florida while I waited out the impasse. The Blazers were still paying me my full salary. Imagine! Paying somebody not to play! Quite a way to start the new year!

Ultimately, Bernie Brown concluded his lawyers couldn't find a loophole to get out of my contract and because no other WHA team would take me off his hands, he'd have to settle by buying me out. I was in Fort Lauderdale when I learned that my lawyer had settled with the Blazers. A media conference was held on January 17, 1973. With Brown looking on, the new president of the Blazers, Dick Olson, read from a prepared statement: "The Philadelphia Blazers and Derek Sanderson have reached an agreement where Derek will be released." The reason cited was "primarily economic."

After trying to force me to quit, which was never going to happen, the Blazers bought out my $2.65 million contract for $1 million.

There was never anything personal between me and Bernie Brown. Money was the determining factor. He contacted my lawyer and wanted to renegotiate my contract. We said no, but he told us he couldn't afford the price. He didn't think I was worth it. He didn't think any athlete was worth it.

Candidly, *no* athlete was worth it. You could take Muhammad Ali, put him on a football field in the morning, a basketball court in the afternoon, a baseball field in the evening and in the ring at night, let him win all four and he still wouldn't be worth it.

The Blazers averaged 4,300 fans per game. You can't make money that way, but I also believe they should have been more patient. I played eight games with them. You can't build a winning franchise in a handful of games. I scored three goals and had three assists in those eight games, and had 69 minutes in penalties.

I was so glad to have had the whole ordeal over with. I know I screwed up. The Blazers expected me to waltz in and be the saviour for the franchise, but if Jesus Christ himself had strapped on some skates and pulled on that gawd-awful Blazers sweater, they still weren't going to fill the rink with fans. The Flyers were Philadelphia's team. They were the Broad Street Bullies, and as much as I hated them, they were still an exciting team to watch. And they were damned good, too, and won the Stanley Cup in 1974 and '75.

The Blazers went on to finish third in the WHA's East Division. And after one season, the team was sold to Jim Pattison and moved to Vancouver. I didn't give a shit at that point.

The WHA really was a minor league. I worked so hard to get to the majors and then there I was, basically in Triple A. There was no glamour in the WHA. There might have been 20 guys who could play in the National Hockey League, and they were just biding their time. The league was a mess. When the New England Whalers won the inaugural WHA championship, which was later renamed the Avco World Trophy after the league secured Avco Financial Services as its main sponsor, the team was forced to skate around the perimeter of the rink with their divisional championship trophy because the Avco Cup wasn't ready yet.

CHAPTER 22

A RETURN TO THE BRUINS: 1972–73

Once I was released from the Blazers, the bashing began. Gary Davidson, the president of the World Hockey Association, was pissed off at my indifference to the league. "The league, as a whole, was very disappointed with Derek's attitude, both since the start of the year and the fact that he hadn't reported to camp with the same degree of interest some of the others had shown." He added, "Sanderson was a liability rather than an asset, and he may be in a position where he has priced himself off the market."

If I had to do it all over again, I would never go to the WHA. Not even for the money. I had always worked hard. I loved to play and I loved to win. Then, suddenly, all that money had an effect on me. I didn't want to put up with the sweat, the bleeding and the pain it took to win. There was no incentive to work harder. All I could think was, "They're paying me $2.65 million, but I can't score seven goals a game. I can't carry the parade." I lost my values. I had so many outside interests that I lost my ability to concentrate on the game. My thoughts were too diversified. I forgot about the sport that had brought me there in the first place. I had no desire. I was just going through the motions. I was so bad in Philly that I wanted to crawl into a hole and hide.

It was during this time that all my troubles really started. Weston Adams Sr. had told me I'd "rue the day" I took the Blazers' money. He explained that I had not been bred to understand money's corruptive power. He told me that someone else should handle my affairs. It was almost as if I felt I didn't deserve the money and had to get rid of it. That's also when I really started drinking heavily.

Even my attorney backpedalled. "In reflection, Derek doesn't think he acted properly. He perhaps didn't do some things he should have done. His attitude was not what it should have been. Derek has some proving to do and I think he feels that way too."

The million-dollar severance I received from the Blazers was nice money, I guess, but it kind of wrecked me. I got more money for not playing than any other player got for playing. But going to the WHA had been a bad move for me and I wanted to move on. For me, the WHA was like buying a motor home. There really are only two great days—the day you buy it and the day you sell it.

Despite that, I am very proud of a number of things we accomplished. Because of the WHA, the average annual salary for National Hockey League players catapulted from $28,000 to $44,000 in the WHA's first year. By 1978–79, when the WHA's last four remaining teams were folded into the NHL, that average annual salary had escalated to $96,000. Harry Neale, who coached in both the WHA and NHL and went on to a stellar career in broadcasting, stated, "Today's players should get down on their hands and knees and thank the WHA. You just have to look at where the game was before it came along and where it was seven years later."

The WHA did a lot of things for the game that we didn't fully realize until years later. Not only did salaries increase, but European players really began coming to North America to play in both leagues. There were also some interesting rules. Hockey is the only sport on the planet that gives an advantage to a penalized team—by allowing the team playing shorthanded to ice the puck. In the WHA, the moment you iced the puck and it crossed the goal line, the whistle blew and it was a faceoff back in the penalized team's end. No-touch icing was another great WHA rule that the NHL never, ever adopted—still haven't, to this day—exactly because it came from the WHA.

And while my time in the WHA was brief, I am very proud to have been part of the abolition of the reserve clause. It is the WHA's most important legacy.

217

While I was playing in the WHA, I was still on the Boston Bruins' reserve list. That meant they owned my NHL playing rights, but I didn't count against the maximum 37 players a team was allowed to have under contract. It didn't look like the Bruins would want me back at first. Harry Sinden said he didn't know where they'd play me, as he was deep at centre. They still had Esposito, Freddy Stanfield and Mike Walton, as well as a kid they were high on named Richie LeDuc. I was frustrated. There were four or five teams who wanted me. I know the New York Rangers wanted me, as did the Vancouver Canucks and the Chicago Black Hawks. If Boston couldn't use me, I wanted them to put me up for grabs in exchange for a draft pick or something.

Things started to turn around in late January, when Harry met with me. He insisted I work out with the Bruins without a contract in order to show him my ability and prove that my back had healed before he'd stick his neck out for me. Everything went amicably. My lawyer told the press, "We agreed that Derek would work out while we're talking about a possible contract."

Just because I was working out with the team didn't mean I was signed, but my lawyer was working on my return to the team I should never have left. But even if a deal had been struck then and there, I hadn't played for two or three months, so I had to get myself back into playing shape.

Finally on February 7, 1973, I signed a contract to formalize my return to the Boston Bruins. I'd had offers from a few teams, both in the NHL and the WHA, but my first choice was always to sign with the Bruins. Boston was the only place I really wanted to play. I signed a two-year deal for $200,000.

Just before returning to the team, I visited Weston Adams Sr. in his hospital room. We had a few laughs and cracked a few jokes, but I knew it was likely the last time I would see him alive. That made me quite melancholy, as I likely wouldn't have played in the NHL had it not been for Mr. Adams. He died on March 19.

My teammates on the Bruins weren't too thrilled about my leaving in the first place. They looked at it as desertion. "You walked out on us, made all that money and now you're coming back." The reception I got when I rejoined the team was cool, at best. Shakey Walton, Wayne Cashman and Phil Esposito were sarcastic, but I expected that. The first thing Bobby Orr said was, "I think you're an asshole for leaving us in the first place, but it's good to have you back. But you have to work at it." He laughed like hell when I threw up after practice, but we were good again. I threw up three straight days when I returned.

Johnny Bucyk told the media, "If he's in condition, he can help." Eddie Johnston said, "A goalie appreciates a good penalty killer and Derek's a good penalty killer. He's a tremendous hockey player." "Time will tell," Dallas Smith told a reporter. "If he wants to play, it'll be all right." Esposito understood what I'd gone through. "Derek has a home with the Boston Bruins," he said. "He took the money. I don't think that was such a bad thing because he sure wouldn't have got paid [by the Bruins] what he got paid to jump to the WHA. His biggest problem was that he didn't have enough brains to handle the money and obviously the people that were helping him didn't help him that well."

The Bruins had been Stanley Cup champions when I left, but I returned to a different team. Cheevers, McKenzie and Teddy Green had jumped to the WHA. We'd lost Eddie Westfall in the expansion draft to the New York Islanders. New faces included Gregg Sheppard, Terry O'Reilly and Fred O'Donnell. Tommy Johnson had been fired as coach just days before I returned and was moved into an assistant GM capacity. The new coach was Bep Guidolin. In the 1940s, a month before his 17th birthday, he became the youngest player ever to skate in the NHL, and he had been coach of the Oshawa Generals during Bobby Orr's final year of junior. More recently, Guidolin had been coaching the Boston Braves. I was warned to watch out for Bep. He stressed conditioning and discipline, neither of which were strong suits of mine.

O'Donnell was wearing my number, 16. He had worn it with the Boston Braves in 1971–72, so it was natural that when he made the Bruins the following season, he would ask for the same number. I wasn't there anymore, so it was available. He said, "Wearing number 16 doesn't make me a better hockey player," and since that was the way he felt, I asked him if I could have it. He offered to sell it back to me for $2,000, which he said he'd donate to charity.

I wasn't paying that kind of money just to wear that number. It wasn't that important, so I took 27 instead.

With Kenny Hodge out with a wrist injury, the Bruins could add me to their active roster without having to lose someone else. Bep dressed me for an afternoon game at home against the Pittsburgh Penguins on February 10. He told me he was just going to give me a few shifts, but I ended up playing on the power play, killing penalties and taking a few regular shifts, too. The fans gave me a loud ovation when I stepped on the ice for my first shift. I played about 12 minutes in a 6–3 win over the Penguins.

Afterwards, the microphones and cameras surrounded me in the dressing room, just like they had in the "old days." I wanted to give the guys a good story, so when they asked me what it was like returning to Boston from the WHA, I said, "Coming back from Philadelphia is like coming back from Vietnam." That was a stupid statement. I certainly never intended to slight members of the armed forces who had served in Vietnam. In hindsight, I'm sorry I made the comparison.

The team started to roll. From the game against Pittsburgh through the end of February, we won eight of nine. I was pressing to score. I didn't want a mental block to keep me from putting one in. I got some points and some chances and then, on February 21, in a game against the Seals, I scored twice to help us win 6–2.

On March 7, while we were in St. Louis, Shakey Walton and a teammate were horsing around and Shakey fell through a plate-glass window. Thank goodness the paramedics got there quickly. Shakey lost five pints of blood and it took 200 stitches to close him up. Walton was a hell of a hockey player and fit so beautifully into the Bruins' lineup, but he was never quite the same player after the accident. He and I were buddies, and while I felt terrible about his accident, Guidolin pointed to me to take Shakey's spot in the lineup.

I was having a drink in Daisy Buchanan's and got talking with some friends. Two of them expressed a desire to try their luck in Hollywood. I said, "Let me see what I can do to help." I helped one get a job at a Hollywood bar. I gave them both a $5,000 loan, and they agreed that they'd pay me back.

At the time, I was hanging out with two Playboy bunnies. These girls were flirting and teasing and asked if I had any cocaine. I didn't have any, so they said, "Go buy some."

I went to Joey Cimino and asked, "Do you know where I can buy some coke?" He said, "No way! Are you stupid?" I said, "All right, all right. Take it easy." Joey would never let me go goofy.

One of the kids I loaned money to got pinched for selling dope to an undercover cop. He came back to Daisy's and slipped a vial in my pocket. I said, "What is this?" He told me it was cocaine. It was a large vial, maybe a third of an ounce. All I could think was, "Holy shit! That's a lot!" He said, "Sell it. It's worth more than I owe you." I left it in my pocket and didn't think any more about it.

I didn't get a date, so I called it a night and left Daisy's around one o'clock and went home to bed. At four o'clock in the morning, I got a phone call from a Boston cop.

"Hey Derek, you awake? Listen, I've got to ask you a question. Are you dirty?"

I asked, "What do you mean, 'dirty'?" I was naive. I had never heard that expression before. My first thought was that he meant I hadn't showered before I climbed into bed.

He said, "Do you have any drugs on you?"

I thought for a minute and then remembered the vial in my coat pocket. "Wait a minute. Yeah, I do." I got up and went into my pocket. "Yeah, I've got a whole vial of coke."

The cop said, "The Drug Enforcement Agency and the local police officials are going to bust you at eight o'clock."

I was stunned. "I'll just pour it down the drain," I told him. "I don't do coke. You know that."

He said, "I know that, Derek. The only reason I'm calling you is because I know you're clean."

"I'll flush the shit down the toilet and then wash the vial," I told him. "Everything will be fine."

"Uh-uh," he said. "No. They want you, and if they want you, they'll get you. They'll fabricate it if they have to. I know these guys and they're vicious. So, here's what I want you to do. Get dressed, get in your car and drive around."

"For four hours?" I asked.

"Yes. At eight o'clock in the morning, I want you to pull up in front of headquarters and then head up to the second floor. I want you to walk into the lieutenant's office—he's the head of narcotics—and knock on the door, put the cocaine in front of him and tell him that last night, somebody approached you, had heard that you made a lot of money in Philadelphia and then gave you that vial," he explained. "That will really mess him up. He won't know what to do."

I walked into the precinct at 7:55 that morning. Every cop knew me and said hello, although I knew they were wondering what the hell I was doing there.

I walked into the lieutenant's office.

"And what can I do for you, Mr. Sanderson?"

I put the vial of cocaine in front of him. He took it, tasted it and looked right at me.

"What are you doing with this?"

I said, "I was in my bar last night and a guy approached me. He said, 'I know you've got money. Here's just a taste. There's a lot more where this came from.' I laughed at him and moved on. I wasn't about to jeopardize my career with something stupid, but I didn't want to insult the guy, so I just took it, but in the back of my mind there were these two girls. That was my motivating factor. I was going to give it to them. I wasn't going to do it." I gave the officer a perfect description of the guy who gave me the coke.

The lieutenant pushed back his chair. "Well, well, well! Isn't this a dilemma?" He said, "I've got more lines on the street than Bell Telephone, and I know you're dirty. This throws a monkey wrench into everything. You come clean out of left field! I don't know what I'm going to do with you." He continued. "I don't know who tipped you off, but I'll tell you this: I've been in this game too long. I'm going to find out who spilled the beans, and both of you are going away!"

I was horrified. "Listen, Lieutenant," I stammered. "I'm a good citizen. I'm a Good Samaritan. I came in here to do the right thing and now you're giving me shit."

He glared. "If you're clean, I'll defend you forever. But if there's something dirty in this, I'll come after you with a vengeance! What are your plans?"

"Right now, I'm injured. I'm not playing," I told him. "I've got a game tomorrow night."

He said, "Okay. Here's what I'm going to do. We're coming up on a long weekend and I'm going away on Thursday afternoon until Monday. Here's my private number. You call me if they approach you tomorrow. Go away, but I want you back here tomorrow morning."

I was fine with that.

The next morning, I reported back as instructed. The lieutenant gave me back the vial. "If you're the dupe in this, I'll protect you, but if you're not, I'll ruin you."

I left. I had the coke with me. I went to the Garden for the game that night. The Bruins were playing, but I wasn't. Between periods, I went into the dressing room. Bobby Orr was on the training table and a few of the guys were smoking. I pulled out my pack of Export As from the pocket of my leather sport coat, but dropped a cigarette. When I bent over to pick it up, the vial fell out of the pocket of my jacket. It hit the floor and Danny Canney, the trainer, grabbed it. The team doctor grabbed it from him, opened it, touched it to his tongue and announced, "Cocaine!"

You could have heard a pin drop.

Harry Sinden broke the silence. "Cocaine! I knew it would be you! The first one in the league busted! Why'd I take you back?"

"Harry, Harry! Calm down!" I insisted. "Everything is fine. Everything is okay. The police know all about it and we're working together."

Confused, he asked, "You're what?"

"I'm working with the police on this," I explained. "Somebody is trying to set me up."

"Who the hell do you think you are, James Bond? You're a goddamned hockey player!"

I said, "Take it easy, take it easy." I explained the whole situation to Harry.

"My Bruins! I've got the first scandal. I don't know what to do." He said, "You're suspended! And I want a meeting with this lieutenant tomorrow morning."

"Okay," I said. I called up the officer and set up a meeting for the next morning at 10 o'clock.

That night, I went to Daisy's. Lo and behold, the two Playboy girls came in. They were all flirty. "You holding, honey?"

I said, "Yeah, I've got a little taste for you, darlin'."

The three of us went into the back room. I put four or five lines out and one of them snorted a line.

"Good stuff!"

I shrugged. "Who knows? I don't do it."

The girls said, "Do it with us or nothing happens!"

"No, no. I'm not doing that," I said. I was thinking about meeting the lieutenant the next morning and wanted to be sharp.

The girls insisted. "Nothing happens unless you join us!"

I did four lines. How stupid was that? When you're drinking, you're not thinking!

The next morning, Harry Sinden, Tommy Johnson and I went to police headquarters. We sat around a big conference table. The lieutenant was sitting at the head of the table. *Bang!* He dropped the telephone down and two cops came in with their guns and their badges and put them on the table. They said, "If he's dirty, then we resign."

Harry jumped in. "See, your own officers trust him."

The lieutenant said, "I trust nobody. If you're so pure, then you won't mind being tested, will you?"

Testing now is commonplace, but back then, apparently there were just two machines in the U.S. that could test for drugs. One was in L.A. and the other, wouldn't you know it, was in Boston.

I knew I'd done the coke the night before. First time in my life! Who was going to believe it was my first time?

God speaks to us in strange ways, and people don't want to believe this. I had the most ridiculous thought in my head just then. I remembered being a kid and sitting with my family, watching a television skit with Imogene Coca and Sid Caesar on *Your Show of Shows*. Sid Caesar was in bed with a girl, and Imogene Coca, his wife, walked into the room and said, "Aha! I've caught you! You're cheating. I knew you were!" He goes, "What, honey? I would never cheat on you." Meanwhile, the girl slides out of bed, wearing just her bra and panties, pulls on her skirt, zips it up, puts on her blouse, tucks it in and grabs her bag. "Her! Her!" said Imogene Coca. "I'm talking about her," and just then, the girl leaves the room. Sid Caesar keeps on denying it.

"What girl? The room is empty, darling."

That's when it hit me. Sid Caesar denied that he was cheating and Imogene Coca couldn't prove that there was a girl there. The girl walked right by her, opened the door and left. "I don't see any girl," Caesar said. "It must be your imagination playing tricks on you."

The moral of the story for me was, when you're in trouble, deny, deny, deny.

I don't know why it popped into my head, but when the officer asked me if I was dirty, I thought, "I'm dead if I say yes, so I'll deny, deny, deny." So when he asked, "Then you won't mind being tested, will you?" I said, "Nope." I figured I might as well bluff it all the way. He made the call and a cruiser arrived out front. They didn't cuff me, but they put me in the back and I was just sickened. It was a cage, and the cops wouldn't even talk to me. Damn it! I was a criminal now!

The police cruiser drove me to Mass General, and waiting there for me were Harry Sinden and Tommy Johnson. The officers escorted me into the hospital and walked me to a room. They took a blood sample and a urine sample and, as quickly as we arrived, we left again. They piled me back in the cruiser and drove right back to the station. The lieutenant was sitting there. "Do you see this phone? When it rings, you'll either be innocent or guilty, and if you're dirty, you go directly to jail."

I said, "Sorry to disappoint you. This is a whole lot of wasted effort. Jesus, I will never do the right thing again!"

Just then, the phone rang. The lieutenant let it ring twice and while he was staring at me, he said, "This is your last chance to come clean. You've got some wiggle room here. I will ask you one last time: Did you do coke?"

Sid Caesar taught me deny, deny, deny, so I denied.

He picked up the phone. "Whaddya got? Are you sure? Absolutely no mistake? Thank you!"

He waited a second before he delivered the news. It seemed like an eternity to me.

"Okay, you're clean."

My mouth went dry and my heart leapt out of my chest.

Harry Sinden jumped out of his chair. "You're harassing my player! Leave him alone! What the hell is this bullshit, dragging him in here? I accused the poor kid and he told me the truth. You made me look like an idiot!"

The lieutenant apologized and let us go.

I could only assume that somebody at Mass General saw that I had been doing coke, was a cokehead themselves, and protected me. But it took me a month to find out the actual story. I couldn't talk to the cop who'd tipped me off for quite a while, because what he'd done was against the law. When we finally spoke, he told me the story.

"Derek," he explained, "we can't give a citizen back cocaine. That's against the law. We gave you back chemicals. When they tested for cocaine, you came up clean. They didn't test for the chemicals that they gave you. If they had, they would have discovered them. Nobody helped you. It was luck, buddy."

I was dumbfounded. "But the broads said it was great coke!"

"The girls didn't know what they were talking about," he explained. "They never gave you back cocaine. The chemicals they gave you give you the same freeze as cocaine." That's how they dupe you when they arrest you.

Thank God I denied using. I told him, "I did the coke with the girls." He said, "Oh, you stupid ass!" I said, "Yeah, and to make matters worse, I was looking to get lucky with the girls, but they left me anyway. They did the coke and then said, 'See you later!' They used me, and giggled out the door and went off to do their thing."

I finished the season with 15 points in 25 games. The Bruins finished second in the East Division. Phil Esposito finished as the scoring leader for the third straight season and Bobby Orr took the Norris Trophy for the sixth time, and finished with 101 points. Nine of our guys scored 20 or more goals in 1972–73.

Our perennial rivals, the New York Rangers, were our opponents in the first round of the playoffs. They finished third in our division, but made short work out of us. They eliminated us in five games. The defending Stanley Cup champions were free to golf.

It had been quite a year!

CHAPTER 23

MY LAST DAYS AS A BRUIN: 1973-74

The 1972–73 season had just concluded, and I was exhausted. I was ecstatic to be back in Boston, having left Philadelphia with a pocketful of money.

It was about 10:30 on a rainy June morning and I was sitting in Daisy's. We had just opened up for the lunch crowd and I was talking with Armand Bianco, my bar manager. I asked him if he'd ever been on vacation.

"No."

"How would you like to go to Hawaii?" I asked.

His eyes lit up. "Great!"

In the bar at that moment were five really attractive girls. Three were stewardesses and the other two were Playboy bunnies. Just for fun, I spun around and asked them if they'd like to go to Hawaii. They all said yes, so I struck a deal. "There are two conditions," I stated. "One, you have to leave with nothing more than the clothes on your back and two, you can't phone anybody."

They all looked at each other and smiled. "Fine by us!"

I hadn't thought it was going to be that easy, but I shrugged and said, "Okay, let's go!"

I had a passing friendship with the chairman of the Sheraton Hotel chain. His office was in the same building as my lawyer. He told me, "If you're going to Hawaii, stay at our Sheraton Waikiki. And if you need anything, let me know."

I put everything on my American Express Gold Card. We flew first class.

It's six hours from Boston to L.A., and another six to Hawaii. We drank all the way there and by the time we arrived, I was feeling no pain.

I had reserved three two-bedroom suites at the Sheraton Waikiki. We decided to go out that night. I thought I could pull it together with a shower, but I was still hammered. The combination of alcohol and heat knocked me on my ass. It had been an extremely warm night and I had taken my shirt off—and *poof!* I passed out on the beach, facedown in the sand. The sun was beating down on me and the tide was rolling up over me when I came to at about 11 o'clock the next morning. The guy who rented the outrigger canoes to tourists was walking around me as he went back and forth, taking the canoes out. I guess the guy must have thought, "Just a drunken fool. I'll leave him there."

I sat up and, after focusing my eyes, realized that the beach was packed—people everywhere—and there I was lying in the surf, oblivious to everything! I cooked the left side of my face and my back. I had a line starting on my forehead, running right down the middle of my nose. I sat on the balcony of my hotel room for three days trying to even it out using vinegar and oil on the burned side. I was in pain!

My travel companions bragged about the water pressure in their shower, but the pressure in my shower was down to a trickle. I could have called down to the front desk and changed rooms or had someone look at the shower, but since the chairman of the hotel chain said, "Anything you want," I was going to force him to step up. I always wanted to call the bluff of someone who was high up in the pecking order. I called back to Boston and got in touch with the guy about my water pressure. Amazingly, it was fixed almost immediately.

My original intention was that this was going to be a little golf vacation. I didn't ask, but assumed that Armand, the bar manager, played golf, which he had never done. But I insisted we play anyway.

Now, of course, we'd all boarded the flight with only the clothes on our back and didn't have golf clubs, so I went into the pro shop and bought two sets of clubs, head covers, shoes—the whole shooting match. And we needed clothes, too, so we had to buy shirts and slacks. In those days, they sold slacks in the pro shop, although we had to make our own alterations by taking a pair of scissors and cutting the slacks to the proper length.

We finished our round and were about to leave. I forgot the clubs in the golf cart. The caddy came out and said, "Excuse me, Mr. Sanderson, but I believe you forgot to pay me."

The kid was standing there and he had my clubs. I said, "Keep the clubs. Not a problem."

Armand couldn't believe what he had heard. "Keep the clubs?!"

Hey, I didn't want to carry them home with us anyway.

I did that a few times. I had a bunch of money and I hated carrying my clubs to the airport. It was the easy way out.

The group of us had a great time. While we were there, we went to see Joey Heatherton's show. That weekend cost me $7,000, which was an exorbitant amount of money at that time. My lawyer paid my bills. He had me on an allowance, but that American Express card sure came in handy. You only live once.

The Boston Bruins still had a good team. Esposito, Hodge, Bucyk and Cashman were scoring, and of course we had Bobby Orr. We lost Eddie Johnston to Toronto to complete a deal that brought Jacques Plante to the Bruins near the end of the previous season, but then Plante was gone at the end of the 1972–73 season, so in order to shore up our goaltending, Freddy Stanfield was traded to Minnesota for Gilles Gilbert. But the biggest change, in my eyes, was the guy behind the bench: Bep Guidolin.

Bep was an all-right guy, but really different from Tommy Johnson and a world away from Harry Sinden. He was old school, through and through. At the first formal practice of training camp in September 1973, I was putting a sweep check on Gregg Sheppard and spun on the ice. I felt that something pulled in my back. It turns out that I had strained a back muscle. I should never have pushed that hard that soon, and I was out of the Bruins' lineup for the first 19 games of the season. I did calisthenics to try to strengthen my back and improve my skating, but it was really bothering me.

On November 5, the Bruins announced they were sending me to the

Boston Braves, their farm team in the American Hockey League. Harry told *Sports Illustrated,* "As he grew more successful, he also grew more talented, but then with more and more success, he got too many outside interests and his hockey began to suffer. Derek isn't foremost a sex symbol or a talk show host or a philosopher. He's a hockey player. I always thought once he got his other interests aside he'd come back to what he was."

I hadn't played a game yet that season. Before I was reassigned, I had to clear waivers, which I did. Luckily, both the Bruins and the Braves played out of Boston Garden, so I could stay in my condo on Beacon Street.

I hadn't yet reached my peak in hockey and had too big an ego to think of retirement. And above all else, I just loved playing the game.

The playing coach of the Braves was Matt Ravlich, whom I had played with for the Bruins over the previous two years. Matt was a good guy. We got along well. But everyone was a step ahead of me. I had only skated a couple of times since hurting my back. I was in walking-the-street shape, but not in shape for hockey. I did two-a-day on-ice sessions under the watch of Jimmy Anderson, a special assistant to Harry Sinden. I worked really hard to get back to the Bruins, and Anderson gave Harry very positive reports about my progress.

I made my debut with the Braves against the Rochester Americans in mid-November. I was more nervous when I first skated out there than I had been before my first NHL game. We won 4–1, and I got a goal and an assist and about 35 minutes of ice time. We played the New Haven Nighthawks next and I got a hat trick in a 5–3 victory. The press gathered around me like they had with the Bruins.

I was quite happy with the Braves, and the Braves were happy with me. Their attendance increased by about a thousand in the game we played at home, we helped set an attendance record in Springfield, and there was a season-high crowd in New Haven when we played there. I ended up playing three games with the Braves, all victories, before I was called up to rejoin the Bruins.

I returned to the Bruins for a game against the Flyers on November 22. The fans gave me a standing ovation when I skated out onto the ice at the

Garden. I didn't get a lot of ice time—Guidolin kept me pretty much to killing penalties. In the second, Gregg Sheppard brought the puck out from behind the net and saw me open in the slot. He flipped the puck to me and I one-timed it past Bobby Taylor. The fans gave me another standing ovation.

All along, there was friction with Bep Guidolin. When I was recalled from the AHL, he told the press, "Derek was recalled because that was the deal we had with Harry [Sinden]. I still don't know if he's in shape. I'm waiting for him to play as great as everyone says he used to. I haven't seen it yet. When he does, he can help the Bruins win the Stanley Cup. He hasn't been playing badly. He looks better every time out. Our communication is better, too. He's doing what I ask him to do. Still, he's Derek Sanderson, isn't he? He has his set ways and that's it."

Bep didn't understand me at all. He hated my lifestyle. He tried to break me, which simply wasn't going to happen. He wanted me to crawl back to him on my hands and knees, but I would never give him the satisfaction. He thought that sending me to the American Hockey League was going to humiliate me. It didn't.

I was barely back when I broke a bone in my right foot against the Islanders and missed 17 more games.

Things weren't the same. The Bruins I played with before I left for Philadelphia were really close. We used to fight together on the ice and then go drinking and carousing together after the game. It wasn't like that anymore.

My drinking had escalated even more since my return from the WHA.

I lived in the penthouse of a 38-storey building in Boston called Harbor Towers. I would pull up to the building in my Rolls-Royce, toss the doorman $20 like a big shot and he would park my car.

One time, as I was taking the elevator up to my suite, I took off my jacket and undid my shirt and realized I didn't have my keys. "Aw, shit!" I was drunk and too lazy to hike back down to street level to get my keys. I thought, "Wait a minute! I can get into my apartment through the balcony entrance."

I climbed out, went up the stairs there and came to a wall. I climbed up on the wall and realized I was now 39 floors up from the street. I looked down, drunk, wobbly and terrified of heights. And the balcony wasn't below me like I had envisioned. "Hmm, this isn't where I'm supposed to be. This isn't my balcony."

I shuffled around and this time when I looked down, I saw a dark rectangle. "That's got to be the balcony," I thought. I could see the sliding glass doors. "Well, I can't stand here all day, can I?" I jumped off the wall.

I had never been airborne that long in my life. I was dropping, thinking, "Holy shit!" and then *bang!* I hit cement and shocked every bone in my body. I didn't do a paratrooper roll like they do in the movies. I landed on my feet and jammed my legs. "Holy Jesus!" I was lying there, afraid to move a muscle. I was sure I had a broken leg or had blown out my back. I systematically went through each body part one at a time—"I can move my neck. I can raise and lower my arms. I can move my legs. I can wiggle my toes." I stood up. Nothing broken. And then I tried to slide open my door. "Shit!" The door was locked.

I was standing on this balcony with the cold wind blowing and I was freezing my ass off. "I'm not staying out here, I'll freeze to death!"

I saw this little hibachi barbecue that I had. I picked it up and threw it at the glass window so I could get inside, but the glass buckled and then exploded out at me. "Jesus Christ!" I was dodging glass everywhere. I then had to climb over the broken glass shards, open the locked door from inside, grab the clothes I'd left in the hallway and go to bed.

I woke up the next day and I was so sore I couldn't move a muscle. I called Harry Sinden and told him I couldn't play that night. "I've got the flu," I told him.

"Yeah, well, you know the rules, Derek. Unless you've got a broken leg, you get your ass over here."

I thought I was dying. I took a few Aspirins, had a hot shower and made it over to the rink. I laced up my skates and went for a couple of twirls around the ice and told them that I'd tweaked my back. I went back to the dressing room and had a massage. I was a lucky boy that sore muscles were all I had.

I figured that I should probably get an X-ray, just in case. I had a couple of beers. Then I scared myself. "What if I had missed the balcony?" There wasn't anybody on the planet that wouldn't think it was a suicide. Everybody. My dad, my mom. "What is the matter with you? Why would you even go there?"

It was around this time that my relationship of several years came to an abrupt halt. She was beautiful and fun to be with, but things started getting strange. I went into the freezer one day and found a box of money. What the hell? I confronted her and she told me that she was putting away a little each week for us. That was really bizarre. I suspected she might have been taking the money I left on the dresser when I undressed at night, but I couldn't prove it, so I set up a trap. I put several hundred dollars in my pants pockets and asked her if she'd take them to the dry cleaners for me. Then, I'd call the dry cleaner and tell him I'd left something in my pants pocket and would he check for me. The dry cleaner would tell me, "No, Mr. Sanderson. There is nothing in the pants pockets that were brought in today." This happened a few times. When I confronted her, she denied everything.

That was it for that relationship. I understand she changed her name and had a couple of minor acting roles, but I haven't heard anything about her in decades.

While I was recuperating from my broken foot, the Bruins went on a road trip. The team made arrangements for me and Darryl Edestrand, who was out with a shoulder separation, to have ice time, but my foot was too sore to skate.

Guidolin went crazy. He accused me of being lazy. He announced the names of his centres for the remainder of the season, and I wasn't one of them. He let the press know that his centres would be Phil Esposito, Gregg Sheppard, Andre Savard and Richie LeDuc. I was fed up with Guidolin, and he was fed up with me. We weren't getting along.

We played the Black Hawks in late January. It seemed as though referee Wally Harris had gone blind all of a sudden. He was missing calls all over the place. In the second period, he finally called a penalty on one of the Hawks. I sarcastically applauded his call and he gave me a misconduct. What?! I don't know what got into me, but I went at him. It took Esposito and Dave Forbes, plus linesman John D'Amico, to stop me. I got tossed out of the game. With 50 seconds left, Orr got hauled down and he thought there should have been a tripping call. Harris gave him a misconduct, too. The Boston fans went ballistic. They tossed all kinds of shit on the ice. It got so bad that Harris sent both teams to their dressing rooms. Most of the fans thought the game was over and went home. When the contest resumed more than half an hour later, there were fewer than 3,000 spectators still in the Garden. When we came back out, beer bottles again descended from the balcony heavens and the police had to toss out a handful of fans. Seems like everybody got tossed out of that game. We lost it, by the way, 2–1.

While we were in Atlanta on an extended road trip in early March, several of my teammates held a meeting to discuss whether I was disrupting the team or helping Boston towards a Cup. Then, it all fell apart. On March 10, I got into an altercation with a teammate while we were in Oakland. It was a silly thing, really, but it boiled over. There was a scuffle in the dressing room, and then, after the game—a 6–2 loss—we got into it again.

I was harbouring a lot of frustration and was dealing with a lot of my own shit. I was mad at myself for ever leaving Boston, regardless of the money. My girlfriend and I were finished. My drinking was getting out of hand and I was partying way more than I should have been. And the Bruins team I returned to just wasn't the same as the one I left.

What happened in Oakland should never have happened. I refused to return to Boston with the team, was fined $1,000 and was suspended. The next day, the Bruins issued a statement: "Derek Sanderson is suspended for the balance of the 1973–74 season and the championship playoffs for conduct detrimental to the proper operation of the hockey team."

"Sanderson has been on probation for quite a while," Harry Sinden admitted. "He has repeatedly violated that probation. What happened in California was the last straw. Other players are not fined for missing flights, but a 30-time loser gets hit with a harder penalty. I thought we'd get him back to what he was a few years ago. I thought we'd need him in the playoffs. It was obvious I was just kidding myself."

Guidolin was my main problem. I was my own worst enemy, but Bep Guidolin had been looking for a way to get rid of me. He was trying to humiliate me to show the team that he was the boss. I called him a $14,000-a-year coach, which was probably true, and predicted that he would not return to the Bruins after that season.

"Sanderson has loads of talent and I feel he could still help this team," Bep said, athough I'm sure it was through clenched teeth. "I have nothing against him as an individual. I'm only interested in him as a hockey player and what he could do for a team." And then he added, "A change of scenery would help him."

At the NHL general managers' meeting, Harry told reporters that he doubted I would ever play for the Boston Bruins again. My attorney was granted permission to negotiate with other clubs for my services, although it was subject to approval by the Bruins. Because the trade deadline had passed, I couldn't play for any other NHL team that season.

It was the most challenging season of my career, and I had just come off a doozy. I only played 29 games. The Bruins went three rounds in the playoffs, dumping Toronto and Chicago before losing to the Flyers.

Those were my final days as a Boston Bruin.

CHAPTER 24

BROADWAY AND THE BLUES: 1974–1976

I didn't want to leave the Bruins, but with Bep Guidolin as the coach, there was no way I could have returned. Our situation would never have worked out. I was the victim of Guidolin's inability to handle the team. I couldn't take orders from a guy like him.

Bep claimed I wasn't in shape to help the team, but I was out with a bad back and then broke my foot. "My job was to get players in shape and play the ones who could help us the most," he stated.

He gave Harry Sinden an ultimatum: "Sanderson goes or I go."

As it turned out, both of us were gone. At the end of the 1973–74 season, Harry dumped Guidolin. I don't like to see any man fired. I bore Bep no ill will, even though I believe he tried to undermine my confidence. We hadn't liked each other since I played against his Oshawa Generals in junior.

The rumour was that John Ferguson might be the next Bruins' coach. I would have loved to play for Fergie. In spite of our battles on the ice, I had the utmost respect for the man. I thought he'd be ideal. Instead, they hired Don Cherry.

I had hoped to rejoin the Bruins, but I had burned too many bridges. Had the Bruins taken me back, it would have appeared as if they were letting the players dictate their policy. My attorney called around to various teams to see if he could place me. I found it ironic that while I was playing with Boston, the Bruins treated me like I wasn't worth much, but as soon as a team talked to them about making a deal for me, I was escalated to a franchise player once again and the Bruins wanted two or three good players in return.

My old friend Milt Schmidt was GM of the expansion Washington Capitals, who were set to join the NHL in 1974–75. Milt expressed interest in having me join his team. The Buffalo Sabres, California Golden Seals and St. Louis Blues of the NHL and Cincinnati Stingers of the WHA all made substantial offers, but Boston wanted an arm and a leg, so they all backed away.

I ended up making a deal myself. I called the general manager in New York, Emile "the Cat" Francis, and asked him if his Rangers needed a centreman. He said, "Be here tomorrow."

After beating the Canadiens in six games in the first round of the previous spring's playoffs, the Rangers had lost to the Philadelphia Flyers in a tough seven-game semifinal. That was supposed to be the Rangers' best chance at the Stanley Cup. Francis knew he had to make substantial changes. The first move he made was to trade captain Vic Hadfield and his million-dollar, five-year contract to the Pittsburgh Penguins for low-budget defenceman Nick Beverley.

Boston, meanwhile, was working on a trade with Vancouver involving me. I told Harry to forget about the Canucks, that he had to trade me to New York. He said, "Derek, they won't give me much. I have a nice deal in Vancouver."

"Yeah?" I shrugged. "Well, I'm going to the Apple."

To be honest, the only place I wanted to go was New York, which is ironic because the fans at Madison Square Garden despised me. But I had great respect for Emile Francis. He and I were worlds apart in so many ways, but he was my kind of guy. He is one of the most knowledgeable hockey men I have ever met. When we were on opposing teams, Francis and I had a love-hate relationship. I wanted to beat the Rangers as much as he wanted to beat the Bruins. He told me he had always admired the way I played the game, and I respected him as one of the best hockey men in the National Hockey League. He gave me a chance that the guys in Boston wouldn't give me. I liked Harry Sinden as a man, but was disappointed that he and the Bruins gave up on me like that.

But there was one more reason I favoured New York. My girlfriend was a model in New York, and it would let me spend more time with her. She was

19 years old and gorgeous. At one time, she had been profiled in *Cosmopolitan* in a feature called "How to Be Totally Gorgeous."

Francis had contacted a few of his players to get a read on what they thought about trading for me. "I told Emile that I didn't think it was a good idea to bring him on board," admitted Brad Park. But Francis had already made up his mind.

My trade was more complex than it seemed on the surface. It was a three-way deal. On June 10, the Rangers left Jimmy Neilson, a defenceman, unprotected in the intra-league draft. The California Golden Seals, choosing first, had agreed to take Neilson, and then the Rangers had the option of taking a player from Oakland or accepting cash as compensation. New York took Walt McKechnie, who was left unprotected by the Seals, and on June 12, the Rangers sent McKechnie to Boston for me.

Harry Sinden knew I had to go, but was saddened that things ended as they did for me in Boston. "All the benefits of being a pro hockey player—the money, the fame, the fan adulation, invitations on the TV talk shows and the recognition—came too easy for Derek," Sinden said. "In the past four years, he's had it all and he hasn't had to work for it. Maybe going to a new team will get him back to square one and having to earn all that again will get him straightened out. I hope so because under all the nonsense, he is a likeable man."

After making $100,000 with the Bruins in 1973–74, the Rangers offered me a one-year deal for $140,000. Perfect! The Rangers were already strong down the middle. They had Jean Ratelle, Walt Tkaczuk and Peter Stemkowski. Where was I going to fit? The Cat assured me that he'd find enough ice time for me. He told me he wanted me for penalty killing first and foremost, but I'd get my share of playing time. He asked me if I had ever played left wing. I'd have played anywhere he wanted me.

Francis warned me that there was one set of rules that applied to everybody on his team. I told him I understood. He also wasn't sure whether I'd be allowed to keep my moustache, as there was a club rule that no player was allowed to have facial hair. If the Cat wanted my moustache and sideburns gone, they would have come off. Whatever he said went, but he never asked.

My attorney warned me that this was my last chance. "The time has come to show you can play hockey like you used to. You have to settle down, keep your mouth shut and just play good hockey."

Nobody knew better than me that the Rangers had stuck their neck out for me. I knew Emile Francis was keeping his fingers crossed that I wouldn't cause him or the club any grief. They hoped I'd be smart enough to avoid making any statements that might embarrass the Rangers. They asked me if I'd do some publicity for the team during the summer, so I went to New York and met John Halligan, their public relations guy. He showed up with all these pretty girls. We went around town getting pictures taken with me and the models in different locations. Everyone wanted to know what was going on, of course. It was a sunny day and great for photo opportunities. A lot of secretaries were outside on their lunch break. The photographer made it look like they were waiting for me. They had no idea who I was, yet it started a buzz: "Oh my God, we've got Derek Sanderson! He's crazy, you know!" That's what everybody was talking about.

When I played in Boston, the Rangers fans hated me. They used to spit on me; they used to throw things at me. They hung me in effigy from the balcony. Twice, I had gone into the stands in New York. When I was traded to New York, the press told me the fans were going to eat me for breakfast, but there's no better friend than a converted enemy. The fans were great! They made me feel right at home. Rangers fans are very knowledgeable, and when you play there, you're a Ranger for life. The fans in New York were every bit as good as the fans in Boston. Both cities have fans that are intensely loyal to their team.

I was packing my things for the move to New York when there was a knock on my door. An agent from the Drug Enforcement Administration and his partner were there with two beautiful girls.

"Can we have a word?" the officer asked.

"Yeah."

"We think you're dirty," he said. "You may have dodged a bullet in the past, but word has it that you're still up to your eyeballs in drugs."

I told them it was bullshit.

"If that's true, then you won't mind taking these two agents and introducing them around at the parties in New York when you go, will you?"

I knew the parties in New York. There were some dealers there, but I had no option. I couldn't *not* take them. So I told the officers I would do it. "Love to work with you ladies," I said sarcastically.

I immediately phoned everybody I knew in New York. I told them that if they were attending a particular gala event at the UN Plaza, that they shouldn't bring any dope. "Don't let anybody have any weight. Tell everybody that the two I'm bringing are heat."

I thought it was a pretty devious plan. If somebody got pinched at the party, they'd eventually find out who testified and realize that they were the girls I brought to the party. I was guilty one way or another. There was no saving grace there.

I took the ladies to the gala. The guys went wild. They partied hard with them, the whole thing, and it didn't seem to bother them at all. Nobody had any weight on them. After two or three parties, the agents said, "Forget it." They realized I was clean.

During the summer, I jogged a lot to get in shape. Instead of driving the car, I walked. I played some tennis, too. The bleeding stomach was over and my back problems were gone. I was feeling good. I cut my hair shorter, but that was cool because shorter hair was coming back into style. I still had my moustache. Emile Francis was okay with that. To be honest, I was surprised—it was the first time he'd ever allowed his players to have facial hair.

I wanted to make a good impression, so I asked Francis if I could come to camp early. I had spoken to Rod Gilbert, and he thought it would be a wise move.

The Rangers' training camp was held in Kitchener, Ontario, which isn't far from my hometown of Niagara Falls, so I left my Rolls-Royce with my parents and took my dad's station wagon to camp. I thought it was better not to come into camp and have my new teammates accuse me of showboating.

I went to camp with the rookies to get into shape and to show everybody I was serious about wanting to do a job for the Rangers. I think that won over a few who questioned the trade. "Derek was one of those guys that you had to be aware of on the ice when you played against him," Brad Park recalled. "Two things could happen—he'd pick your pocket and steal you blind or he'd embarrass you. The past run-ins that we had are things that you put behind you when you become teammates. It's a team game no matter whether you like or hate the guy sitting next to you in the same sweater."

You couldn't get away with a thing with the Cat. He treated us all the same. For inspiration, he showed us Vince Lombardi's film *Run to Daylight*, a made-for-television documentary about the Green Bay Packers' 1964 training camp.

Boston's training camps were a picnic compared with New York's. The Rangers were on the ice from 8:30 to 10, and then back on the ice from three to four in the afternoon. I threw up three times the first two days of camp.

After being part of the Boston organization for so long, and part of a group of guys who were really, really close, I wondered how I'd be accepted. You have to remember that our playoff series had been intense affairs full of fights and venom. I thought, "This could prove interesting."

It actually worked out very well. I really liked the guys on the team.

Rod Gilbert was already a great friend. We spent a lot of time together as we were the only Rangers living in Manhattan at the time. Jean Ratelle was a true gentleman. I would say of all the people I've ever met in hockey, Ratty was the most moral, decent and family oriented. He was quite religious, but never forced his beliefs on anyone. Ratelle went out and played the game very cleanly.

I got along really well with Bert Wilson and Teddy Irvine. Eddie Giacomin and I had had that run-in in 1970, but he became one of the guys I liked best on the Rangers. He and Gilles Villemure were our goaltenders. Great guys and both fiercely competive.

It took a while for me and Pete Stemkowski to warm up to each other. We didn't like each other at first, but I soon found out Stemmer was a good guy. Same with Brad Park.

We used to call Steve Vickers "Sarge." The two of us were watching the Belmont Stakes on TV in June 1973. That day, Secretariat won, completing the coveted Triple Crown that also included the Kentucky Derby and the Preakness. I casually mentioned that Secretariat was the first horse since Northern Dancer to win the Triple Crown.

Sarge said, "Turk, I don't think Northern Dancer won all three races."

I argued, "Oh yeah, the horse absolutely did. Won them all. In fact, I'm so sure that I'll place a wager on it with you."

He said, "Sure. How much?"

It only took me a second to respond. "How about $10,000? That's how sure I am."

"You're out of your mind, Turk," he countered. "I'm not betting that much. I've got an idea. We both have moustaches that are part of our identity. I'll bet you your moustache that Northern Dancer didn't win the Triple Crown."

"You're on," I replied. I was anxious to make shaving off Sarge's moustache a spectacle.

We called over to the sports department of *The New York Times*. While we waited, some guy over there went into the archives to check out the question.

"Hey guys, I've got your answer," he said on his return. "You ready? Northern Dancer won the Derby and the Preakness but came in third in the Belmont Stakes. Who won the bet?"

If he had listened carefully, he'd have been able to tell. I was cursing like a sailor while Sarge laughed his ass off. I surrendered my moustache—the one I had fought for and that had become my trademark—at the hands of my victorious teammate. Damn, I'd been so sure Northern Dancer took all three! Vickers took great pleasure in shaving it off. I started growing it back right away, and don't think I've shaved it off again to this day.

Ricky Middleton and I became pretty good friends through the course of that training camp. We both liked the nightlife. In Emile Francis's opinion, we both liked it just a little too much.

There were so many great guys on the Rangers, but there were cliques. When I was with the Bruins, Bobby Orr would never allow cliques to form. Part of the Rangers' problem was geography. Guys lived all over the place, so it was tough to build the family feeling we had in Boston. Gilbert and I lived right in the city, but we had guys in Long Beach, elsewhere on Long Island—all over the map.

In Boston, if one guy went someplace, everybody went. We had Bobby's two-drink rule and everybody had to go. We were all family. Other teams didn't do that. "Oh, my dad's here. Catch up with you guys another night." Not in Boston. We made everyone absolutely comfortable. When I went to New York, after a game, I said, "Okay, where are we going?" And the guys asked, "What do you mean, where are we going?" Everybody went their own way. It was an entirely different feeling.

Guys would go out in groups of two or three, but there would never be 20 at a time. And the rookies were always left on their own. They never felt like they belonged. As one of the team leaders, Brad Park was part of a clique he never even believed he was part of. He had his go-to guys that he went out with all the time.

I flipped out on the guys in the room one time. I stood up and threw a glove in anger. "I'm sick and tired of this fucking team. Get on the same page. You guys aren't together. You don't know how to win." Eddie Giacomin and Gilles Villemure agreed with me. They wanted to win so badly. Everybody wanted to win, but they just didn't know how. In Boston, we had the greatness of Bobby Orr, and he had the amazing ability to unify, to show that no one was more or less important than anybody else. Everybody was important to Bobby. That's what a leader does. You lose because you don't have a leader.

Our practice rink was out on Rockaway Boulevard on Long Island, which was a pretty good haul from where I was living in Manhattan. I used to ride in from Manhattan with Rod Gilbert. I woke up one morning and realized I'd missed my ride. I guess he honked and honked and when I didn't come out, he figured I had found another way there. I ended up taking a cab from Manhattan to Long Beach, which was something like $70. I didn't have the cash, but figured that when I got there, I'd ask one of the guys to loan me the money.

I walked into the locker room and the cab driver followed me in. He wasn't taking any chance that I might stiff him. I guess the guys picked up on what was going on, so they decided to bust my balls. When I asked if I could borrow 70 bucks, nobody seemed to have any money. "Sorry, Turk. I'm a little short until payday." "Didn't bring my wallet, Turk. Sorry." "I've only got four bucks and I need it to buy a sandwich. Sorry, Turk."

This went on for 10 or 15 minutes. I was shitting bricks and the cab driver was hounding me. "I want my money, guy!"

Finally, the boys in the room started to laugh and ponied up the cash for this poor cab driver.

Got me good!

After practice and games, a few of the Rangers would go to Il Vagabondo, our hangout. There'd be seven or eight of us. Before I came along, they always split the bill, but when I arrived, I couldn't believe that they were so cheap as to be figuring out who owed what and who drank more. I said, "Give me that bill. I'll get it this time."

"No," they insisted. "Just put down a ten and you're good."

"Look, guys. Money is not that important. You can't take it with you." With that, I pulled out a $100 bill and lit it on fire with my cigarette lighter. We all just watched it burn away. I thought the waitress was going to kill me. Her eyes almost popped out of her head. I left her a $100 tip that night.

People had this image of me—the devil-may-care playboy who went through cash (and women) like water. I guess I fed it, but it really was exaggerated. I was insecure, pure and simple. I liked to be liked. Sometimes, I did crazy things to get attention. There were two Derek Sandersons. There was the public one who was crazy, admittedly, and did things to get noticed. Then, there was the private one, a guy who is actually quite shy and insecure.

People kept telling me I was a millionaire. Hell, I might have been a millionaire on paper at one time, but I was blowing $150,000 a year and I had no idea where it was going.

Rod Gilbert had suggested that I live in Manhattan because it was closer to the action. Emile Francis was afraid that New York's nightlife would eat me alive. Let me tell you that what they say is true: New York never, ever sleeps! Emile was right and I was not prepared.

I loved New York. I kept my private life as separate from my professional life as possible, but the media never let me forget I was Derek Sanderson. I wore a full-length fur coat through the winter and squired beautiful women around town. That was my life.

Gilles Villemure said, "Derek was outspoken and the media was after him all the time. He was the guy nearest the door in the dressing room and all the media was there. Nineteen other guys? No problem. They wanted Derek. He had that personality. He was a natural with the media. He got all the attention. We didn't have to say anything because they all wanted to talk to him."

"Derek was a beauty," said Stemkowski. "If you got him in a group, Derek had to be the centre of attention. He had to tell a story and would top anything you had. But if you got Derek one on one, he was a good guy. He got along with everybody. There was no one who didn't like him. You just put up with him and shook your head at the way he was."

I was stunned one night while watching *The Tonight Show* to hear Johnny Carson say, "When Derek Sanderson was playing hockey in Boston, he was one of those people that brought excitement to their sport, like Joe Namath to football, Ilie Nastase to tennis and Muhammad Ali to boxing."

Wow! Heady praise.

I started the season wearing number 4, but when Rod Seiling was waived early in the season, I switched to my old number 16 and Ron Greschner took 4. The same fans who used to hate me quickly adopted me when I started wearing their colours. They used to chant, "We want Derek! We want Derek!" Every time I stepped on the ice, they gave me a nice round of applause.

Every team had their systems. The Rangers believed in a very short passing game coming out of our own end. The Cat hated the long pass from corner to wing. That pass got picked off a lot because it was so easy to anticipate.

I was happy to be in New York, but didn't get much playing time because they already had three good centres in Ratelle, Tkaczuk and Stemkowski. I got the chance to play more when Stemmer went down with a charley horse. They put me out on a regular shift between Jerry Butler and Ted Irvine and I responded with two goals in three games. Then, Francis put me on left wing with Ratelle and Gilbert on the top line. Later, Tkaczuk broke his leg. When they played me full time, I had 18 points in eight games.

People asked me how my game was different from five years earlier. It was simple: I was more intelligent. Back then, I thought that fighting was what was happening, but any moron can go out and beat up on guys. It takes no talent. I hadn't mellowed, but I had learned how to play. When you first come up to "The Show," you want to prove yourself—show that you belonged. You hit guys. You fought guys. You were really hungry. You were making $11,000 or $12,000 and could make $19,000 by winning the Stanley Cup. You wanted it badly!

When you're a veteran, I wouldn't say you were complacent, but you didn't feel that you had to prove anything. You still had to work hard, but I was making $140,000 in New York. Life was different. I didn't need to fight anymore. It's not that I wouldn't, but why did I want to get into it with a guy like Eddie Shack, who was a pal of mine? For what? I went out and played the game without wasting the extra steps on dropping the gloves. Besides, the Rangers were a tough team. Steve Vickers, Teddy Irvine, Bert Wilson, Jerry Butler, Ronnie Harris, Gilles Marotte—these were tough kids. Pete Stemkowski was tough. Walt Tkaczuk and Billy Fairbairn didn't back down from anything.

During a game against the Flyers, Emile Francis came into the dressing room between periods and was steaming. I think we had lost three in a row. We were way too good to lose three in a row. He put his hands on his hips like he always did and was standing there in his blue blazer. "Okay, let me see what I've got here," he began. "This seems to be the best that the New York Rangers can put their hands on." He looked around the room. "Gilles Marotte. Captain Crunch. You couldn't crunch a Dixie cup. And Ronnie Harris, you're supposed to be a hitter. What have you hit? You can barely hit the floor, for Christ's sake!"

He went around the room and then came to me. "And Sanderson. Rabble-rouser. Tough guy. You've turned into a powder puff! You've let your social life get in the way of hockey."

He said, "What is it with you guys? I went and got a team that's the toughest team in the league on paper. What happened to you guys?" He took a dramatic pause. "Okay, tonight, I don't care about the two points. Tonight, I only care about one thing and that's finding our toughness. I don't care what else happens, but I don't want this team to get into the double-digit-second mark without a brawl."

He started the next period with Johnny Bednarski, Bert Wilson and me at forward and Ronnie Harris and Gilles Marotte on the blue line. The moment the puck dropped, Bednarski ran at Don Saleski. It started a donnybrook. You didn't push the Broad Street Bullies around at home without retribution. For that matter, you didn't push them around on the road, either.

I worked really hard in New York. "Sanderson showed the guys he wanted to belong," Brad Park confirmed. "He worked his butt off."

My hips and back were killing me. I was taking my prescription medications, but found that drinking dulled the pain.

The second-to-last game of the season was a do-or-die match-up with the Atlanta Flames. At the end of two, we were down 2–0, but we scored three in the third to win the game. I got the winning goal that night. Then, we beat the Islanders in the final game of the season to earn a spot in the playoffs.

I scored 25 goals and 25 assists as a spare part with the Rangers in 1974–75. I led the Rangers in penalty minutes with 106.

Bobby Orr led the NHL in scoring again in 1974–75. It was very strange to play against Bobby after all those years of playing together. When we played against the Bruins, he'd be cradling the puck behind his own net and I'd taunt him. "You aren't going anywhere, kid." He'd get pissed. He'd stand behind the net with the puck and I'd go, "Go ahead. You're going to pass it because you ain't carrying it." I did that to him in practice for eight years. Davey Keon taught me that—dance a little left, dance a little right, and the guy with the puck behind his own net can't go anywhere. You don't want to piss Bobby off too much, though, or he'll make you pay. I was just busting his balls a little.

We faced the Islanders in the first round of the playoffs. Before the first game, I gave an edict that nobody was to shave until we either won the Stanley Cup or were eliminated. Everybody agreed, and if anybody shaved, they were fined $100. Emile Francis agreed to our plan. This may very well have been the start of the tradition of the playoff beard.

The beards didn't last long. We were eliminated in three games by our local rivals, the Islanders.

I met a girl at a small bar in New York. After a few glances, she seemed interested and I was intrigued. I had just broken up with my girlfriend and this girl seemed willing. After some back and forth, the bottom line was that she wanted some coke. "I don't do that shit," I told her.

"I do," she said.

We bantered a bit, but she figured I was a holdout and moved on. A dealer came in and she began to flirt with him—all the while, glancing at me. I got the message pretty quickly. For the first time in my life, I bought cocaine, although I had no intention of using it. I got it for her. We went back to her place and things were going well. She wanted the coke, so I broke it out. "I don't want to do it alone. It's no fun," she said. Drunk, and with no safeguards of reason in place, my logic was, "Who's going to know?"

The fact was, I would.

I crossed the line. The beginning of the end: a pretty face with a great body started me on cocaine.

I discovered that cocaine gave me the ability to continue my favoured pursuit, which was drinking, for longer periods of time. Coke allowed me to stay awake longer so I could drink more. The combination was lethal for me. I was predisposed to being an alcoholic, and here I was combining copious amounts of alcohol with pain drugs and cocaine. I was out of my mind.

I was really looking forward to my second year in New York. I loved the city and the fans. I was coming off a good year, but losing to the Islanders in the first round of the playoffs had been devastating. Emile Francis was crushed and we all knew that changes were coming.

It started with Teddy Irvine, Jerry Butler and Bert Wilson being dealt to St. Louis for John Davidson and Bill Collins that summer. In August, Ron Stewart was named coach, and all I could think was, "Oh shit, I'm dead." He had taken Springfield to the Calder Cup championship over New Haven the previous spring. I knew my days in New York were numbered. I thought Ron Stewart was one of the biggest jerks who ever walked the face of the earth.

Ever since he and I had a fight when the Bruins brought me up for a couple of games in 1966, I'd hated him.

The Rangers selected Wayne Dillon with their number one pick in the draft that summer. He had won a Memorial Cup with the Toronto Marlboros in 1973, but had played two seasons in the WHA and been a 30-goal scorer. The Rangers then had five centremen: Ratelle, Tkaczuk, Stemkowski, Dillon and me. Emile Francis, who was still the GM, said, "We can't afford you all. One of you has to go."

I went to camp, but Stewart buried me. I knew it wasn't going to work out because of our mutual hatred. We played the St. Louis Blues during the preseason, and Stewart benched me and Ricky Middleton. It wasn't hard to see the writing on the wall.

Before the game, I went to my pal Eddie Johnston, who by then was the Blues' backup goaltender, and told him, "I gotta get outta here, E.J. Can you get me to St. Louis?"

He asked, "I'm sure I can, Turk, but will you come? You're not going to hold them up for extra cash or anything, are you?"

"No, none of that shit," I said. "Just get me out of here!"

We played the game and afterwards, Popsy told me to meet him and Sid Salomon, the Blues' owner. I did, and we came to an agreement. I told them I had no intention of making a scene or asking for more money. "What I'm making is all I need." We shook hands on the deal.

The next morning at practice with the Rangers, I acted as though everything was normal. Emile Francis called me into his office and said, "I don't know if I've done you a favour."

I said, "Where'd you trade me?" Then I blindsided him. "I don't mind St. Louis. They've got a good team."

His jaw hit the floor. "How did you know?"

I winked.

"Players are making their own deals now?" He was pissed off. "I had a feeling there was something behind this!"

On October 30, 1975, the Rangers traded me to St. Louis for future considerations, which turned out to be the first-round draft pick in 1977 that they had given the Blues earlier. The Rangers used the pick to select Lucien DeBlois.

While I was sitting with Francis, I said, "Cat, let me tell you something. The best player you have on this team is Ricky Middleton. He's a diamond in the rough. He has a tremendous hockey mind and a set of hands like I've never seen."

Francis just shook his head. "Great! Now you're a manager and a coach, too!"

"Just doing you a favour, Cat," I said. "You've been good to me and I'm just giving you the facts. This kid has an unorthodox style, so he's going to be his own type of player. Don't try to make him something he isn't. He will be one of the best ever, so don't lose him. He's not tough, but he is afraid of no one. Just let him play and watch how good he is."

Francis didn't acknowledge my suggestion. He just shrugged.

My trade was just one of the deals New York made that week. They traded both of the goalies that had carried the team for several years. They had picked up John Davidson in the summer, so they sent Gilles Villemure to Chicago on October 28 and then traded Eddie Giacomin to Detroit on October 31. But the Rangers weren't done dismantling the team yet. A week later, they announced a blockbuster. On November 7, they sent Brad Park and Jean Ratelle to the Bruins for Phil Esposito, Carol Vadnais and Joe Zanussi.

I was really surprised, but by then I was with the Blues, so I didn't really care what the Rangers did.

By the way, they went and traded Ricky Middleton, too. Ron Stewart wanted him gone because he thought I had been a bad influence on him. They sent him to Boston for Kenny Hodge at the end of that season. It was one of the all-time worst deals ever made in the National Hockey League. When a writer later asked Rick what he thought of the trade, he said, "Oh, it was a good trade! Twenty pounds for 10 years."

Esposito wanted Hodge in New York. He wanted to try to recreate the magic of the Bruins, but Hodgey was on the far side of the mountain by then. Kenny played just 96 games before they sent him to the American Hockey

League, and he never came back. Ricky Middleton played for 12 more years. All he did was score 402 goals for the Bruins.

As much as I'd loved playing in New York, I looked forward to a fresh start in St. Louis. I knew it was a good hockey move for me. With the Rangers, I was often playing left wing on the fourth line. As a player, I was going nowhere.

I knew a few of the guys on the Blues. My old friend Eddie Johnston was playing goal. I had also played with Rick Smith in Boston. Ted Irvine had played with me in New York the year before. The Blues were Garry Unger's team. He'd been with them since 1970–71 and was their consistent scoring leader. I had played against Garry in junior when I was in Niagara Falls and he was with the London Nationals, and we both broke into the NHL in 1967–68. Garry was a great guy and had a flair about him both on and off the ice. Bob Gassoff was a tough competitor for the Blues. I really liked Bob, and after I left St. Louis, was devastated to hear that he was killed in a motorcycle accident on Unger's property in May 1977.

And I certainly knew Bob Plager.

The Plager boys were tough sons of bitches. I played against the youngest one, Billy, when I was in junior. When I was with Niagara Falls, he played for the Peterborough Petes. The three brothers—Bill, Barclay and Bob—had once played for St. Louis at the same time. By the time I arrived, it was just Bob and Barclay.

Bob and I hated each other. One night while I was with Boston, we were in St. Louis, and towards the end of the game, after a whistle, I stuck out my knee and caught him. He was in agony. There was no penalty called, but I had hurt him. He left the rink on crutches. As our bus was pulling away, I saw him heading to his car and couldn't help myself. "How's the knee, Bob?"

He yelled back, "I'll get you! Your time will come, Sanderson!"

Later that season, we played the Blues again and Plager was back in their lineup. Every time he skated past me, he said, "I owe you one, and I'm going to get you!" We'd be in the corner and he'd smirk, "It could be tonight, Sanderson. And it won't be pretty!"

About a year later, he caught me with a hip check that sent me ass over tea-kettle. Busted up my knee pretty good. When I came back and we next played the Blues, I smiled at him and said, "I guess we're even now."

"Uh-uh," he said. "My hit was clean. Yours was dirty. I'm still going to get you and I'll remind you, it won't be pretty."

This went on for years, even after I got traded to the Rangers. We were playing the Blues and Claude Larose and I got into a scrap. Plager came over and we collided by their bench. He grabbed me and said, "It could be now."

I just stared at him. "You've been saying that for years! I don't think you have the guts!"

"Really?" he said. I closed my eyes and waved at him. When I opened them, his entire fist was in my face. He pounded me pretty good. I took a lot of punches and no one came to bail me out. I never went down and never bled, but asked him, "Is that all you have?" When I left the ice, I held my hands up in the air as if I'd won. The crowd went crazy!

The next season, we were playing together in St. Louis. It's never fun to go to a team where there is built-in animosity, but Bob came over, shook my hand and said, "What happened to you in New York will never happen to you in St. Louis. We're family here." Gassoff also came up to me and said the same thing. I appreciated that. I was getting too old to fight young kids anymore.

You hate guys when you play against them but respect them when you play with them. But once one of you leaves, you hate the bastards all over again.

Pierre Plante was wearing number 16 and had been for a few seasons, so I took 19.

When I got traded to St. Louis, Garry Young, the coach, asked me into his office and said, "Who would you like to play with?" Other than in the WHA, I had never in my life been asked who I wanted as linemates.

Chuck Lefley had been a 20-goal scorer with the Canadiens. One night, he was winding up for a slapshot and I kept coming at him. He high-sticked me as I wiped him out. I took a cheap shot at him and blew out his knee. He sure didn't like me, even though he didn't have a mean bone in his body. And

Claude Larose had been a valuable player for the Canadiens and North Stars and always tough to play against. What I loved about him was that you could absolutely trust that Montreal Canadien heart, courage and discipline. Word was that he was going to be waived. I ended up saying, "If I can, I'd like to play with Lefley and Larose." They put us together on a line and I was resurrected.

In Boston, I was a third-line centre, but with the Blues, they looked at my line as one-two with Garry Unger's line. Other than my games in the WHA, I hadn't been a first-line centre since junior. That changes your game substantially. In Boston, I played against all the big scorers, like Mikita and Beliveau. In St. Louis, I was expected to score, so I had checking lines shadowing me.

Lefley and I had real chemistry. He could skate like the wind and had a great shot. I was able to draw players to me and then dish the puck to Chuck, who was a great finisher. Our line took a regular turn, but I was also paired with Chuck on the penalty kill. I scored in my first game with St. Louis. It was October 30, 1975, against Boston.

I hadn't played much in shorthanded situations in New York, where Tkaczuk and Fairbairn were the principal penalty killers. Lefley and I really clicked on the PK. In our first 16 games together, I had two shorthanded goals and Chuck had six. It seemed that we got about three shorthanded chances in every game.

Lefley was really easy to play with. We really connected, and the proof was on the stat sheet. That season, Chuck led the Blues with 43 goals and 85 points. Garry Unger had 83 points, and I finished third on the Blues with 67, the most I ever collected in my NHL career. Neither Chuck nor I ever enjoyed a better season.

We faced the Buffalo Sabres in the first round of the playoffs, but they eliminated us two games to one.

I really worked hard to put my efforts into playing the game on the ice rather than making headlines off it. I worked hard to curtail my drinking. The bright lights of St. Louis were a great deal dimmer than in New York or Boston, and that helped. I had used drinking to forget my problems, but it was a good season and I had fewer problems in 1975–76. One of the things I discovered—and you'll laugh at this—is that instead of excessive drinking, I took up playing Monopoly instead.

I loved Monopoly. When most people play, the game goes on for hours, but I found that a properly played game could be over in 25 minutes. Hockey players are traditionally card players, but instead of poker, I used to have four teammates playing Monopoly, and everything had to be paid in real dollars.

But in truth, the games had only just begun.

Whenever I visited my parents in Niagara Falls, I played golf with my old neighbourhood buddies. During the summer of 1975, I went home and got together with Tommy Cottringer and the guys for a day at Cherry Hill, a great golf course in Ridgeway, just outside of Fort Erie.

The booze was talking one time when I told Tommy about my dream of one day settling down with my girlfriend on a ranch with lots of acreage and a few horses. I had this romantic notion that I could be a gentleman farmer.

On the way to the golf course, we stopped at a convenience store and Tommy picked up one of those real estate magazines.

"Hey Turk, here's a place you should buy. It's a ranch in Fort Erie, so you can play golf at Cherry Hill."

I wasn't really thinking of buying a place at the time, but the idea was intriguing. We looked at the picture and description. It was a gorgeous 10-bedroom ranch on Windmill Point Road, right at the mouth of the river. There was 400 feet of beach and the property extended 400 feet into Lake Erie. Cherry trees lined both sides of an 1,150-foot driveway that led up to this palatial estate. There was a fenced-in corral for horses on one side and a three-car garage on the other. There wasn't a nail in the house. It was constructed completely using wooden pegs.

We played our round of golf, but the boys agreed that we should go out and take a look at the property. I called the realtor and he told us we could meet him at 4 p.m. to look at the place. We drove over and the place was even better than it was described. We weren't able to go inside, but we peeked into the windows. The house was absolutely beautiful, and while I wasn't necessarily ready to fulfill my dream, it was a place I could envision living in.

I inquired about the asking price. The realtor said it was listed at $475,000. In 1975, that was huge money—about the same as a couple million today. There was no way I was paying that, so I looked at him and said, "How about if I offer $425,000?"

The realtor took me aside. He had a secret he wanted to share. "My client is going through a divorce. His wife will be freezing his holdings on Friday at noon. Offer him $160,000 cash. Take a chance. He can hide the money. Nobody around here has got the kind of money that he's asking for."

I couldn't believe what I had been told! The problem was, I couldn't put my hands on that amount of cash so quickly. I figured I could scrape together about $130,000, but the rest of my money was in escrow. I called around to a few friends. A few were blunt and told me they were doing me a favour by saying no. "Derek, you're living pretty fast." By then, word of my drinking and drug use were everywhere throughout the hockey community. Nevertheless, I somehow got the full amount and on the Wednesday, I went to the seller's office and offered him $160,000 cash.

He threw his pen at me. "Get out of my office, you thief!" he yelled. "Do you think I'm stupid?"

I told him it was the best I could do. Real estate wasn't really hot at that time. I handed him my phone number in case he reconsidered.

"To hell with you and your phone number."

On Thursday afternoon at three o'clock, he called me.

"Get in here." He really loved that home, but he wanted to liquidate as quickly as he could before his wife got it. As mad as he was at me, he knew that it was the best offer he was going to get before the clock ticked down. No one else was going to be able to pay him even that much money—and in cash—on the spot.

He signed the offer. "Give me the money!"

I wrote him a cheque. I owned the place for $160,000.

I dreamed of sharing this amazing place with Jill, so that weekend, I brought her up from New York to take a look. I said, "Consider this an engagement gift!"

She said, "Yeah? But who's going to clean it?"

Men don't think like women do. I wasn't prepared for that comment. I thought "gorgeous mansion." She thought "too many rooms to clean."

So now I had this beautiful ranch. I gazed out at my property and all I could think was, "Wow! I'm out of my league here. I've got no cash, but I've got this amazing huge ranch." It didn't really matter because I was certain that I was going to play in the NHL for another 10 or 12 years and I was starting to make some serious money. But I couldn't see the forest for the trees. At that time, I wasn't very together. I was all about fun, and when you're a professional athlete, it's got to be about dedication, focus and concentration on your sport.

There was an immaculate horse barn at the ranch, so I bought a few horses. A local guy, Pat Keating, had a small construction company about a half-mile away and I hired him to bring his backhoe over and clear some land for me. I asked him, "Do you know anything about horses?"

It turned out that he did.

I bought four horses. Three of them were great, but one was crazy. It was a little cutting pony. When the vet came over, he said, "I'll shoe and run those three, but I'm not going anywhere near that other one."

I gave the pony to the Fort Erie racetrack to take care of, but Pat informed me they weren't taking proper care of him and that the horse had thrush and could die. Thrush is a bacterial infection that horses get in their hooves from unclean stalls.

I had had too much to drink one night and came up with the brilliant solution that I'd steal my horse back from the track. It was wintertime, and I snuck in, got the horse, and as we were crossing the property, he went over a three-foot ledge into a large pond . . . with me under him. *Kaboom!* I sobered up pretty damned quickly! The horse couldn't get up and thrashed about wildly, and I was certain I was going to die, either from drowning, hypothermia or being kicked by the horse. In desperation, I grabbed his tail and pulled as hard as I could. He reared up and, in doing so, pulled me out.

The horse bolted away and I had to walk home. It had to be 10 below, and I was soaked to the bone. I froze my ass off. By the time I arrived at the ranch, that horse had found its way back to the barn at the house.

I liked to invite my friends from Boston and New York to come up to Fort

Erie and chill out. It was a great refuge. There was a huge billiard room with an antique pool table and a massive stone fireplace that got a lot of use. We'd be out of our minds, but talk for hours, solving the world's problems. The parties were legendary. I was hanging out at Studio 54, the legendary New York disco, and invited several stars, including Rod Stewart, to use my home to hang out. I don't know whether he ever did, but he had a key.

I remember one time I invited a bunch of people up to my place and then realized I didn't have enough beds. Even with 10 bedrooms, only two were furnished. I called Pat and we bought at least a dozen bedroom sets—beds, mattresses, pillows, bedding. They were used that weekend and never again. I never even thought about the cost. I was going through money pretty good in those days.

I had this beautiful split-rail fencing all down my property line. It cost me a fortune, but because some of my friends couldn't find firewood one weekend, they stupidly tore down the fencing and burned it in the fireplace.

My girlfriend, Jill, used to come up from New York, and there were several times when she couldn't find me. She'd panic and call Pat Keating in the middle of the night to help her look for me. More often than not, they'd usually find me in the barn, wasted and sleeping in the stall with the horses.

I still had my Rolls-Royce at the time and I put it to good use. The locals used to see me driving the Rolls through the fields, bouncing over the furrows with the back seat full of straw and the trunk full of beer. It didn't bother me. I was living the life I had dreamed of.

CHAPTER 25

WILD IN THE WEST: 1976–77

Two old pals, and two of the brightest hockey minds of the era, found new employment to start the 1976–77 season. Emile Francis joined the St. Louis Blues as general manager, and John Ferguson took his place with the New York Rangers.

Francis had dealt me from New York to St. Louis the season before; the Ranger coach, Ron Stewart, wanted me out and Francis said he never overruled his coach. I went on to have a career year, with 67 points in 65 games. My linemate Chuck Lefley scored nearly twice as many goals as he ever had before. And then, in February 1977, the Blues let me go! Francis told me they couldn't afford me. I was making $200,000.

There was more to the decision. Emile and I clashed. I hadn't played a lot through the first half of the season, collecting 21 points in 32 games, and it hurt—physically and emotionally. I pouted. My hips were perpetually sore and it was terribly painful to walk or skate. I had gone back to drinking heavily, and I was hooked on painkillers.

The Blues had had enough. "We went along with him as long as we could," Emile commented. Just after New Year's, they decided to send me to the Kansas City Blues of the Central Hockey League, but to do so, they had to waive me through the league. Any NHL team could have plucked me off the waiver wire for $30,000.

No one did.

"You're a great player with lots of talent, but you have to block out your personal affairs," the Cat warned. He told me I was welcome to make my own

259

deal if I could find a team that would take me. I contacted the Bruins, the Rangers, Buffalo Sabres, Los Angeles Kings and Vancouver Canucks. No luck. The teams believed I represented too much of a gamble for a $200,000-a-year contract.

On January 11, 1977, I was sent down to Kansas City. It was very humbling for this 30-year-old, but the Blues had to pay me my NHL salary, so I couldn't be too resentful.

I scored the winning goal in my first game in Kansas City. Then, it was a six-and-a-half-hour bus ride to Oklahoma City for the next game. It had been a while since I'd had to endure one of those ball-busters. It was depressing. I needed to develop a positive attitude and not feel sorry for myself. I never talked about money. I just tried to be one of the guys. The kids on the team told me their troubles and asked me what it was like in "The Show." When we got to Oklahoma City, they held a press conference for me. That was where I'd got my start in the pros, and I appreciated their loyalty to me.

There were two things that helped buoy my spirits while I made my home in a hotel room in Lenexa, a suburb of Kansas City. One was that I flew in Jill, my fiancée, on weekends. The other was that there were scouts at the games. I had hoped that a playoff-bound NHL team might have a player injured down the stretch and make a deal for me.

I took the opportunity to mentor some of the young guys playing with KC. I really worked with Bernie Federko on his faceoffs, and he has often expressed his gratitude.

In my third game, I broke some ribs. I was certain that the injury ended any hope of joining an NHL team that season, but I was very pleasantly surprised to be acquired by the Vancouver Canucks on February 19. I had played eight games during my exile to the Central League, and scored four goals.

Phil Maloney, the Canucks' GM, had made a special trip to Kansas City to watch me play against Tulsa. We met for about an hour after the game and he told me he was impressed by the way I handled myself on the ice. He knew I had something to prove and he agreed to give me the opportunity. The Canucks purchased me from St. Louis.

Maloney had been both coach and GM of the Canucks, but in December, before I arrived, he gave up the coaching job to concentrate on the manager's portfolio. He had hired former team captain Orland Kurtenbach as coach. I don't want anyone to think I did not like or respect Kurtenbach. I did, but I was cocky and he was a very conservative coach. We may have clashed a bit, but that was more my fault than his.

In Vancouver, I was reunited with my friend Mike Walton, who had returned to the NHL the previous February when his WHA team, the Minnesota Fighting Saints, went out of business. The Canucks had me centring a line with Don Lever and Rick Blight. Blight was a really heady hockey player and Lever deserved all the publicity he got. They were two great talents, but because they played in Vancouver and no one east of the Rockies read the local papers or saw their games, their talent went unnoticed. I felt I had to go out and play my best for Maloney. He put his job on the line in bringing me to Vancouver.

I wore number 19, just as I had in St. Louis. In my first game, we were playing the Atlanta Flames. I picked up the puck at the red line, skated through their defence, deked Phil Myre and scored on a backhand. We won 5–1.

The Canucks were eliminated from playoff contention in the next-to-last game of that season. We lost to the Colorado Rockies, who hadn't won in 18 games. And we had been leading 3–1 going into the third.

I was backchecking and Paul Gardner had the puck. I reached for it, but in the process, I tripped him. Bruce Hood, the referee, called a penalty on me. I flipped out. There was no way he should have called that penalty. I was going for the puck! When I argued the call, he immediately gave me another minor for unsportsmanlike conduct and started laughing when he did. He gave me a misconduct and then threw me out of the game. I felt like punching him. I probably should have!

The Rockies came back and scored during my second minor. They ended up winning 6–3 and we were out of the playoffs. We finished the season tied for third with Chicago, but they got the nod because they had more wins. We finished fourth in the Smythe Division.

And that was it for me in Vancouver.

I was really upset because the Canucks deserved a better fate. We had a surprisingly good offence and power play, but the problem with Vancouver was that you were always in an airport. I seem to recall that we practised 32 days fewer than anyone else in a season because of the travel. That hurts your conditioning and the team suffers.

I played 16 games as a Canuck and had 16 points. It had been a turbulent year. When you add in my points from St. Louis, I had played 48 games in 1976–77, scored 15 goals and 37 points. Not bad. Plus, I had those four goals and seven points in eight games with Kansas City.

Vancouver was the beginning of the end. I had a terrible summer. My mind was racing. I was torn in a hundred different directions. I had a lot crowding my mind.

I was hanging out with some bad guys and partying 24 hours a day. I was also hanging out with rock stars at Studio 54, the best-known nightclub in the world at the time. My colitis flared up and the tranquilizers the doctors gave me made me hungry all the time. I couldn't sleep and I had a lot of time to eat, so I ended up putting on some weight. My dad got sick, and I was scared that I was going to lose him. I lost money in a real estate deal and I wound up in a lot of financial trouble. There was overdue tax on my Rolls-Royce going back to 1972.

A while after Judy and I had broken up, James Caan, the actor, introduced me to a beautiful girl named Jill. She was a New York model who had represented North Dakota at the Miss World–USA pageant in 1972. She was wild and totally gorgeous. The most impressive thing about her, though, was that there was not a mean bone in her body.

Jill was trying to get me to stop drinking, but the more she tried, the madder I got. I was angry—angry at her, angry at the world and, if I had stopped to think about it, angry at myself. I put myself in that position, but thought I was invincible. One thing I have learned, though, is that when someone close to you tries to help you and tells you something, you can't get angry at them. Why? Because you know deep down that they're right and you are wrong, but you're just too stubborn to admit it.

I had been with Jill for five years and decided I was ready to settle down. Jill and I were supposed to get married on August 13 that summer, but she dumped me two weeks before the wedding date. That messed me up badly. I was intolerable and I knew it. I was a drunk and a drug addict. I drank myself out of a beautiful woman. She found somebody else on the rebound.

I put Jill above hockey, but that was a mistake. It was the only time I put anything before the game. It was only possible because I was losing my ability to focus and compete the way I once was capable of. If I used Jill as an excuse, I could blame someone else for my failure. However, it took a few years and getting sober for me to realize that.

I didn't report to the Canucks' 1977 training camp in great shape, but when I took my physical, I was declared fit to play. After one of our practices in camp, five or six of the boys went with me to Number 5 Orange, a famous Vancouver strip club. Nobody was flirting with the girls. There was none of that nonsense. It was just a place to have a few drinks and let our hair down.

This big guy in a surly mood came over to me, moved right in close and said, "You don't look so tough."

I said, "I'm not, but I bet I'm crazier than you are! If you give me a licking, I assure you, it won't end here. I'll find you somewhere. It won't end like that."

He said, "Yeah?"

Larry Goodenough stepped in and replied, "Yeah! And if you want him, you've got all of us."

The guy was looking for a fight and away it went! They tore out the tables and chairs. Punches were being thrown. It was a donnybrook. I was with some pretty tough guys, but I should have backed down—not for me, but for them. It brought them a lot of trouble that they didn't need.

Larry was wearing sandals and in the scuffle, he lost one and stepped on a broken beer bottle. I took him to the hospital for stitches. While there, they tested my blood and found the alcohol content ridiculously high—plus they found evidence of cocaine, sleeping pills, Seconal and Valium.

"I can't condone his attitude," was what Jake Milford, the new GM of the Canucks, told the press on September 30. I was relieved he didn't reveal the entire truth.

The guy who had brought me to Vancouver, the guy who deserved my loyalty, Phil Maloney, had been fired after the 1976–77 season. And Milford had decided, before he even saw me play, that he wanted me out of there. I didn't help my case. I gave him the reason that he needed to get rid of me. The Canucks sent me down to the Tulsa Oilers of the Central League.

I had had a lot of "last chances" before, but I felt that the Vancouver shot was truly the final one. I wanted a chance not only to play but to prove I wasn't as bad as everybody claimed. I wanted to be remembered as a hockey player, and a good one.

I didn't resist being sent down, although I lasted only four games. Then one day, I simply walked off the ice. I was done. I told my lawyer to settle the contract, and I got what I wanted. They gassed me. On October 20, Vancouver bought out the final year of my $160,000-a-year contract. I was a free agent.

At that point, alcohol had taken over my brain. Alcohol creates selfishness and belligerence. You're no longer patient and kind. You have no more moral values, no scruples. Your principles are all gone. It became all about me— what *I* wanted, and what I wanted in the next six hours, not what I wanted 10 years from then. I was just going from day to day, letting the cards fall where they may.

It was a stupid way to live and, I might add, a lonely one. It certainly didn't endear me to anyone, but I didn't realize that. I do now, but I didn't know then. You couldn't have told me that then.

I had nothing in my life—no hockey, no girl. I hit the skids.

I did some things that were crazy. I'm lucky I'm still alive.

CHAPTER 26

ROCK BOTTOM

I was really messed up when Vancouver dumped me. My career was over. The girl I loved was gone. I felt overwhelming despair and panic. I was unable to hold a thought or complete a sentence. I was in a fog and nothing made sense.

"How did I screw up my life so badly?" That became a daily question. "Where did it start and how?"

I was 31 years old. I should have been in the prime of my life, and yet there I was, quickly sinking down into the dark abyss of alcoholism and substance abuse.

I should still have been playing hockey. As a defensive specialist, I could have lasted until I was 40. I could continue to win faceoffs and kill penalties for years to come. And the money hockey players were making had just started to get good, too.

Deep down, I was really a one-woman guy, and I had found the girl I wanted to spend the rest of my life with. She had been everything I wanted in a woman, and I'd let her slip through my fingers like sand.

God damn it!

Maybe I wasn't ready to learn. God works in mysterious ways. Maybe my life was not about hockey but a struggle to learn how to live.

I was focused solely on instant gratification—material things—and not real life at all. But what was it that I had to learn?

Everything was against me. I just said, "Fuck it!" I was selfish and vicious. I was in a place of complete denial about how foolish I was. At that moment,

I would have stolen your wallet and then helped you look for it. I didn't give a shit, no matter what happened.

I was lost. Mentally and physically. I didn't know where to start or how I'd finish. My drinking and drug use went wildly out of control. I went on a three-year binge that was the worst kind of merry-go-round you can imagine; out of control with fear that you might never get off.

I descended into the depths of a hell I could never have imagined.

I took the settlement money from the Canucks and went to Dallas. My partners Joey Cimino and Jimmy McDonough and I had put together a deal to open a club there. We put up $400,000 and another party was to float a $400,000 loan until the Friday at noon. By Thursday, we hadn't heard anything. No returned phone calls. We tried to find our contact all day Friday, but then at noon, they closed the deal without us.

We were distraught. "I should have known," Joey said.

We lost our investment. We discussed what we should do, but ultimately, put our tails between our legs and skulked away.

Joey would do anything for me—he is a true and dear friend. But, even though I wasn't the cause of it, he was pissed off at me because the deal fell through. "You're all messed up," he growled, referring to the fact that I was so deep into drinking and drugs. "Get out of here."

So, I did. I entrusted Joey with whatever money we had at Daisy's and our other bars and, in a stupor, I took off for Chicago to meet a teammate and a Playmate.

Bobby Orr was with the Black Hawks at the time. He played only six games before he came to the crushing realization that he couldn't continue playing. His knees were shot, and at 31, his NHL career was over. The Hawks gave him a position as assistant to general manager Bob Pulford.

I really wasn't dealing in reality. I thought, "I'm going to go to ask Bobby to help me get a job coaching the Black Hawks." I arrived in Chicago and looked him up. "Hey Kid, it's Turk," I slurred. "How about getting me a job coaching the Hawks?"

He knew that I was drinking heavily and doing drugs and that I needed help. "Let's talk about it," he said. "Want a coffee?"

I met Bobby and right away he saw that I had the shakes. I couldn't even hold the cup of coffee steady. He knew I was in big trouble and that he had to get me into detox. Bobby is a clever guy. "Listen, if you want to coach, you'll want to see what the dressing room looks like. Let me show you."

As I was walking out, Bobby pulled the door closed. That's the last thing I remember. I blacked out, and when I woke up, I was in a hospital with three doctors and Bobby staring at me.

Bobby didn't pull any punches. "You're an alcoholic and a drug addict. You need help. You're going into rehab."

All the guys were really good to me when I was out of my mind, but they didn't understand me like Bobby did. You can't put anything over on him. He was the only one who said, "You've got to get sober. You've got to grow up." There is no halfway with Bobby. He knew what I needed.

I told him I didn't have the money for rehab, but he told me not to worry. He found a place that would take care of me. It was really expensive, but Bobby was going to pay for the whole thing using cash because he didn't want there to be a record of it.

Ludicrously, I was thinking I could walk into a coaching job with the Black Hawks. Bobby said, "Listen, Derek. You get straight and sober and I'll give you the benefit of all the credibility I've worked so hard to establish. I'll make sure you're taken care of. When you get back on your feet, I want you to find something that you're interested in and I'll back you."

That is a friend!

He was the one guy I never had a doubt about. When Bobby says he's going to do something, he's as good as his word.

But I didn't last in rehab in Chicago. I bolted. I met up with two friends of mine—both were Playmates. They were looking for a score. By this time, I was well down the road—out of the game, finished, destitute. I was dealing and stealing.

My dealer asked, "Can you help me?"

I said, "You holding?"

He said, "Yeah. I need some help. I've got a lot of customers and I've got to bag and cut."

I told him I'd help. I took the girls to his place. He rang us in and up we went. I found him in a bedroom that he had converted into an office. There was a dining room table in there that he used for "business." He had two kilos of coke. Peruvian flake. Beautiful. He was flaking it off, cutting it up and crushing it. He was cutting it with baby lactose and a jump of strychnine to give it a bite. Guys cut cocaine with baby lactose, baby laxatives or even baby powder. Coke is bitter. If you smell coke and it's sweet, it's likely cut with lactose or baby powder. Cocaine is supposed to be granular, flaky. You can see the flakes in Peruvian. If it's cut too much, it gets powdery.

I was sitting there bagging up 8-balls—an eighth of an ounce—for my dealer, wearing a mask because if you're inhaling the fumes and the flakes for any length of time, you get stoned out of your skull. While I was talking to him, I glanced up and knew something was very wrong. His eyes were as big as saucers. He completely stopped. Frozen.

I felt the cold metal of a gun behind my ear. Fuck! I thought it was a robbery. If it was a hit, we were both dead. There was a kilo of cocaine there on the table.

"Freeze! Don't move! You're under arrest!"

I had just left detox and was devastated when it turned out to be a cop. All I could think was, "Two keys of coke—that's a federal offence, and they'll also nail us for intent to traffic. Great! Now I'm an international drug dealer. I'm going to jail for 15 to 25 years. I ain't walking from this."

I wanted to puke.

I said to the cop, "No, no. No trouble, officer. I just got out of detox. My friend needed help bagging and I'm just helping. Test me. I'm good."

I continued. "Look, he's a friend of mine. I'm helping him out." In my head, all I could think was, "Holy shit! What do I do? Jesus."

My mind started to race. We were on the third floor and there was a tree outside. I started to wonder: If I ran to the window and dove, could I hit the tree? And If I hit the tree, could it break my fall. And if it broke my fall, could I run?

Trust me, it seemed there was no getting out of that situation. I was going down for 25 years in the joint. If I had had a gun, I'd have killed everybody there. All I knew was that I wasn't prepared to do Cook County hard time. I'd seen the TV shows.

Everything had been so good. Bobby had given me the opportunity to take the first few steps towards getting my life in order. I was with two Playmates. All I could think at that moment was, "What the fuck are you doing, you stupid asshole?"

Then the cop looked at me kind of weird, and with his head cocked, he asked, "Is your name Sanderson?"

I started to ramble. "Yeah, I'm Sanderson, officer. I'm sorry. I'm so sorry. I just got out of detox. I came over here to help my friend bag. That's it."

"Come with me," he demanded.

They already had the kilo of coke that had been out on the table. The cop took me into the kitchen. They knew there was more coke somewhere in the apartment. They had already gone through the storage locker downstairs, but the second key wasn't there. It was hidden in the kitchen, at the bottom of a brass pot, one of a set that stacked together. The cop took me into the kitchen. These brass pots were on top of the cupboard, above eye level—unless you were six foot four. And this cop was a tall guy. He was a Chicago cop, probably narcotics, but not a federal Drug Enforcement Administration agent.

The cop, a sergeant, introduced me to his lieutenant, saying, "Look at what we've got!"

The lieutenant shook his head. "What are *you* doing here?"

"Listen," I pleaded. "You've got to believe me. I came here to help a friend."

"He told me a story about getting out of detox and bagging," the sergeant said. "He might be clean. I don't know."

Meanwhile, the lieutenant was searching for the second key. He started turning over the pots. "Holy shit!" I thought. "He's going to find it!" He got to the big one. I knew that when he found it, we were screwed. As he was searching, he said, "You tell me where the other key is and we'll let you walk."

I couldn't give up my dealer. I would never rat him out, so I acted like a dummy. Deny, deny, deny. If they found the other key, I would have been implicated—and wouldn't get out of jail until I was almost 60 years old.

The lieutenant was holding the pot that held the cocaine, and he turned towards me and asked, "Is your name Sanderson?" He was looking at me, and not the pot, at the very moment that he exposed the kilo of coke. But he didn't see it.

"Mother of God," I thought, "he didn't find it!"

"His name isn't on the warrant, is it?" the lieutenant asked.

The sergeant said, "No, it's not."

"If we bust him, this thing goes from quiet to public," the lieutenant stated. "We don't need that." He looked at me. "Who's out there with you?"

I said, "There are two girls—my friends. They had nothing to do with this."

"Grab them and get the hell out of here!"

"Yes sir."

I corralled the girls, hurried out the door and down the stairs and into the car. "Shut up," I demanded. "Don't say a fucking word."

I never saw my dealer again.

I had hit rock bottom. There I was, shivering on a park bench in Central Park—broke, cold and tired.

I had gone to a girl's apartment and before I knew it, I had given her all the cash I had and been locked out. With nowhere to go, I was resigned to sleeping on a park bench in Central Park.

I was only in the park for a week that time. Never once did I think I was fated to spend life on the street like that. I knew I had my faculties, so I looked at it more as a lark the first time—a life experience. I knew I would be able to get out of my situation. I knew I could go back home to my mother and father. I had the greatest parents in the world, and I had that in my back pocket. I simply didn't want them to see me like that.

The words from the drunk whose booze I tried to steal rolled around in my head. That's when I knew I needed help. I searched out a friend.

"I'm sick," I told him.

"Yes, you are," he said. "Look at you."

My front tooth was gone. I had dropped a bunch of weight. My hair was a mess. I hadn't shaved and I looked like hell. It was freezing out but I was sweating like a pig.

Mickey was a dealer, but he refused to deal to friends.

"Why don't you do this coke with me?" I asked. "I don't want to do it alone."

"I deal it," he answered. "I don't use the shit."

"Try it, you'll like it," I suggested. "You've gotta know what you're dealing."

"No I don't!" he replied. "I'm not that stupid." He said, "You're a good person, Turk. The drinking and drugs are going to kill you. You've got to get out. I don't care about the other people, but I've known you for 10 years. You deserve to get straight. You've got something to offer. Most people don't. We'll put you into detox, get you back on the straight and narrow, get you off the streets and get you back home to Canada. Don't break your mom's heart. Get straight, man."

This was a hard-core drug dealer who had killed, and yet, he was trying to save me from myself. He arranged for me to detox at some place in Manhattan. What a pigsty! If the cockroaches had a union, they could carry you out of the place. At the detox, they had to deal with the DTs—*delirium tremens,* uncontrollable tremors of the extremities and secondary symptoms such as anxiety, panic attacks and paranoia—but my colitis was also acting up, so they isolated me and took pretty good care of me. The staff was good, but I didn't feel like I had anything in common with the people who were there getting treatment. No one understood what I did or where I'd come from. I had the "poor-me's." I was blaming everybody else for my being in detox. A guy asked me, "Do you see what you're doing? You're telling me it's not your problem."

I said, "I know. If I hadn't done this, if I hadn't done that, if my girlfriend hadn't left me . . ."

He demanded, "Can you get back to *you?*"

I listened to him but I didn't hear him. I only stayed for four days and then I left. I did learn a couple of things, but I had to get away.

CHAPTER 27

THE BLIZZARD

Detox taught me a few things about myself and a little bit about my addiction, but I didn't stay long enough to get the help I really needed. I was back to old habits—drinking and cocaine.

I was beholden to a friend. At various times, he had lent me money, found me a place to stay and given me cocaine. He was the guy who checked me into detox in Manhattan. He said, "I've got a deal going down and I could use your help."

"Sure, I'm there for you, buddy."

I felt obliged to him, but I wasn't thinking straight. Mentally, I was out of it. I was using more street values than common sense.

He explained, "I'm about to go into something kind of dicey and I need some backup. I've got to buy some shit from some Colombian guys I haven't dealt with before."

I didn't think about what would or possibly could happen. I didn't consider the repercussions of failure. The macho tough guy in me took over.

He handed me a gun and said, "Put this in the inside pocket of your coat, leave your hand on it and when we get there, I want you to stand in the corner. I'm expecting two guys to come in. If a third guy comes in, then shoot and we run."

I tucked the gun in my pocket. It was seven o'clock in the morning. We went down to a seedy bar in Spanish Harlem. The ceilings were low, the lights were dim and the stench of stale beer and urine permeated the joint. As wasted as I was, all I could think was, "What the fuck am I doing here?"

273

I took my post in the shadows as instructed. My friend sat at the bar with a whack of cash. In walked two guys. My friend nodded at the guys who had just entered and they nodded back. They placed a package on the bar and my friend put the money beside it. It was only then that I realized my role in this scenario. If either side didn't trust the other and made a move that would compromise the deal, I had to fire that gun and make no mistake in taking out those guys with the cocaine. This was not exactly what I was expecting!

I could feel the sweat drenching my shirt but didn't dare move. If the guys noticed me, I could be the thing that compromised the transaction. I prayed that the deal would go off as planned so I could get out of there.

The Colombian guys counted the money, nodded and left. My friend waited for a moment, grabbed the drugs and motioned to me.

"Come on, let's get out of here!"

I sat in his car, barely able to breathe. I was gulping air as we sped away.

"Thanks, Turk. I appreciate your help."

I said, "Not a problem," like it was no big deal, but I was scared to death. I was more frightened of getting pinched than what could have happened in that bar. I said to myself, "I'm getting out of here! This ain't me. I'm a hockey player, not a drug dealer."

He was going to give me some coke, but I told him, "To hell with the coke. Give me money. How much have you got?"

He handed me all the cash he had: $180.

I said, "Do whatever you want to do. I don't need this shit. I'm outta here."

A couple of weeks later, some guys put a bullet behind his ear.

Booze and drugs were ruling my life. Most days, I was drinking four bottles of wine before lunch and two bottles of liquor later in the day. I was doing coke so that I could stay up for longer periods of time so I could drink more. And if I couldn't get a drink, I'd polish off three bottles of Nyquil. Then, I'd take 20 milligrams of Valium to try to get to sleep. At that point, anything that would give me a buzz would work.

I truly never realized at the time how much I was drinking. It catches up to you. And I never realized what all the booze will do to you. Funny, but I hated the taste of booze, yet I loved the feeling. For a while there, I was really firing it back.

If it sounds like a horror story, it absolutely was. I was riding the wild horse, and lucky to be alive. I put it all down to the grace of God. My mother prayed for me every night. I didn't even know my mother was that faithful a person.

There's something about the grace of God, isn't there?

After the terror of my involvement in the drug deal sunk in, all I could think about was going home to my ranch in Fort Erie. With the $180 I got from the drug deal, I decided to fly home. I had to get away—my life was spinning wildly, completely out of control.

I bought a one-way plane ticket to Buffalo for Thursday, January 27, 1977. The weather reports for western New York State were terrible. An arctic front was sweeping through the area. It was the beginning of the worst blizzard ever to hit Buffalo. We were lucky to be able to land. It was absolutely brutal in Buffalo. I didn't have any luggage and all I was wearing was a thin jacket. I still had to get from Buffalo to the ranch in Fort Erie, which was 30 kilometres (about 20 miles) away. I jumped in a taxi and said to the cabbie, "I need to get to Fort Erie. This is all the cash I have. How far will it take me?"

He said, "You might make the Peace Bridge."

I got in and he drove to the Peace Bridge. "That's it," he declared as he pulled over and let me out.

The snow was really blowing, and as I walked along, I was freezing my ass off. I still had 10 kilometres (six miles) to go before I got home. "You stupid bugger." Even though I was frozen and broke, I was glad to be away from that drug scene.

I walked over the Peace Bridge. That's when I considered climbing over the side and just ending it all by jumping into the Niagara River below. What stopped me? It would have devastated my mother and father, and I couldn't do that to them. "I'll kill myself when they're dead," I thought.

After my brief thoughts of suicide, I walked into the hotel at the foot of the bridge. I was anxious and frozen. I went into the bar. I didn't have a cent, but I told the bartender to give me a double Johnnie Walker. "I'll be right back," I told him. "I've got to go to the men's room."

He poured it, assuming that I was going to stay. I peeked around the corner and when he wasn't watching, I came back, fired the double back and split. He was too busy to notice.

I quickly left the hotel bar and started walking. I had a long way to go before I could sit in front of that fireplace and thaw out. It was snowing like a bastard. The wind had really started to blow hard and the soft flakes of snow had turned into whipping wind and a blizzard.

I walked all the way from the border to my house. It took me hours, and as I wasn't dressed properly, I was frozen to the bone. The second I walked in the door, I had to have a drink to warm up, so I finished the last of the vodka. I went around looking for any other booze I had in the house. I drank a couple of fingers that were left in one bottle, emptied that, emptied another and passed out in a deep sleep.

The snow had left Buffalo immobilized. The National Guard had been called to clean up the city, but visibility was so poor that they sent everyone, including the National Guard, home. The temperature dropped like it was falling off a cliff. In four hours, it fell from 26 degrees Fahrenheit (minus-3 Celsius) to zero (minus-18 Celsius). By Friday afternoon, the accumulation of snow was ridiculous. Roads were impassable and travel was impossible.

I wasn't going anywhere.

When I woke up that morning, I took a steak out of the freezer and threw it into a fry pan with some bacon grease. It splattered away and I threw in a handful of fries. I had a kimono my girlfriend brought back from a modelling assignment in Japan. My mother had always taught us to turn the handles of pots and pans inwards, but I didn't. When I reached for the spatula to flip my steak, the wide silk sleeve of my kimono got caught on the handle of the frying pan and pulled it off the gas flame. I saw it falling. I reached out to grab the frying pan, but the boiling grease sloshed over my left hand. And the french fries fell out, landing on my left calf and foot. I tried to jump out of the way but couldn't avoid the sizzling contents. The steak and the rest of the grease hit the handle and landed on the countertop. Had it landed on me, I would have been cooked alive.

All my life, I had conditioned myself to believe that pain was a state of mind, and this was no different. I thought, "This doesn't hurt," but I got dizzy, lost my balance and fell down. The pain was overwhelming. God help people who die in a fire. I looked at my leg and I saw the skin bubbling—actually bubbling into blisters and popping. I was holding on to my left wrist, trying to cut off all the circulation, but I saw pieces of meat stuck to my skin. I was taking the meat off my wrist and the french fries off my feet and skin was peeling off with it.

"I'm in trouble!" I gasped.

My dad had always told me that whenever you're in a crisis, you mustn't panic. Panic will kill you. I sucked up the pain as much as humanly possible. "State of mind, Derek. You can handle it." But oh Mother of God, it hurt! I was in excruciating pain.

"Ice," I thought. "I need ice." I looked out the window and it was nothing but snow drifts from the blizzard. It was unbelievable! I couldn't see my car— the Rolls-Royce was covered. "When did this happen? Overnight?"

I held on to the counter and manoeuvred my way around the corner. I had four refrigerators at different spots in the house. I managed to get to one, reached in and grabbed an ice cube tray. I took the ice cubes, put them in a towel, smashed them and then held the towel to my throbbing foot. I wrapped another towel covered with crushed ice around my hand. I used three or four trays of ice cubes, and in my mind, I thought I had control of things.

I went to make a phone call for help. The phone line was down. "Shit! How long can I last here?" I looked around for something to numb the pain. I needed a drink. Nothing. I didn't have any booze left in the house. I didn't even have an Aspirin. I had nothing.

I started to talk to God. "You've put me here for a reason and I haven't figured out why just yet." I might have been hallucinating, who knows? "I always thought I was above all this, didn't I? Pain, state of mind, I can handle it. I don't need this. I don't pray, God, but I just don't get it."

The pain wasn't subsiding and I ran out of ice, so I crawled to the front door. All I had on was the kimono; I was naked underneath. There was a big, heavy tapestry on the back of the couch, so I wrapped myself in it. I pushed open the front door and stuck my burned left leg and my left hand in the snow. I don't know how cold it was. I'd guess five below.

I was lying there, trying to ease some of the extraordinary pain. I said to myself, "I'm all alone; totally, completely, absolutely alone. I don't have my parents. I don't have Jill. I don't have friends. I don't have money. I don't have drugs. I don't have booze." And then it hit me—this was it. I was going to die. It was 10 o'clock in the morning and there I was, stranded in a snowbank in excruciating pain with nothing but a tapestry to protect me.

Pain was nothing new to me. I'd had more cuts and operations than I could ever have counted, sustained broken bones and a broken heart, struggled with colitis and bad hips that ached with every step. But this pain was unimaginable.

I lay there for what seemed like an eternity. The silence was made more eerie by the drone of the blizzard whipping around outside. Never before had I wanted to die, but I half-hoped that if I closed my eyes, the pain, and my life, might peacefully drain away.

How did I find myself here in the first place? How did a good kid, raised well by loving parents in a nurturing home, the same talented kid with the skill to make it to the National Hockey League, the storytelling hockey player liked by most everyone who knew him, find himself a hopeless alcoholic, broke and defeated and praying for a quick and peaceful death?

I had let myself lose track of what was meaningful in life. I'd let booze, drugs, sex and money control my life—not the values instilled in me by a loving father and a doting mother. On the occasions when I thought about it, which was almost never, I could think of a million excuses for going off the rails. The way I was defining myself had diverged from what actually defined me. This 90-degree excursion was proving to be fatal.

You hear stories about the afterlife and the things people experience— soft, white glow, warmth. My eyes were closed and I could see the white glow. I had my left foot and some of my left shoulder outside the tapestry. I was in a very uncomfortable position because I had to pull my right leg up under me to stay reasonably warm. Just like they say, my whole life passed before me— all the dirt, the guns, the fights, the bullshit, the lying, the cheating, the bragging, hurting Jill, hurting people, using people. I thought, "I am not a good person!" I prayed and I wept. I can remember a tear. And I thought, "God, I am going to freeze to death here, aren't I?"

God is inside your head. I know He's inside my head and He's inside my heart. I don't know what a soul is because I'm just not that smart, but I was lying there and I prayed. "God, get me out of this. Get me out of this like you have every other time I've asked you. I promise I'll help people. I'll help kids."

I was getting more and more desperate and I was getting colder and colder. Then, all of sudden, I stopped shivering. All of a sudden, it was warm. I realized I could let go. I accepted that I was going to freeze to death. I was comfortable after getting past the intense shivering and chattering and panic.

I had a decision to make. If I got a break, would I do what I promised and live up to it? That's when I learned that it can't be 99 percent of the commitment and one percent con; it had to be a commitment of 100 percent.

In my mind, I said, "God, I will. Please! I need help."

I was inordinately cold, and then I realized I couldn't bend my fingers. It was probably the burn. By my estimate, I had passed out for at least an hour in that blizzard.

The only thing I could move was the big muscle of my right ass cheek. I could tense that muscle. I worked my ass cheek repeatedly and soon, the snowbank gave way. I rolled down. That got my blood circulating a little. God may have been testing me—"Okay, let's see what you're made of."

No pain.

I crawled up the stairs. The door was unlocked and I got in. I crawled across the kitchen floor and pulled myself up so that I could lean my back against the lower cupboards.

The phone rang. I glanced across the floor, and there it was on the floor. Wait a minute! The lines were dead!

It was Dr. William Hogg. He was calling to ask if I would hand out trophies at a banquet for the Fort Erie Minor Hockey Association.

A doctor! I was incredulous. "Doc, I will do anything you want me to do, but I need you right now. I've had an accident in my kitchen and I'm burned really badly. I'm at Windmill Point Road—"

He interrupted me, "I know where you are. But there's a blizzard."

I responded, "Call Pat Keating. He's got a backhoe. He'll get you in."

"I'm on my way," he said.

I realized that I could move and it didn't hurt anymore. Everything was frozen. I crawled up the stairs and I flopped onto my bed. I remember thinking that pain really was a state of mind, just like my father had so often told me.

Just then, the pain went from my left foot to my left ear like a sword. It was so intense, it nearly blew the top of my head off!

"God, I'm sorry. I'm really sorry. I promise I will never be cocky again!" For me, that would truly be a test. Being humble might have taken more strength than I had. But the pain remained as intense as ever. It pounded and throbbed and I was writhing on the bed. I was getting panicky. I could hear the backhoe in the distance digging out the driveway, but the damned driveway was 1,150 feet—nearly a quarter of a mile—long.

Fear came and went. Patience and calmness came and went. I kept praying. "I can't see You but I feel You here with me."

Not long afterwards, Pat Keating arrived at my door with the doctor. They took me to Douglas Memorial Hospital in Fort Erie. I have no idea how I got there, whether by ambulance or Pat's backhoe. I was put in a private room at the end of a hallway. I don't remember a lot. I was there a couple of days. I was being treated for the serious burns and frostbite, but my colitis was also acting up and I had psoriasis that left me with blotches on my face and hands. They gave me some tests—some psychological tests and some detox tests. I was getting pain medication, so it wasn't your basic detox, and while you're getting the pain medication, you don't miss the booze.

On the third day, I got a knock on the door. I couldn't imagine who it could be. My parents didn't even know I was there!

There stood Rudy Krulik.

Several years before, the juvenile hockey team in Niagara Falls needed a coach and my dad had agreed to help out. At that level (17- and 18-year-olds), it was strictly recreational. If you hadn't made it to junior by then, you weren't going to. It was too late.

I was 13 years old and my dad asked me to be the stick boy for his team. I said okay.

On that team, there was a born-again Christian. The guys loved him but were ruthless in their teasing, yet he never got angry. Whether the team was all over him or not, he always smiled. On the ice, he played tough and hard. He was a good defensive player.

The guys were relentless. When my dad would enter the dressing room, he'd say, "Hey, come on you animals! We've got a 13-year-old boy here. Whaddya think you're doing? Settle down or I'll knock somebody out!"

The second my dad left, they'd be all over the kid again.

That kid they teased was Rudy Krulik.

I never talked to Rudy back then but I was struck by this placid face that was always smiling. He'd ruffle my hair with his glove once in a while, but that was about it. That was all the interaction we had other than me watching him play.

I was lying in the hospital bed debating whether I should call my parents. There was a sign on my door saying, "No Visitors." I had two nurses who each worked 12-hour shifts and I had Dr. Hogg, so when I heard a knock on the door, I thought it was unusual. I opened my eyes and there was that kid, Rudy Krulik.

"Holy shit!"

He smiled and asked if I remembered him.

"Do I remember you? Of course!" I replied. "But I haven't seen you since I was 13."

"Yes, you're right." He still had that same smiling, placid look. He put his hands in the air. "And look—no Bible! I'm not here to convert you. But when I was shaving this morning, God told me to go to a room at the end of the hall at Douglas Memorial. I didn't know who I'd find there, but I was to deliver a message to the person in that room, and that message was that God wants you and He's going to get you. That's all I was supposed to say."

And with that, Rudy left my room and disappeared down the hallway.

I hollered after him. "Rudy! Get your ass back here! Rudy, don't leave without giving me answers!"

He was gone. I had no idea how to get hold of him. He left me with the message and left.

I turned the television on to kill some time. What should be on but *100 Huntley*

Street, a Christian program out of Toronto. I changed the channel and it was *The 700 Club,* another Christian program, out of the U.S.

I turned the TV off after a while, but I noted how content everyone was on those programs.

While I was in the hospital being treated for second- and third-degree burns to my arms and legs, the doctors weaned me off my drinking and barbiturate problem. I got healthy and when I was released, I returned to my house with my parents, who made sure I didn't drink. Everything was good. And then my dad said, "You can't live like this. You're too young not to work. I'm going to the plant tomorrow and I'll get you a job sweeping floors. It's time you grew up."

"Dad," I sputtered, "I'm not a bum and I am not going to be sweeping floors at the plant!"

"Oh yeah, big shot?" he countered. "Whaddya think you're going to do?"

For the first time since I was 15, I didn't have a job.

I said, "I'm going to call Ted Lindsay and see if I can't catch on with the Detroit Red Wings."

The only person in the National Hockey League who hated me was Ted Lindsay. His name just popped into my brain; I wish I knew why. After he retired, Lindsay was a hockey analyst with NBC and in 1973, he went on national TV and stated that the Bruins were crazy if they took me back. In '77, he was named general manager of the Red Wings.

I picked up the phone, dialled the Detroit Red Wings and asked for Ted Lindsay. I told the receptionist it was Derek Sanderson. Moments later, Ted barked down the line, "What do *you* want?"

I said, "Ted, I know that we've had our differences in the past but I've learned a lot through the past few years and I need a break. I want to play hockey again. I'll pay my own expenses, but I just need somebody to give me a shot."

There was dead silence. Finally, Ted spoke. "You'll pay your own way?"

"Yep."

"It won't cost the Detroit Red Wings anything?"

"Right."

"You've got skates?"

"Yeah."

"Will you do what you're told?"

"Yes sir."

"If you lie, you cheat, you drink or you swear, you're finished. Got it?"

"I do."

"If you're late for a meeting or late for practice, even once, you're done. Got that?"

"Yes."

He said, "I need to think about this. Give me your number. I'll call you back."

Lindsay called me back, and didn't mince his words. "Okay, the Detroit Red Wings will give you a tryout if you abide by our rules. I know you'll need conditioning. Be on a plane tomorrow at 11 and we'll talk."

I flew into Detroit and Ted picked me up at the airport. He shook my hand and looked me straight in the eye with that determined look that made him one of the NHL's most feared wingers. "You know something? I ought to be committed for this! Derek Sanderson . . . what the hell am I doing? The only player I've ever known who didn't respect the game, and here I am reaching out and helping him! I cannot believe I am doing this!"

I was humbled. "Ted, I just need a chance. That's all I want."

Lindsay mumbled and grumbled all the way from the airport to the hotel. "Here's what I'm going to do with you," he started. "You're going to do what you're told. You are not coming to Detroit for glamour and glory and television. You're going to go to Wayne Maxner and the Windsor Spitfires (a team in the Ontario Major Junior Hockey League). You're going to get in shape with them and relearn the whole process all over again. We will offer you a contract if you get into shape, have the right attitude and if we feel you can make a contribution to the Detroit Red Wings hockey club. If it appears that you can't or won't get in shape, then the possibility of playing with the Detroit Red Wings is over. Have you got that?"

It was made abundantly clear and I certainly understood the conditions. I just wanted to start skating again.

If I had to be humbled that way, I was glad it was under the eye of Wayne Maxner. He was a couple of years older than me, but I knew him through the Niagara Falls Flyers. In 1962–63, he was the OHA scoring champion, just like I was four years later. During that season, I would practise with the Flyers once in a while. And in 1965–66, we both played a handful of games with the Bruins, although I don't think we were there at the same time. He played a couple of seasons with Boston and then floated around the minors. When he retired from playing in 1973, he was hired to coach the Spitfires, where, in this most unusual way, our lives intersected again.

Back in those days, Wayne had an affiliation with the Red Wings. He used to do some scouting for them in the junior loop. He was a really good guy.

It was early February 1978. Ted took me to the old Windsor Arena and introduced me around. It was good to see Wayne again, and while he was friendly, he was all business.

I was also introduced to Real Chevrefils, who had been a good player in the National Hockey League and was now the Zamboni driver. He looked a hundred years old. He warned, "Don't end up like me."

I said, "Real, you were great! What happened?"

He shrugged. "Ego. Women. Thought I was better than I was. I don't know. It's over, but don't let it happen to you."

Tragic story, and it really struck home with me. Everybody predicted that Chevrefils was going to be one of the best to ever play the game, but alcohol got in the way. He had been an NHL All-Star in 1957–58 after scoring 31 goals. By the next season, he was out of the league. He bounced around the minors for a while and ended up playing senior hockey in Windsor. After he retired, he stayed in Windsor, but life didn't get any easier for him. He got a meagre pension from the league, but Jimmy Skinner, an executive with the Red Wings, arranged for him to get a bit more from a special fund for ex-players who needed some help. Real spent a lot of time at the Mission, and people would see him shovelling snow to make a couple of bucks. He never got hockey out of his system and they gave him a part-time job at the arena driving the Zamboni. He was only 49 when he died in 1981.

Before I checked into the riverfront hotel not too far away, Lindsay said, "You be at practice on the ice at four o'clock."

The clock was really ticking slowly that afternoon, so at about 2:30, I thought I'd go over to the rink and see Maxner. I had my skates, the same ones I wore in 1972 when we won the Cup. They were tube skates, and all the juniors were now using Tuuk blades.

I walked down the corridor and it felt the same as the Niagara Falls Arena. Cold building; just a typical Canadian rink. Real Chevrefils had just lectured me, and I got to the dressing room and stopped. I stood there, staring at the door. I ran my hand through my hair, clutched my skates and took a deep breath. And then I said, "Jesus Christ! I can't do this," and I turned and walked away.

I walked 15 or 20 steps and then started to tear up. I was overcome by emotion. I realized that if I didn't go back and walk into that dressing room, my life was over. I didn't know how it would end, but my life would be over.

I had a decent man giving me a shot and a friend in there as a coach. "Grow up, Derek." I turned around and went back towards the dressing room. I spotted Real Chevrefils as I was walking down the hallway. "Feels good." That's all he said.

I knocked on the dressing room door and somebody yelled, "Come in." I opened the door and my jaw hit the ground. Every single player was already dressed. It was an hour before practice! You could have heard a pin drop!

I wanted to crawl into a hole. I wanted to cry, to be honest. Not one of them looked up at me. Wayne Maxner was sitting in the coach's room. "Hey Derek, come get dressed in here." That was the kindest thing anybody could possibly have done for me at that moment.

I had never had to worry about equipment before, and there I was in borrowed gear. There were holes in the socks, the garter belt was shit and there was stuff missing.

I got dressed. The equipment mostly fit and I stepped onto the ice. All the guys were already out there. I gingerly put my skates down onto the ice surface. "Good, you're back on ice. That's where you belong," I said to myself, feeling a little uncertain on my skates. It felt like I had never skated in my life. "This is not going to be easy," I thought. I hadn't skated since Vancouver. I took my time, using baby strides, and went around the perimeter of the rink, minding my own business. I did that a couple of times, feeling more confident with every stride. And then Maxner blew his whistle. "Okay, between the lines!" That's a drill where you skate as fast as you can between the blue lines, glide around the net and then, when you hit the opposite blue line, skate as hard as you can again.

I got to the blue line and fell down. I slid to the opposite blue line, got up, made my turn around the net, and when I hit the blue line this time, I fell again. I didn't know what to do. One of the Spitfires laughed, not derisively, and said, "If this is how good you have to skate to play in the NHL, I'll be a first-round pick!" The guys giggled and I just smiled. "It's a little tougher than that," I said. But those were the first words spoken to me.

My legs weren't there yet and neither was my wind, but my weight was stable. I knew if I could get my timing back, I'd be able to get back to the NHL. It took me a while, but after a couple of days, I was feeling pretty good while I was skating and I scored once in a while. And then, the players started asking me questions. They didn't ask me about girls or parties or good times. They wanted to know about faceoffs—positioning and how to set up a draw. I stayed out with the centremen and, in teaching them, I started to come back.

I practised with the Spitfires on a daily basis, and if they weren't practising, they would arrange ice time for me. I was basically regarded as a member of their team and got along very well with the players. I kidded around with them and told them it was the first time I'd been with a first-place hockey team in 10 years! I am very grateful to all the Windsor Spitfires for their kindness. Even though this entire experience was to help me, I hope that I helped the junior kids, too. They knew my story. I was an in-the-flesh example of what could happen if you didn't look after yourself. I occasionally talked to some of them about my demons. In fact, I think that really helped me.

I was quickly getting into shape. Maxner had me on the goal line doing stops and starts. He said, "I'm not going to put my team through this because they're already in shape and I don't want them tired, but you stay here and keep doing them." And I kept on doing them.

The Red Wings were going to give me a month or so and then evaluate my progress to see if I was ready to make the jump back to the NHL. Wayne Maxner would give Lindsay regular progress reports, as would Billy Dea, Detroit's special assignment director. He told me he was impressed with my diligence and dedication.

I was feeling pretty good about things. Ted Lindsay came to me and said, "Listen, you were paid off by the Vancouver Canucks and are a free agent right now. So, anybody can sign you. Here's what I'm asking you to do. If a team approaches you and makes you an offer, be man enough to give me a chance to match it."

"That's a promise," I vowed. "No problem, Ted."

I continued to work out with the Spitfires. I was training hard but really having a good time with the kids. The team was about to head off on a northern Ontario road trip, playing the Soo Greyhounds and Sudbury Wolves. Lindsay came to me and said, "Billy Dea is going on a scouting trip and I'll be at a general managers' meeting in Florida. The team will be away for a few days. You'll be stuck here alone."

I offered to go with the Spits on the road trip, but Ted said, "No, I want you to stay here and practise from nine until one every day."

All I could think was, "I've done that before. Hap Emms used to make us do that when I was with the Flyers. That's a long time! You get bored silly!" I used to entertain myself, firing pucks at the net: left post, right post, crossbar, backhand. You can only entertain yourself for so long.

As Lindsay was leaving, he said, "There'll be no one here. If you need anything, talk to Real Chevrefils."

I waited to see the team board the bus and wished the guys good luck on their road trip. They thanked me for the help I'd given them.

Empty building. The team was gone. Lindsay was gone. There was nobody around. I went back to the hotel and had dinner. Then, I called my old girlfriend Jill to tell her I was back on my feet again. I thought I'd get some respect from her and we might be able to get back together, but when I called, a guy answered. There was a guy living with her! I was pissed off! I heard the guy say, "That asshole drunk wants to talk to you, Jill."

I went out of my mind! "Gimme that guy's name 'cause I'm gonna come through this fuckin' phone and kill him!"

Jill heard that and said, "You haven't changed."

"Yeah? Well that guy's an asshole," I shouted. "Who is he?" And then I heard another voice. "What the fuck, are you living with two of them?"

She said, "Yeah, but they're just friends. Stay out of my life," and then she hung up on me.

I had all that emotion in my gut. I had done all that hard work to get back on my feet and I realized I was doing it for all the wrong reasons. I was doing it to get my girl back.

I went to the hotel bar and, against my better judgement, ordered two beers and a shot. I took the drinks to my table, but just then, in walked some referees. They had officiated the Red Wings game and were going to have a quick bite to eat in Windsor before heading off to Toronto. All I could think was, "If they see me, they'll tell Ted."

I bolted out the back door and went up to my room and ordered three bottles of wine from room service. I hadn't had a drink in weeks and now I was in the bag. "Fuck her! Fuck him! Fuck them! Fuck everybody!" My ego came back as big as ever. "I'm gonna make it back 'cause I still can play. I'm tough, I'm mean, I'm good! I'm fast, I'm hitting, I'm scoring! Fuck everybody!"

I looked outside and the snow was coming down hard. "No way am I going to get up early tomorrow." I called reception and said, "I've got a wake-up call for eight o'clock tomorrow morning. Cancel it." I figured I'd get up when I got up. I wasn't going out on the ice by myself at nine o'clock. Who'd know? And I certainly wasn't going to practise for four hours by myself!

I rolled over, grabbed the pillow and went to sleep.

At eight o'clock the next morning, I heard a knock on my door. "Who can that be?" I thought. "I told them I didn't want a wake-up call!"

"I'm good. Don't need towels! Leave me alone," I shouted towards the door.

The knocking continued.

"What the hell, are you deaf?"

The knocking continued.

My head was pounding. My mouth was dry. I felt like shit. I ripped open the door to scream at this persistent maid . . .

There stood Rudy Krulik.

"I went to bed last night at 10:30 and I couldn't sleep. God said, 'Derek needs you in Windsor.'"

He said, "I'd have been here a lot sooner but there was a blizzard. I couldn't go any faster than about 20 miles per hour. I left St. Catharines last night at 10:30 and I'm just getting here now. I drove all night."

I said, "It took you that long to get from St. Catharines to Windsor? It's usually a four-hour drive!" He said, "Oh yeah! When you take the back roads and you don't get on the 401, you hit all kinds of roads that aren't plowed. Took forever."

I was confused. "Rudy, what are you doing here?"

He said, "I know! Every single mile, I asked God what the heck He was asking me to do. Every time I've asked God a question, He has given me an answer, but I prayed to Him all night and He abandoned me. All I knew was that I had to get to you, but I couldn't figure out why. On TV, they said you were doing great and you were getting offers, so you certainly don't need me here. I don't know what I'm doing here!"

I shook my head. "Come on in, Rudy. You need a cup of coffee." He said, "Yeah, I better before I head back." I asked him if he needed to crash for a while, but he said he just wanted to get home.

And then he asked me what I was supposed to be doing.

"The general manager went to some meetings, the special assignment guy went on a scouting trip and the team went on a road trip," I replied. "I'm supposed to skate from nine to one.

"Have you ever skated from nine to one?"

He laughed. "Yeah. That's boring."

It was about five after eight. He said, "Let's get a coffee." I agreed. We told stories over several cups of coffee, and then he said, "Now that we're awake, why don't we head over to the rink?"

I said, "There's only the Zamboni driver there." He said, "Come on, let's head over. I want to see the arena." So we arrived at the old barn and Real Chevrefils gave me the key to the dressing room.

Rudy admitted that he was confused that God had let him go to Windsor and I seemed fine. "It's a first," he told me. "But you look great, Derek. In fact, you look terrific. I'm glad everything is going so well." Then he asked me again what it was I was supposed to do.

"I'm supposed to be on the ice from nine to one," I shrugged.

He said, "Well, since you're here, you may as well put on your equipment and do what they asked. Don't go breaking rules, Derek. Why don't you find me a pair of skates and I'll go out there with you?"

We found a pair of skates that were close to his size and I pulled on my equipment. I did it solely because Rudy had stuck out his neck coming that far. I owed him that much. "You promised the man you would do what you were asked to do. That means not going back on a promise."

I dumped some pucks out onto the ice and looked up at the old clock, right by a big picture of the Queen. *Boom!* It was nine o'clock sharp.

"Are you happy now?" I asked Rudy. And just then, Ted Lindsay came around the corner by the penalty box.

"You're one lucky boy that you're here," he snarled. "We all bet that you wouldn't show up, and if you hadn't been here, you were through. Finished."

He fished around in the inner pocket of his sports coat and pulled out a plane ticket. "Here you go. There's no need to hang around here this morning. Go get dressed and don't miss your flight. You're going to Kansas City tonight."

From behind me, I heard Rudy softly say, "Thank you, God!"

I said, "Mr. Lindsay, I'd like you to meet my friend."

Rudy just waved and walked away.

CHAPTER 28

THE COMEBACK: 1977–78

There were only a couple of months left in the 1977–78 season. The Detroit Red Wings had liked my progress and felt that if I continued to work hard and played a bit with their farm team in Kansas City, I'd be better prepared to step back into the National Hockey League.

I flew into Kansas City and met my new teammates. Even though I'd played there the year before, the roster had turned over almost completely. In 1976–77, the team, then called the Blues, had been affiliated with both St. Louis and the Red Wings. It seems like an unusual set-up, but in those days a few clubs either didn't have enough money or extra players to operate farm teams of their own. In the off-season, St. Louis hooked up with Salt Lake City and moved their players there. Now, the team was called the Kansas City Red Wings and was linked solely with Detroit. Only a few guys remained from the previous year's lineup.

They gave me number 9 because Fern LeBlanc was wearing 16, and they put me on a line with J.P. LeBlanc. We were flying. In the first minute of the first game, I assisted on a goal by J.P. In that first game, a win over the Fort Worth Texans, I assisted on all three goals that J.P. scored. He said, "Holy shit, I've never played with anybody as good as you!"

Our coach, Larry Wilson, used me on a regular line, on the power play and on the penalty kill. And the team really worked hard in practice, too. I nearly died when I first went out, but I showed them how badly I wanted to play.

You have to remember, I was still paying for this tryout out of my own pocket. I think I was the first guy in the history of hockey who was paid not to play, and then the first guy who had to pay to play! I think Detroit paid for my hotel room. That was $12 a night. Big deal.

After four games, Ted Lindsay told me that they liked my commitment to hockey and they wanted to bring me up to Detroit. The thing was, I really didn't want to leave Kansas City. We were lighting up the league and I was having a blast.

I practised with Detroit, but was told I wouldn't play in any of the 18 games remaining in the regular season, although if they made the playoffs, they would consider using me.

Ted said, "Derek, I can't put you straight away into the Red Wings lineup. You'll think hockey is too easy. You won't respect all that you've been through to come back. What you have done is quite remarkable. None of us thought you could climb back from where you were."

J.P. LeBlanc and I joined the Wings in early March. I was there as a spectator but J.P. had earned a spot in the lineup. But behind my back, players were bad-mouthing me, talking about how I was bad for the team. Ted Lindsay came into the dressing room, and it was then that I appreciated just how tough he was. He paced back and forth, and then suddenly stopped. "Somebody on this Detroit Red Wings hockey club has one big mouth and I'm going to find him. Whoever it was said that the man sitting right there, Derek Sanderson, was a cancer and that if he was to dress for us, he'd destroy this hockey team. Let me tell you, that man right there has accomplished an incredible amount to get here—more than all of you combined. You can't appreciate what he's done to make it back to this point. And now, somebody has shot their mouth off and is out to destroy him. When I find out who it was, I will trade you immediately. You will be off this hockey club. No conversation."

Whether it was a coincidence or not, one of the players was traded within days.

The next day, I got a call from my lawyer. The Pittsburgh Penguins had offered me a contract to play the remainder of the season for them. Prorated, they were offering the equivalent of $185,000 a year. Because I had yet to sign with Detroit, I was technically a free agent, and I opted for an immediate return to the NHL with Pittsburgh rather than serving an extended stint in the minors and playing for Detroit the next season.

The Penguins were playing the Kings that night, so I had to catch a flight from Detroit to Los Angeles. I called my lawyer and asked him if he had informed Ted Lindsay and the Red Wings that I had signed with the Penguins. He claimed that he had. He told me Lindsay didn't fully appreciate what I had done. After being out of shape, badly burned in a fire and suffering from frostbite to my extremities, it was an extraordinary accomplishment to come back, get into shape and be ready to help an NHL club. The Detroit Red Wings wanted to pay me $500 a week and give me a summer workout program so I could come back fresh, strong and sober and be the player I should be. But there was some serious money and an immediate job waiting for me in Pittsburgh and I took it.

Years later, I asked Ted if my lawyer had contacted him back then.

"No, he never called me," he replied. Ted had actually been quoted in the media at the time as saying, "Sanderson's lawyer ruined him the first time around and he's going to ruin him again. This kid trusts this guy for some reason and I don't know why."

Lindsay charged that the Penguins had tampered with me, but NHL president John Ziegler told the Red Wings that he would not interfere with my comeback. Ted was upset and said that he felt the Penguins and I had destroyed his faith in people.

I was so embarrassed that I ducked Ted for years. It took me until the NHL All-Star Game in 2001 to finally face him and apologize. He glared and said, "It took you long enough!" I told him that that was how scared I was and how little I thought of myself, and that I regretted letting him down.

Support from the fans in Pittsburgh was overwhelming. In an interview before I suited up for my first NHL game in about a year, I expressed my appreciation. "I owe all of this to the people who wrote me letters, the people who had hope that I could overcome the stumbling blocks I put in my own way. I don't want to let down the fans, the people in Pittsburgh, and I don't want to let myself down either. I will help Pittsburgh in any way I can. I owe that to Mr. Savill [Al Savill, chairman of the Penguins]."

I also publicly thanked Ted Lindsay. "I want to make this very clear. I'm very grateful to Ted Lindsay for his unselfish effort on my part. He was first class all the way and I'm grateful for that."

The Penguins' coach was Johnny Wilson, whose brother was the coach in Kansas City. When Johnny asked Larry about my progress, he was told I was ready and could contribute. Baz Bastien, the Pittsburgh general manager, intended for me to spell off Peter Mahovlich, who was the Penguins' number one centre. A writer for the *Pittsburgh Post-Gazette* cracked, "The Penguins needed a center in the worst way, and that's exactly what they got—a center in the worst way."

I played the rest of the season with the Pittsburgh Penguins. My number 16 was available and I was glad to have it back.

In my first game with the Penguins, we lost to the Kings in L.A., but it felt like I had never been away. I thought I'd only see spot duty, but I took a regular shift, killed penalties and was used on the power play. It did, however, feel like I needed another five or six games to build up my endurance. Vancouver beat us the next night, but early in the first period, I scored my first goal as a Penguin. It also happened to be my 200th NHL goal. I really wanted that goal. I didn't want to end my career with 199. I kept the puck as a souvenir. We came from behind to beat the Maple Leafs in Toronto in my third game and while playing 30 minutes, I scored again. I also took a puck to the forehead, good for 13 stitches. Wayne Maxner told me it was the best game he saw me play after my time in Windsor.

Then, in Chicago, the roof caved in. My body collapsed. I blocked a shot and bruised my foot and didn't play after the first period in a 9–1 loss to the Hawks. But it wasn't just my body that collapsed. Minnesota snapped a 12-game winless streak by dumping us 7–1. Then, the godawful Colorado Rockies ended a 32-game winless streak with a 5–2 win over us.

Curfew was midnight and one night, I got in at a quarter past. The Penguins kept me out of the next game, a 2–2 tie with Detroit. We couldn't find a win no matter what we did. Montreal and Boston both beat us soundly and then, we hosted Toronto and only 6,000 came to the game. Just as well— we lost 6–3.

The Penguins were bleeding badly. The franchise lost $2 million that season. The day after our loss to Toronto, the ownership changed for the fifth time in 11 years. The new ownership group was headed by Edward DeBartolo, whose son owned the San Francisco 49ers. That night, as a welcome gift to our new owner, we beat the North Stars, 7–2. But a loss to Detroit followed, and we were officially eliminated from playoff contention.

In a meaningless game on April 8, we lost 6–4 to the Washington Capitals. I scored my third goal of the season at 5:14 of the third period against Jim Bedard, another Niagara Falls kid. It turned out to be my last goal in the NHL. We rounded out the 1977–78 season by edging the Cleveland Barons 3–2.

The Penguins finished fourth in the five-team Norris Division. I played 13 games and finished with three goals and an assist.

Colin Campbell, one of my teammates in Pittsburgh and now a VP with the league, commented, "We didn't have time to get to know Derek. He was looking for another 'last chance.' He still had ability and talent but was pretty beaten up. He still had issues—he missed a practice, had an awful-looking body and he fell apart quickly. We all felt bad for him, but his demons were too ingrained to overcome and his stint with Pittsburgh was short-lived."

The Penguins had a 60-day window after the conclusion of the season in which to exercise an option to negotiate a contract. On June 6, 1978, GM Baz Bastien decided not to re-sign me.

I wasn't sure what to do. Was it over? Was I through?

In the fall of 1978, I was skating with the Boston Bruins once again, hoping I might catch on in a defensive role with them, but on October 5, the team announced I had retired. I had talked to other teams in the NHL as well as in Europe, but there were no other opportunities.

Secretly, I made one final, desperate attempt to come back. In September 1979, I contacted my old friend Glen Sather and asked him if I could try to find a spot with the Edmonton Oilers. Slats thought there just might be some hockey left in me and invited me to his Storm Mountain Lodge in Banff to get into shape, with the intent that he would introduce me at the Oilers' training camp at the University of Alberta.

"I did it more for human reasons than for hockey reasons," Sather admitted. "He really wanted to make a comeback and get his respectability back. He convinced me that he wanted to prove he could take the hard way back. I agreed to go out running and hiking with him and help him get in shape, but he didn't last long. He hopped in his $40,000 motor home and went down the road."

I realized it was over. I had to try to accept that I was done.

CHAPTER 29

SOBER AND STRAIGHT

To an alcoholic, the bottom is every day. Every day, you try to quit. You know that you've got no control. You're really pumped—you have four hours under your belt. And then you have seven hours. It's one o'clock in the afternoon and you're proud: "I haven't had a drink since three o'clock this morning!" And then it's happy hour and you have a beer. And then another beer. And then a shot and a beer. Bingo! Gone again!

For me, that was every night. Every night, I'd swear I was never going to drink again, and then I'd go back.

I went to detox 13 times before I was admitted to rehab, and it was there that I was finally able to give up my addictions to alcohol and drugs.

To be absolutely candid, I was in such a drug-and-alcohol-induced haze that I don't even know how I got to Hotel Dieu in St. Catharines, Ontario. In the scheme of things, it doesn't matter. What does matter is that I met a man there who saved my life in 1980.

I don't even know his name, although I sure wish I did. I told him I was sick and tired of being sick and tired. He got me on my knees and convinced me to let God into my life. That made all the difference.

He said, "Derek, I've been doing this for 18 years." I asked him why he chose to be a rehabilitation counsellor. He told me, "I do it because it's a calling. I have to do this." I asked him why and he replied, "Because I know what fear is and I think that alcoholics are inherently good people who simply don't know how to handle fear."

I didn't fully understand, so I asked him what he meant. He said, "Okay, let me ask you: How old were you the first time you drank?"

"Nineteen or 20," I answered.

"No, no." he said, stopping me. "I don't mean the first time you drank to get drunk. I mean the first time you drank."

I thought about it for a moment. "I played on this softball team one summer. Fast pitch. I was 16, maybe 17. I was the youngest guy on the team; I was the catcher. The team bet me I couldn't drink 30 seven-ounce draft beers in 30 minutes. I chugged 16 or 17 of them and then I puked everywhere. The guys thought that was hilarious. That was the first time I drank."

"No. You don't understand," he continued. "Not the first time you got drunk. I mean the first time you drank."

"Hmm," I thought. "Right! My girlfriend dumped me when I was 12. She was the first girl I ever kissed, but she practised on somebody else. That hurt me, so I went to the fridge and drank one of my dad's beers. One made me feel better, so I had another one. And when I felt even better after two, then I thought that three would make me feel great. I drank three beers. And then I put the caps back on the bottles and put them back in the case, thinking my dad would believe that he received three empty bottles by mistake.

"When my dad came home, he asked me how I was doing. That day, I said, 'Heh.'

"'What kind of answer is that?' he asked.

"'You heard me,' I answered cockily. 'Your ears don't overlap.' That was a line my father used often—mostly under his breath to my mother. It didn't seem as funny when I said it. He pulled me towards him and smelled my breath. 'Have you been drinking? Get upstairs! Now!'

"I stumbled up the stairs and did a face-plant onto my bed. The room was spinning around."

The guy at Hotel Dieu sighed. "That's a good story, Derek, but I want the first time you ever drank."

I had to dig even further into the recesses of my memory. "Well, my uncle gave me a beer at Christmastime when I was seven. Does that count? That was the very first time I ever tasted alcohol."

The counsellor leaned in. "What do you remember about that time, Derek?"

"My uncle handed me a beer," I recalled. "And what does any seven-year-old do when he gets something new to eat or drink? He smells it. I remember thinking, 'Beer stinks.' I took a sip and it was bitter, so I held my breath like any smart kid does when he has to eat or drink something he doesn't want, and I guzzled it all down. My uncle said, 'You're old enough and big enough to drink it all.' I got two compliments in a row from him and I became putty in his hands. I drank that beer. I was the life of the party. Instead of being the shy kid in the corner, I was laughing and jumping around. Everybody laughed. 'Look at Derek. Isn't he cute? He can't even stand up!'"

"What do you remember about the laughter?" the counsellor probed. "Were they laughing with you or at you? There's a big difference."

I thought for a moment, and then continued the story. "Then, my dad came around the corner of the kitchen and took one look at me. 'Son, what's the matter?' I could always tell when my father was concerned. He had a special look—not blame, but genuine concern for me. I felt like I had 'DRUNK' stamped on my forehead. I wondered how my dad knew. 'What's the matter with you?'"

"I pointed to my uncle. 'He gave me a beer!'"

With all drunks, it's always someone else's fault for the position they're in. It is never your fault.

"My dad grabbed his brother-in-law and threw him off the porch into the snow. 'Who are you to give my son a beer? Don't you give my kid a drink again or I'll break every bone in your body!' Then my father wheeled around and pointed at me. 'You! Upstairs!'"

My room was upstairs. It was small and square and the chimney ran through my room. There was a small chest of drawers and a single bed against one wall. There was no TV, no computer, no Internet, no iPod, no books. All you could do was sleep or look out the window. It was like jail to a kid. I spent no time in my room unless I was sleeping or being punished.

"I remember the feeling and I remember being punished," I told the counsellor. "And I didn't care."

I was surprised at how vividly I remembered the incident. I asked, "Why is this so important?"

"It was an event," he explained. "To a social drinker, it was nothing." He paused. "You were an alcoholic when you were seven. It didn't matter what occupation you chose—ditch digger, doctor—you were going to be an alcoholic."

I stared at him. "You have got to be kidding." Hockey, fame and fortune had absolutely nothing to do with it.

He continued. "Give me your first impressions of the drug."

I stammered, "What do you mean, 'drug'? It wasn't a drug, it was beer!"

"It's the most abused drug in the world," he stated. "Everybody thinks it's harmless. Now that you know that beer is a drug, a poison and an anesthetic, I want your first impression of the drug. And make no mistake, from now on, alcohol is a drug, okay?"

I reluctantly agreed.

I distinctly remembered my first impressions of the drug. I hated the smell and I didn't like the bitter taste. But I loved the feeling, and that was the problem.

I was still, however, a long way from being a believer. I recall thinking that I might be able to learn something from this guy so that I didn't end up in rehab again. I figured I could learn to drink responsibly.

He gave me that perfect lecture on being honest and told me I wasn't going to be able to con him as I had so many others before him. "I want you to understand how denial works. When I first asked you when you had your first drink, you told me you were 20. When I prodded you a little, you mentioned baseball, and the age decreased. When I pushed you further, you mentioned a girlfriend and the age decreased again. I finally got you down to seven years old. And you remembered the event quite vividly. You were in denial. Because if you admit that you realize the damage done to you and to others, it is a terrifying thing. You have to face the realization that you are at fault. That is the core of denial."

"Why is it so important?" I asked.

He said, "Because whether you started drinking at seven, at 17 or at 27, to us, it's an event—a place where we can hide away. And we know it. Now you've got to learn how to control it. I'm going to help you control it."

He studied me for a moment or two. "Derek, do you want to get well?"

I said I did.

He asked if I was finished fighting, and I replied, "Yes."

"Have you ever prayed?" he asked.

"When I was young," I replied.

He smiled. "All you have to do is submit, be honest and not hold anything back."

"I may not be a good enough person."

He said, "We all are when we are humble."

"Why is that important?" I asked.

"Because that is going to make all the difference in your recovery."

He asked me if I was self-conscious about praying with him in the room. I wasn't. "I'm scared enough that I don't mind the help." He explained that all I had to do was get down on my knees and ask God for patience, courage and understanding. After that, the rest would come easy.

When I was in Boston, I'd been living the life. I was a single guy playing for the most popular hockey team on the planet, beautiful women all around me. The image I projected was that I was this crazy playboy, and I believed my own hype, but the truth was that I was just an insecure kid from Niagara Falls.

During my rookie year, I had a crush on a really cute girl. She was one of the first two or three girls I ever slept with. After a Sunday night game, we were in bed. "I can't believe that I'm with Derek Sanderson," she said with this monstrous grin. "I can't wait to tell the girls at work tomorrow!"

I was horrified. All I could think was, "Holy shit. She's going to tell people about my performance. Uh-oh. If I'm not great, she could ruin my reputation." So, we made love all night long. That way, if she told her friends, they'd hear about how great I was in bed. That was my motivating factor. For a while,

I tried to be a superman with everyone I was with, going all night long. But I was killing myself.

I later met another girl I really liked. We got together and it was the same thing—all night long every night. One night, I went for round two and she stopped me cold. "Hold it! I don't know who you're trying to impress, but once is sufficient!"

Out loud, I said, "Thank God!" At last, I could finally get some sleep!

The truth is, I was really inexperienced sexually when I arrived in Boston. I was a small-town kid. The girls attracted to professional athletes in Boston were prettier, sexier and more experimental than any girl I knew in Niagara Falls. These girls didn't seem to care who they slept with. A year before, when I was tearing up junior, I couldn't get a girl to even look at me, but here I was, the same guy, but now as a Boston Bruin, and there were any number of women who wanted to sleep with me. I could never figure that one out. For a young guy with raging hormones, it could have been a female buffet. Morally, this freely available sex ran totally against what my mother had ingrained in me. I was always taught to respect women, but here they were, offering up their bodies seemingly without regard to anything but being with a Bruin. I was afraid that if I wasn't a hero between the sheets, these girls would spread the story that I was lousy in bed.

Fear.

I became a kid in a candy store. I was educated quickly in Boston. I learned about love and I learned about drinking.

I started drinking a bit when I was a rookie with the Bruins, too. I really hadn't been a drinker before that. I might have had a beer or two the odd time. I didn't even like the taste of booze. I had a choice: to drink or not to drink. I chose the wrong one in order to belong and to please other people.

Air travel, still a bit of a rarity in the era of the six-team NHL, became an absolute necessity once the league expanded to places like Los Angeles and Oakland. And flying scared the hell out of me. The whole idea of having to depend on something heavier than air—suspended in the air—to get me from place to place unnerved me. I hated not having any control over my destiny and I got really anxious and panicked before every flight we took.

The Bruins sent me to a shrink, and that was the first time I ever had drugs. Valium mellowed me before a flight, but it made me groggy and irritable and interfered with my play. I was finding it all too much. The doctor took me off the Valium, but I still needed something to calm me before a flight, so he suggested a couple of shots of Scotch. That took the edge off, but after a while, it wasn't enough. The next thing I knew, I was getting so hammered just to be able to fly that I was passing out and had to be poured off the plane on the other end.

That was really the start of my drinking problem. I ended up self-medicating. Alcohol masked my fears—fear of flying, fear of not being accepted, fear of not being liked enough. I used alcohol as a coping mechanism for fear, and I feared things I couldn't control. The problem was, once I began drinking, I didn't know how to stop. It was like a snowball rolling down a hill. It started small and picked up speed and volume as I went along. It drove me down a dark road.

My fears were exaggerated by my surroundings. Owning four bars was the worst thing that could have happened to me. I wanted to be the genial host, so I was there, first at Bachelors III and then at Daisy's, from the end of practice until closing time when I was in town. I bought the world a drink, and I joined them to be cordial.

I started as a social drinker and before I knew it, I was drinking constantly. Others around me started to notice that my drinking was becoming a problem. Most of my teammates didn't see it because I was living downtown, but Bobby Orr took me aside a few times and talked to me about what I was doing. But I didn't think I had a problem. I was in denial. I sloughed it off.

It doesn't take much for your life to unravel. I would have been an alcoholic anyway, but it was a fear of flying that really led me to heavy drinking. The bars in Boston set me on a path that accelerated my addiction. The money in Philadelphia was superfluous. What kind of ego trip was that? I was lonely.

The drugs really started to take hold of me in 1973. I was taking barbiturates for the pain in my hips and to help me sleep. Barbiturates are opiates. They were for a legitimate medical conditions, and prescribed by reputable doctors. But then, on top of that, I began experimenting with bennies. When you play a physical, violent game like hockey, all that speed does is nullify fear, and fear is God's way of honing your instincts. I never did anything too crazy and I never hurt anybody. I was always generous to a fault. I didn't get mean until near the end—1978, '79, '80—and that's when I was really bad.

There's a lot of bad in all of us. The struggle between good and evil is the battle we all fight every day. We each struggle to be a good person. It's not always easy. I can be very mean. If you hurt me or mine, I can kill you, but I don't want anybody to make me mad enough to hurt them. That isn't civilized behaviour.

We were young and foolish, and readers must try to relate to the temperament of those times. One thing that will always remain is that relationships will be helped along by alcohol. It is a lubricant and a truth serum. I am not certain that things people say when drunk are not actually what they really want to say, but suppress when sober. It certainly was a tool that males used to loosen up their dates back then.

And when I was playing, most of the guys smoked. You could cut the smoke in our dressing room with a knife. When Mike Walton joined the Bruins, the first thing he said was, "You guys are all nuts! You know you aren't supposed to do this, don't you?" There was no alcohol or drug-awareness program in the league when I played. A couple of guys hired by the NHL came around during training camp to talk to us about gambling, but that was it. Now, the league and the Players' Association provide all kinds of programs to help players who need assistance. There are great counselling programs in place, and the stigma of needing help no longer exists. When I played, you would never show weakness in any area of your game or your life. You didn't want to give the owners any excuse to move you off the team.

I never drank the day of the game. That was my rule of thumb, but I was often so drunk from the night before that I didn't sober up for two days after the game. But it wasn't just the alcohol that was my problem, although it certainly was the biggest part of my challenge. By 1975, I was drinking much more than usual. I was drinking unnecessarily—if it was there, I drank it. I was going to that place where your mind goes to seek the truth about yourself; a place you don't visit often because it scares you. I knew I was in real trouble, and to not drink was to admit that.

There isn't a lowest low for alcoholics. There is a turning point where you realize that you need help, that you can't control the thing—that you are absolutely powerless over alcohol. That is the first and most important step. The rest is simply to give up control—to let go and let God.

Alcohol is a drug. Alcohol abuse is a disease. It doesn't discriminate. It ruined my life at the time. Once the drug has you by the throat, then you have to listen to someone and get their help.

I can look back now and see the sequence of events. As the counsellor showed me, it didn't really matter what line of work I was in, I was going to be an alcoholic.

Why was I an alcoholic?

I learned that fear is what rules our lives. And what constitutes fear for me may be different than what fear is to you, but fear is at the root of our problems, and fear was at the root of why I was an alcoholic and addicted to drugs.

Like everybody, I had my fears. I had a lot of insecurities. I was confident when I was on the ice because there, for the most part, I could control my surroundings. But even there, I had fears. I had a fear of failing—failing as a hockey player, failing as a lover, a businessman, a friend, a son and a brother. Fear of flying. Fear of success. Fear of becoming an adult. Fear of relationships. Fear of life.

I was loved by my parents. I was a good kid and I had great friends. I was an A-student until I quit school to play hockey, but the reason I ultimately quit school was because I had a fear of public speaking. Ironically, that's what I ended up doing after my playing days were over.

No matter what you do in your life, you try to avoid fear or the things you fear. That first girl you fell in love with broke up with you and you don't ever want to face rejection again, so you're afraid to get involved again. I danced with that girl in high school and she laughed at me. That was the last time in my life I ever danced. Fear of being laughed at and fear of rejection.

Fear carves us. It's what makes us. Life is about learning to deal with it. Parents will try to teach you that it's okay to feel fear, that it will go away or be overcome. But fear can be insurmountable. For a drunk, fear can be amazingly difficult, so fear combined with despair creates panic. When fear overwhelms you, you become suicidal and then all you need is access.

The sole purpose of alcohol, because it is a drug and an anesthetic, is to numb the pain of fear, feelings and emotion. The fear does not go away. That's why, when you sober up, you need it again.

You're afraid of being rejected by a girl, but after a couple of drinks, you're full of liquid confidence. You think you're funny and interesting and lose your fear of talking to girls. But then you start to believe that you can't be what you want to be without booze—you can't be funny or you can't be a good lover without a drink. That's what alcohol does. It anesthetizes those fears.

Do you know why alcoholics are mad at other people? Because in their heart of hearts, they know that the people are right. "You're a drunk." "You can't drive." They say, "Friends don't let friends drive drunk." No, friends shouldn't let friends *get* drunk. Then we wouldn't have this problem. But that would kill an industry, and the alcohol lobby is far too powerful. During the 1920s and early 1930s, prohibition was tried. From 1919 to 1933, there was a national ban in the U.S. on the manufacture, sale and transportation of alcohol. All that resulted in was corruption among politicians and within police forces and the rise of organized crime.

In the halls of Alcoholics Anonymous, they know that people, in their struggle, sometimes take what is known as a "geographical cure," where you get away from the people and troubles you're encountering by getting a fresh start in a new location. I decided to go to a family cottage near Napanee, Ontario, about a half-hour's drive west of Kingston.

I jumped into my van, joined by my dog, and drove all day from Boston to Napanee. I made certain I had no booze with me because I knew it was a distraction that might prove tempting.

By late afternoon, I began to get anxious about being without alcohol. I crossed the border into Canada at four in the afternoon and knew that the provincial liquor store closed at five. I pulled in and bought a bottle of wine, just in case I needed it.

The dog and I slept in the van, at the side of the road, and continued the drive the next morning. Before we got far, I stopped at a liquor store and grabbed a gallon of vodka and then picked up three quarts of orange juice at a grocery store.

I pulled into Bon Echo Provincial Park on Mazinaw Lake around two o'clock. I pulled out a cup, the orange juice and the vodka, and by the time I'd finished drinking, around 10, there was maybe a finger left of that gallon of vodka. I realized I should get back to the cottage and get some sleep, so I turned the corner, and as I drove over a hill, I saw a car coming towards me. It looked like he was on my side of the road, so I panicked and cut left, but the approaching car cut in the same direction. He ran off the road and I ran into a ditch. Just then, flashing lights went on. It was an Ontario Provincial Police cruiser!

Oh, shit! The officer walked towards me and I knew I was in big trouble. I simply hung the keys out of the window and he ripped them out of my hands. I could very easily have killed the man.

He was angry, but in control. "Get in the cruiser!" he barked.

I fell down a couple of times walking from my truck to the police car. He threw me into the back seat and took me back to Napanee. I spent the night in a jail cell. The next morning, I went before the judge. My blood alcohol concentration was 0.34—today, you can be convicted of impaired driving if your level is higher than 0.08. I used to function at 0.2 and you wouldn't know I was drunk.

The judge said, "With this alcohol concentration in your blood, you should be dead! A social drinker would have died. You are a full-blown alcoholic, son. This is not a joke. Get help!"

I wish I could remember what happened. Actually, maybe it's better that I can't. I can only guess that I paid a fine, probably had my licence suspended and was ordered back into detox.

When I was in New York with the Rangers, my drinking was bad and I was using cocaine on a regular basis. In St. Louis, I kind of straightened up a little bit, but not enough to really notice. My drinking just got worse and worse, exacerbated by the drug use. I was in self-destruct mode and didn't realize it.

I never thought I drank that much and never realized what it could do to you. For a while, I was really firing it back. Add to the mix cocaine, prednisone, Valium and whatever else I was using, and I was out of control. I never smoked pot and I never used needles, but I was an addict. I let myself lose track of what was meaningful in life.

I used to do cocaine strictly so I could stay up and drink more, but I couldn't stop after a line or two. If I had an ounce of coke and there were four of us sitting around a table, none of us would leave until it was all gone.

I began using cocaine when I was in New York. I was running with a fast crowd and we all did it—recording artists, film stars, models, athletes. Names you would know. We hung out at Studio 54, the famous disco where the "beautiful people" gathered, and at Plato's Retreat, a swingers' club. Do you think a little boy from Niagara Falls could walk in there straight? Not a chance. If I had been sober, I'd have been horrified; but drunk and stoned, I thought I was king of the world. I could be anybody I wanted. That made things easy for me.

Cocaine fools you. You think you have it together, but you don't. It causes confusion and paranoia and your ability to reason goes out the window. Cocaine seems to go hand in hand with money. It's for fast-living people. We big shots rolled $100 bills to snort the coke. We were too self-important to roll one-dollar bills. Coke is an insidious, ravenous snake. One spit of its venom grabs you and it won't let you go. And cocaine is never 100 percent pure. In order for dealers to make money, it gets cut with anything sparkly and shiny that will burn the nose, including rat poison, strychnine and even crushed glass. You don't know what kind of shit you're putting into your body. It's likely about 10 percent cocaine and 90 percent adulterants. Yet people think they are getting a great high.

I once visited my mother so high on cocaine that I got into what I thought was an intellectual discussion with her, in which I tried to convince her I was the Second Coming of Christ. She was horrified. "Oh my God, son. You're delusional! You've lost your mind! You can't be the Second Coming!"

"Why not?"

"Because you're not a good enough person."

That was a wake-up call! Her response hit me like a cold bucket of water. My poor mother didn't know I was high. She thought I was having some kind of intellectual or emotional breakdown.

If it sounds like a horror story, it was. And all of it was true.

It took me several tries before I finally beat my addictions.

In my first seven detox visits, I tried to control my drinking and drugging. I was taking little tidbits of information and tailoring them to my own use. At the first detox, the only word I heard was "toxic." I figured that it was a simple matter of not drinking and drugging together. So I decided I'd just drink beer. *Boom!* I was in trouble again.

I went to another detox thinking, "Okay, I'll just drink wine." *Boom!* I was back in trouble and soon back in another detox. I tried straight vodka. *Bang!* Another detox.

Make no mistake: alcohol is a drug. The only difference is that it is legal at a certain age. Alcohol gives an entrée to other drugs. Nobody does drugs straight out of the box. You're drinking beer and then you start smoking grass or you do a couple lines of coke.

I had tried Alcoholics Anonymous. It's an amazing program, but you can't pick and choose which of the steps you are going to adhere to. You have to accept all 12 steps.

The first step of Alcoholics Anonymous is to admit that you are powerless over alcohol. You have to admit that you cannot control your life. Once you admit that, you go on to step 2, which says that you have to believe that a power greater than yourself can restore you to sanity. Now that you've accepted steps 1 and 2, you go to step 3, which is to make the decision to turn your will and your life over to the care of God as we understand Him. When you do that, life is very simple because all God wants when you get up in the morning is for you to be a good person.

Step 4 is to take a moral inventory of yourself. The next step is to admit to God, yourself and to another person the exact nature of your wrongs. Step 6 insists that you be entirely ready to have God remove all your character defects. Next up is step 7: humbly ask God to remove your shortcomings. Step 8 says to make a list of all the persons you harmed in any way while you were drinking and make amends to each of them.

Once you have accomplished those steps, it's step 9: to make direct amends to the people you've hurt, except when doing so would hurt them or others. Step 10 is to continue to take personal inventory and when you are wrong, not to be afraid to admit it. Step 11 demands that you improve your contact with God, as you understand Him, through private conversations that ask for knowledge of His will for you and the power to carry them out. The final step, number 12, is to have a spiritual awakening as a result of these steps, and to practise these principles as part of your day-to-day life.

In reality, and simply put, everyone would be a better person if they lived by what AA espouses.

I bought into AA's 12 steps, but only when it was convenient for me. That's why I failed at sobriety so many times before I finally went to rehab.

During one of my visits to detox, I was experiencing horrible withdrawal symptoms and needed something to take away the pain. I craved something to make me feel better, so I went to emergency in Albany, New York, and, in order to get a shot of Demerol, I told them about my ulcerative colitis. They would examine me, discover that it was active and I would tell them about the awful cramps and pain I was experiencing. They would give me the Demerol, which I actually needed for the painful withdrawal from alcohol I was experiencing.

While I was waiting for the doctor to arrive with my Demerol and sensing the relief it would bring, the guy in the bed next to me pulled back the curtain and announced, "If you take that, you're finished."

I looked at him and remembered the 12 steps of Alcoholics Anonymous. "You're right," I said. I thanked him and asked the staff to take me to detox. I didn't care if I died, but I didn't want to die. That's how alcoholics think.

They took me to the detox floor. A liver expert ran some tests and told me my liver had all but shut down. He explained that I was a step away from having a full-blown case of cirrhosis. "Do you think we're going to give you drugs so you can get high and die that way? Let me tell you something: when you have cirrhosis, it affects the ability of your liver to function. Have you noticed lately that the alcohol isn't working and your drugs aren't working?"

I said, "Yeah, but I thought it was just tolerance."

"No," he continued. "Your liver is not functioning properly. You get high because of your liver. It transforms the alcohol, breaking down the drugs and poison. When that function is gone, you will die an extremely painful death from cirrhosis of the liver. You won't get any drugs to kill the pain. They won't work without your liver. Derek, it's a horrible way to go."

I sure didn't like the sound of that.

"I've always wanted to say this," he said. "The next drink you have will kill you."

I left the hospital, and then crossed the street to a bar and proceeded to get hammered. I thought, "You aren't scaring me!"

Never talk to a drunk about his drinking when he's using. You've got to wait until he has a sober moment. When he has cleaned up a bit, then you can talk to him.

After he's one day sober, a drunk needs to think, "Why don't I do another day?" That's how it starts. I would get close. At 10 o'clock at night, I'd realize I only had a few hours to stay sober until it was a fresh, new day. I'd try to go to sleep, but would toss and turn. I'd get up and it'd be four o'clock in the morning. "Let me just take a shot of whiskey to help me fall asleep." And I'd fall back into drinking again.

My mother always told me that if I couldn't sleep, I should get up and do something—watch television, read a book, do push-ups, go for a walk. Anything. The worst thing you can do is just lie there.

There were many who tried to help me. The Phil Esposito Foundation attempted to get me the help I needed. Phil tried to corral me and get me into a substance abuse program, but I put the kibosh on that. I knew what they were trying to do, but I went there looking for cash instead of assistance for my addictions. The intent of the foundation was morally right, but I wasn't having anything to do with it. I wasn't ready.

There are two stages to addiction. There's the "I want it" stage, called first-stage addiction, and then there's the "I need it" stage, or second-stage addiction. That is where you really need help to get out of it. I was in second-stage addiction when I was checked into Hotel Dieu. I discovered that there are an awful lot of good people who will help you if you will just admit you need it, and I thank God for them.

While I was in rehab, I learned that it is imperative that you do everything they tell you. There are no shortcuts. The toughest thing is to put your ego away, take the cotton batting out of your ears and put it in your mouth. That's what people don't understand: Shut up! You are in rehab because you are a drunk and want help. You want a better life. You may think your reason is for your wife, your child or someone else, but you are in rehab to get sober for you and you alone. With the help of a higher power, being sober for the rest of your life will be all that you had hoped for. Be strong. Be patient.

There are three types of drinkers: social drinkers, problem drinkers and alcoholics. The social drinker enjoys alcohol for the camaraderie it brings. These social drinkers usually sip their drinks and don't like the feeling of being impaired. The problem drinkers like the feeling of drinking for effect. They drink to get drunk and plan their drunks—"Oh boy! It's Friday. I can drink all weekend!" The alcoholic needs alcohol to function. And there are subsets, too: binge drunks, maintenance drunks (so much every day) and blackout drunks.

The statistics on alcoholism are mind-blowing. Alcoholism is an extremely serious problem in today's society. If we are ever going to see a reduction in injuries, fatalities and other problems directly linked to alcohol addiction, it is extremely important that the public receive as much knowledge as possible about its effects.

The Institute of Medicine of the National Academy of Sciences estimates that alcohol abuse in the U.S. costs society from $40 billion to $60 billion annually—for health and medical care, social programs that address alcohol problems, lost production in the workplace, motor vehicle accidents and violent crime. Alcohol contributes to 100,000 deaths every year, making it the third leading cause of preventable deaths in the U.S., following tobacco and diet. Half of all traffic fatalities and one-third of all traffic injuries are directly attributable to alcohol.

I used to drink three quarts of vodka and consume cocaine through the course of weekends. My friends had to try to force me to get some sleep because they were afraid my heart was going to blow up. The heart is only a muscle, and cocaine destroys heart muscles.

There are no such things as recreational drugs. That's a myth. Who invented that little fairy tale? The dealers and those who want to justify its use! There are many different chemicals in marijuana, and the medical world does not know what most of them do to body parts like your pancreas, heart and liver. They do know what tetrahydrocannabinol, or THC, does. It destroys depth perception, it destroys your ability to pick up moving objects, it stops short-term memory from passing knowledge to long-term memory and it makes you lethargic. The marijuana smoked in the 1960s and 1970s pales in comparison to the pot grown today. Sophisticated growing methods, like growing marijuana indoors, feeding the plants with chemicals and heating them 24/7 with ultraviolet lights has enhanced the quotient of THC, the main active substance in the cannabis plant. As a result, daily smoking in 1972 would take months before the user was addicted. Today, daily smoking can get users addicted in days or weeks, not months.

When I finally found my way to rehab at Hotel Dieu in St. Catharines, the counsellor was the right guy at the right time for me. He explained the role of God in my recovery, and I was ready. I got on my knees and said, "God, please help me. I can't live like this anymore." That was the difference for me. I had struggled with the spiritual side of Alcoholics Anonymous, but when I accepted God, I was saved. I was never suicidal, but my unwitting death wish was becoming a self-fulfilling prophecy.

The despair is overwhelming and totally consumes your entire thought process. The only thing that can get you through this is faith. I truly know that there is a God, but I also know that God is not going to come down in the shape of a flaming bush and talk to Derek Sanderson. He speaks to us through other people.

It is never too late to re-create your life. Wipe the slate clean, start fresh, get on your knees and humble yourself. Ask God for help—"Just give me strength." That's all it takes—one day at a time. Every hour of every day, we all come to forks in the road that force us to make decisions. God gives you two choices: yes or no, left or right, right or wrong. Life is very, very simple. There's no grey area here. It doesn't matter what religion you are, the higher power asks but one thing from you: to be a good person. We only have to make the right decision.

Spirituality is at the foundation of everything. I am very comfortable with it. I still would get on my knees and thank God for giving me the strength for another day and to go about my business. I'm comfortable with Jesus Christ because I'm a Christian. Some people in AA can never get sober because they can't deal with the spiritual part. They think it means you have to be religious and you have to go to church. No, you don't. The house of the Lord is in your heart. It's wherever you are.

Through life, we all have to deal with pain, hurt and rejection. Those are human emotions we face every day. And once you have faith, you're not afraid to die. Since I've been sober, I am no longer afraid to fly. When I was scared, weak and trying to stay sober, I had the "Serenity Prayer" from Alcoholics Anonymous: "God, grant me the serenity to accept the things I cannot change, the courage to change the things I can and the wisdom to know the difference."

The priority for any addict is to anesthetize the pain of living to ease the passage of the day with some purchased relief. After I went to rehab, I never considered having another drink. I took it very seriously. I went to AA meetings. I had a sponsor. I had my last drink in November 1980. There was a point where I had to get off the medication, too. I had been diagnosed as a schizoid manic-depressive with psychopathic tendencies. That was pretty heavy! At one time, my anger could have gotten to a point that I could kill, but not now. I've had 10 hip surgeries and am in constant pain. Doctors gave you something to numb the pain, but I've been clean from drugs, including prescription drugs, since 1985. I was a pretty heavy smoker, too. I'd smoked a pack and a half a day since I was a kid, but I had my last cigarette in 2002.

I am always just one arm's length away from drinking. You white-knuckle it for a while. Now I know what life is like as an addict and I can stop myself. Once you've been sober awhile, it becomes a lifestyle. You get used to it and then you're fine. I live every day by the things Alcoholics Anonymous taught me. And it's spiritual, too. I don't know anybody that can get through this without it being a life-altering experience. Getting clean and sober was victory enough, but making the climb back was just as miraculous.

As we get older, our bodies start to break down. My hips still give me problems, but after 10 surgeries, there isn't enough bone left to go back in for anymore. I'm a prostate cancer survivor. Prostate cancer can be an insidious thing, and I encourage men over 40 to get checked out. And beyond that, as we age, we wake up and everything hurts.

Now that I look back, maybe my addictions were meant to happen. I was fortunate—I didn't go to jail and I didn't die, so now I grow up and go onward. Today, I no longer try to have the world revolve around me. I live a simple life and take care of my family, my friends and my clients the best I can.

Arriving at rehab in Hotel Dieu was the best thing that could have happened to me. My romance with drugs and alcohol was over. For 10 years, I had lived on the tail of a comet.

CHAPTER 30

STARTING OVER

Working my way out of the fog of booze was a long battle. It was April 1980. I had been sober close to four months and was living with my parents in Niagara Falls.

My dad said, "Your career's over, son. You pissed it away. Life isn't all about watching television and staying in your room, Derek. It's time to turn the page."

I had begun working with my lawyer in 1969. He set me up so that he would pay my bills, invest my money and give me an allowance to live off of. I would drop by his office when I needed money and he'd give me $5,000 or $10,000. But he mentioned, "Each time you come in, I have to send my assistant downstairs to the bank to get the money. If you give me power of attorney, I can just sign and the cash will be here. All you have to do is phone and we'll save all that time in between."

That sounded efficient to me. I said okay because I trusted him.

It was the worst mistake of my life.

My lawyer always told me that he wanted to see me independently wealthy and financially secure for the rest of my life after hockey. "I'd like him to be prepared to go into business at the executive level. He has a sharp mind and he can be articulate. His problem, perhaps, is that he comes off a little rough," he said.

He stood by me through the World Hockey Association debacle and through my moves from Boston to New York and St. Louis. But when things were really going bad in 1977, '78 and '79, when I was drinking heavily and into the drugs, all of a sudden, he disappeared.

I got suspicious. I got to wondering about the status of my investments. I really needed the money, but my lawyer had assured me early on that I was well taken care of and had no financial worries. I had certainly spent recklessly, but I had no concept of whether my money had been invested and if it had been, why I didn't have any of it. I would have had a nervous breakdown if I'd ever sat down and truly added up how much I lost.

I figured if I was going to start over again, the best place to do that was in Boston. I knew Boston. That was where I had lived for many years and where I had enjoyed my best professional successes. I had friends there. Bobby Orr was there and I knew he would help me.

I returned to Boston, flat broke. I called Bobby. He said, "Play your cards right, Derek. Be honest. We'll get you back on track." He used to come and see me two or three times a week.

Bobby had his hands full with Frosty Forristall at that time. Frosty had been our trainer with the Bruins, and he and Bobby were close. They had lived together before Bobby married Peggy. Frosty had drinking problems, too, but he was a great guy and really had a lot to do with the success of our team.

I phoned Spike Boda. He had been the golf pro where I used to play at the International in Bolton, Massachusetts, but had moved to the Andover Country Club in Andover, Massachusetts. I called him about a job and we got together to talk about possibilities. Why Spike's name popped into my head, I'll never know. I hadn't talked to him in six years, but for some reason, I remembered his phone number. God speaks to us through other people, and for some reason, I was directed to Spike.

Spike knew everything I had been through, but he was a good friend. I had known Spike, his wife Angela and their children since they were small. Spike told me he couldn't afford to pay me. "I've got my sons as assistants, but I'll talk to Ivan Cormier and see what we can do." Ivan owned the Andover. They offered me a position working in the pro shop. They couldn't pay me, but they would provide three meals a day and lodging in a loft above the shop. Spike and Ivan took a big leap of faith by taking me on. Spike told me that the key to life was humility, and golf would teach me that. I would get up at 6 a.m. to wash golf carts with a sponge and hose and clean clubs for the members who liked to play early. The first tee time was eight o'clock, so I would open up the pro shop and sell items that members needed.

My routine each day was to wake up early and put in a full day. I'd be exhausted, so I'd go to bed early. The next morning, it was up and at 'em again. There was no life outside the golf course, but because of where I was in my life, it was a blessing in disguise. Working at the golf course really kept me on the straight and narrow.

When you're sober and you've got no money, you learn to be resourceful. There was a group of women who wanted to learn how to golf. The pros didn't have time, so I recognized a need and filled it. I read *Harvey Penick's Little Red Book,* which is the Bible of golf instruction, and I charged the ladies $20 per lesson.

Mondays were my day off, so I would go out and golf. I'd also go and play when it was raining. Nobody else wanted to play in the rain. I would holler over to Spike, "I'm going out," grab a cart and play by myself using just two irons and two woods. I'd play a little game with myself and I kept a scorecard. It really was a good test of my ability, and I got to be really good playing in the rain.

I worked at the Andover from April to November of 1980. Ivan and Spike were great to me. Spike never lectured me. He was a true friend.

I paid off some debts and then my friend, Larry Ansin, helped me find a studio apartment on the ground floor of a building in Winchester. Rent was only $400 a month. I had occasionally played golf with Joe Bellino, the 1960 Heisman Trophy winner, who happened to be from Winchester. At some point, he mentioned that he often went to auctions. "Do you ever come across any cheap cars?" I asked. It turned out that he did. He found a big red, beat-up '65 Chevy Impala. It had a bench seat so that when you turned a corner, you slid right across. It was $750, but Joe bought the car for me.

Spike registered me in the PGA. They teach you how to run a pro shop, how to market, how to re-grip clubs and all that kind of thing. That was the plan, but my hips betrayed me. After my second summer at the Andover with Spike, I went to see a doctor about why I was in such pain. After examining me, he told me I had arthritis.

318

"You're kidding me, Doc! I'm only 34."

He said, "Yep, arthritis. I'm going to send you over to Massachusetts General."

I went straight to the hospital with my X-rays, but the doctor there informed me, "This isn't arthritis. It's avascular necrosis."

"What's that, Doc?"

"You've got bone death, and one hell of a lawsuit. Who gave you the prednisone?"

I just looked at him. "You guys at Mass General did."

He immediately shut up. I think he nearly had a heart attack.

In 1982, a magazine was doing a story on me, going over the path I had taken following my hockey career. I told them about getting sober in 1980 and working at the Andover Country Club.

They said, "That's great. And whatever happened to your lawyer?"

I told them, "I no longer have a relationship with him."

The writer was astonished. "Didn't he set up a trust for you?"

"No," I said, shaking my head. "I'm completely broke. Wiped out."

The writer submitted the story and I didn't think too much more about it. I was working at the pro shop at the golf course. I'd get my duties done at the course first thing in the morning. The mail would come in around 10 o'clock. One day, I was sitting there with Spike Boda and his family. While sorting the mail, I was surprised to find a letter for me. It was from Boston Capital, an asset management company where I once had my investment portfolio. I ripped it open and started to read: "Dear Mr. Sanderson. We understand that you no longer have a working relationship with your attorney, so we will redirect your quarterly dividend cheques. In addition, we apologize for the amount of this cheque but due to tensions in the Middle East, your oil wells have been capped."

I owned oil wells?

I called Boston Capital. "I just read your letter and I'm confused," I began.

I had received a cheque for $126,385 and they were apologizing for the size?! I was absolutely stunned. As the conversation continued, I was told that the company had paid me no less than $385,000 each year. They told me, "We are terribly sorry, but we thought you had a working relationship with your attorney."

I said, "No, our relationship ended some time ago. Probably 1978 or so."

There was a long, silent pause on the phone.

"We have been sending your quarterly cheques to your attorney."

My lawyer had been taking the dividend cheques for years and never told me. I never even knew I owned things. I still don't have a record of any transactions. None, zero, zip.

I immediately went to my lawyer's office on the 45th floor of the Prudential Tower, walked right in and grabbed him. I had every intention of throwing him to the street below. Lucky for him, there were bars on the windows. The other lawyers in the office must have suspected I was about to go ballistic. They stormed in, and it took all of them to pull me off.

Through gritted teeth, I snarled, "You son of a bitch! You give me my money!"

He said, "You're broke!"

I was stunned. "How the fuck am I broke?"

He said, "You're broke because I paid all your bills!"

I snarled, "Oh you have, have you? You could have fooled me! The IRS is all over me. They're trying to arrest me for past taxes! You paid shit! Listen here, you son of a bitch—pay me!"

He said, "You're broke."

"Fuck you!"

He then turned to one of the young lawyers who worked with him and barked, "Back-charge the bastard all the way to 1969, when we started working together!" He went and billed me monthly fees that he promised he'd never charge me. Thirteen fucking years! It came to millions of dollars. Whatever might have been left in my accounts was wiped out completely.

I trusted him with my life. I didn't have any idea what I had. I had given him power of attorney.

I was flat broke and hopelessly crippled. The doctors told me I had to have my hip joints replaced because of the avascular necrosis. Osteotomies are surgical procedures where the bones are cut, reshaped or partially removed to realign the load-bearing surfaces of the joint. Disease had separated my leg bones from the hip sockets. Doctors claimed that it was likely caused by the prednisone used to quell the pain of the colitis. The FDA had approved the drug, but no one had any idea it would cause avascular necrosis where hip sockets dry out. I didn't know it. The doctors didn't know it. No one really is to blame. Candidly, I would have taken the prednisone anyway, even if I'd been advised that it would shorten my career. That's how dedicated I was to the game.

I was scheduled for surgery on the assumption that I was covered because I had played for the Bruins. Three days later, my hips were still bleeding and I was still hooked up to all the fluids when the accounting department came into my room and confronted me. They told me that, in fact, I was not covered, so they gave me some Percodan and threw me out. I was still bleeding, for God's sake!

The hospital asked me if I had a place to stay. The day before, Dr. Max Offenberger, the NHL's sports psychologist and a good friend, had come by to say hello. I told the people at the hospital that I'd be staying with Max. He let me stay with him for a while at his summer home in Saratoga. My hips were sore from the ride in his sports car, but it was great to have a place to recuperate for a while.

The realignment osteotomies hadn't worked out and I was in agony. I later moved in with a friend in Winchester and spent almost all of my time in bed because I could barely walk.

I phoned Bobby Orr and told him I needed surgery on my hips. Through the NHL Players' Association, it was arranged for me to go to Toronto for my surgeries. I don't know the full details, but I do know that the NHLPA paid for the operations. I believe there might have been some compensation from the Ontario Health Insurance Plan.

Dr. Gordon Hunter, a consultant orthopedic surgeon in Toronto, examined me during my first appointment. I was in terrible shape, both physically and mentally, and he refused to operate on me. The Players' Association then contacted Dr. Allan Gross, an orthopedic surgeon at Mount Sinai Hospital in Toronto. Dr. Gross is one of the top orthopedic surgeons in the world and was one of the pioneers in hip transplant surgery.

Dr. Gross agreed to see me. My Ontario health insurance had been activated, so we went ahead with the appointment. "When we got in there, there was no question that he did have avascular necrosis," explained Dr. Gross, who agreed that the problem was likely related to the steroid use. "Derek had had surgery on both hips in Boston. They were called realignment osteotomies, but they just didn't work out at all. When he came up to Toronto, he had to have hip replacements, which we call difficult hip replacements because of his previous osteotomies."

Dr. Gross and his team were wonderful to me. I ended up having two hip operations with Dr. Gross in Toronto—in 1985 and 1988. He is truly a top-notch surgeon. The Boston surgeon who did my last three hip surgeries—Dr. Joe McCarthy—is also internationally renowned. He is vice-chairman of the Department of Orthopaedics at Massachusetts General Hospital, past president of the American Association of Hip & Knee Surgeons and is on the board of directors of the American Academy of Orthopaedic Surgeons.

In 1983, after my first hip surgeries, I was home in bed in excruciating pain. I could barely move, but I tried to play golf. I took my crutches to the course and—without using my legs, just my arms—taught myself to hit balls with surprising accuracy through the trees using a 3-iron. I could eventually hit the ball through a four-inch space from 70 yards away. I was still around the pro shop at Andover, but I couldn't do much.

I was living in my studio apartment and was friendly with a guy on the third floor. My hips were so bad that I could barely move, so he and I worked out a system so that I could eat. I'd crawl out of my apartment and yell up to him. He'd come out with a rope and lower some cereal and milk down to me. I would go into my apartment, pour the cereal and milk, and then hoist it back up to him.

I was really living day to day. I didn't even have enough money to eat. The weight was just falling off me. Sometimes, my friend and his wife would go out and they'd bring me home Chinese food. That was a real treat. I gradually started to feel a little bit better but was going stir crazy. I wasn't able to shower or bathe. My friend tried to help me have a bath by wrapping me in Saran wrap, but I couldn't lift my leg over the tub. And to make things even worse, my leg got infected. "I've got to get out of here," I decided.

At a party a few months earlier, I'd met a guy named Anthony. He called me "Flash." He said, "Listen, Flash, come by any time you want for dinner." I was so hungry that I decided I'd try to drive out to see him.

I wasn't able to drive very well. In fact, I was going 12 or 15 miles an hour on Route 16, a major artery, winding my way through all the towns on my way to Revere. I had my four-way flashers on the entire way. I got honked at and sworn at and people swerved by me and cut me off. It took me 40 minutes to go the nine miles from Winchester to Revere.

I finally got to Anthony's house, but there was an upstairs and a downstairs and I didn't know which level he lived on. Standing there with my crutches, I was unable to knock on the door, so I stood out front and simply yelled, "Hey, Anthony! Anthony!" Finally, his mother came to the door. She took one look at me and said, "Oh, my God! Get in here. You could use a meal. Come on in here right now!" She fed me and I ate like a pig. Anthony's dad was a super guy, too. They asked me to dinner and I stayed there for three years. I never went back to my apartment.

I had my own room upstairs. I'd lie there by the hour. Anthony's father finished work by mid-afternoon, so we'd play gin until supper. He was really good. He'd tease, "Buck a point, Derek?" I laughed. I didn't care. I had no money. I think the game ended up being $485,000 to $312,000 for him.

Once I felt up to it, Anthony took me to the track at Suffolk Downs. We went every morning. I was terrified. I didn't have any money and Anthony was heavily into gambling, but he taught me about horse racing and I started to understand a bit.

He said, "I've got a horse standing in Toronto," which meant it had been foaled there. It was a one-year-old running as a two-year-old, and it was posting great times in time trials. His plan was for me to go to Canada, which would give me a chance to hang with some friends, and then I'd bring the horse back with me to Suffolk Downs. Anthony named the horse Unlucky Flash. This thing was a bullet.

"Here's what we're going to do," Anthony explained. "We're going to wipe out the trifecta."

"What do you mean?"

He said, "I'm going to run the horse in the trifecta in Maryland. We'll wheel him on top to win, place and show, but we need about $40,000 in order to win $200,000 to $300,000." You can do that with a trifecta as long as your horse wins. The horse we were betting on had run in 13 races, but had come in second 11 times.

We begged and borrowed the money. A dear friend of mine, Larry Ansin, a fabric manufacturer, loaned me some money. Anthony came up with some money and we were ready to execute his scheme.

"I can't believe we're going to do this," I told him. "It's ridiculous!"

He took all the money and bet it. He bet some with the book in Boston, which I was against. You don't let wise guys know you're betting this kind of horse, but his ego wanted to show off. All of Anthony's cousins came down and we stayed in a single hotel room, sleeping on couches, the floor and anywhere you could find a spot. They gave me the bed because of my surgery.

The horse was running at 14–1. Each of the cousins placed a $100 bet on the trifecta at different windows so no one would catch on to what we were doing. They couldn't discover that we were trying to fix the race because it was just before post time and it would be impossible to compare bets from different trifecta windows. Our only fear was that someone else might be doing the same thing.

Anthony and I were sitting at the finish line. "Come on, Flash, get excited," he prodded, but I couldn't. I was a nervous wreck. That was a ton of money for a guy who didn't have any. I thought the scheme was insane, but Anthony kept reminding me that we could win more than $200,000.

"All we have to do is break out on top," Anthony reminded me.

They were at the starting line and the bell rang. "And they're off," the announcer called. "It's Unlucky Flash leading the pack."

The horse opened it up on the backside and was ahead by three lengths.

As thrilled as I was to win a second Stanley Cup championship in 1972, I was even happier for my dad, seen here with me and Lord Stanley's legacy.

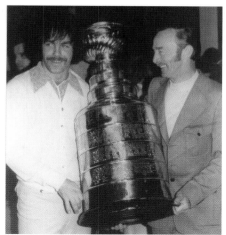

Who would have thought that the three of us would lead the exodus to the World Hockey Association? In 1972, I joined the Philadelphia Blazers, Bobby Hull (*centre*) became a member of the Winnipeg Jets and Gerry Cheevers (*right*) jumped to the Cleveland Crusaders.

BETTMANN/CORBIS

I never wanted to leave the Boston Bruins. They were family as much as they were friends and teammates.

I became the highest-paid athlete in the world in 1972 when I signed with the Philadelphia Blazers of the WHA for $2.65 million over five years.

HOCKEY HALL OF FAME

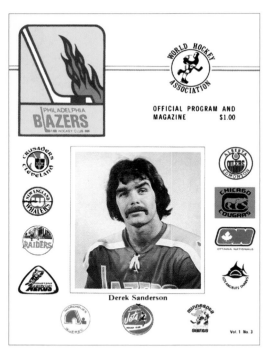

The Blazers regarded me as the saviour of the franchise, but one guy couldn't draw the kinds of crowds needed to make money in the WHA, especially with the NHL's Philadelphia Flyers already established in the city. That's teammate Dave Hutchison in the background.

COURTESY OF RON TOWNSEND

My career in the World Hockey Association lasted all of eight games. Worst decision I ever made. They tried to get me to quit and finally gave me a million-dollar severance package to walk away.

I returned to the Bruins during the 1972–73 season, but things were different. I couldn't even wear my old number, 16, as it had been given to Fred O'Donnell.

I hated leaving the Bruins for a second time, but coach Bep Guidolin and I just couldn't coexist, so I joined the Rangers in 1974. After playing with Bobby Orr for so many seasons, it was strange to play against him.

Although my brawling tailed off as my career went on, I never backed away from a fight. Linesman Matt Pavelich stands guard as I rearrange myself after a scrap.

AL RUELLE/KEVIN SHEA COLLECTION

I'm ignoring Bobby Schmautz (*right*) as I retrieve my glove in a game between two archrivals.

AL RUELLE/KEVIN SHEA COLLECTION

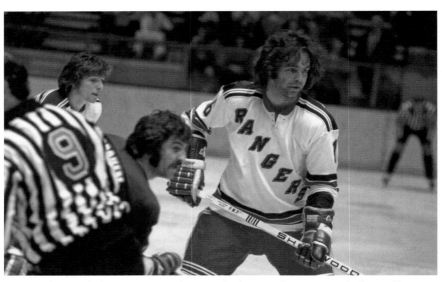

Steve Vickers and I bet our moustaches on whether Northern Dancer had actually won the Triple Crown. I lost and had to shave my trademark 'stache.

MECCA/HOCKEY HALL OF FAME

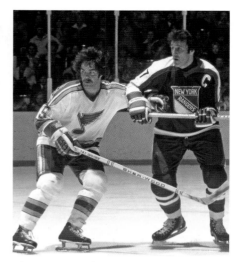

I really enjoyed my time in St. Louis after I was traded from the Rangers in October 1975. Being paired with Chuck Lefley (*left*) was great luck. We both had career seasons. He scored 43 goals and had 85 points, and I scored 24 goals and had 67 points.

PORTNOY/HOCKEY HALL OF FAME

Playing against former teammates is a fact of life in hockey. Once on the ice, they're all opponents. By 1975–76, neither Phil Esposito (*right*) nor I were in Boston. I was in St. Louis and Phil was with the Rangers.

PORTNOY/HOCKEY HALL OF FAME

I traded plane travel for bus rides when I was sent to the Kansas City Blues in 1977. Having jumped straight from junior to the NHL, it was a strange experience to play in the minors. I played only eight games for KC that season. As I worked my way back into the NHL after Vancouver, I ended up in Kansas City again, but this time, the team was renamed the Red Wings.

GERALD ESKANAZI/*THE NEW YORK TIMES*/REDUX

Even though the demons had a firm hold of me while I was with the Canucks in 1977, I still contributed 16 points in the 16 games I played for Vancouver. Here, I'm being hit by Rod Seiling of the St. Louis Blues.

PORTNOY/HOCKEY HALL OF FAME

The Canucks cut me after blood tests showed I was drinking and doing drugs. My world had fallen apart—my dad was sick, my girlfriend had dumped me and my health was not good. I skulked home to my place in Fort Erie, which I'd bought while I was with the Blues.

STEVE WAXMAN

After being dumped by the Canucks and suffering terrible burns in a kitchen accident, I fought back and convinced the Red Wings to give me a shot. They sent me to the Windsor Spitfires of the OHA so I could get in shape and they could observe me.

WALTER JACKSON/*WINDSOR STAR*

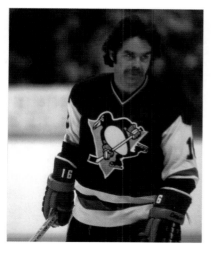

Most people had written me off, but the Pittsburgh Penguins signed me as a free agent in March 1978. I had worked hard to make my return, but the Penguins didn't renew my contract at the end of the season, and that was the end of my NHL career.

On my 50th birthday, I got together with some of the people who mean the most to me. Left to right, there's Johnny Lombardi; my sister, Karen; me; and Tom Cottringer.

Here I am with my beautiful wife, Nancy. When I met her in 1984, I knew right away that I was going to marry her. We did just that on December 28, 1986.

Three generations pose for a picture: my boys, Michael and Ryan, with Nancy and her father, Don Gillis. Don was a popular sportscaster in the Boston area for years.

Life after hockey is challenging when the game is all you know. Through the support of great friends like Bobby Orr, I was able to redeem myself, and since hitting rock bottom, I have enjoyed three careers: speaking to school kids, broadcasting and being a financial advisor.

I've always loved to golf, and while on my road to recovery, I worked at a golf course. Despite having hips ravaged by operations, I still get out as often as I can. Here I am at the Bobby Orr Golf Tournament held annually in Parry Sound, Ontario.

In 2011, I really enjoyed being part of Road Hockey to Conquer Cancer, for the Princess Margaret Cancer Centre in Toronto. Ron Ellis (*left*) and Scotty Bowman (*centre*) also supported the cause.

Nancy and I love spending time with one of our favourite couples, Bobby and Peggy Orr.

Around the clubhouse turn, he led by four lengths. The entire field trailed Unlucky Flash, and he was running comfortably. I started to get pumped. I could smell big money.

Anthony shouted, "Flash! This is it! We're going to win!"

I had been looking at the ground, unwilling to look at the track, but just then, the crowd rose to its feet and cheered. I lifted my head and the horse turned and—I swear to God—looked right at me. He lost his momentum and was edged in a photo finish by about a quarter of an inch. The horse finished second, so we didn't lose our shirts, but I said, "Never again."

Anthony talked me into trying again. This time, Unlucky Flash was running in New York. We were seated, $35,000 in bets placed, and I looked down—our horse wasn't on the track! "Scratch it! Somebody's messing with us!"

Just then, Unlucky Flash came out. I was a nervous wreck by that point. It turned out our usual trainer had the flu so we had a backup trainer. Unlucky Flash was the last one into the gate.

The bell rang and they all took off. All, that is, except our horse. Nothing! He finally got out of the gate, but by this time, the other horses were 15 or 20 lengths ahead of him. But he just picked up and started building momentum. He went wide and went around everybody. By the home stretch, he was neck-and-neck with the leader.

And once again, he lifted his head. He lost by an inch.

"That's it! I am never going to gamble again," I told Anthony. "I learned my lesson. To hell with this!"

In 1984, while I lived with Anthony, *60 Minutes* did a story about me. Harry Reasoner accurately depicted me as having once been the highest-paid athlete in the world but now needing to rely on the kindness of friends after losing everything, including my health, to alcohol and drugs. By the way, that piece was nominated for an Emmy Award for excellence in television production.

I will forever be grateful to Anthony and his family for helping me out when I needed a hand, but I realized I had to get away from the gambling. Suffice it to say I didn't need any more trouble in my life.

CHAPTER 31

VISITING SCHOOLS

As I was walking out of Daisy's in November 1984, I ran into Joe Timilty. He was in the Massachusetts Senate and had previously been on Boston City Council.

"Hey Joe, how're you doing?"

"Doing okay, Derek," he said. "You're limping. What happened?"

"I just got out of the hospital after hip surgeries, Joe. But I screwed up. I didn't have any insurance. If it wasn't for friends coming up with the money, they'd probably have put me in jail."

He looked at me quizzically. "Are you kidding me?"

"No, I'm not, Joe."

He asked, "Why don't you go see your partner, Joey Cimino? Together, you guys owned the bars. He must owe you something."

"No," I replied, shaking my head. "Joey's been working them himself for years. He has no obligation to me."

But I decided to give it a shot and went to see Joey. I walked in sober and he welcomed me warmly. "Nice to see you back," he said with a smile.

We chatted for a while. I said, "Listen, Joey, I know we've got nothing in writing, but do you think you could throw me a bone here?"

He nodded. "Yeah. I think I should buy you out. After all, you did start it and you did work it. It was your reputation that put us on the ground and you're the one that got the licence." He said, "Come with me."

We walked over to the bank. He got the key to a safety deposit box and asked me to join him. After opening the box, he pulled out two small packets.

326

"Here you go, Turk. I saved these for you."

I opened the packets, and there were my Stanley Cup rings from 1970 and 1972. He had saved them for me. He had saved them *from* me. "You were drinking so much that I know you would have sold those rings for a song and lived to regret it. There you go. I want you to have your rings back."

Then, he also gave me $35,000. He didn't have to give me a penny. We had been friends a long time. I appreciated Joey then, as I do now, more than he'll ever know. Joey stood by me when others gave up hope.

Just out of the hospital, I briefly stayed with Dr. Max Offenberger. The pain I was experiencing was excruciating, but I knew I had to get past that. I was sober, but the Percodan made me feel a whole lot better. Max reminded me that a drug is a drug, and he wanted me weaned off the Percodan. "Well, it's also survival right now, Max. I'm too old to be brave. Bravery is for the young, and I'm in pain." But I gradually took longer and longer in between Percodan and soon, I didn't need them.

When Joey gave me the 35 grand, I had money in my pocket for the first time in years. I was all set, getting better by the day and going back and forth to the golf course. I was living with my friend's family, eating well, and life was good.

Joe Timilty kept in touch with me. "Derek, do you have to have any more surgeries?"

"Yeah," I answered. "But I've got to get myself insurance. I've got to get a job."

He asked, "What can you do?"

I said, "Joe, I was a hockey player. The only thing that kept me out of college was high school! I don't really know what I can do."

I told him I had been a good student until I quit in Grade 11 to play hockey. He said, "I have an idea, Derek. You have been through a lot the last several years. You know a lot about alcohol and drugs from the inside. I just left Mayor Ray Flynn and he told me that a report had just been issued that stated that

Massachusetts is the worst state in the union for alcohol and drug abuse in schools. Derek, I have an idea. Let's set up a meeting with Mayor Flynn."

The meeting took place the next day. After we exchanged pleasantries, Mayor Flynn cut to the chase about the report. "I don't want to believe it, Derek. What I have in mind is hiring you to go and talk to the kids. Visit as many schools as you can, evaluate the situation, and by year end, I want you to give me a report."

I reflected back on Fort Erie and my promise to God that if he spared my life, I would talk to kids about alcohol and drug abuse. It's curious how life works. I had never spoken to kids before unless they asked me for an autograph, but I needed a job and this fulfilled my promise. I agreed to the mayor's plan.

I didn't know anyone when I went to the schools—not the principals, the teachers or the superintendents. I went to the first school and was introduced at an assembly. The kids refused to pay attention. I was talking at them; yelling at times so I could be heard. They were eighth- and ninth-graders. Why would they care? The school was three-quarters minorities and here I was, an old white guy, standing up there telling them my story. They had no common ground with me, and I couldn't command their attention to deliver my message. I failed. Badly. The third school I visited was in Bunker Hill. There were about 300 seventh- and eighth-graders. The principal was on the stage telling the students, "You must listen to our guest today. He's going to give you a lot of information about decision-making and the pitfalls of alcohol. At one time, he was the highest-paid athlete in the world . . ."

While he tried to gain respect for me with his introduction, I ducked behind the piano at the back of the stage and, as much as it hurt, I got down on my knees. "God, please help me. Please take over my mind and my body and use me as a tool to deliver Your message. I don't know what to say to these kids. I've done three schools and it just isn't working."

" . . . a former Stanley Cup champion with the Boston Bruins, please welcome Derek Sanderson!"

I got up and as I walked to the front of the stage, under my breath I said, "I need Your help, Lord."

I decided not to stand on the stage this time. Instead, I put my crutches down and sat on the edge of the stage. I politely asked the principal to have all the teachers and monitors leave the auditorium. He refused. "Derek, no. First of all, you have an expensive ring on your hand and I don't want any temptations. And secondly, they have never been left unattended before."

I calmly told him, "Something tells me I'll be fine."

He shrugged and said, "Okay. I'll watch you from outside the door."

"Uh-uh," I said. "Don't get caught watching because when we get to the question-and-answer part, I don't want any of these students to feel as though they can't ask me anything. I don't want them to think they'll be penalized if they talk to me about something illegal or wrong."

I liked to tell stories to the students. It helped me gauge the pulse of my crowd. For example, I'd talk about a guy walking down the hall going to his locker, stoned, and as he's walking he says, "This is the longest corridor I have ever been in!" If you smoke dope, you know that's funny because marijuana distorts your perception of distance, so if they laugh, you know you've got an experienced audience.

The kids were a bit unruly at first, but I noticed this one kid in the front row. He was in the eighth grade, but he was bigger than the rest of the kids. From my experience, I could tell that he had control of the kids in his grade.

"Excuse me, I want to talk to you alone over here."

"Okay."

"How many of these kids are yours to control?"

"About 30," he replied.

I said, "Okay. How about you keep your 30 and give me the rest?"

He looked at me, trying to figure out where I was coming from. I told him I wasn't trying to get one over on him, but that I needed him to help me. He held up his hand. You could have heard a pin drop.

I thanked him. He nodded and sat down. I talked for an hour and a half.

"I'll tell you what," I began. "I can sit here and try to talk to you guys, but if you're not listening, it doesn't do any of us any good. I once had a TV show and the first line of the theme song was 'Everybody's talkin' at me,' and that's exactly what I'm doing here with you today. I'm talking at you. I don't want to do that. I'm giving you a few facts, which you probably already know anyway, but we've got to get to the reason why you guys choose to do wrong."

I said, "Let me pose a situation. I've got a gold pen here and after I write with it, I leave it on the stage when I leave. You know the pen is worth a lot of money, so you grab it. Once you get it, what do you do with it?"

Every kid had an answer. "Sell it." "Keep it." But the kid with whom I had started the morning surprised me. "It's your pen, so I'd give it to the teacher. She'd return it to you. She'd know how to get hold of you since she got you here."

I said, "Ah! So you do know right from wrong! Why do you choose to do wrong?"

He answered, "Because life sucks."

There was a chorus of yeahs.

I said, "You're what, 12 or 13? Life doesn't suck. Life is what you make it. I know that people beat you over the head with that all the time, but it's true. You've got to learn to read, write, add and subtract or you aren't going anywhere in this world.

"You can be a criminal. To get drugs, you either steal or you deal. Both ways are illegal. You go to jail. First offence, second offence—they'll try to give you a break, but you won't listen because you're not afraid of the system. But let me tell you, you can't be hired by anybody. You've got a criminal record. Nobody wants to hire a criminal. And who wants to live in an eight-by-ten-foot cell? Do you want to be fresh meat for somebody? You don't want to do that."

These were tough kids. They took their lives in their hands every day just by going home. The projects are bad. Hearing gunshots is an everyday occurrence. The cops told me that if you are driving through the projects and come to a red light, you should stop 10 feet behind the car in front of you. That way, if a gang jumps off the corner to carjack you, you can pull out and drive through the light. The gangs won't jump out and get you because they know what you're doing. But if you're boxed in, all they have to do is walk up to your window and then they can do anything they want.

It's a different world. We shouldn't judge them the way we tend to because individually, they're pretty good kids. But when they're in a group, it's a pack mentality. They show off to impress their friends.

It took me 50 or 60 schools, but I realized that kids are essentially all the same. I went to schools in poorer areas and I went to schools in affluent suburbs. Polar opposites, but every one of the kids is afraid of what their peers think. Students want to fit in. It is dangerous to be the oddball. Everyone wants to be perceived as cool, but cool has a price tag. There is immense pressure to drink, do drugs and have sex. These students are extremely vulnerable.

I figure I've spoken at about 800 schools, and probably talked to 480,000 kids through 12 years. In every case, I had to tailor the speech for the audience I'd be talking to.

I would ask that the school not mix the grades. After a while, you get to know your audience, and I had talks geared to each grade. When I spoke to fifth- and sixth-grade kids, it was all about decision-making. Trust, loyalty, respect and honesty. They're still kids. I didn't get into booze, drugs and sex. It was too early. The message you want to convey to them is that decision-making is a skill; that you must make the correct decisions or there are penalties.

In the seventh and eighth grades, the kids are starting to show that their hormones are awakening, and they are beginning to experiment. Ninth-graders are in a whole different ballpark. These students are in a new school, so after being the top dog in Grade 8, they're now pieces of shit in Grade 9. The seniors and juniors push them around. The sophomores just want to avoid contact with them. The ninth-grader has nothing in common with the other students. They're just hanging on for dear life, trying to survive without getting picked on. Ninth-graders have raging hormones, and if you give them sex education, they want to practise. How do you get a girl to do what you want them to do? Get them drunk or stoned. Ninth-graders are in an awkward spot. They can't drive. They are still a couple of years too young to get a licence. It isn't cool to ride your bicycle. You're a nerd if you've got a bike and a helmet, so they're walkers.

Tenth-graders are just marginally cooler than ninth-graders, but their network is a little wider and their curiosity a little deeper. Kids in the eleventh grade, in many cases, are now old enough to be licensed, so they might occasionally have access to a car, which opens up all kinds of possibilities regarding sex, drugs and drinking. They can go to parties where there is access to all three. Seniors have the car more regularly, whether it's their own or a family car. They've got a girlfriend or boyfriend. They're at all the parties. They can get into bars or beer stores. They're the big man on campus or the happening girl. And if they're an athlete, they are everything in their school.

A very small percentage of students possess true confidence in themselves, and it is almost exclusively an athlete, a pretty girl or a straight-A student who doesn't give a shit about the stigma attached to being smart. The vast majority of students are B and C students, unsure of themselves and their place in the hierarchy of student life and still growing into their bodies. They're growing in leaps and bounds and their hormones are rushing beyond control. You're not yet what you're going to be when you're out of college. You pick up all your bad habits and all your mistakes in the seventh, eighth and ninth grades.

The education system doesn't have anything in place for these kids, so where do they fit in? Some go to the drug culture. Maybe they become dealers. They've got to be cool somehow, and if they can't do it through athletics, are only so-so at school and they don't look like models, they find some other way to be popular. People always like you when you're holding. Once you discover that, you can become cool pretty quickly. You take that scary step—"I'm going to buy this shit and put it in my pocket and sell it to friends." Next thing you know, you're selling inside the school. If you get caught, you get a juvenile record, but as long as you're an adolescent, they don't throw you in jail.

That is terrifying. But it's so easy for kids, and they don't think.

It's the same with sex. I was at one girls' school talking to a Grade 8 class and I asked them, "How many of you have not—I repeat, *have not*—had sex or done drugs?" There were only eight of them. And then they started telling me stories that ripped me apart.

These are kids who have just become teenagers! I didn't know whether I was on foot or on horseback when I was 17. We never saw anybody naked. Our biggest thrill was seeing a topless woman in *National Geographic.* Back then, I wondered why breasts weren't pointed like the sweaters we saw in the Eaton's catalogue.

My dad sat me down when I was 12 and said, "I'm going to teach you the facts of life."

I said, "Forget it, Dad. I'll pick up what I need to know in the pool room."

He growled, "Those friends of yours know nothing. You've got another 12-year-old telling you what to do? Guess what? You're in trouble."

I couldn't believe the sexually oriented questions and comments that came up when I spoke at the schools. I was talking to a girls' Grade 9 class in Connecticut. There were four girls, good-looking and dressed much older than their age in short skirts. They asked if they could talk to me confidentially after my talk at that school. They confided that they traded sexual favours with businessmen for cocaine at lunch hour. They didn't see it as a big deal. I looked at the girls square in the eyes and said, "This little sex ring has got to stop. We have to get you off this path you're on. If you think you can use sex as a tool, then everything breaks down." I explained that what they were doing was, in fact, prostitution. When they heard that, they were upset, and they argued with me, but that's exactly what it was. They told me they would never have sex for money, but a trade was okay. They couldn't come to grips with the fact that if it didn't hurt and was even occasionally fun, it was wrong. "It's wrong because these men are using you, and they should go to jail."

I had to get the principal involved and I understand that the police were notified. They ended up arresting the guys.

There were a lot of stories similar to that. It was eye-opening.

My drug and alcohol discussions opened up all sorts of conversations, and I found myself being a combination of social worker, psychologist and mentor. I appeared in the schools for free, and therefore, I was in great demand. I would love to get back at it, but I'm afraid that I have a mortgage, too.

I was talking to seventh- and eighth-graders at a school when a kid came in late for assembly, all upset and crying. A teacher was trying to quell some commotion at the side of the stage. I went over and asked, "What's the problem?"

The teacher asked, "Can you help us?"

"With what?" I asked.

She said, "His friend is outside and he says he is going to kill himself."

"How old is he?"

She said, "He's only in the seventh grade."

Suicide in the seventh grade? Really? Kids haven't even begun to live yet! How bad can life be at 12 years of age?

I said, "Look, I was a hockey player and I'm an alcoholic. I am not a Ph.D. I am not a psychiatrist, and I am certainly not a child psychologist. What if I make a wrong decision? The liability of me going out there and helping that kid—"

She interrupted me. "Derek, you are head and shoulders better prepared for this than any of us."

Something inside me told me I wasn't alone on this, so I agreed. The principal sanctioned it. He said, "If I call the superintendent, then the kid will have a stigma for life."

"Give me a few minutes," I asked. "Let me just talk to him."

I saw him sitting alone at the ball diamond behind the school, so I calmly walked over to him. "How're you doing?"

He was sullen. I could tell by his expression that he wanted to know who I was.

"What's the problem? Your friend is worried about you."

"He shouldn't have said anything," the kid replied.

"Something wrong at school?"

"No."

"Home?"

Bingo! He didn't say a word, but I knew I had my answer.

Finally, he asked, "I don't see a way out of this. Does it get better?"

"Not really," I admitted. "I could probably tell you here and now that if you eat your vegetables and do what you're told that everything will be fine, but I'd be lying to you. You have to get your game in order."

He huffed, "They never let me do what I want to do!"

"What do you mean?"

He explained. "My father wants me to play Pop Warner football. Look at me! I'm 70 pounds!"

I said, "Yeah. What position did he want you to play? Linebacker?" I thought a joke might help, but it didn't, so I shut up.

I invited him inside the school with me. "Come on. We'll talk." I asked the principal if I could use his office, and then the kid and I sat and talked for quite a while. I threw out a blue-sky scenario. "If I was a magician and could wave a wand and make things right, what would you want me to do?"

"I'd want you to tell my dad that I don't like football," he answered.

"Why?"

"Because they don't understand me," he explained. "My dad wants me to be a football player because they make a lot of money."

I said, "Well, that doesn't have a lot to do with a seventh-grader, now, does it? There's a long way between now and the NFL." I asked him, "Do you have the heart for it?"

"No. I don't like football. In fact, I hate it."

I had to crack the veneer a little bit and came up with an idea. "Everybody's good at something. What are you good at?"

His eyes lit up. "I can draw."

I saw a total change in him as soon as he saw that someone cared. I said, "Let me see your work." It was very important to use the word "work," because to an artist, that's his work. That one word meant I was giving credence to his passion.

He rummaged around in his bag and whipped out a series of cartoons. I couldn't believe how good they were! All the characters were original. The haircuts were different. The characters were of different ethnicities—black, white, Asian. They were really funny. They had good times, tough times, failures. The kid was a sensational cartoonist.

I realized that this kid had a rare talent, and I didn't want to lose him. "How would you feel if I called your father?"

The kid shrugged, so I called the dad. He came over to the school and I enthused about the talent his son exhibited. Then I got serious. "Do you have any idea how much Charles Schulz makes?"

Neither of us truly knew, but we knew it was a fortune—syndicated comic strips, books, merchandise. His father realized how much money cartoonists can make. Last time I heard, the kid had gone to a special school for the arts and flourished.

I would talk with the kids about drinking. "Why would you put booze, which is an anesthetic, a drug, in your body?" I asked that question in every school I visited. The odd time, I'd get some smart alec kid saying, "Because it's fun!" I'd respond, "You can't have fun straight? If you can't, you've got some serious issues to deal with. What's fun? Laughing like the village idiot? Jumping off buildings? Throwing rocks through windows? Tell me what part of that is fun. You wouldn't do that stuff if you were sober. You're too smart for that so you have to get stupid first.

"If you want a girl to do the things you want her to, you have to make her stupid, too. Girls can make love sober. Some need love, some need like, but they can have sex. Why, as men, do we need to numb our emotions first? The sole reason for drinking is to suppress feelings. That's all it does.

"If one drink is good, you figure two must be better. And if two are better, then three must be great. And then you start to overdose on the drug. And people are no longer laughing with you, they're laughing *at* you. There's a big difference.

"And you start to lose your real friends because alcohol is more important to you. And you start to hang out with a second tier of people who have the same issues you've got. You're not afraid anymore. Your friends have moved on. You've got to figure it out."

Drugs, alcohol, sex—it's about decision-making. I talked about repercussions of their behaviour. Kids don't always think their choices all the way through. It's all about the moment. It's all about fun. They think they are invincible. We all did.

I spoke very bluntly, and maybe that's why the kids warmed up to me. They asked questions—really candid questions—and later, the principal would comment, "I have never seen these kids so quiet for two hours. I never even thought it was possible."

It worked great. What I learned is that you don't do alcohol and drug awareness lectures—you do alcohol and drug awareness discussions. The discussions were a common-sense approach to life. I was candid and honest and I found the kids reacted well to that.

I challenged them to think. I told them, "All through your life, you are going to have one of two choices—yes or no, right or wrong, good or bad. Those are the only choices you get. Think about things before you do them. If you make the easy choice, things can get bad really fast. Make the right choices."

My personal opinion is that common sense is a gift. At birth, you're given a set of tools. Some people get looks, some get intellect, some are born beautiful and some have common sense. If you're really lucky, you might get a bit from several categories. People say that everybody's got good in them. I don't believe that, but I do believe that everybody's got ability in them. You have to find out what it is. Find your passion, and when you find it, do it. Sometimes it takes a while. All God wants of you is to be a good person. If you get rich or famous in the process, great, but as long as you work at being a good person, you will be happy.

I did a lot of parent awareness talks as well. Parents are in denial, too—"Not my kid!" I tell parents that children only have the right to safety, not privacy. If you suspect that they're doing drugs, search their pockets when you do the laundry; search their rooms when they aren't there. That is only good parenting, because once they try booze or drugs and they know it works, stopping them from going to the next stage is really tough. Most of you have likely seen that television commercial where the mechanic is selling an oil filter and says, "Pay me now or pay me later." Well, later costs a lot more in this circumstance, too.

Bullying is another thing that many kids encounter. I remember an expression from my childhood: "Sticks and stones may break my bones but names will never hurt me." What a stupid, mindless expression! We are all a product of name-calling. The hurtful joking and so-called lighthearted jabs still hurt. We are all feeling people who can still be hurt by a thoughtless remark no matter how old we are. Those insults we heard as children remain with us for a lifetime. Here I am in my 60s and I can still recall who said what to me and why.

We all remember the bully of our neighbourhood or schoolyard. He or she usually had a couple of hangers-on. Bullying has always been a pet peeve of mine. I hate people who push others around—people they know can't or won't fight back. When it happened to me, my father told me, "There's only one way to handle this. When you see him tomorrow, walk right up and punch him in the face." Bullies don't like to be confronted and, as a rule, they are cowards as well, so when you stand up to them, usually the bullying comes to an end. By the way, I confronted my bully as my dad instructed. I walked up to him from his blind side, called his name and then hit him as hard as he was ever hit. I did take a beating, but after that, he never bothered me again.

Bullying today can also take on a different look because the Internet is a perfect place for cowards to hide. They can type whatever lie they want and then sit back and anonymously watch the damage they've caused. They are, in my mind, like the drug addict who steals your wallet and then helps you look for it.

You wouldn't believe the people I meet. People in their mid-30s approach me to tell me that they remembered my talk from 20 years earlier and the impact it had on them. It's very rewarding.

I took away every bit as much from the schools that the students, hopefully, took away from my visits. It was the greatest experience of my life—not hockey. The seven years I spent in Boston with the Bruins was the greatest fun I had in my life. I won two Stanley Cups with the greatest guys in the world. But the most rewarding experience of my life was talking to kids at the schools.

CHAPTER 32

THE LOVES OF MY LIFE

When I was drinking heavily and close to rock bottom, my mother prayed for me. She also told me to straighten up, find a nice girl and get married. I asked her, "Why would I want to do that?" My time was my own. My money, what little I had, was my own. I had no one to answer to. I came and went when I wanted.

I now know that, where women were concerned, my courage came from drinking. I was loquacious, but at the same time, women scared the crap out of me. I had been terrified of rejection since I was a kid. I had a girlfriend when I was in high school and one day, *boom!* We broke up. I had another one and thought I loved her, and that didn't work out. That girl in high school laughed at me when I tried to dance. That hurt more than anyone ever knew.

I had nice girlfriends over the years. There were even a couple of times when I entertained the thought of settling down and getting married. But when it hadn't come to pass, I was certain it would never happen. And I certainly had no intentions of having children. Now I can see that I was selfish and I knew it. I didn't want the responsibility. It was all about me and what I wanted when I wanted it.

When I first got sober, I was living in Andover. I didn't date anybody for two years. There was a big hole in my life. But in 1984, my life took a completely different path.

I was working with kids, talking to them about the dangers of alcohol and drugs, and had a little office at City Hall. I was writing, doing my charts and making schedules. I was being paid $17,000 a year. I could cover my rent, and that was about it.

Nancy Gillis was a Boston College communications graduate and was working for the city government. She was the liaison between the city and Cablevision when it first came out. Cablevision had channels set aside for community content, and one day she walked into my office along with a producer and a cameraperson. "I'd like to interview you for our program." She was very businesslike about it.

Well, the moment she sat down, I knew I was going to marry her. That was it. She was statuesque, and had the prettiest, happy face, the most wonderful eyes and dark, curly hair.

We had a couple of meetings, and the third time we met, I said, "You didn't have to go through all this, you know."

Nancy looked at me quizzically. "What?"

I said, "We're probably going to end up living together, so we probably should have a first date."

She gave me a look that hinted she was going to be angry, but then smiled and said okay. We went to dinner that night.

I left work to get ready. I was living at Anthony's place, and when I arrived home, his mother was putting out a big Italian spread, which she did every night.

She looked at me and said, "Where are you going?"

I said, "Don't set a place for me. I'm going out tonight."

The entire family just looked at me.

"I've got a date," I explained.

"You're kidding?"

I said, "I'm not kidding. I'm taking her to dinner."

Lily said, "But I cooked all this just for you. It's your favourite." Lily did guilt really well.

I said, "Well, then, put it aside and save it for me."

"No," she insisted, "we've got to share it."

I sat down and ate pasta fagioli, lasagna, and bread and butter. I was so full I thought I'd explode. I drove to Dorchester to pick up Nancy. As we drove away from her house, I asked, "So, what do you want to do?"

She was dressed to the nines and, with a furrowed brow, answered, "I thought you said we were going to dinner."

I said, "Ummm, I want to talk to you about that." She looked at me strangely, and I knew I had to bluff. I said, "Of course. Where do you want to go?"

We went to a great place owned by a friend of mine, so I knew we'd get good treatment. They gave us a quiet table for two. Nancy ordered the salmon and I ordered a steak, but I was just picking at it.

"What's wrong with your steak?" Nancy asked.

"Nothing," I replied. I gave her some silly line. "I was too busy looking at you!"

"Don't do that," she warned. "Seriously, why aren't you eating?"

When you get sober, you learn to be honest. I said, "Well, to tell you the truth, I went home, and even though I told them I had a dinner date, the family I live with had already made supper. I felt so bad that I ate it."

"Didn't you tell her you were going for dinner?" Nancy asked.

"Yeah, I did, but you don't know Lily."

Nancy shrugged. "If you were full, why would you order a steak? Why didn't you just order a bowl of soup or a salad? You shouldn't have wasted your money."

I said, "I thought I could get away with it, but I'm full."

So we went out for a drive and then went back to her place. We sat on the couch and talked, and then I went home. We went out again on another date, and then another and another. Every time I went to her place, I wondered where her roommates were. It turned out they were hiding upstairs and didn't want to disturb us. "Tell them to come down," I said, and we all talked and laughed. And then I left.

It was a long time before we got into anything. But I knew I was going to marry this woman. It was just a matter of time. I even told her early on. "You know we're going to get married, don't you?"

She chuckled. "Let's just take this one date at a time."

I told her friend Teresa, "You know Nancy and I are going to get married, don't you?"

Teresa laughed. "Yeah. I've been told you've said that before!"

I visited three or four schools each week as part of the alcohol and drug awareness program, and then I'd see Nancy at night. I felt like I was dating for the first time all over again. She was intelligent and honest, decent, good and trustworthy—all qualities that I admire in a woman. Nancy was different than the other ladies that I'd dated. I never for a second believed that Nancy wouldn't be part of my life.

I was sober when I met Nancy. She would never have stayed with me if I had still been a drunk. She kept asking me, "Who is this person everybody tells me about? You're not the wild and crazy guy I keeping hearing about."

I lowered my eyes. "You don't want to meet him."

I was in a different space. That guy had been part of a different time in my life.

I remember walking along the beach. I was trying to be romantic, but because of the way I had to walk with my metal hips, I kept hip-checking Nancy every step of the way. She just looked at me and laughed. "If this relationship is going to continue, this isn't going to work." I even put my arm around her to walk, but *boom! boom! boom!* My hobbled gait made it almost impossible to walk with class and grace, no matter how hard I tried.

"Okay," she said. "Time out!"

At any other time with any other woman, I would have been mortified that my walking was so awkward that I kept bumping into her, but she laughed, and I started laughing with her. She made me feel comfortable enough that it didn't matter how I walked. I was no longer self-conscious.

I realized that Nancy had everything that I didn't have. She was my rock. Women are gifted. The patience—oh my God!

As time went by, Nancy was concerned with my living arrangement. Anthony was gambling a fair bit, and she realized I had to get out of there.

"Okay," I said. "Then why don't we get married?"

Nancy said yes and we made plans for a wedding. When I told Anthony, he blurted out, "You can't!" That made me angry.

Nancy and I had our wedding at the Andover Country Club on December 28, 1986. My longtime friend Spike Boda took great care of us there. We moved into an apartment in South Boston and my friend Larry Ansin bought us some furniture as a wedding gift.

The master plan was always that I would give Nancy anything she wanted. Nancy wanted children, so we started a family. She blessed me with two boys, Ryan and Michael.

Michael was born first, on May 28, 1991.

Being pregnant was Nancy's dream. That was her Stanley Cup! She didn't drink, smoke—none of that. Whatever the obstetrician told her, she did. But it was a tough pregnancy. Nancy was on bed-rest for five months before she gave birth to Michael.

I was on the 13th green, walking to the 14th tee at the Ridge Club in Sandwich, Massachusetts, when I saw the pro come over the hill. I told my golf partners, "This is for me, boys!"

Sure enough, he said, "Mr. Sanderson, you've got to go to the hospital right away. Your wife is in delivery."

"Holy shit." I was an hour away. I don't even remember getting to the hospital, but I walked in and they threw a gown on me. "Come on in."

It was a C-section. I went in and I got to see Michael first. It was absolutely amazing! I didn't get all emotional. I was just worried about Nancy being happy. That's all that mattered to me. And the baby looked good—ten fingers, ten toes. And healthy at six pounds, 10 ounces.

He was six weeks premature. They sent Nancy home but kept Michael in the neonatal intensive care unit. He was jaundiced and had some trouble learning how to feed and breathe at the same time. Nancy was terrified. I just held her all night while she cried. You've got to give those neonatal nurses a bed in heaven. They're the heroes. They show patience and kindness to every parent that comes through the door. They took amazing care of Michael. Those nurses gave us a wonderful gift.

The next day, Nancy and I drove back to the hospital to see our baby. I pulled over and told Nancy I had to make a quick phone call. I called the hospital and said, "Do not attempt to keep that child another day." No way was Nancy coming home that day without that baby.

Michael was still a little jaundiced when we brought him home. They told us to put him in his crib by a window so that he'd get enough sun. His start in life certainly didn't affect his growth. He's six foot four and smart as a whip today.

Our second child, Ryan, was born on June 8, 1993. Thankfully, his birth was uneventful. Ryan, too, has grown up to be a strong, talented and extremely intelligent young man.

All of a sudden, having two little guys changes your life. The carefree life I had once known was now officially over. Every man has to realize that caring for a wife and children is a huge responsibility.

I'm very, very proud of both boys. They are extremely good students and great kids. They're intelligent. They're witty. They have mean streaks in them, but that is all self-preservation.

Both of them are very aware that alcohol is a drug and that I simply can't drink. I'm full of fear. My biggest concern is that they don't get the disease. In this country, alcohol is portrayed as being cool, but it's the most abused drug in North America.

I told the boys early on that their father was an alcoholic, and warned them that they had a 300 percent greater chance of being predisposed to this disease by birth. I wanted them to have a healthy respect for alcohol, not a curiosity. There's a big difference. They are going to drink, going to have a beer, going to be with friends, but I want them to remember that the disease is always hanging around their neck. And if they find themselves using any excuse at all to get drunk, then there is a problem. It has to be addressed, and addressed quickly.

From the time the boys were small, I spoke freely about being an alcoholic. One day, when he was about 12, Ryan said, "Hey Dad, Mom drinks wine." She has a glass, maybe two on occasion, and then puts it away. He asked, "Why can't I have her genes?"

"I don't know," I answered. "I don't know if science has got it down to that art yet, but I wouldn't run the risk."

All we can do is arm both boys with as much knowledge as possible . . . and pray.

In February 2011, *GQ* magazine picked me as one of the 25 coolest athletes of all time. That blew my mind. I was the only hockey player among a group that included the legendary boxer Muhammad Ali; race-car driver Mario Andretti; tennis stars Arthur Ashe and Bjorn Borg; soccer's George Best and Pele; football players Tom Brady, Jim Brown, Joe Namath and Kenny Stabler; basketball stars Julius Erving, Walt Frazier, Allen Iverson, Michael Jordan and Pete Maravich; baseball pitchers Bob Gibson and Tim Lincecum; two-sport star Bo Jackson (football and baseball); skier Jean-Claude Killy; daredevil Evel Knievel; golfers Arnold Palmer and Gary Player; surfer Kelly Slater; and Ted Turner, a world-class yachtsman before becoming a media mogul. That's some pretty heavy company!

A friend of mine called. "You won't believe it, Derek. I'm at a checkout counter in Florida and this woman in front of me said, 'Hey, look at this. Derek Sanderson's been picked as one of the 25 coolest athletes of all time by *GQ*.' I couldn't believe it!"

The next morning, I came down the stairs for breakfast in my underwear and ripped T-shirt. Ryan looked at Michael and said, "*This* is the coolest athlete?"

I said, "There was a time. There was a time."

They laughed and said, "No, Dad. Sorry. It just can't be done."

I thought they would cut me a little slack, but they didn't.

We sent both boys to a private, boys-only Christian school. It's a great school where everything Nancy and I teach them at home is reinforced on a daily basis. They've learned to be great writers and speakers. They've learned to respect themselves as well as others. They are both class acts.

A single-sex school is good for teenagers. The kids don't have to worry about the distractions that are inevitable when boys and girls are together in the same school. When you've got the raging hormones, you don't need that on top of everything else.

As bad as things got when I was heavily into drinking and drugs, I never once thought that I couldn't get back on my feet, but I knew I couldn't do it on my own. You need friends, you need family and you need the love of a good woman. Whatever emptiness there is in a man is filled by a woman. A woman gives you purpose. It was when I met Nancy that I finally had purpose. I had enough trouble taking care of myself; I certainly didn't think I would ever have a family. Nancy gave me children, and all of a sudden, I was responsible for lives other than my own. Suddenly, I had a whole set of problems completely different from any I had ever known. I had to get up each day and go to work because I now had to support my family.

It was the greatest thing that ever happened to me. The miracle of seeing your children born and develop into outstanding citizens is absolutely overwhelming. Having children nailed me to the ground and gave me a responsibility.

I owe it all to Nancy. She's the love of my life.

CHAPTER 33

TV BROADCASTER

Fred Cusick was a broadcasting legend in Boston. He was a Boston boy who played hockey while attending Northeastern University. After serving in World War II and the Korean War, he returned to Boston, and between 1952 and 1960, he did play-by-play of Bruins games on radio station WHDH. He also called Bruins hockey over the station between 1965 and '67. For the first several years, former Bruin Johnny Crawford served as his colour commentator.

In January 1957, Fred broadcast the first nationally televised Bruins game—a contest against the Rangers, on CBS. He did both colour and play-by-play on CBS's *Game of the Week* for a few years. For a couple of seasons in the 1960s, when the Bruins appeared on *Hockey Night in Canada,* he arranged for tapes to be sent to Boston, where he added his own commentary. The games were then shown on Sunday morning on local TV.

I first got to know Fred in 1969–70, when he was doing play-by-play on WBZ radio. That year, Johnny Peirson, who had starred with the Bruins in the 1940s and '50s, did colour commentary. The next season, Cal Gardner was in the booth with Fred. Then, in 1971, Fred permanently crossed over from radio to television when WSBK-TV, channel 38, began broadcasting the Bruins' games. Peirson was his partner again, and they remained a great team right through 1984–85. They also worked on NESN (New England Sports Network) broadcasts in 1983–84. In 1985–86, Terry O'Reilly and Dave Shea took Peirson's spot, and Peirson became the studio analyst.

Thirteen games into the 1986–87 season, the Bruins fired Butch Goring and hired O'Reilly as the new head coach. "Taz" was just starting his second season in the TV broadcast booth. His place wasn't filled right away, and there was no shortage of hopeful candidates: 11 guys were up for the job, and six of them had agents! At the time, I was working for the City of Boston, talking to kids in the schools and not making a lot of money. Friends suggested I would be a great partner for Fred. A friend of mine, Billy Skinner, even called the station—claiming to be me—and got an appointment for an interview. If not for that radical move, I never would have applied for the job.

I phoned Kenny Harrelson, who had been my roommate years earlier when he was with the Boston Red Sox. He had done commentary on Red Sox baseball games from 1975 until 1981, when he was let go. He moved on to Chicago White Sox telecasts. I asked him, "What do you think, Hawk?" He told me to go for it.

I asked him if there was money in broadcasting. He said, "There can be good money if you're good. But I don't care what you ask for—pay them if you have to—just get on that television. The most important thing in your life will be to be on that television every night when the Bruins play." His advice was sterling: "Treat the viewers like they are your friends and you're sitting in their living room, talking about the game. Say the same things you would say to a group of guys sitting around having beers and watching a hockey game."

Channel 38 interviewed me, and one of the first questions they asked was, "What's your philosophy? What would your approach be to the game?"

I said, "Well, first of all, it's my experience that hockey is a game of mistakes. Goaltending notwithstanding, the team that makes the fewest mistakes usually wins. In baseball, they give you the ball. In football, they give you the ball. And in basketball, they give you the ball. But in hockey, you have to take the puck away. So the referee drops the puck and it's fair game from there. There are no written plans. It's a bouncy piece of rubber and you are going upwards of 25 miles an hour on frozen water. Trust me, it's a very difficult game to play.

"I am not going to bury players," I continued. "If you expect me to go on and insult the Bruins, then I'm not your guy. I would guess that 99.5 percent of the people watching the broadcast are Bruins fans. Why would I tell them that they have a terrible product? I will recognize individual efforts and all positive signs, but when the Bruins aren't playing well and are getting shelled, I will extol the virtues of the other team. It isn't always that the Bruins are bad. Sometimes, the other team is playing well. You are appeasing your fan base, but you've got to give them knowledge."

They really liked that theory. I got the job on November 22, 1986. They hired me at $50 a game. I never would have gotten the job if Fred Cusick and Harry Sinden hadn't also given me their endorsement.

I was told to arrive at the rink at 5:30 that afternoon. I got there and sat with Fred. He had the rosters out and we went over names and pronunciations. He said, "Listen, Derek. I know you're kind of new at this, so why don't we just ease you into it? I'll do most of the talking, and you jump in every once in a while when you feel you've got something to contribute. But you must conclude what you're saying by the time they drop the puck. Be succinct. Be quick with your thought and don't run off at the mouth, okay?"

The Bruins were playing St. Louis and were down 3–0 at the three-and-a-half-minute mark of the first period. Fred said, "Well, that's a rather inauspicious beginning."

I said, "Oh, I'm not worried."

He looked at me quizzically. "Why?"

"The Blues don't even know they're up 3–0," I said. "The only good thing about being down 3–0 is that you have 57 minutes left to play." I said, "All the Bruins need is a pretty goal, a power play and a fluke."

Before the eight-minute mark, the Bruins tied the game on a fluke, a pretty goal and a power play. Thank you!

The game ended in a 6–5 Boston win.

That first night, Fred told me, "Add anything to the broadcast if it's interesting." After three minutes, he couldn't shut me up and we continued doing the TV broadcasts for 11 years until Fred retired at the end of the 1996–97 season.

Kenny London was the finest producer/director I ever worked with. We worked together for eight years, and we did both the home and away games. Kenny and I didn't get along very well the first two or three games I worked because he was trying to tell me what to do. I finally said, "Kenny, I'll tell you what. You teach me good television and I'll teach you good hockey."

He said, "I like that."

I told Fred and Kenny upfront that there would be times when we would have differing opinions. I believed, and still do, that fighting has to stay in the game. Intimidation has to stay in the game. I don't know whether either agreed, but they never tried to stop me from voicing my opinion.

I have to credit three guys for really helping me become a good broadcaster.

Harry Sinden was a disciple of Lloyd Percival, and the most knowledgeable hockey man I ever met. Harry is a genius, but the beauty of the guy is that he has the ability to listen. It's not all his way. If your argument holds water, he'll listen. You had to state your case and stand up to him. He respected that. He has no ego. That's what made him the perfect general manager.

On the road, Harry travelled with Tommy Johnson, who was the assistant general manager and part of the Bruins organization for more than 30 years. As a player, Tommy won the Norris Trophy in 1959 as the NHL's top defenceman when he was playing on that Montreal Canadiens team that won five consecutive Stanley Cup championships. He was our coach when we won the Cup in 1972. He was a fun guy to be around and a big help to me, too. If you were a hockey player, he'd go to the wall for you.

And Fred Cusick? God, did he have energy! I'd come in to the broadcast booth, just dragging my ass. I'd have my usual pregame meal—two hot dogs with Caesar salad dressing. Fred would say, "You can't eat that. That's bad for you!" He'd be eating his bowl of soup.

Fred was a wonderful person to be around. His mood rarely changed, except when he had had enough of me on the broadcast. Then, he'd just shut off his hearing aid. I met a lot of people who thought he wasn't very friendly, but he had difficulty hearing and if he didn't see you to gauge your interest in him, it appeared that he ignored people, which was far from reality. Fred was the sweetest man I've known—kind and considerate to everyone.

There might be a two-week road trip, so you'd have to pack accordingly. I would be limping through the airport because of my bad hips and Fred would be carrying both of our bags. He was 70 years old! Fred was a big, tough guy. He was six foot two and strong. He was an old navy captain, and he used to just pick the bags up like they were nothing and tell me to meet him out front. He'd walk through the whole airport and arrive at the taxi stand 10 minutes before me.

Those three guys knew more about hockey than just about anybody in the business. All three were senior to me and each of them knew and loved the game. It became contagious. Hanging out with Fred, Harry and Tom was as good a 10-year run as I've ever had.

The four of us—Harry, Tommy, Fred and I—played golf anywhere and everywhere we could when we were on the road. Because I was the junior guy, it was my job to book the course. We played some great courses. Then, when we finished broadcasting the game, we went back to the hotel and the four of us had dinner. We'd talk hockey until 1 a.m.

I gained knowledge about the intricacies of the game from my father, but where I really learned the game was as a broadcaster. You have an entirely different perspective on the game when you are seeing it from the broadcast booth. I got the reputation for being a homer, but why not? I had been a Bruin and we were broadcasting in Bruin country. But I could certainly be analytical. I could do a game with any team and tell you exactly what happened.

I saw games with five different coaches behind the Boston bench. Terry O'Reilly brought passion to the games he coached. Mike Milbury thought too much. Rick Bowness was a very knowledgeable hockey man and just as good a person. Brian Sutter had a really strong work ethic, similar to Terry O'Reilly's. Steve Kasper knew the game but took over the team during a period of transition.

I saw some great hockey and some hockey that wasn't as good. I was in the booth when the Bruins went to the Stanley Cup final in 1988 and 1990. But just as exciting for me was observing Cam Neely mature into the best right winger ever to play the game. While Gordie Howe played in the NHL and WHA for 32 years, Cam's career was abbreviated by injuries, but no one I ever saw could pass, shoot and carry the puck as well as Cam. And he added pure toughness and was an unbelievable hitter.

During the 1995–96 and 1996–97 seasons, I worked with Fred Cusick on WSBK while I was paired up with Dale Arnold on NESN. At the end of the

1996–97 season, Fred retired from broadcasting Bruins games, and that was the end for me, too.

Fred did continue broadcasting, though. He did the home games for the Lowell Lock Monsters of the American Hockey League and finally retired for good after the 2001–02 season. He was 83.

Fred Cusick was the Bruins' play-by-play announcer on either radio or TV for 45 years. The Hockey Hall of Fame presented him with the Foster Hewitt Memorial Award in 1984 as "a member of the radio and television industry who made outstanding contributions to their profession and the game during their career in hockey broadcasting." In 1988, he received the Lester Patrick Award for his outstanding contributions to hockey in the U.S.

I was so proud and blessed to work with Fred. One of the many highlights for us was to cover the final Bruins game at the old Boston Garden, which was a preseason exhibition game, as well as the Bruins' first game in the Fleet Center—their home opener against the New York Islanders.

Fred died peacefully on September 15, 2009, at his home in Barnstable, Massachusetts. He was 90 years old. He was blessed to have lived a full life and was proud of being married to Barbara, one of the classiest women I've ever met, and of his four children.

So many broadcasters just want to shock. It was my belief that you should teach the game, mainly pointing out situations on replays. I told the station, "If you want to teach tomorrow's fans, you have to teach the kids positional play." Once a play is over, it's tough for fans to recall without the visual help.

I can't stand these broadcasters who pontificate about what a bad play a player has made. My style was to give credit to the opponent for making a *good* play. The only pet peeve I had with a player was if he was not giving it his best effort and if he backed away from a one-on-one battle for the puck because of laziness or self-preservation.

Those days broadcasting the Bruins' games were very special. I enjoyed every one of them. I learned so much and, hopefully, gave viewers food for thought and added value to the broadcasts.

CHAPTER 34

FINANCIAL INVESTOR

Clive Fazioli was a marketing genius. Clive and Fred Cusick, his good friend, used to broadcast the Tucker Anthony Golf Classic on Cape Cod, which featured team competition between New England's golf clubs. It was a local show for local sponsors. One day, Clive asked me if I'd be interested in earning some extra money by doing the show with him and Fred.

NESN was in its early years, and cable was in its infancy. The station needed programming and the Tucker Anthony Golf Classic was a good fit. They had their broadcast truck there to tape all the activity. Fred Cusick and I were in the booth and Clive Fazioli was on the course. We filmed over the course of three days. Sixteen teams competed in the tournament.

My first interview was with Jack and Mary Gale. Mary was the Massachusetts women's amateur champion and competed in the U.S. Women's Open. Jack, her husband, was Mary's coach as well as a member of the PGA. Bruce Devlin, who played on the PGA Tour and who was designing the Ridge Club on Cape Cod, where Bobby Orr and I now live, happened to be in town, so it was decided that he'd help me with my first interview.

I had the only microphone. Bruce Devlin was to my left and I said, "Welcome back, ladies and gentlemen. Today, we're speaking with Jack and Mary Gale." I turned to Mary and went completely blank. I didn't know what the hell to ask her. I was okay on the intro, so I asked, "We can edit this, right?" But once I started thinking we could cut the tape, I lost my train of thought and went blank. I started to stumble and stammer.

Bruce Devlin could sense my panic. He was a professional and had done a lot of interviews on the senior tour, so he stepped in. "So, Jack, we understand that you're Mary's coach." But I had the microphone in front of me, listening to them like a fan. When I realized the interview was being conducted, I thrust the mic in front of Bruce, but Jack was answering the question. By the time I figured out that I had the mic in front of the wrong guy, and put it in front of Jack, he had just finished his answer and Bruce was asking the next question. I was so flustered that the microphone was never in front of the right person.

Bob Whitelaw, the NESN producer, leapt out of the truck. "Derek! What are you doing? When people's lips move, put the microphone in front of them!"

I felt like an idiot. "Bob, it won't happen again."

He said, "I can see this is going to be difficult." I had signed a contract with them for the next year as well, and I knew he was thinking, "I hope he's not going to continue being my interview guy."

Somehow, I got through the Tucker Anthony Golf Classic. Clive called me up and asked me to meet him at his office. I thought he might ask me to do another golf show or something. When I arrived at his office, he introduced me to John Goldsmith, the chairman of Tucker Anthony, a regional brokerage firm based in Boston, with 38 offices on the east coast. At the time, the company was owned by John Hancock Financial.

John, who is one of the smartest, sweetest guys I've ever met in my life, told me, "I was in New York when you were with the Bruins. I hated you then."

I was a bit taken aback. "Most people in New York did," I replied.

"Oh no, I wanted to kill you."

We laughed. The ice was broken and then he stunned me with his next question.

"How would you like to come to work at Tucker Anthony?"

I had done alcohol and drug awareness for the City of Boston for three years and then went to Browning-Ferris Industries—BFI Waste Management—and worked with them for three years. I ran the BFI Cares program in the schools free of charge, so it was in demand. I was also involved in community relations for BFI in Canada. When John asked if I'd like to join Tucker Anthony, I loved the idea, but I had no clue what I could do there.

"I want you to learn the business."

I was perplexed. "I don't know anything about it, John."

"I understand," he stated. "You're no good to me if you don't understand the industry. I'd expect you to go back to school." He added, "Derek, I want you to really think about this. You can't be telling hockey stories for the rest of your life. You've got to start a career."

So, at 40 years of age, I went back to school to prepare to take the Series 65 exam that permits you to be a financial adviser. I hadn't studied for a test since I was 16. The week before the exam, I took a crash course in "Mathematics Made Easy." The exam itself lasted six hours and was conducted online. Not only had I not taken math in 24 years, but I knew nothing about computers. There I was, sitting in one of the cubbyholes by myself—no cheat sheet, nobody sitting next to me.

I really had to work hard at it. I was quite intimidated by the jargon at first, but once I learned about investing, I realized it was based on sound judgment, and while I didn't always exhibit it, I was blessed with good common sense. I learned that the industry really comes down to two questions: "What are you doing for me?" and "What am I paying for?" I like to simplify everything.

After I finished taking the exam, I told John I wanted to start a sports group. The idea was that I would protect players from the sharks that were out there, because I didn't want any of them to end up broke, like I had been at the end of my career.

John said, "It's ambitious, but I like the idea. Write your mission statement and give me a business plan by the end of the week."

I wrote down the services I wanted to provide. John took a look at them and told me, "You can't offer these services for that price."

There were three pillars to the mission statement of my sports group. One was to protect the athletes from themselves. The second was to take the athletes out of the hands of the Philistines—those who would take advantage of them. After I was ripped off by my lawyer, I swore it would never happen to another player as long as I lived. I had been worth millions at one point, and then my health was gone, my hockey career was over and the person I trusted to manage my assets told me I had no money. That was a rude awakening. The third pillar was to educate players.

Glen Wesley and Bobby Orr were my first clients, and both are still with me today. In actuality, I have to call Glen my first client because his money came in first. Bobby invested with me the same day, which was amazing, of course. He said, "So, you're in the investment game? Okay. When do we start?" He told me I could use his name to secure other clients. That was huge! Bobby's got great integrity and credibility. When I say, "Bobby Orr is a client," people say, "If Bobby thinks you're okay, then we do, too." His is an endorsement that I've always used. Shortly afterwards, Keith Tkachuk became not only a client but a good friend.

After I initiated the Sports Group, I spoke with John. "This isn't going to work," I said. I had been using individual brokers, who were only too happy because I was giving them found money, and I had picked the broker to match the personality of the player. But I quickly realized that I needed the benefit of professional money management. John took me to Freedom Capital, the largest money manager for cities and towns in Massachusetts. They predicted that the Sports Group was going to be a cost centre, losing money the first year and, as a result, their bonuses would be affected. "What can I do to alleviate that?" I asked. They suggested I could help the sales team in order to take pressure off the Sports Group. That way, I could get what I wanted for my players.

Players make good money these days. If managed properly, they shouldn't have to worry about working when their playing days are done. We put people on a budget. In my day, nobody ever put me on a budget. I want to give my players the best advice possible. That is paramount to me. Athletes as a rule are insecure and overconfident. I trusted my lawyer with my life and gave him power of attorney. I believed that I had my money invested for me, but when I talked with him after I hadn't been in contact for a couple of years, I was dumbfounded to discover that I was broke. Whatever had been left in my accounts was completely wiped out. I got vicious when I realized that I'd lost millions of dollars. When I was sleeping under bridges and begging for money because I didn't know where my next meal was coming from, I sure could have used the money. Even some of it. But it was gone.

Believe me, that isn't going to happen to the players I represent.

I was one of the lucky ones. Because of the love of friends and family, I scratched and clawed my way back. I can't agonize over what was, but I can control what will be. I wish I had the money and investments I earned through hockey, but I don't. It's water under the bridge now. I've got my sobriety, my family and great memories. I'm rich in all the important ways now.

The Sports Group started slowly. Early on, I went to John Goldsmith and told him I needed an assistant with exceptional organizational skills. I hired Susan Ritval. She was absolutely brilliant. She was not only a lovely person, but she never made mistakes. She was diligent and saved me more than once.

I used to go into the office at seven o'clock in the morning and work until six at night, then went and did the Bruins' TV broadcasts. I travelled with the Bruins a great deal, but that gave me the opportunity to talk to athletes. I'd grab three or four of the guys, take them golfing or take them to dinner. It was a lot of fun and I was always absolutely honest with the guys. I reminded them that I once played the game and was taken advantage of by my adviser, and told them I didn't want that to happen to another athlete. I care too much to let them get railroaded.

When the Sports Group really got going, we had 21 percent of the National Hockey League as clients. We eventually extended the group beyond hockey players, picking up race-car drivers, baseball, football and tennis players.

People forget that the government takes half of what an athlete earns. If he is making $6 million, it means he really is only taking home $3 million. The problem is, many of the guys spend as if they've got $10 million. I will not let the players I work with go crazy and buy four cars. And they don't need an 8,000-square-foot mansion. You don't need to build a monument to yourself when you're 28.

Something I was especially proud of was called the Athlete's Fund. It was aimed specifically at young prospects who weren't yet making a great deal of money. A kid needs financial advice but isn't really making enough to warrant an adviser. How do I get him under management? I get him in the educational program and on the mailing list and start taking care of his life. The Athlete's Fund was my vehicle to get young players to gain confidence in me and the company, and get them in early. By the time they had made the big time, we were well on our way. It allowed the player to have professional money management, tax sensitivity and access to an educational process.

It was a big hit and we had $31 million in the fund from guys putting in $40,000 to $50,000. I always believed in snob appeal and exclusivity. Nobody could buy that fund except a professional athlete and those designated by the athlete—mostly parents and siblings.

We learned that *Barron's,* the leading financial magazine, was going to do an investigative piece on the Athlete's Fund. Everybody at the firm was horrified at the prospect, but I sat down with the writers, told them how I was an ex-player who got robbed by my adviser and didn't want it ever to happen to one of the players I represented. I explained the Athlete's Fund to them in detail and *Barron's* ended up putting us on the cover and calling the fund one of the most brilliant ideas anyone had had in the marketplace in years.

The Athlete's Fund was a starter vehicle. Once an athlete was making big money, I moved them into an individual stock and bond portfolio. We plucked the stocks that were the best up-and-coming ideas. I wanted players to see how investing in growth and not spending could turn saving into a hobby. I wanted them to pay attention to hockey, or whatever sport they were playing, pay attention to their family, have a nice vacation and maybe a summer cottage and not have to worry about their money. At the end of 15 years, they'd have 10, 12, 15 million—depending on how much they were making.

The pyramid of wealth is the way I construct a financial plan. The base of the pyramid is cash in your pocket. The next level up is the savings account, and on top of that is a chequing account. Then, it's fixed income bonds. The next level up is equities, large-cap growth, buy and hold. Then you get into Nasdaq. The pyramid is now pretty narrow at the top because that's where all the risk is. Understanding the financial pyramid is an important part of financial planning. It is a great way for the players to visualize the importance of certain stages. If they build the financial pyramid in the specific order I lay out, one level at a time, they will have a solid financial plan. They'll be able to weather short periods of financial hardship without jeopardizing their long-term goals.

The challenge for an athlete is that they have a short window in which to make good money. It takes them years of dedication and sacrifice to get there, and then they make good money for six or seven years, if they don't get hurt. Athletes deserve every penny they make. I don't begrudge the salaries made by today's athletes. Just like my generation built careers on the backs of those that went before us, today's athletes have built their careers on my generation. We opened a lot of doors for the players of today.

I moved companies four or five times, but I always moved with an eye towards providing my players with more services for lower fees. Smarter people than me are managing the money, but I question them every single day to protect my athletes. There is that tug and pull every day, but the team I'm with is second to none.

After witnessing my own fortune thrown away in alcohol and poor investments, I wanted to help fellow athletes avoid that. If someone would have told me back then that I'd one day be sitting in the boardroom of a prestigious Boston-based investment firm, I would have said, "You're nuts!" I was a high school dropout who lost millions of dollars at the height of my career. It's funny how life works. That's one of the things I tell my clients: you have no idea where you're going to be and what you are going to do when you're 50 or 60 years old.

CHAPTER 35

MY DAD

My dad used to tell me, "The heroes in this world are the people who move people." He was referring to teachers or police or coaches or even parents—someone who has an impact on your life. Every kid has a hero, but there has only been one hero in my life and that was my father.

My dad was a little guy with a huge presence. He weighed 150 pounds soaking wet and stood five feet, eight inches. If someone commented on his height, he'd say, "I'm happy. I'm an inch taller than my wife. That's all I care about."

The funny thing is that both my boys are well over six feet. I'm six foot two and Nancy is nearly five-ten. Both of my grandfathers stood six foot six, but my dad didn't get the height gene in our family. Yet, in spite of his size, he was tough. He controlled the neighbourhood. He was surprisingly shy, but was really good to people and had a big heart. He was very generous, but if you crossed him, that was it. He was done with you for life.

My dad coached my hockey teams when we were kids. He loved hockey and he loved kids. If anybody needed something, he'd get it for them. Even though he was only taking home $28 a week, if a kid couldn't afford a stick or a pair of skates, my dad would buy them for him. So when the Bruins gave him a hundred dollars for my rights, that was a month's pay for my father.

Through my career, people occasionally questioned how much I really cared. I can guarantee that I cared as much as anybody who ever played the game. There wasn't one single game that I ever went into where I thought we were going to get beaten. It didn't matter who I was playing with—the Bruins,

New York, St. Louis, Vancouver or Pittsburgh—I always thought we'd win every game. My dad taught me that lesson when he was coaching my team of eight-year-olds. I've never known of any other way to approach a game. My dad was my yardstick. He was my rules committee. He taught me to work hard and play hard, and to never abuse the game.

For a guy with a limited formal education, he was extremely intelligent and very opinionated. When he returned from World War II, he turned into a letter writer. He was always sending letters to politicians, including the prime minister. "What are you doing with our tax money? Why are our taxes so high? You're giving the world away." He believed that as a veteran, it was his God-given right to ask pointed questions of politicians. No one ever answered his letters, so he determined that all he had the power to do was protect his family. "I pulled my life in around this little sidewalk, this driveway, that fence, that backyard and that's it. I take care of you, your sister and your mother and the world be damned." His entire life revolved around my mother, my sister and me.

He always resented not having an education, and that's why he wanted me to have one. He told me, "You'll regret never going to college," which I do, but choices have to be made in life. In spite of lacking education, both my dad and I loved to read, especially books about the Second World War. He insisted that I try to get various viewpoints in order to give myself a real understanding of a situation.

When I was young, I would often bring up topics to discuss with my dad because it would buy me a few more minutes before I had to go to bed. There was nothing my father loved more than the chance to express his opinion. If you asked my father a question, pack a lunch! You'd get the most in-depth answer you could ever imagine. One evening, my mom, Dad, my sister and I were watching *The Rifleman* and I threw a challenge to my father. "Dad, if you were sitting around and a guy walked in the door with a gun right now and said, 'You've got to make a choice. Only one lives—your wife, your daughter or your son,' who would you choose?"

My sister was biting her fingernails, afraid to hear my father's answer because she was sure he'd pick me. I was the apple of his eye, and I was certain he'd pick me, too.

A quizzical look came over Dad's face. "There's nothing I can do? I'd let him shoot me if it meant the three of you were okay. I would do that in a second."

"No, Dad. You have to choose," I told him.

"Then I choose your mother," he said.

I was shattered! "You'd pick Mom?"

My dad said, "Yes, son. Your mother can give me more of you, but you can't give me more of her."

I asked my mom, "What would you do?" She said, "Oh, I'd take the two of you kids. I couldn't choose between you and Karen. If I can't take both of you, then that's it, let your father go."

It never bothered him a lick.

My dad was an extremely wise man. He boiled his moral code down to three basic tenets. The first was never come home drunk. The second was to never bring the law to the door. He'd say, "I don't ever want to have a policeman standing on my porch asking for you, no matter where you are." And the third was to treat women with respect. My dad would tell me, "It doesn't make you a man to make a girl cry." He said, "If you live by those three rules, you're going to be a good guy. Help the weak, help those who stumble to get up, and then, when *you* are weak and stumble, somebody will help you."

Not a tough set of rules. That moral code was flawless as far as I'm concerned. My father lived and died by it.

When I was playing with the Bruins, no one was prouder than my dad. In fact, when we won the Cup in 1970 and 1972, I was happier for my father than I was for myself. When we won the Cup in '70, I used my bonus money to buy him a car, a boat and a colour TV. He wanted to see me play in colour. Winning the Stanley Cup was the culmination of achieving a dream, and my father really respected success. He would have been proud of me no matter which career I had chosen, but if you're going to be a player in the National Hockey League, the epitome of success is the Stanley Cup.

He always told me to be the best I could be, but he added, "You're never going to be your best until you're not afraid of anybody." He said, "Fear can destroy you. It can debilitate you. I have no fear." He told me stories of serving in the Second World War. "When those German shells were coming in and you'd be lying there with little more protection than your uniform, *that* was fear."

My dad just shook his head at the press I was getting. He said, "Son, I'm telling you, you've got this image and it's going to eat you up. You are not like that." Eventually, I had to admit that he was right. But I said, "Dad, they won't let me stop."

"Son, keep your mouth shut. They want you to be that person you've invented. It's good for selling papers. Writers are only human. It's more sensationalistic to write about you, your comments and your exploits. They want you to be that person. They don't really care about your opinion. It's better to write about the craziness than to say, 'He's a good guy.' Only you can change the direction the press has taken with your image." He didn't have an education, but he had a ton of common sense.

To my father, everything was mental. He was a psychologist. I think the same way.

He taught me that no matter what the circumstances, you must always give a man the opportunity to back down. I learned that if you give someone a chance to back down as a way to save face, they'll take it 99 times out of a hundred. If someone pushes you and then they push you again, in your head you say, "That's twice." When they push you a third time, if it's worth fighting over, it's worth winning. You do anything you have to do to win that fight. Use anything you can get your hands on. You bite, you kick, you hit them with a rock—whatever it takes to win. There is nothing fair about fighting.

Another of his lessons to me was that pain is all a state of mind. He'd say that your brain will never retain pain, or else no woman would ever have a second baby. Funny, but men would never have a child at all!

A third lesson, and one that I absolutely agree with, is that life is all about conquering fear, and fear is different for every one of us. This was quite possibly the most important lesson I ever took from my dad. It is very much the reason for my turning my life around, and the reason I decided I wanted to write this book.

I started thinking about fear when I was about 11 years old. I realized that everybody's fears were different. Why did some guys play soft and some play dirty and some play tough? There are reasons for this, and fear is the common denominator.

Fear is all about self-preservation. My dad used to tell me that fear was a gut instinct, and that if you've got a feeling that something's going to happen, get the hell out of there.

My father and mother always, and I mean always, believed there should be a united front. They backed each other completely. I could never get away with playing one off the other. Never once did I ever go and ask my dad for something without him saying, "Well son, I've known your mother a lot longer than I've known you, and I don't think your mother would say that," or "I don't think she would allow that. What do you say we go talk to your mom?" I was always a bit of a con artist, trying to find an easy way out. I always did that, and he'd say, "Son, you think you're so smart. I'll tell you this: don't ever try to put one over on your mother and me. If you lie to me, I'll break every bone in your body." That was his favourite expression.

He taught me to be loyal, and to be a man of my word, which I was, whether it was in hockey, in business or in my relationships. He warned, "Don't get married if you have any intention of cheating. Don't you ever break your promise to her. When she bears you children and then you cheat on her, you're cheating on her, your children *and* yourself. The whole structure of the family falls apart. That's civilization, so you've got to hold the line. Once you're married, don't cheat."

When I first laid eyes on Nancy, I knew I was going to marry her. I was 38 years old. I doubted I would ever get married. I knew I was selfish. I didn't want children. I knew all that. But once I met Nancy, all of that changed. We got married a year and a half after that first meeting, and I would never, ever cheat on my wife. I had my parties and crazy times. I had no need for any more of that. My father's words resonated in my head. If I wasn't ready to be loyal to just one woman, then I wouldn't have married Nancy. Did I have opportunities? Absolutely, but never once did I cheat or even come close to cheating on my wife.

Loyalty? Here's how loyal my father was. He used to sneak behind my mother's back and buy lottery tickets because she never let him gamble. She thought it was throwing good money away. "Oh, Harold. You've got no chance of winning."

He would shrug and say, "Caroline, you can't win if you don't play."

My dad always bought Lotto 6/49 tickets, but on one occasion, he forgot, and the draw was that night. One of the guys he worked with said, "Sandy, I've got 10 lottery tickets for tonight. Do you want to buy five?"

"Oh, that would be great," my dad replied. "I'll buy five and if I win, I'll give you half."

"Fine by me," his co-worker said. My father was always a good guy and well-liked by everybody. He was a guy people trusted. He didn't win that night, but it started a pattern between the two of them. It wasn't as though they were close friends. They never went golfing, never broke bread, none of that. But for two or three months, the two of them bought lottery tickets and vowed to share the prize if either of them won.

My dad and my nephew, Derek, were at the Maple Leaf Village Mall in Niagara Falls, picking up something for my mother. They went into a store to buy lottery tickets and my nephew saw one of those plastic devices that help people select their numbers. "Here, Grandpa. Play these."

My dad would never disillusion my nephew—never—so he said, "Okay, I'll play those numbers, Derek. Let's see what you've got." He bought a lottery ticket using those numbers.

Mother of God, those numbers came in. My dad won $1,472,000!

He took the winning ticket in to a kiosk to claim his prize. Not long afterwards, the lottery office in Toronto called him. "Are you Harold Sanderson? Can you verify your address for us?" He confirmed the information, and they confirmed that he had won. "Jesus Christ! How much?"

When they told him, he cupped the phone and called to my mother, "Son of a bitch, Caroline! We hit it! We hit the jackpot!"

My mother asked him what his plans were. "Well, first of all," he said, "I've got to give the guy at work his half. There's plenty left for us."

I was ecstatic for my folks. "Dad, what are you going to do with the money?"

He told me of his plan to share the money with his co-worker. The guy was away on vacation when the numbers came in. He had no idea that my dad had played, let alone won. He had no idea that he was in for a huge payday.

I couldn't believe it. I was in Boston, flat broke, living on the good graces of a family in Revere, struggling and just getting on my feet. I could have used a break.

"Dad, why are you sharing with him?" I asked. "Would he do it for you?"

"Son, we made a deal," he explained. "I told him if I won, we'd split. My word is good. I did what I said I'd do." It never crossed his mind not to pay this guy.

I said, "Dad, I could use a few shekels."

He told me, "Son, you've had your go-round. You pissed away your money and it got you nothing but trouble, hurt and pain. God doesn't want you to have easy money."

And that was it. I was stunned.

"What do you want me to do?" he asked. "Break my word and give it to you over a guy I promised?"

When you think about it, just the sheer simplicity of it was right and there's no other way to look at it. I talked to my mother about it and she simply shrugged. "That's your father. That's the way he is." Once Mom said that, it was fine by me. I could have used some money, but that was my dad.

His co-worker was fishing somewhere near North Bay. Somehow, my father got hold of him and said, "Hey, we won the lottery." He gave the guy $736,000. My mother gave my dad three days off, and then he went back to work. She said, "You'll go through that money in lottery tickets alone, trying to win it again."

He laughed. "At least I'm vindicated."

"Well, that you are," she chuckled.

They didn't do anything extravagant with the winnings. Not a new car or anything.

That truly explains what my father was all about: the simplicity of honesty. He'd say, "If you're lying, you're only lying to yourself. Getting something from somebody isn't worth it if you're lying to yourself." He told me, "You'll learn the value of that one day, and I'll tell you why. All the money you win, all the money you make—you're not taking it with you, son. All you've got is your word. You lose that and you lose everything."

That's how he raised me. Those lessons spilled over to me. If I've given you my word, it's done.

My dad never did anything to hurt me in my life. He just wanted me to be stronger, that's all. What he taught me was that I had no foundation for success in place. No matter what career I chose, I was going to be an alcoholic and I was going to have to deal with that. I had to get sober before I got started again, and that's one of the reasons why I decided to change my life for good in 1980.

Until I was about 27 or 28, I think I only saw my dad cry once or twice. My sister was going through some marital difficulties. I was going through my darkest days. At work, they had taken him off the tools that he so loved and made him a foreman. He loved tools, loved solving problems involving those tools. He was miserable at work and he was sad at home. He blamed himself for my problems. I told him repeatedly that my troubles had nothing to do with the way I was raised, and that he and my mom were the greatest parents a kid could ask for, but he was very sad.

My father suffered from emphysema for 15 years. Everybody said it was from smoking—he always had a cigarette in his mouth—but I think working in the foundry had something to do with it, too. He wore an oxygen mask, although he'd take it off so he could have a smoke.

One day, my mom called me in Boston and told me to hurry home because we were about to lose Dad. I wanted to say goodbye, so I flew into Buffalo, rented a car and drove straight to the hospital.

My mother and sister were there in my dad's room waiting for me. He had slipped into a coma by that point and was unable to respond. There was nothing we could do but sit around and wait. We sat in that room and just looked at him. That was strange. He would have hated that.

The doctor arrived and told us we could lose him at any time. He asked us if we wanted my father resuscitated should his vitals fail. We didn't know what to think. I finally said, "Mom, Karen, why don't we go home, get some sleep and come back tomorrow?" I wanted everybody out of the room. We walked down the corridor on our way out of the hospital. My mom was upset and

Karen was in tears. I stopped and said, "You guys go ahead. I'm going to talk to the doctor for a second."

I asked the doctor how long my father had, and he told me it was difficult to say, but his opinion was there wasn't much time left. And then, by the next day—and much to our astonishment—my dad came out of the coma. In fact, a few days later, we took him home. I told him, "Dad, do you know that I was going to have them pull the plug on you the next morning at 10 o'clock?"

He lived another three years after that. And he would say, "Next time, don't be so quick to pull the plug. Give me three or four weeks!"

Realizing how close we were to losing him prematurely scared the shit out of me.

We knew Dad didn't have a lot of time left. His breathing was really laboured, which made talking all but impossible. It would take him 20 seconds to gasp enough breath to spit out a seven- or eight-word sentence. You couldn't hold a conversation with him because it was just too taxing on him.

With great difficulty, he said, "This is not good, but I don't mind. You've got to go your own way at the end of the day."

My father died in September 1998.

With all due respect to my mother and sister, my father was my hero and played the biggest role in helping guide me through life. If I spend more space talking about him, it's only because of the immense importance he held for me growing up.

He was the greatest man I ever met in my life.

CHAPTER 36

AGAINST THE WIND

One of my friends used to tell me, "Hanging out with you is like living in a movie. It's never dull and it never ends. Whether the sun's up or the sun's down, it doesn't matter to you, does it?"

"No, to tell you the truth, it doesn't," I said. "You can have just as good a time with the sun up as the sun down."

The *Los Angeles Times* once described my lifestyle as "part Errol Flynn, part King Farouk." I never fully appreciated that my life was that wild, that turbulent or that colourful, because every single day was like that for me. As soon as I got up, each day was a new adventure. That was my life and I assumed that everybody lived that way. I later discovered how wrong I was.

In the span of an extraordinary life, I made the National Hockey League, won two Stanley Cup championships, became a trendsetter, gained celebrity status, became a millionaire, descended into addiction, was homeless, almost died, asked for salvation, kicked booze, drugs and cigarettes, climbed back from the wreckage, met an amazing woman who gave us two great sons, taught kids about the evils of addiction, was a broadcaster and now advise athletes about their finances. That's a lot to pack into one life!

How my life took such twists and turns, I'll never fully understand. I was a kid from a middle-class family from Niagara Falls, loved by my parents and raised to know the difference between right and wrong. I was a good kid with good friends. I was a good student until I quit to play hockey.

So with all that love and all that support, how the hell does booze catch you by the throat and spin your life around?

Fear.

This book is about conquering fear. Fear to you is not the same as fear to me. Everybody's fear is personal, and we all have a personal definition for fear. We avoid fear at all costs. Your career path is defined by your fears. If you're afraid to fly, you're not going to be a pilot. If you are afraid of water, you don't become a sailor. Fear is God's way of keeping you tentative about something that will harm you. That's natural. When you're standing on the blue line in a hockey game and you have that feeling in the pit of your stomach, that's fear. When you meet a girl you really like and you really want her to like you, you get that feeling in your stomach. That's fear, too.

Courage is the ability to deal with fear. It took a lot of courage for me to face my demons. In 1972, I was the highest-paid athlete in the world and, because of addiction, fed by ego, the era and more money than I knew what to do with, I was living under bridges, panhandling and eating out of dumpsters six years later. At one time, I could write my own ticket. I owned bars. I was a guest on several national TV shows—I even had my own show. International magazines did features on me. Even after being away from the spotlight for more than 30 years, *GQ* still named me one of the 25 coolest athletes of all time—the only hockey player on the list. The fans loved me. Even though the media called me a third-line centre in Boston, I always thought of myself as a first-line centre. Harry Sinden told me I was the best defensive forward he had, and as a result, he asked me to take on the role of penalty killer and turn it into an art form. "This is a team game. Nobody can win faceoffs like you and faceoffs are the key to killing penalties," he said.

I never understood it all. I never understood what it was about me. Why was a penalty killer getting so much attention? I was never a star. I was never a great player. What really turned me on about hockey was winning faceoffs, making smart little plays and being around Bobby Orr as he was picking up all of his records.

People told me I had "it" (whatever "it" was). They said I had charisma. I was a kid; I didn't even know what charisma meant. I just went along with it all. My biggest thrills during my hockey career weren't championships or hat tricks or magazine covers. My favourite moment was just making it—officially making the Bruins in 1967.

And then I destroyed a great career.

I never had any ambition to be a star. I never had ambition to be a millionaire. I never dreamed of being rich and famous. When I was on the ice, I just wanted to be a good teammate and contribute to my team to the best of my ability. Off the ice, I just wanted to have a good time. I had no plans. Maybe that's why I floundered—I just lived one day to the next. My life was totally ad-libbed.

I lived well and I lived hard. I look back and realize that I made some really stupid mistakes, but I learned from each one of them. My life wouldn't have gone where it did without them. Life has these little turns and twists, and you can't guarantee anything.

People ask me about my life's problems all the time. They try to dissect my comments and come up with the reasons why I had alcohol and drug issues, but they are always wrong. They say it was the early fame, the money and the inability to handle the big life.

The truth is, every day is a bottom when you know you can't quit. Alcohol has you by the throat and won't let go. There are many bottoms—some worse than others—and it is a dark, ugly place you do not want to visit.

I do not take pride in the things I did, but I have had to come to terms with them with a lot of help from family, friends and faith. The "three Fs" are what life is all about. You do very little in this world alone. Even if you think you are singular, personal accomplishments are useless and empty if you have no one to share them with. Humility is the key to success.

It's only by the grace of God that I am not dead or in jail, but that craziness came before I met my wife. Once I met her, everything got better.

I realize that hockey made me. I don't spend any time thinking about what could have been. Why would I? I can't do anything about it now. Does everything happen for a reason? I happen to think it does. Had I not been a hockey player who succumbed to his addictions, I would never have had the opportunity to speak to thousands of young men and women about alcohol, drugs and sex. And who knows how many lives or careers I saved because of that. And that led me to broadcasting, which eventually opened doors to my current career as a financial adviser to athletes. As Tom Brokaw pointed out on NBC, I am the only athlete to have it all, lose it all and then work my way back again without being arrested (I guess he didn't know about my drunken escapade in Napanee). My experiences are invaluable to the athletes who are my clients. I want to insure that they are properly prepared for life after hockey, and I use my story as a warning to athletes about the need to plan for the future.

Being a hockey player was my dad's dream for me, but it was a dream that I am so grateful was realized. For years, I spent my life running against the wind, and today, I'm the better for it.

I spent my career crossing the line. Had my life not been like a movie, there'd be no need for this book. I lived fast and unapologetically, but the lessons I want to resonate are ones of redemption, conquering fear and the value of family, friendships and faith.

It's a powerful message.

ACKNOWLEDGEMENTS

We have so many people to thank for their contributions to *Crossing the Line*.

The book would not have seen the light of day had it not been for Bill Swinimer. After introducing Derek to Kevin, he helped guide the book through both business and editorial channels. We can never thank you enough, Bill!

Huge thank yous to Jim Gifford and the family at HarperCollins Canada, as well as Mitch Rogatz and his team at Triumph Books. In addition, we were very pleased to work with Lloyd Davis, an extraordinary editor.

The authors express deep appreciation to their wives—both named Nancy—for their help (and patience).

Sincere thanks to Bobby Orr for friendship, for consultation and for agreeing to provide the foreword to *Crossing the Line*.

Paul Patskou provided invaluable research assistance. Thanks, too, to Matthew DiBiase, Cathy Kinast, Jay Moran, Andrea Orlick, Marko Shark and Ron Townsend for going the extra mile. The Society for International Hockey Research (SIHR) also delivered outstanding research assistance.

Childhood memories of Niagara Falls were provided by Tom Cottringer, Brian Greenspan, Rudy Krulik and Rob Nicholson. Pat Keating shared memories of Fort Erie. Great thanks to all of you.

Hockey memories about Derek were contributed by John Bennett (WHA), Johnny Bucyk (Boston); Colin Campbell (Pittsburgh); Gerry Cheevers (Oklahoma City, Boston); Steve Davies (WHA); Ron Ellis (NHL); Doug

Favell (junior, Boston); Eric Morris (junior); Brad Park (NHL), by way of Thom Sears; Harry Sinden (Boston); Rick Smith (junior, Boston, St. Louis); and Ed Westfall (Boston).

Ron Friest and Wayne Maxner supplied interviews about Derek's time practising with the Windsor Spitfires and preparing for his return to the NHL. Bob Duff of *The Windsor Star* was extremely important to our research on this period of Derek's career.

We thank Mike Anscombe as well as Jim Hough and March Thompson of CBC's *Hockey Night in Canada* for furnishing us with video footage and transcripts of interviews with Derek.

For their memories of *Face-Off*, we thank stars Art Hindle, Trudy Young and Jim McKenny as well as casting director Karen Hazzard. Jean-Patrice Martel also provided research material on the film.

For information on Ted Green's head injury, we thank Dr. Michael Richard of Ottawa General Hospital. Dr. Allan Gross of Mount Sinai Hospital and Dr. Gordon Hunter (formerly of Sunnybrook), both in Toronto, were instrumental in supplying information on Derek's hip surgeries. Information on head injuries was given by Dr. Charles Tator of Toronto Western Hospital.

WordWrap Associates Inc. provided transcription assistance.

Thank you to Craig Campbell at the Hockey Hall of Fame for helping us with photographs spanning Derek's hockey career. Assistance with photos was also provided by Karen Sanderson, the Niagara Falls (Ontario) Library, Ron Townsend, Steve Waxman, *The Windsor Star*, Getty Images, Corbis Images and *The New York Times*/Redux.

From Kevin:

I thank my partner, Nancy Niklas, for extraordinary patience; my mother and stepfather, Margaret and Gerry England, for constant encouragement on this and every project; my brother Dale for support beyond the call of duty; and all those friends and family members who shared my enthusiasm for the creation of this book. And thanks to Derek for allowing me to share his story with the rest of the world.

From Derek:

I would like to thank Nancy, Michael and Ryan for their ongoing love and support. I had a great childhood, thanks to the love of my mother and father (God rest their souls) and my sister, Karen. Sincere appreciation goes to Bobby and Peggy Orr and family for their friendship and support. There are so many people who have made important contributions to my life, and alphabetically, I'd like to recognize Bob and Sandy Bahre; Spike and Lynne Boda and family; Joey Cimino; Tom Cottringer; Hap Emms; Phil Esposito and the Phil Esposito Foundation; John Goldsmith, who sent me back to school and helped me create the Sports Group; Gardner Jackson, my partner in the Sports Group; Pat Keating; Rudy Krulik; John Lombardi; Bill Long; Jimmy McDonough; Harry Sinden; the Spencer family; George and Gene Survillo; and Mark Ventre. I'd also like to thank past teammates both in hockey and in business. These are people who never gave up on me.

No one chooses to be an alcoholic. I'm the last person in the world who would ever have dreamed that I'd end up that way. Through family, friendships and faith—discovering that there is something stronger than all of us—I was able to restructure my life. The people who really cared gave me the strength to get back on my feet, and I am eternally grateful.

BIBLIOGRAPHY

BOOKS

Brunt, Stephen. *Searching for Bobby Orr.* Toronto: Knopf, 2006.

Bucyk, Johnny, with Russ Conway. *Hockey in My Blood.* Toronto: McGraw-Hill Ryerson, 1972.

Chapin, Miriam. *Contemporary Canada.* New York: Oxford University Press, 1959.

Cole, Stephen. *The Canadian Hockey Atlas.* Toronto: Doubleday, 2006.

Davidson, James. *Killer: The Brian Kilrea Story.* Burnstown, Ont.: General Store Publishing House, 1993.

Eagleson, Alan, with Scott Young. *Power Play.* Toronto: McClelland and Stewart, 1991.

Eskenazi, Gerald. *The Derek Sanderson Nobody Knows.* Chicago: Follett Publishing, 1973.

Esposito, Phil, and Peter Golenbock. *Thunder and Lightning: A No BS Hockey Memoir.* Toronto: McClelland and Stewart, 2003.

Kreiser, John, and Lou Friedman. *The New York Rangers: Broadway's Longest-Running Hit.* Champaign, Ill.: Sagamore Publishing, 1996.

Lapp, Richard, and Alec Macaulay. *The Memorial Cup: Canada's National Junior Championship.* Madeira Park, B.C.: Harbour Publishing, 1997.

Lautier, Jack, and Frank Polnaszek. *Same Game, Different Name: The History of the World Hockey Association.* Southington, Conn.: Glacier Publishing, 1996.

Ludzik, Steve, with Steve Wilson. *Been There, Done That.* Niagara Falls, Ont.: Ludzy Inc., 2010.

McFarlane, Brian, and Kevin Shea. *Team Canada 1972: Where Are They Now?* Toronto: Winding Stair Press, 2001.

McFarlane, Brian. *The Bruins: Brian McFarlane's Original Six.* Toronto: Stoddart Publishing, 1999.

Moran, Jay. *The Rangers, the Bruins and the End of an Era.* Bloomington, Ind.: AuthorHouse, 2009.

Percival, Lloyd. *The Hockey Handbook.* Toronto: McClelland and Stewart, 1951.

Plager, Bob. *Tales from the Blues Bench.* Champaign, Ill.: Sports Publishing, 2003.

Plimpton, George. *Open Net.* New York: W.W. Norton, 1985.

Sanderson, Derek, with Stan Fischler. *I've Got to Be Me.* New York: Dodd, Mead, 1970.

Sports Illustrated: The Hockey Book—A Tribute to the Game. New York: Sports Illustrated Books, 2010.

Surgent, Scott. *The Complete Historical and Statistical Reference to the World Hockey Association.* Tempe, Ariz.: Xaler Press, 1995.

Vantour, Kevin. *The Bruins Book.* Toronto: ECW Press, 1997.

Villemure, Gilles, with Mike Shalin. *Gilles Villemure's Tales from the Rangers Locker Room.* Champaign, Ill.: Sports Publishing, 2002.

Willes, Ed. *The Rebel League: The Short and Unruly Life of the World Hockey Association.* Toronto: McClelland & Stewart, 2004.

MAGAZINES AND PERIODICALS

Action Sports Hockey, February 1975

Action Sports Hockey, April 1975

Action Sports Hockey, February 1978

Canadian Magazine, December 7, 1974

Hockey Digest, April 1973

Hockey Illustrated, May 1971

Hockey Illustrated, May 1974

The Hockey News

Hockey Pictorial, March 1970

Hockey Pictorial, November 1971

Hockey Pictorial, November 1974

Hockey Stars of 1971

Hockey World, March 1975

Inside Hockey, 1970–71

Life, April 9, 1971

Maclean's, November 1968

Maclean's, April 1972

Sports Illustrated, October 17, 1970

Sports Illustrated, December 21, 1970

Sports Illustrated, April 26, 1971

Sports Illustrated, November 6, 1972

Star Weekly, December 6, 1969

NEWSPAPERS

The Boston Globe

Chicago Tribune

Daily Times (Delaware County)

The Evening Bulletin (Philadelphia)

The Gazette (Montreal)

The Globe and Mail

Hartford Courant

Indiana Evening Gazette (Pennsylvania)

Los Angeles Times

The Lowell Sun

The Montreal Star

The New York Times

Niagara Falls Review

Ottawa Citizen

The Philadelphia Inquirer

Toronto Star

The Washington Post

The Windsor Star

The Winnipeg Tribune

INDEX